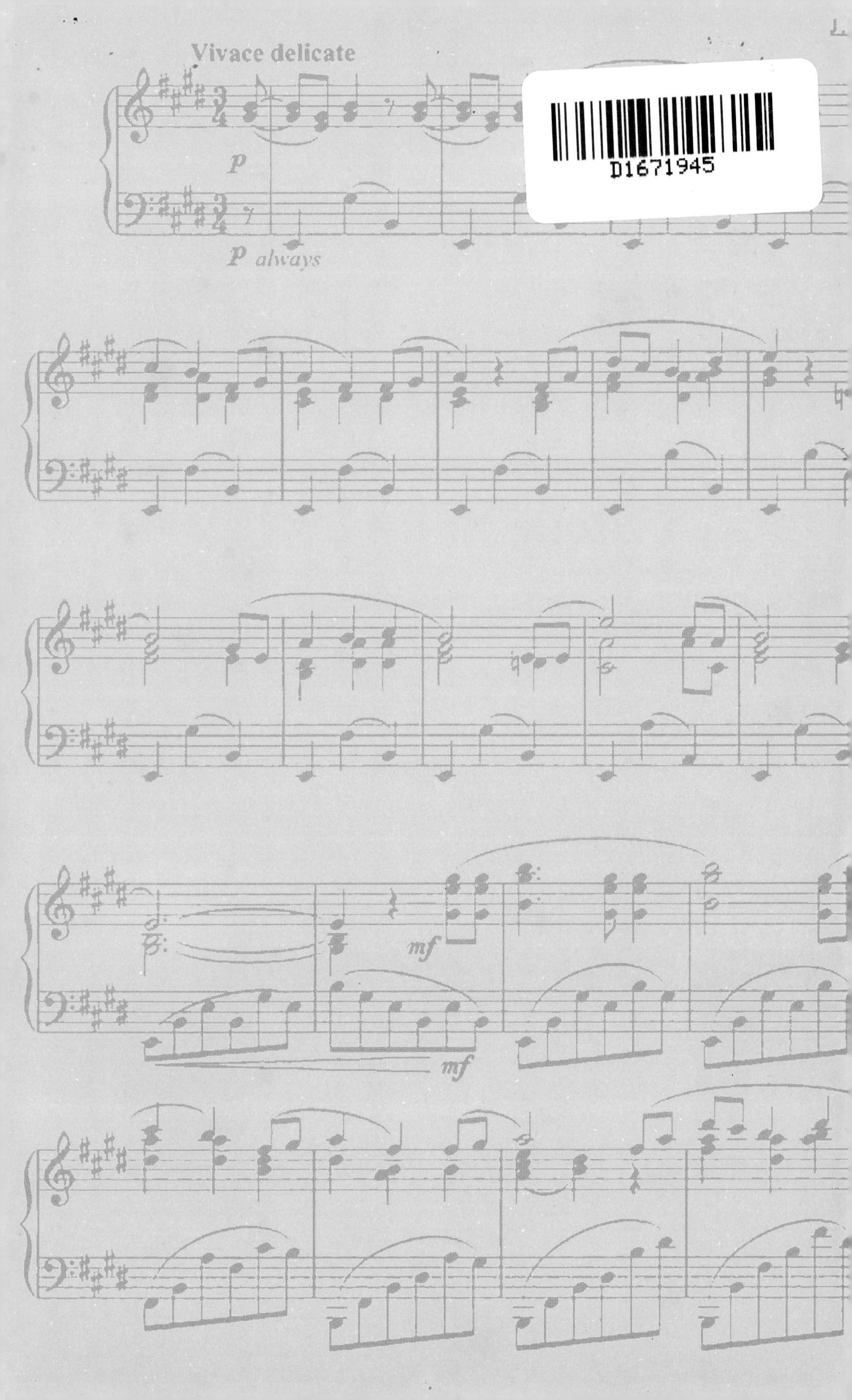

D1671945

Zubin
Mehta

# Zubin Mehta

## A MUSICAL JOURNEY

BAKHTIAR K. DADABHOY

PENGUIN
VIKING

VIKING
Published by the Penguin Group
Penguin Books India Pvt. Ltd, 7th Floor, Infinity Tower C, DLF Cyber City,
Gurgaon 122 002, Haryana, India
Penguin Group (USA) Inc., 375 Hudson Street, New York, New York 10014, USA
Penguin Group (Canada), 90 Eglinton Avenue East, Suite 700, Toronto,
Ontario, M4P 2Y3, Canada
Penguin Books Ltd, 80 Strand, London WC2R 0RL, England
Penguin Ireland, 25 St Stephen's Green, Dublin 2, Ireland (a division of Penguin Books Ltd)
Penguin Group (Australia), 707 Collins Street, Melbourne, Victoria 3008, Australia
Penguin Group (NZ), 67 Apollo Drive, Rosedale, Auckland 0632, New Zealand
Penguin Books (South Africa) (Pty) Ltd, Block D, Rosebank Office Park,
181 Jan Smuts Avenue, Parktown North, Johannesburg 2193, South Africa

Penguin Books Ltd, Registered Offices: 80 Strand, London WC2R 0RL, England

First published in Viking by Penguin Books India 2016

Copyright © Bakhtiar K. Dadabhoy 2016

Page 473 is an extension of the copyright page

All rights reserved

10 9 8 7 6 5 4 3 2 1

The views and opinions expressed in this book are the author's own and the facts are as reported by him which have been verified to the extent possible, and the publishers are not in any way liable for the same.

While every effort has been made to trace copyright holders and obtain permission, this has not been possible in all cases; any omissions brought to our attention will be remedied in future editions.

ISBN 9780670088690

Typeset in Bembo by R. Ajith Kumar, New Delhi
Printed at Thomson Press India Ltd, New Delhi

This book is sold subject to the condition that it shall not, by way of trade or otherwise, be lent, resold, hired out, or otherwise circulated without the publisher's prior written consent in any form of binding or cover other than that in which it is published and without a similar condition including this condition being imposed on the subsequent purchaser and without limiting the rights under copyright reserved above, no part of this publication may be reproduced, stored in or introduced into a retrieval system, or transmitted in any form or by any means (electronic, mechanical, photocopying, recording or otherwise), without the prior written permission of both the copyright owner and the above-mentioned publisher of this book.

A PENGUIN RANDOM HOUSE COMPANY

*For Ma*

# Contents

# Prologue

## Who Is a Conductor?

'Above all he is a leader of men. His subjects look to him for guidance. He is at once a father image, the great provider, the fount of inspiration, the Teacher who knows all . . . He has but to stretch out his hand and he is obeyed. He tolerates no opposition. His will, his word, his very glance, are law.'

–Harold C. Schonberg

WHAT DOES A CONDUCTOR DO? All musical performance, whatever the size of the group involved, must be controlled by one person. In chamber music it is usually the first violin that leads but an ensemble of more than eight players is usually directed by a conductor who uses a baton to communicate his direction.

The conductor as he stands today emerged over one hundred and fifty years ago and really came into his own around the last quarter of the nineteenth century. Today the prime function of the conductor is interpretive but till the mid-nineteenth century, he served primarily as someone who kept the beat, a kind of human metronome.[1] Before the nineteenth century, the beat was given either by the first violinist or by the keyboard player, or both. Initially the fiddlers were loath to give up their power. When the German genius Felix Mendelssohn conducted with a baton in 1832 in London, the violin-leader and the clavier-leader were distressed at being upstaged. Mendelssohn offered to withdraw, but was talked out of it.

The baton is an innovation largely credited to Ludwig Spohr, a violinist and conductor. Initially, Spohr used his bow and then graduated to a roll of paper for keeping time before introducing the baton in Hamburg in 1817. In April 1820, he conducted the London Philharmonic with the baton, and the orchestra, after its initial alarm, quickly realized the merits of the innovation. From this early custom of using the violin bow came a title still used today—concertmaster. In a modern orchestra, the concertmaster is the principal first violinist who sits to the conductor's immediate left. He plays the solo violin parts that occur in symphonic works. He also supervises the tuning of the orchestra before the conductor appears.

Initially viewed with suspicion, the cult of the virtuoso conductor has come to stay. The conductor has emerged as the one figure who interprets music in toto and draws together the individual skills of the musicians and even of the composer. It is, after all, the conductor who interprets the score of the composer. Since musical notation is an inexact art, and symbols and instructions are subject to differing interpretations, the same piece of music may sound different when performed under different conductors. Every conductor, indeed every musician, has as his point of departure the score. What makes him a better or worse musician is the way he translates the musical notation from the printed page to his instrument. In the case of a conductor, the whole orchestra is his instrument. But musical notation can no more be translated in a precise or fixed manner than can the spoken word. Given a dozen pianists, each might play the notes differently.

A score can be likened to a skeleton with notes and rhythmic patterns, along with a few non-specific directions about volume and tempo. It is the conductor's job to flesh out this skeleton according to his own knowledge and training, by deciding on the right volume, tempo, emphases and other subtle nuances. The conductor has great scope for self-expression since a work is capable of different interpretations. Even a conductor's own repeated performances of the same work do not necessarily remain the same. Faithfulness to the spirit knows no rigidity and should not be confused with faithfulness to the letter. The spirit of a work of art is flexible and elastic. Without the varying interpretations different conductors offer, music would be stale, flat and boring. The famous Franz Liszt, who was a pianist, a composer and a conductor, knew how inexact the printed note could be. He said it would be illusory to believe that one could put down in black and white everything that gives a performance character and beauty. The secret, according to Liszt, lay in the talent and inspiration of the conductor and the players.

A conductor, above all, is a leader of men. He must have an innate talent to lead. A conductor must always beat a fraction of a second before the orchestra, not behind them. But that fraction of a second can never be taught. It is an innate talent. With leadership comes authority. A conductor must take it for granted that people are going to do what he says. Again, a sense of authority is innate and can be acquired only to a limited extent. And all the leadership and authority are useless if the conductor does not know his music: he must fully understand what a piece means and what its message is. He must know what its architecture is, where its major melodies lie and where it stands stylistically in the history of music. He must know when to create tension and when to let it flow, but no matter what he does, he must always be in control and have the technique to communicate his point of view to the orchestra. Some veteran musicians who have played under every renowned conductor living have a 'show-me' attitude. 'Any hint of weakness, any indication of bluff, any evidence of immaturity, and the players lose all respect for their leader. Once that has happened, it is next to impossible for the conductor to rehabilitate himself.'[2]

As the American conductor Leonard Bernstein once said, 'The conductor is a kind of sculptor whose element is time instead of marble; and in sculpturing it, he must have a superior sense of proportion and relationship.'[3] The difference between a mediocre conductor and a good one lies in his ability to get what he wants. The best conductors know how to put across their ideas to the orchestra and use the rehearsals to do just that. They have the ability to prod artistically; to enthuse an orchestra to play the way they want. If an orchestra is faced with a real leader, it will follow gladly and without complaint.[4] But a conductor must also be a good psychologist, knowing just how much to prod and when to leave the orchestra alone.

A conductor is a father figure, teacher, administrator, executive and musician, all rolled into one. He is the controlling force, translating musical symbols into meaningful sound. It is the conductor's mission to interpret other men's thoughts. Each conductor reads the symbols differently. Just how fast is fast? Is an allegro a pace, a trot or a gallop? Conductors have their own ideas based on years of experience and study.

While soloists have only their own parts to contend with, a conductor's responsibility encompasses the entire work—he has everybody's parts to worry about. He has to perfect an enormous number of notes and parts before he can concern himself with how they should all sound when played together. A conductor hears in his mind the sound he wants the orchestra to produce. And his real challenge lies in trying to cajole, charm or threaten a group of 100 or more musicians—each with his own ideas about how the music should be played—to perform the way he wants. While all the players (with the exception of the percussionists and double basses) are able to sit during rehearsals and performances, and all of them have a chance to relax when they have no notes assigned to them in the score, the conductor's job is far more demanding. He has to be constantly alert, guiding, correcting, coaxing and even scolding as the situation demands, ensuring that the players express his ideas and not theirs.

It is essential for the conductor to earn the respect of the orchestra. It is said that it takes a good orchestra about fifteen minutes to determine if a conductor is a good musician, a great one, or just a poseur. The musicians are also likely to test the conductor. They know when their mistakes (sometimes made intentionally) are allowed to go unnoticed and will respect a conductor who calls them sharply to heel. A conductor's job is complicated enough but he also has other onerous responsibilities that add to his mental and physical strain. Apart from leading 100 musicians and making them play harmoniously, he must also have a working knowledge of every instrument in the orchestra. (Most conductors play at least one instrument well.)

A conductor must not only be able to read the score like a book, he must also assimilate its structure and inspire his orchestra to achieve what he thinks was the vision of the composer. The architecture of a work is of fundamental importance and it should be imprinted firmly in the musicians' minds by the conductor so that they convey it to the audience. He must also be well acquainted with all the standard works of the symphonic repertoire (and many non-standard ones as well).

Above all, he must have the ear that can spot, in Harold C. Schonberg's words, 'one wrong note in a welter of orchestral noise'.[5] A conductor must also master the art of assembling programmes which further the cause of art and at the same time cater to popular tastes so as not to alienate the audience. Schonberg feels that a conductor, in addition to his many virtues, must also have the quality of projection: the ability to project his physical and musical personality to the orchestra in front of him and to every listener in the audience behind him.[6] This brings us to the question of interpreting a piece of music. To many, this question lies at the very heart of conducting. It is impossible for two people to conduct a score in exactly the same way.

♫

Conductors have different styles: some stand motionless, moving the tip of the baton in tiny gestures (Richard Strauss). Others do not use the baton at all. Gasparo Spontini who was the star of the Berlin Opera from 1820–41 did most of his conducting with his eyes. As he told Richard Wagner who was much impressed with his conducting: 'My left eye is the first violins, my right eye the second violins and if the eye is to have power, one must not wear glasses, as so many bad conductors do, even if one is short-sighted.' And Spontini was terribly myopic, confessing to Wagner that he could not see twelve inches ahead of him.

The Hungarian-American conductor Eugene Ormandy did not use a baton for the greater part of his career. Pierre Boulez, Leopold Stokowski and Dimitri Mitropoulos preferred to conduct with only their hands. This method is common with smaller groups and choral conductors. Whether or not conductors use batons, it must have direct relevance to the music being performed. Bernstein is quoted as saying, 'If [the conductor] uses a baton, the baton itself must be a living thing, charged with a kind of electricity, which makes it an instrument of meaning in its tiniest movement. If the conductor does not use a baton, his hands must do the job with equal clarity. But baton or no baton, his gestures must be first and always meaningful in terms of the music.'

The German composer and conductor Carl Maria von Weber would drop his hands and let the orchestra conduct itself for long stretches. Mendelssohn was also known to put down his baton and stand motionless. Later, Hans Richter did the same but this was more in the nature of a gimmick. Felix Weingartner who first started out as a choreographic figure on the podium later became known for the sobriety of his gestures and his baton. His style was most reserved and economical, and he boasted that he could go out to a party after a concert without changing his collar. Conductors vary a good deal in this respect and it isn't the one who is hottest under the collar who achieves the greatest success.

Otto Klemperer used his fist, while Arturo Toscanini made circular motions, left hand pressed against his heart. Fritz Reiner held the baton between the thumb and the third finger describing miniscule motions.[7] As a young conductor, Gustav Mahler indulged in extravagant gestures but later switched to a simpler beat with a motionless body. Richard Strauss was perhaps the most restrained of all the important conductors. He used a tiny baton and his beat was delivered in tiny arcs.

But not all believe in such economy of motion. At the other end of the spectrum are those who flail about, with arms, shoulders and even legs being used to convey instructions (Bernstein and Leon Barzin). Bernstein, the only native-born conductor to be music director of a major American orchestra and the most important conductor the United States has produced, was known for his clenched fist, swivelling hips and pelvic thrusts. A showman par excellence, he was one of the most choreographic of all conductors. Whatever the visual impact, all conductors are trying to project an overall concept of a musical work.

The Hungarian Arthur Nikisch, who is considered one of the

founders of modern conducting, was the first to guide the baton with fingers and wrists rather than fists and arms. He also used his left arm more than any previous conductor had done. Adrian Boult (later Sir), the British conductor who studied in Leipzig and was in constant attendance at Nikisch rehearsals and performances, said that the latter 'made his stick say more than any conductor that I have ever seen'. Every orchestra sounded different under the simple beats of Nikisch. He combined economy of motion with a miniscule beat; he could pull the orchestra up or send it along with a flash of his eye or the slightest motion of his baton.

Most great conductors rely on their memory to conduct a musical work. Mendelssohn conducted from memory but since in those days it was considered disrespectful to the composer to do so, he used a score. There is a story about how, at one of his performances, the wrong score was placed on his desk, but Mendelssohn gravely turned the pages as if nothing was amiss. Hans von Bülow's powers of retention were extraordinary: he automatically committed to memory every musical score he read. As he famously told Richard Strauss years later: 'You must have the score in your head and not your head in the score.'[8]

Nikisch almost always conducted from memory, although he invariably had a score in front of him. He could evoke the beauty of sound from any orchestra, even one he had never worked with before, and seemed to possess mesmeric powers over the musicians. Angelo Neumann, an impresario from Leipzig, was preparing a company to tour with Wagner operas, and Nikisch was recommended to him. After Nikisch was appointed, Neumann received a telegram from the intendant of the opera informing him that the orchestra had refused to play under him because he was too young. Neumann telegraphed back ordering a rehearsal, with instructions that the members of the orchestra could resign if they did not like the conductor. Nikisch, as was his wont, charmed the orchestra. There was no question of anyone resigning.

However, Georg Solti defied the craze: he always conducted from a score. He blamed Toscanini for the fact that many conductors think they must conduct from memory: 'Why did Toscanini conduct from memory? Because he was nearsighted. Of course, he had that fabulous memory, but that wasn't really why he never used a score. Today we have an entire generation of young conductors who think they must conduct from memory—all because Toscanini was nearsighted. It is total lunacy.'

Reiner, the Hungarian-born American conductor who was believed to have the best baton technique, acknowledged Nikisch as the creator of his style. It was Nikisch who told him not to wave his arms while conducting and to use his eyes to give cues. Reiner tried to achieve maximum musical results with minimum effort. He used a big baton in a tiny beat and the tip of his baton would move in tiny arcs. Reiner, like many others before him, was an autocrat. He expected perfection and could be acerbic and cutting to his musicians, many of whom called him a sadist.

♫

The relationship between conductors and orchestras has undergone a change over the years. A conductor today is considered to be someone who helps the musicians; dictatorship on the podium is a thing of the past. Toscanini, Szell and Reiner were all podium tyrants who would stop at nothing to get the results they desired. Toscanini, by his very presence, was able to move both the orchestra and the audience to the point of idolatry. The musicians were terrified of his wrath and played for him with unique involvement. Szell was revered, feared and sometimes loathed but he was able to build his Cleveland Orchestra into a world-class ensemble.

Reiner was known for his perverse desire to belittle his musicians but was nevertheless hailed for his impeccable baton technique and the glorious sound he produced from the Chicago Symphony Orchestra. However, the days of the tyrant are long over and no international maestro would ever contemplate employing the brutal tactics which the likes of Toscanini and others got away with.

If the era of tyrants is over, then so are the days when a conductor remained with an orchestra for a full season or seasons. Today there is not only the dual-post syndrome with conductors guiding the decisions of more than one orchestra, but also a mad rush for guest conducting. Thus, it is a rare conductor who does not allow his talents to be shared by more than one orchestra.

In the past, conductors used to regularly change or retouch scores. In the eighteenth century, the creator and the performer were one. It was only in the second half of the nineteenth century that the new lot of musicians regarded themselves as interpreters and not creators. Wagner was not as concerned with the letter of the score as he was with its spirit. He once thoroughly revised Christoph Willibald Gluck's *Iphigénie en Aulide* in 1847 to get the sound he desired. What Gluck had in mind when he composed the piece did not really matter. For the Romantic school which Wagner exemplified, the performer became the creator, and one's self-expression took precedence over fidelity to the composer's score.

Wagner opposed the literal attitude to the realization of a score. He wanted the conductor to put his personal stamp on the music rather than simply 'let the composer speak for himself'. During the entire nineteenth century, there was a carry-over from the eighteenth-century practice of embellishing and improving scores. Musicians thought nothing of changing scores to suit themselves. Wolfgang Amadeus Mozart knew that his operas and other works were never going to be performed after his death exactly as he wrote them.[9] Wagner was the strongest conducting force of the nineteenth century and was the one who, more than anybody else, launched the cult of the conductor. According to Schonberg, he was a 'conductor of remarkable force and imagination who attempted to *create* in his interpretations'.[10] He shaped a generation of not only composers but also conductors.

Wagner's interpretations, which were highly personal, deep and intense, were unique in Europe. A supreme subjectivist, his reading of a work was as expressive of his own self as of the composer. During the period of the ripest Romanticism, most successful conductors leaned heavily towards the Wagner camp: Bülow, Richter, Nikisch and Mahler and, up to recent times, Wilhelm Furtwängler. There also evolved an antagonistic school led by Weingartner, Karl Muck and

Richard Strauss. The high point came with Toscanini who is considered the ultimate literalist.

While most great conductors tend to be autocratic, Mahler was an absolute despot. Where all conductors do a certain amount of changing and editing, Mahler all but rescored. He was under constant attack for heavy modifications in the symphonies of Ludwig van Beethoven and Robert Schumann. But what was heartening was that he had the same attitude towards his own music. Klemperer quoted Mahler as saying that if his Eighth Symphony did not sound good enough, anybody could 'with an easy conscience' make changes in it. An unpleasant, neurotic, sarcastic man, he was also a genius. Orchestra players hated him, that was a given. But Mahler also happened to raise the hackles of fellow conductors whom he treated with contempt. He became a legend in Vienna and his ten years as chief of the Vienna Opera are now called the golden years. Always seeking perfection, he completely reorganized the Vienna Opera. He conducted every performance as though it was a matter of life and death.

Toscanini had the greatest influence on contemporary conducting. The modern development of the conductor's art which has promoted him from the position of a time-beater to that of an interpretive virtuoso reached its culmination in the genius of Toscanini who seemed to know instinctively how to express the thoughts and feelings of the composer. He changed the concept of conducting, marking the final transition from the Wagner style to the more objective twentieth-century style. Toscanini represented objectivity as intensely as Wagner, Bülow and Mahler represented subjectivity. The emergence of Bülow marked the rise of the re-creative rather than the creative musician, the man whose job it was to interpret the works of others—which is the norm today.

Conductors before Toscanini used the score as a means of self-expression; for Toscanini the *only thing* a musician had was the notes which had to be followed as scrupulously as possible. Conductors who over-interpreted in the name of style drew his scorn. Tradition, according to Toscanini, was to be found in only one place—the music. Commenting on Beethoven's *Eroica* Symphony, he said, 'Some say this is Napoleon, some Hitler, some Mussolini. For me it is simply allegro con brio.'[11] Critics said that he made music which was little more than ordered sound, lacking any kind of emotional appeal. This was not true. Toscanini's literalism did not make him a sterile technician or a blind purist. He believed that 'music must breathe' and despite his own tenets was quite capable of infusing his personality into his interpretations. 'His phrases were long and aristocratic, his climaxes stupendous, his handling of melodious elements gracious and lyric. Above all the feature that marked his conducting was intensity.'[12]

In dispensing with the entire Romantic style and demanding that everything be played as written, Toscanini's method came to be regarded as revolutionary. The standard analogy compared him with a restorer cleaning great paintings that had never been seen in their original colours by modern viewers. Toscanini always conducted from memory: his eyesight was too poor for a score to be of any use to him. Like other audience cynosures, he threw tantrums. His rage was legendary and he would stamp and scream.

The renowned Austrian conductor Herbert von Karajan[13] was a literalist and completely objective in his interpretation but also conveyed a great deal of excitement and electricity. His theories involve letting the orchestra share the responsibility for a performance. 'For a concert with my Berlin Philharmonic, I first achieve rehearsal perfection—complete mastery of detail and mechanization. Then I let the men play freely during the actual performance, so that they are making music as much as I am—sharing the emotion which we all have together.' Karajan had no theories about baton technique. He believed that a conductor must feel the tempos and rhythms before an orchestra can do so. Inner rhythm—actual and psychic—is more important than arm and body movement which is merely the carrier. This rhythm, a mysterious force which every conductor of merit possesses, radiates from the conductor to the orchestra.

Furtwängler, who carried the old Romantic tradition to the middle of the twentieth century, had the most unorthodox beat of all. His baton was inexpressive and difficult to follow. His beat which was every musician's nightmare was extremely puzzling. There were often several beats at once which made the audience wonder which of the repetitions would be chosen by the orchestra for the impact of the sound. Someone asked a player in Berlin how the orchestra knew when to start with Furtwängler, and he said it was easy: when the players first saw him appear in the wings they would count forty beats and begin.[14] It was a miracle that they did, in fact, come in together. But it was this tension, this uncertainty, extended over an entire concert that contributed a great deal to the magnetic power and warmth of the tone quality that one came to expect from his performances.

If an orchestra doesn't quite know where it is, it plays with a certain intensity, an excited vitality, that contributes something remarkable to the performance as a whole. Furtwängler was fully conscious of the problem his beat gave musicians but he believed that 'standardized technique creates in turn standardized art'. He demanded the utmost concentration from his players and believed that the conductor's worst enemy is routine. After all, a classic is a piece of music that endures over time by revealing new and unexpected aspects in diverse contexts of interpretation and performance.

The witty, if sometimes acrimonious, British conductor Sir Thomas Beecham, who was poet, savant, financier and musician, also conducted from memory. He had no baton technique to speak of and music critic Neville Cardus once reported how his baton got entangled in the back of his coat. He was an ungainly sight on the podium, yet he managed to achieve amazing results from orchestras. Performances of the same work could vary from concert to concert and there was always the feeling that something unexpected would happen.

Seeking to transcend the printed note, the German-born American conductor Bruno Walter believed that if a conductor's personality is unable to fulfil the spiritual demands of the works he performs, his interpretation will remain unsatisfactory even though his musical execution may be excellent. He believed that a really good conductor has in his ear an ideal sound which he seeks to impose on the orchestra. He also highlighted the manual talent for conducting, saying that a clumsy hand would prevent even a highly gifted musical mind from making the correct impression. A democratic conductor, he looked on his musicians as his colleagues and, like Furtwängler, expected them to have their own musical ideas.

♫

Ultimately the debate about the literal versus the passionate school of conducting boils down to a matter of interpretation or opinion. And interpretation is a matter of degree. Toscanini 'interpreted' less and Furtwängler more, but there is no right or wrong. Even the simple marking 'allegro' is open to interpretation and can never be defined in black and white. Some conductors, including Zubin Mehta, are of the opinion that their interpretations are so distinctively their own that they become 'like handwriting', impossible not to recognize.

The conductor has to instruct and command but he should not be unduly bossy. He is still the servant of the composer, and Toscanini talked of Beethoven, and Walter of Mozart, with the profoundest reverence and humility. The best interpreters venerate the composers they serve, and delight in the new beauties that continually emerge from the greatest pieces of music.

Similarly there never has been any firm agreement on the question of tempo: one only has to note the disparity between the time it takes different conductors to play the same symphony. Just as there is no right or wrong interpretation, there is no such thing as true or right tempo. There are times when a conductor will want to alter the tempo by employing *rubato*, changing the duration of notes, playing some a little slower and others a little faster, or shortening one beat and lengthening another.

Beating time falls into the purely physical nature of conducting—the ability to convey meaning by a movement of the hand, the body and even the eyes. What a conductor does physically affects an orchestra. So if a conductor wants a 'pianissimo' from his players but waves his hand and arms vigorously, then he is likely to get something quite different. Both in the mechanical and non-mechanical aspects of conducting, and in the relationship between the orchestra and the conductor, what is important is that indefinable quality called 'chemistry'. Conducting is a question of communication by whatever means possible. There is no way of explaining why the same orchestra or the same piece of music sounds different under different conductors. This aspect is dealt with at some length in the last chapter.

Does an orchestra really need a conductor? Many uninformed concertgoers are not at all sure what it is a conductor really does. Zubin Mehta recalls a woman asking him after a performance if he ever met the orchestra before a concert. Conducting is deceptively simple and it operates consistently in the realm of the abstract. There have been experiments with conductor-less orchestras, the most famous being the Persimfans, founded in Moscow in 1922. Even in those early days of communism, it turned out that some players were, to use George Orwell's famous phrase, 'more equal'. At the beginning of a piece, all eyes would turn to the concertmaster just as in a string quartet. The Persimfans concertmaster ended up being the conductor in all but name. Somebody has to lead, assume responsibility and hold it all together—in a word, the conductor.[15]

Technical perfection seems to be an aim which has grown in importance in modern times. In the past there was no obsession with an orchestra playing together or otherwise. What was interesting was the spirit, the attention, the tempo. It is said that Beethoven, when he conducted his own Ninth Symphony, had only three rehearsals. Judged for technical perfection, it would have been a terrible performance. But it made a great impression because the audience heard the essence. The very fact that a conductor is an interpreter means that there will always be something new, an element of surprise, of fresh discovery and new insights: when the mood of the music and that of the conductor coincide, one can expect magic.

It is unfortunate that a conductor's job looks misleadingly simple. In fact, he has sometimes been called the world's greatest charlatan. According to Hungarian violinist Carl Flesch, who played under all the acclaimed conductors until his death in 1944, conducting 'is the only musical activity in which a dash of charlatanism is not only harmless but absolutely necessary'.[16] It also appears glamorous, for it gives a great sense of power. Summing it all up, Sir Adrian Boult made a list of qualifications for the practising conductor: he should know a few instruments well and should also have played in an orchestra or sung in a chorus; he must possess a comprehensive understanding of the whole classical repertoire and have sound knowledge of music history; he must be a leader with great patience and an iron constitution ready to deal with the maddening frustrations he is likely to face; he must have a good baton technique; and lastly, he should be a connoisseur of many other forms of art.[17] Little wonder then, that there are just a handful of men who are considered top-notch conductors. Zubin Mehta, the subject of this biography, is undoubtedly one of them.

# Introduction

ZUBIN MEHTA IS INDIA'S most famous immigrant to the United States of America. A citizen of the world with an Indian passport, the jet-setting Western classical music conductor has been an ambassador of the country for the past fifty years, the embodiment of cultural globalization, and the perfect advertisement for cultural synthesis.

His musical career has been a long series of 'firsts'. *Time* magazine featured him on the cover of its 19 January 1968 issue, an achievement for any conductor, let alone one who was only thirty-one years old. Zubin 'precociously stormed the most daunting redoubts of European music',[1] becoming one of the youngest conductors to lead both the Berlin and the Vienna Philharmonic orchestras. At twenty-four, he became the conductor of the Montreal Symphony Orchestra. A year later, he was named conductor of the Los Angeles Philharmonic, thus becoming not only the youngest conductor of a leading American orchestra, but also the only man ever to direct two major orchestras in North America at once.

His debut in London in March 1961, with the Royal Philharmonic, was the first time someone from the subcontinent had directed a major British orchestra. Zubin is also the first and, thus far, only music director of the Israel Philharmonic. Indeed it seemed that he had been born under a lucky star which always managed to steer him towards the right people and opportunities. By the time he was thirty, he had done enough to raise the Mehta name into the sunlight of undying fame.

Along the path from prodigy to *éminence grise*, he has emerged as perhaps the most flamboyant personality in the ostensibly staid world of Western classical music. His performance partners have ranged from Frank Zappa to the Three Tenors, his venues from the Hollywood Bowl to the Jerusalem Theatre where the audience donned gas masks during a solidarity performance he gave amid the Persian Gulf War. His populist approach—sweeping productions of late Romantic favourites, the battlefield-morale concerts, a requiem in a bombed library in Sarajevo—has won him many admirers. At the bottom of it all is his belief that music can help in fostering peace. He has on occasion been dismissed as having more show than substance, of being an outstanding performer but rarely an innovative interpreter of classical music. He has also been accused of putting into his music more personality than finesse, more vigour than virtuosity—criticism which, at this stage of his career, seems less than academic. After almost six decades in the profession, Zubin's musical experience and knowledge are formidable and incontestable.

Zubin might have conquered the world but he is still a Mumbai boy at heart. His commitment to the milieu of his birth is as sincere as his pride in being an Indian citizen is genuine. Despite his phenomenal international success, he has never severed his links with the country of his birth—he retains his Indian passport—and remains proud of his Parsi heritage. Although inconvenienced by his Indian passport, he has never relinquished it for more convenient travel documents.

The maestro was born on 29 April 1936, the day Toscanini conducted his last concert with the New York Philharmonic, which coincidentally was also the first anniversary of the founding of the Bombay Symphony Orchestra. Zubin's extraordinary journey from Bombay to the most prestigious podiums of the music world is a saga of genius and dedication. Zubin himself has confessed that he made his career by jumping in at the last minute when he substituted for the big names that dropped out. But as he says, one has to be ready when the chance comes and make the most of the opportunity. Western classical music as a career was not an option in the upper-middle-class, close-knit Parsi family in which Zubin grew up in the 1940s and 1950s. In fact, Zubin was being groomed for the medical profession, just as his father, Mehli, had initially taken up accountancy, though his real love too was music.

Mehli, a gifted musician in his own right, was a self-taught violinist (later studying under Ivan Galamian in the United States) who founded the Bombay Symphony Orchestra in 1935 and played in the Bombay String Quartet. Mehli honed his son's talent and eventually permitted him to go to Vienna to study music. Zubin was surrounded by music from the time he was born. The constant exposure to recordings and Mehli's unyielding dedication to his craft nurtured the highly gifted child into a precociously mature, adolescent musician: much of Zubin's subsequent brilliance and achievements were the result of this intimate collaboration between a father and son who were also connected as teacher and pupil.

In Vienna, young Zubin discovered the joys of listening to a real orchestra in the great concert halls. Till then, his exposure to orchestral sound was limited to his father's vast collection of scratchy records of inadequate quality. Zubin tells us how he felt when he first heard the Fourth Symphony of Pyotr Ilyich Tchaikovsky being played by the great Karajan. 'And again, I was familiar with the piece from one of my father's records of the Boston Symphony Orchestra under Serge Koussevitzky. However, what I heard through the doors sounded completely different.'

Zubin's musical career and his interactions with the great names of the twentieth-century world of music make for a fascinating story. His meteoric rise to international stardom from the ranks of a lowly apprentice in the blink of an eye when he was in his mid-twenties is equalled perhaps only by the trajectory of Bernstein's ascent to fame when he was Zubin's age. Zubin is especially close to the pianist and conductor Daniel Barenboim, a friendship which began when he met him, only twelve at the time (and a prodigy to boot), at Siena when both were taking classes at the Accademia Musical Chigiana.

It was at this time that Zubin also met Claudio Abbado, who went on to become an influential name in the world of conducting. Zubin supported the attempt by Barenboim and the late Edward Said to bring together young Israeli and Palestinian musicians in the West-Eastern

Divan project. He was also a good friend of Barenboim's first wife, the cellist Jacqueline du Pré. Zubin counts among his friends musicians such as Itzhak Perlman, Pinchas Zukerman and Plácido Domingo to name only a few. Zubin has been on the scene for the past fifty years and there is no one in the world of Western classical music whom he does not or did not know. He is, after all, the 'upper crust of a rather small loaf'.[2] Past associations ranged from the great Karajan to Karl Böhm who gifted him the Nikisch ring in his final testament.

Without doubt, the biggest romance of Zubin's musical life has been with the Israel Philharmonic Orchestra. Zubin first conducted the orchestra when he filled in for Ormandy in 1961. When the Six-Day War broke out in 1967, Zubin dropped all his international commitments and flew to Israel to conduct the orchestra that had been left stranded by the sudden cancellation of Erich Leinsdorf. He flew to Tel Aviv on an aircraft which was carrying ammunition, with the governor of the Bank of Israel and a *Newsweek* correspondent for company. A subsequent conflict in 1971 and the 1991 Gulf War elicited a similar response, with Zubin rushing to Israel to demonstrate his solidarity. Zubin has always identified with the Israeli nation and its people during their crises.

In Los Angeles, Zubin was often criticized for his flamboyance and 'Hollywood attitude'. His magnetic personality, charisma and drop-dead good looks made him a huge hit with women, and over time the playboy image grew. This image irked him as he thought it came in the way of his being considered a serious artiste, which he undoubtedly was, and still is. Zubin spent sixteen long years with the Los Angeles Philharmonic and nobody would deny his stellar role in its all-round improvement.

Zubin has also never shied away from experimentation, be it his infamous concert with Zappa, the NBC crossover concert on TV, or conducting the Three Tenors for the World Cup final in Rome. In the early 1980s, Zubin and Ravi Shankar took part in a fusion experiment which was successful abroad but greeted less enthusiastically in India.

Later, Zubin gave another example of his *Sitzfleisch*, spending thirteen years (1978–91) as the music director of the New York

Philharmonic, a tenure which represents the longest incumbency of any chief conductor in the orchestra's history. Before he took over, there was the famous contretemps with the orchestra's musicians when his remarks about the ensemble soured his relationship with them. In December 1967, Zubin had rather tactlessly said, 'A lot of us think, why not send our worst enemy to the New York Philharmonic and finish him off once for all.' Though it was a remark made in private, a *Newsweek* reporter overheard it and it became Zubin's most celebrated verbal gaffe, the skeleton that rattled in his cupboard every time the New York Philharmonic was mentioned.

Zubin apologized, but it took years for the wound to heal. Later, even as music director, he hardly received a uniformly favourable press. Zubin, in fact, received a very poor press, especially in his last few years in New York. He also had an adversarial relationship with music critic Martin Bernheimer in Los Angeles. He bore it all with shoulder-shrugging resignation, voicing his indignation only when he found that the criticism was based on appalling ignorance. But most conductors seem to have been given a hard time by the press in New York. Bernstein was the favourite whipping boy of the New York critics; before him, both John Barbirolli and Dimitri Mitropoulos were given a hard time. Also, many agree that Zubin's place-to-bury-one's-worst-enemy remark was only a reflection of the standard opinion of the New York Philharmonic as a band of hard-boiled musicians who were capable of giving any conductor a hard time. But his interpretations of Anton Bruckner and Mahler while at the helm in New York came to be regarded as definitive, and his mastery of the music of Richard Strauss rivalled that of George Szell who led the Cleveland Orchestra for many years. As his career matured, Zubin became an accomplished opera conductor and even made a memorable foray into the popular repertoire, making history conducting the first of the Three Tenors mega concerts in Rome.

While Zubin's appeal is linked with the Israel, Los Angeles and New York philharmonics, his musical legacy remains deeply rooted in the Central European tradition. For Zubin, who commands a clean, precise beat, the 'true sound' has always meant the Viennese sound.

Musically, Zubin is equally adept with Mozart, Mahler and Arnold Schoenberg, and capable of recreating that unique Viennese sound with orchestras as far apart as the Israel Philharmonic and the Maggio Musicale Fiorentino. He has protested against Vietnam and Bosnia with his music, and attempted to perform Wagner in Israel (in 1981). Zubin has also been actively involved with the Maggio Musicale in Florence for decades and was the music director of the Bavarian State Opera from 1996 to 2006. Thus, as Homi K. Bhabha put it, Zubin brings vast and various worlds with him—Vienna, Montreal, Los Angeles, Tel Aviv, New York, Florence and Valencia—each of which has contributed a theme, a transition, a rhythm, a voice to the score of his life. Vienna, of course, holds a special place in his heart and he has sought to replicate that ideal Viennese sound in the orchestras he has led all over the world.

Zubin views music as a complement of not only personal fulfilment but also public purpose. 'As a conductor, I express myself through music. I try to help, and also to protest or to make people think. This I think is a wonderful responsibility.' The responsibility to make people think demands the courage of one's convictions, something Zubin has never lacked. Nor has he lacked the gumption to speak out freely and, at times, even indiscreetly, when it comes to causes dear to him. When he made the brave decision to play Wagner in 1981, it provoked a huge furore but he did so out of 'a belief in the democratic aspirations of Israeli civil society and the role of the finest orchestral music as part of such a democratic dialogue'.[3]

All through his musical career, Zubin has chosen to stage concerts in politically tense areas on the borders of Israel and Palestine or in Israeli zones where Arabs and Israelis coexist. He has long been fond of making political points. He goose-stepped off a Leningrad stage during the Soviet era and stayed away from Greece when the army was in power. He repeatedly refused invitations to perform in South Africa because of apartheid, before finally making a trip to Durban which he says was worth it because it gave Indians a chance to see an Indian being given a standing ovation by a white audience. He refused to lead the Israel Philharmonic in Germany's national anthem—a traditional courtesy at the Berlin Festival—because it remained 'Deutschland über alles'. He led the orchestra in a performance of Mozart in the bombed-out shell of Sarajevo's library and conducted at the sixty-fifth anniversary of the Warsaw ghetto uprising in 2008.

More recently, he played in Kashmir in 2013, seeking to apply the balm of music to the wounds of that troubled state. That performance too was not without its share of pre-concert controversy. At the bottom of it all is his conviction that music has a mission to provide the occasion for 'self-searching ethical reflection on the unforgiving political predicaments of our times'.[4]

♫

There are two kinds of biographies. In one, the subject is deceased and the biographer reconstructs as clear a picture as possible of the subject's life and personality, through letters, personal papers, books, newspaper articles and interviews. Such a biography tends to be a scholarly work, often undertaken by a historian. Since the subject is dead, all can be revealed.

In the second type of biography, the subject is living, which on the face of it is a great advantage as nothing can replace the value of personal interaction with the individual one hopes to portray. But there are disadvantages as well. Personal papers and letters are still locked away. Friends, acquaintances and even enemies are reluctant to speak candidly about a person worthy of a biography. Such a person is generally also highly influential. In addition, there are certain boundaries of decency that must be observed.

The living biography is a journalistic undertaking. Such a biography implies close collaboration, a relationship between the writer and his subject. This book, however, falls into neither of the two groups and is somewhat difficult to categorize. Since I had neither unrestricted access to documents and papers, nor indeed more than peripheral contact with the subject of the biography, it is important for the reader to know how the book came to be; how a person with no musical credentials at all had the chutzpah to write a biography of one of the world's greatest conductors. I have long been an admirer of Zubin Mehta. My first interaction happened when our entire family went backstage at Siri Fort Auditorium after Zubin finished conducting a concert with the New York Philharmonic in New Delhi in September 1984. We posed for photographs with him and his wife, Nancy, more than pleased at our family's flirtation with immortality, with *aapro* Zubin.

Over the years, I followed his career thorough reports in the media and attended most of his concerts whenever he visited India with some of the orchestras he has been intimately associated with. In 2006, I started working on a book, *Sugar in Milk: Lives of Eminent Parsis*, which had biographical profiles of twelve personalities who in my opinion were among the greatest Parsis of all time. Zubin, of course, found a place in it. In the process of writing that profile, I came to know a lot more about him and his musical achievements, and though I may not have realized it then, it is possible that the seed for this book was sown at that time. We corresponded briefly on email and he answered the questions I put to him, but not before verifying that he was indeed in eminent company. The only thing he wanted to know about the book when I first approached him, was who were the other worthies with whom he would be sharing publishing real estate. The profile was written and the book was published in early 2008. (I also put the New Delhi photograph from 1984 in the book after 'Photoshopping' the rest of the family out of it.)

I sent the book to Zubin through the good offices of his childhood friend Dr Yusuf Hamied. He indicated his appreciation of what I had written and told me so in person when we met at the launch of his autobiography in Mumbai in October 2008. While it would be impertinent to comment on the memoirs of an international celebrity, I could not help thinking that his life (even the little I knew of it) was far more interesting than his memoirs indicated. The tone of the book seemed to be one of deliberate understatement. It was published in German in 2006 and subsequently translated into English in 2008. I had a professor of German translate most of it into English and used it when I was writing my profile on him.

Soon after the launch of his autobiography, I was consumed by the idea of writing his biography. That I was not remotely connected with Western classical music either as musician, critic or aficionado did not bother me in the least. Maybe it should have, but it didn't. A rational examination of my candidature as Zubin's biographer would have brought the project to a premature end right at its inception, and I am glad that I never undertook such searching self-examination. I plodded on, regardless of my limited knowledge, developing a ravenous appetite for, and devouring any article on Zubin that the online archives of numerous magazines and newspapers seemed to have plenty of. Armed with information gleaned from hundreds of articles, I started writing the book.

I contacted Zubin and asked him what he thought of the idea. Predictably, it did not find favour, given that he had just published his autobiography. I was disappointed but continued with my labours sporadically and, in the span of a few years, had completed the first draft of the book. There the matter lay for a few years. The research and writing of another book intervened; my pet project, indeed idée fixe, had been banished from my writing table but not my mind. Late in 2014, I came to know that Zubin was bringing the Israel Philharmonic Orchestra to Mumbai for a concert at Brabourne Stadium in April 2016 to celebrate his four score years on this earth. A biography published on one's eightieth birthday isn't such a bad idea, so I contacted Zubin again with renewed optimism, knowing that now there was some chance of his agreeing to 'put his life in my hands', so to speak. He agreed to answer some of my questions with the proviso that I was not to ask too many (i.e. not make a pest of myself), to which I had no choice but to agree.

A biography of Zubin contends with two potentially overwhelming facts: that the subject is a celebrated international conductor almost relentlessly in the spotlight, with much of his life already in the public domain; and that he himself has published his memoirs. This biography attempts to outline Zubin's life in music; it is not an examination of his personal life. Personal insights come incidentally, they are not central to the biography. Thus the biographical thread exists only to give continuity to the reflections on music and on the relationship between music and life. Admittedly, the events are not new, but I would like to believe it is akin to turning a kaleidoscope—the pieces remain the same but they fall differently each time, forming ever-changing patterns. This book tries to link music and life, history and biography, the professional and, to a very limited extent, the personal, as it weaves in and out of Zubin's life so as to situate him and his musical achievements at the centre of international Western classical music.

My main worry when I started researching this book was that I am neither musician nor musicologist; neither music historian nor critic. Nor can I consider myself knowledgeable about music. I would be guilty of adding pretence and untruth to ignorance if I projected myself as a dyed-in-the-wool aficionado of Western classical music. Many would say that I am eminently unsuitable for the task I have undertaken and they might just be right. When the English translation of Zubin's autobiography was launched, I reviewed it for a magazine and ended the piece with the words: 'One can't help thinking that this book is merely an appetizer; a definitive and full-length biography of this extraordinary life remains to be written. In his book Mehta has shown us the music; we would like to see the man as well.' Little did I dream at the time (or maybe I did, the subconscious mind is a funny thing) that I would be the one to write a full-length biography of Zubin; it, however, deals largely with his life in music, though it does have many more personal details about him than his own memoirs contain.

That Zubin has read the manuscript, made corrections and given his suggestions has been a huge bonus for which I am most grateful. His authorizing this biography is, of course, the icing on the cake.

Notwithstanding all its imperfections and the limitations of its author, this biography will have served its purpose if it succeeds in igniting interest in the life of a remarkable artiste whose service to music has been marked by undying passion, great virtuosity and exceptional longevity.

# A Child *of* Music

IT IS SAID THAT Zubin Mehta learned to sing and speak at almost the same time. He was surrounded by music from his first attempts at lisping phrase and toddling steps. A prized possession was a pair of drumsticks he received at the age of two. Nothing in the house was safe from them and when they were confiscated for an inappropriate attack on household objects, he substituted two of his mother's spoons for sticks and resumed the assault. At an age when a child's amusements are limited to toys and toes, musical instruments seemed to attract him the most. He would identify records by the colour of their labels and ask his *ayah* to play them for him on the wind-up gramophone they had at home.

Fate often chooses incongruous birthplaces and families for genius. Western classical music was almost non-existent in Bombay (now Mumbai) or, for that matter, in India, till the end of the nineteenth century. The little that existed was restricted to amateurs who played in the privacy of people's homes. It spread to India very slowly through European settlers who were mainly English or Italian. As a close-knit community that has jealously guarded its own ethnic identity, the Parsis (with some notable exceptions) have rarely developed an intimate understanding of Indian classical music. As with many other things Western, they have, however, embraced Western music most willingly.

If Bombay was a less than perfect place for launching the career of an internationally famous classical music conductor, Zubin could not have asked for a more appropriate father or a more supportive mother. It was to Mehli Mehta and his wife, Tehmina, that Zubin, indisputably the world's most famous Parsi and one of the most famous Indians alive, was born in Bombay at 2.50 a.m. on 29 April 1936. He learned music, or at least heard it, as he learned to talk. He could have been nothing but musical in the atmosphere that prevailed in his home. His world was one of harmony and, from his earliest days, he felt life through music.

♫

Of the groups which constituted the Western-educated class, the Parsis were one of the most prominent. With their progressive outlook, they had been quick to learn English; now they were quick to take advantage of the new culture, with Parsi families taking to Western classical musical enthusiastically. Some attained great virtuosity at the piano and the violin, an achievement made more remarkable by the fact that they were entirely self-taught or had very little musical tutelage.

Parsi musicians soon started making their mark both as performers and as teachers, and one of those who rose to early prominence was the pianist Bhikhaiji Palamkote (1867–1954), the first music teacher in the Parsi community, and indeed the first Parsi to receive recognition in the field of Western classical music. She passed the examinations conducted by Trinity College London, and had the unique distinction of being made a life member of that institution.

Her name was associated with Trinity College in the form of a scholarship awarded to Parsis who passed its diploma examinations with honours. In 1921 she established a fund to set up a concert hall in Bombay. When it became clear that the fund would never be rich enough to achieve its objective, it was decided that the money collected (Rs 23,000) would be transferred to Trinity College to use the interest to give cash prizes and medals to meritorious Parsi students. She even received a letter from Mahatma Gandhi who, while praising her achievements, said that he would have been very pleased if she had rendered her services for the cause of Indian music as well.

In 1922, a Parsi philanthropist, J.B. Petit, decided to fund Bombay's first symphony orchestra: the Bombay Symphony and Chamber Orchestra. Most of the musicians were Goan and, in a pattern which lasted many years, the audiences were largely Parsi. But the new orchestra folded in 1928 once its benefactor withdrew financial support. Clearly, it was easier to build a band than an audience; Parsi passion alone was not enough to sustain the orchestra.[1]

Though the Parsis were among the first to develop a taste for Western classical music, not many actually became professional musicians. The two Mehlis, Mehli Casinath and Mehli Mehta were perhaps the best exemplars of this musical embrace. Born in 1894, Merwanji (Mehli) Bomanji Casinath, like many others of his time, was an autodidact. After teaching himself the violin, he went on to become proficient in the piano, the cello and the saxophone. He also played the harmonium on which it is said he would often play Indian ragas. The six-foot-tall Casinath, who was almost as broad as he was tall, started giving music lessons and, as his fame as a teacher spread, he attracted pupils from all over Bombay. According to Bomi Billimoria, one of those who came to him for lessons was Mehli Mehta, Zubin's father, who made the journey to the imposing Casinath Hall, a palatial mansion by the sea which was the ancestral home of that genial giant. According to Billimoria it was Casinath who taught Mehli how to tuck the violin under his chin.[2] When I asked Zubin about Casinath he said that though he remembers the name, he does not recollect Mehli ever talking about taking any lessons from him.[3]

In 1930, Casinath formed the twelve-piece Young Men's Parsi Orchestra. Dressed in spotless white *dagli*s (Parsi wedding shirts) and Parsi caps, this ensemble was especially popular at *navjote*s and weddings where they would play Johann Strauss's waltzes and other Parsi favourites. Casinath was not only a versatile musician and an inspirational teacher, he was also a composer of some merit. He wrote many marches, including one called 'Parsi Loyalty to Royalty' in 1921 to commemorate the visit of the Prince of Wales to India. In 1926 he wrote the 'Pahlavi March' to commemorate the coronation of Reza Shah Pahlavi of Iran. He also composed the 'Sanjan March' and the 'Zoroastrian National Anthem', the latter being played at the end of every musical evening. (In the 1940s a certain Nani A. Palkhivala played the violin in this orchestra. Palkhivala is considered by many to be India's greatest lawyer.)

Another Parsi notable in the world of Western music in Bombay was Phiroze M. Damri who played the violin in Casinath's orchestra. He, however, courted fame not as a violinist but as the greatest harmonica player India has ever produced. In November 1937, a German by the name of Matt Hohner came to Bombay in search of a musician to promote their harmonica in India. He was introduced to Damri and it proved to be a turning point for both. It is said that Damri mastered the book *Teach Yourself Harmonica*, which Hohner gave him, in just three days! He founded and ran the Hohner Harmonica Club for six decades, starting in 1937, and by the time he died at the ripe old age of ninety-one in 2005, he had trained generations of harmonica players.

## BORN TO THE BATON

Zubin (which means 'powerful sword') shares his birthday with two famous English conductors, the inimitable Sir Thomas Beecham (1879) and Sir Malcolm Sargent (1895). Tehmina had Zubin's horoscope cast and the first hints of his future greatness came from an astrologer who predicted that the child would be a leader of a group of people (he was, however, unable to indicate what kind of group). At the bottom of the chart he wrote: 'The child born on this day will be changeable, over-confident, and much too sure of himself. He will desire to lead but requires training in judgement and moderation.'[4] A second son, Zarin, was born on 28 October 1938, two and a half years after Zubin's birth.

Mehli was musical both by temperament and by vocation. Of generous enthusiasms, he spread the love of his art throughout his community. Sons with famous fathers and fathers with famous sons share a similar predicament. A son's claim to fame often rests solely on his famous father and a father is sometimes remembered only because of his renowned son. Mehli faced that predicament all his life, though it is doubtful if he ever viewed it as such: nothing gave him more pride than the achievements of his son Zubin. He himself was a musician and conductor of no mean merit.

Whether Zubin could have become a great conductor without his father's influence is a matter of speculation. What is certain, however, is that music entered his physical and intellectual system so completely at an early age that it became his nature. Listening to music was as natural to him as breathing and, as a child, he would often be a 'pretend' conductor. In a TV interview many years later, Mehli gave Zubin all the credit saying he was a musician from the time he was in his mother's womb. But it was obviously the admiration of a doting father which made him play down his own contribution. Zubin is inconceivable without his father; just as Zubin is a unique phenomenon, Mehli was a unique father. The two created each other. As Zubin has observed in his memoirs, 'Moreover, I had a very special relationship with my father based on music. He was and remains for me a model of willpower, energy and stamina.'[5]

Born in Bombay on 25 September 1908 to Nowroji and Piroja, Mehli discovered Western classical music through the records of Jascha Heifetz, Fritz Kreisler and Efrem Zimbalist (who went on to head the famous Curtis Institute in Philadelphia from 1941–68). He was inspired by the great violinists Heifetz and Jan Kubelík who passed through Bombay in the late 1920s on their way to China or Australia. There were also Italian opera companies that came to Bombay and toured parts of India in the early nineteenth century. Difficult as it is to believe, Gioachino Rossini's opera *The Barber of Seville* was performed in India in 1835![6] (In an interview Zubin narrated how Mehli saw Heifetz at an exhibition match of tennis between Bill Tilden and Henri Cochet in Bombay in the late 1920s and wondered if playing the violin was so easy that one could attend a tennis match in the morning and play the violin at a concert in the evening!)

Nowroji, who was a manager of the New Islam Cotton Mills, Bombay, encouraged his son's interest in the violin. At the age of seventeen, Mehli was allowed to study under Oddone Savini, leader of a salon orchestra that played in Bombay's British hotels. Savini was also perhaps the only violin teacher in Bombay.

Undaunted by the fact that his passion had little or no future in India, Mehli taught himself to play the violin after having learned the basics from Savini. Learning the violin is no easy task; beginners, especially, are known to produce sounds that are unmusical to say the least. Zubin says that such was Mehli's talent and dedication that he memorized Beethoven's Violin Concerto, one of the most challenging works for the violin, note for note, from a Heifetz recording. He recalls that his father was fanatical about his playing. His achievements become even more praiseworthy when seen in the light of the fact that recordings were hardly high fidelity in those days, and had a rather feeble sound.

Mehli received his bachelor of commerce degree from Sydenham College, University of Bombay, before being employed as a tax collector for the government. But the world of accountancy or, for that matter, a career in the mills, held no charm for him. Mehli, according to Zubin, was given the odious task of collecting taxes from the egg vendors of Crawford Market. He recalled how Mehli used to complain bitterly about the peculiar smell in those shops. Then, one day, he decided to give it all up to pursue Western classical music. In the 1920s and 1930s a career in Western classical music for an Indian was something out of a fairy tale, even though it was more likely to have gained acceptance as a profession among the westernized Parsis than among other communities. In a decision that must have taken much courage, Mehli bravely decided to live his dream.

The dream of giving Western classical music a home in Bombay was a cosmopolitan one and Mehli was in the vanguard of those who wanted to make this happen. His talent and expertise were to provide the city with a range of musical institutions: A Palm Court Sextet at the Taj Mahal Hotel, the Bombay Symphony Orchestra and the Bombay String Quartet. 'Mehli's rich, eclectic talent caught the changing moods of the city perfectly: a bit of glitz; some razzmatazz; the serious intimacy of chamber music; and the grand orchestral occasion.'[7]

## THE BOMBAY SYMPHONY ORCHESTRA

When Anna Pavlova toured Bombay with her ballet company in 1935 to perform for the British aristocracy, the need for an orchestra became all too apparent. There were no musicians available to accompany her and they were forced to enlist the services of Bombay's pre-eminent Parsi amateur, Mehli. His experience until then had been limited to living rooms, playing solos with his friends and an occasional radio performance. Having attained some local recognition as a violinist, Mehli saw this as a golden opportunity to establish himself. He quit his job as tax collector and formed a makeshift orchestra, appointing himself as concertmaster and soloist. Pavlova and the orchestra performed throughout India over a three-week period, and these were Mehli's first paid performances. They did *Giselle* and *Raymonda* among others, and Mehli played every single one of the violin solos.

At about this time Mehli married Tehmina, a marriage that was to last sixty-seven years. The two were married on 6 March 1935, and Mehli would have happily missed his own reception if he had been allowed to have his way: he was scheduled to play in the ballet orchestra at the same time. Mehli even told a disappointed Tehmina that she would have to welcome the guests on her own. But Mehli's boss at All India Radio came to her rescue. He told Mehli that if he missed the reception he would never play for All India Radio again. The threat worked. And since Mehli was the only man who could play those violin solos, those parts had to be cancelled for that evening's performance.[8]

After the tour was over, Mehli realized that he could form a symphony orchestra with the musicians he had gathered and thus was born the Bombay Symphony Orchestra on 29 April 1935, exactly a year before Zubin was born. He co-founded the Bombay Symphony with Belgian-born conductor Jules Craen, who had studied at the

Brussels Conservatory. At its inception the Bombay Symphony comprised, Jewish refugees, British navy musicians and Craen, who often featured his concert pianist wife, a Goan named Olga Athaide.[9] Mehli was the concertmaster. He auditioned musicians who earned a living performing in hotels and restaurants, or played wind and brass instruments in navy and police bands. He also single-handedly managed a host of logistical issues: transporting musicians who could not afford a cab in his own car and purchasing suits for them. While the amateur and professional musicians played in tuxedos, the navy musicians performed in their uniforms! The orchestra was a sight to behold.

Zubin, Zarin and Tehmina assisted Mehli in any way they could. 'We prepared the programmes together, and saw to it that they were published. My father would mark in the score the instructions for the violinists and I would then copy them into the other parts. In addition, the orchestra did not have all the instruments. For instance, there were only two horns. The other two horn parts were played by a saxophone, and we had to transpose the music for saxophone.'[10]

As we have already noted, in a curious coincidence, Zubin was born on the first anniversary of the founding of the Bombay Symphony. It was also the year in which the Israel Philharmonic Orchestra was founded, while the day marked the legendary Toscanini's last performance with the New York Philharmonic. The Bombay Symphony gave concerts once every six weeks at the Sir Cowasji Jehangir Hall, in the heart of Bombay's cultural district. Katy Gundevia who grew up in Cuffe Parade in the 1940s recalls how she and her mother used to take a walk on the seashore (it had no encroachments then) and sit on the bench opposite the Mehta bungalow, where they enjoyed hearing Mehli as he practised his music in the evenings.[11]

Western classical music played little part in the tumultuous city of Bombay but this did not in any way diminish Mehli's ardour. He created an oasis where classical music flourished and, five years after he founded the Bombay Symphony Orchestra, he formed the Bombay String Quartet. It consisted of Adrian de Mello, Russi Mody and George Lester apart from Mehli himself. Mehli is known to have observed: 'The string quartet has been the prime basic factor of my entire musical philosophy.' One of those whom Mehli taught, and who went on to make a name for himself in England, was the violinist Homi Kanga. After taking his first lessons from Mehli, Kanga went to Paris for further studies and eventually settled in London where he played in both the London Philharmonic Orchestra and the Royal Philharmonic Orchestra. Kanga also founded a number of ensembles, including the Kanga String Quartet.[12] (Hindi film music composer Pyarelal, of the famous duo Laxmikant–Pyarelal, also used to train under Mehli and the Bombay Symphony Orchestra.)

After some years Mehli took up the baton, teaching himself conducting just as he had the violin. His audiences were almost exclusively white, something which he deeply regretted. Mehli eventually had to leave Bombay because there wasn't enough encouragement or funding for Western classical music. He always felt the hurt about leaving 'that beautiful home by the Arabian Sea, that beautiful country, all my friends and all my music circles'. In an interview, Mehli was once asked if he had made his peace with Bombay. He said, 'I have no quarrel with Bombay. When I came away from Bombay, they gave me parties, they gave me receptions and a good send off. But my life, my main aim and my goal is my music. A man stands for his work and my work was not appreciated or accepted.'[13] (Many years later, Mehli was a much loved and respected music director of the American Youth Symphony in Los Angeles for thirty-three years.)

Mehli felt understandably miffed at the lack of enthusiasm for his work, but he, being Parsi, could at least avoid the secondary status assigned to other Indian musicians. In the 1920s and 1930s Hindu and Muslim musicians were still seen as subjects of the royal courts and were accorded a very low social status. This became clear to Mehli when he observed one of the top female classical vocalists of India being treated as a lowly servant when she performed at a private dinner at a residence in Bombay's tony Malabar Hill. Mehli who was present at the dinner noted the casual manner in which the singer was dismissed from the room once her recital had been completed. While her art was appreciated, she would never be a social equal in the eyes of her patrons.

The Bombay Symphony Orchestra went from strength to strength, growing in numbers and improving in quality. It continued to grow during the Second World War, evolving into a diverse group, and included many European players who were escaping the war. It was truly a wartime League of Nations: a Prussian violinist, a Czech cellist, an Italian flautist, an Albanian bass player and a Greek who played the oboe and bassoon. Goans and Parsis made up most of the strings.[14] By now Mehli had become the central figure for Western classical music not only in Bombay but also across India. (Just how driven Mehli was can be judged from the fact that he had played more than 400 chamber-music concerts before he left for the United States.)

Mehli also performed regularly at the Taj Mahal Hotel in Bombay from 1939 onwards. At a time when many jazz bands performed at the Taj, Mehli provided classical performances playing light music with his 'Melody Trio' during the businessmen's luncheon in the ballroom. A British observer remembered with admiration how Mehli played Mendelssohn's Violin Concerto, remarking that he was the finest instrumentalist in the East. Zubin does not remember accompanying him to these concerts. Mehli also played at certain exclusively British establishments such as the Breach Candy Club and smarted at the fact that Indians were not allowed. He was a nationalist at heart, according to Zubin, and even though he was an erudite musician, it was no coincidence that he never performed the music of English composers.

A programme of a matinee concert at the Excelsior Theatre in February 1937 for the Consulate of Poland was discovered in 2004. It had Mehli on the violin, Egidio Verga on the cello and Walter Kaufmann on the piano. First Verga, and then Lester brought the magic of the cello to Bombay. Kaufmann, a Jewish composer and pianist from Karlsbad, was also in Bombay at the time, and is today best remembered in India for having composed the famous signature tune announcing All India Radio's Western classical music broadcasts.

It was executed by Mehli and Verga, 'a soaring violin heard over a cello drone pretending to be a tanpura'. Kaufmann even composed a score, 'Slavonic String Quartet' (*Romantischer*), and dedicated it to Mehli.

## 'MUSICAL PLEASURE GARDEN'

Tehmina recalled in an interview in 1988 that Zubin had two or three favourite records and, as a child, he would pick out only those. 'When he was sick or in pain, if we played a record he would just put his head on my shoulder and be quiet. As soon as the record finished, he would remember his pain and start crying.'[15] A tango with a refrain sung in German was one of his favourites. Zubin recalls that Mehli possessed a large collection of records which exposed him to a variety of music at an early age. He listened to symphonies and was soon familiar with Beethoven, Johannes Brahms and Mahler. He says that sometimes he even missed his game of cricket when there was new music to listen to at home.

Zubin was surrounded by classical music right from the cradle. In an interview to NDTV in September 2008, Zubin said that he had no choice. 'Of course I don't remember the first time I heard music in my life because it was always in my home . . . I think I learned music and Gujarati at the same time.'[16] Since the Mehta living room was the venue of rehearsals with the orchestra or with the Bombay String Quartet, Zubin got to know many of the pieces by heart and would often hum melodies by the great composers. This seed, sown in a sensibility fashioned by his father, was to flower in adult life in a manner no one could have foreseen.

On one occasion Mehli and his group played Franz Schubert's *Death and the Maiden* and the *Trout* Quintet for a radio broadcast. Since the music was about a minute too long, the little variation in the slow movement of the *Trout* was deleted believing that no one would miss it. But young Zubin immediately spotted the omission and asked them why they had not played that particular part. Later, he witnessed his father's lessons and chamber-music rehearsals, and was soon whistling Niccolò Paganini caprices in the original key, cycling or playing cricket. Silloo Billimoria, whose tenants the Mehtas were at 21-A, Cuffe Parade, recalls that Zubin could whistle beautifully as a boy.[17] The fact that his father was a musician and possessed a large collection of records, Zubin says, ensured 'a very early access into paradise' and, since his entry into 'this musical pleasure garden' as a boy, no one has been able to drive him out of it.[18]

India at the time was still under British rule and the Indian National Congress and Mahatma Gandhi were at the forefront of the freedom struggle. Zubin's youth, however, was untouched by developments on the political front, though he did recount in a recent interview how familiar he was with the words 'Quit India' and how they would invariably leave the theatre before the English anthem 'God Save the Queen' was played at the end of a film. He grew up, in his own words, 'sheltered and cheerful' with a caring and loving mother, and a wonderful father. As a lad he got into scrapes just like any other healthy young boy, earning his first scar at the age of three! He indulged in the usual childish amusements and later developed an interest in cricket, which remains an abiding passion.

He attended Campion School and, along with NCPA Chairman Khushroo Suntook, was one of its first students. At that time it had not moved to its premises at the Cooperage and operated out of a rented apartment in Marine Lines. Suntook joked that each classroom had an attached bathroom. Zubin moved to St Mary's in Mazgaon in the fifth grade. (Zubin inaugurated the 150th-year celebrations of his school in September 2013, where he unveiled the logo, and he and his wife, Nancy, gave short speeches. It proved to be a memorable occasion for the students and the teachers.)

In the summer of 1944, Zubin suffered a bout of spinal meningitis. It was a most trying time, but Zubin bore the pain cheerfully. Luckily, the sulfa drugs that had just been introduced at the time provided a cure and, within a week, he improved. But he had to miss school for two months to recuperate and the only thing he really enjoyed during those difficult days was his father's music.

## THE MOVE TO AMERICA

The limits of pragmatic self-instruction soon became apparent to the self-taught Mehli. He decided that the only way he could improve his skill was by getting formal instruction. In 1945, thanks to a grant from the Tata Endowment Fund, he arrived in New York to study the violin. (Zubin says that Mehli left for America on the very first ship that left Bombay after the Second World War ended.) The Tata grant was a chance he could ill afford to miss and Tehmina supported him fully even though it meant that she would have to manage their two boys alone for four years. When asked by a friend how her husband could leave them alone for that long, she simply replied, 'How can he *not* go?'[19]

Since he was too old for the famous Juilliard School, he had to take private classes. But his luck held and the legendary Galamian, one of the most influential violin teachers of the twentieth century, took him under his wing. Galamian was of Armenian origin and taught violinists like Michael Rabin, Perlman and Zukerman who went on to become big names in the world of music. (Perlman and Zukerman still are; Rabin passed away prematurely in 1972.)

Notwithstanding the fact that Bombay had little to offer Mehli by way of encouragement, it still gave him a heart-warming farewell when he left for America in 1945. A packed Sir Cowasji Jehangir Hall saw the Bombay Symphony conducted by Mehli perform pieces by Claude Debussy, Beethoven, Schubert and Tchaikovsky. A newspaper report acknowledged Mehli's contribution to the Western classical music scene in Bombay:

> Someone must take over. And at once. The future of music in India requires it. But whoever may now be placed on the podium, the figure of Mehli Mehta will remain gigantically projected in the background as the one who succeeded in bringing the symphonic coordination of the musicians of Bombay to its present high degree.[20]

It was unquestionably Mehli's pioneering efforts that kept Western classical music alive in the country. He was everywhere. He selected programmes with an eye to enticing newcomers into the classical music fold. At the same time there was also enough on the programmes to demonstrate to music lovers that he and his ensembles were capable of meeting the challenges of more difficult works. Instructions were issued to close the doors of the concert hall once the performance started—classical music had to be respected. Latecomers were admitted only after the first composition had been completed. Mehli also placed two large boards at the ends of the stage which bore the words: 'Please do not clap between movements.'[21] (This is something newcomers to Western classical music in India still need to be educated about.)

In New York, Mehli started from scratch or 'open string' and perfected his violin technique with Galamian; until then he had judged it 'no good'. Tehmina had to manage on her own for the four years that Mehli was away. It was difficult raising two young boys (Zubin and his younger brother, Zarin) on her own. Since Tehmina came from a reasonably well-to-do family, finances were not an overwhelming problem. They also had a tenant whose rent was a welcome addition to the family finances.

Mehli arrived in New York in the summer of 1945 and almost immediately attended his first concert—an outdoor event at Lewisohn Stadium with Alexander Smallens conducting the New York Philharmonic in a performance of Giacomo Puccini's *La Bohème*. It was his first opera. It was also the first time he was hearing an orchestra other than his own.[22] Mehli wrote in detail about learning the violin all over again and his experience of the many concerts he attended. From his apartment on Fifty-Seventh Street and Lexington Avenue he sent home every programme of the New York concerts that he attended, complete with commentary on the pieces and the artistes. On many occasions his programmes were his letters. He attended concerts of Artur Rodziński, Mitropoulos and Walter and was most impressed with the performances of the violin virtuoso Heifetz whom he called 'God'. Mehli had moved to New York hoping to become a world-class violinist, but there was too much competition in a field bursting with talent. 'It was the heyday of great conductors and virtuosos. At my best, unhappily, I was no match for Milstein and Heifetz,' he said.[23]

Another artiste who greatly impressed Mehli was the conductor Leopold Stokowski. He called his strings 'silken perfection' and promised to bring back some of his records conducting the Philadelphia Orchestra so that Zubin could also experience, at least vicariously, his virtuosity. (Neither Mehli nor Zubin could have dreamed that it would be Stokowski who would provide the latter with the opportunity to make his American debut with the Philadelphia Orchestra.) Young Zubin looked forward to Mehli's letters and programmes, and began to dream of one day becoming an international musician himself. When listening to music at home he began to pretend that he was a conductor.

After Mehli left, there was less music at home. Zubin played the piano and listened to recorded music incessantly. By the time Mehli came back, he knew at least by ear most of the major works of the symphonic repertoire. His father had built a little cupboard for their records and every night after dinner Zubin would pick a symphony or tone poem to listen to. He would sit on the sofa in the living room and sometimes get up and conduct in his own way. He did not have a baton and had no idea of what he was doing, but he was 'conducting'.

Since Mehli had the entire collection of Heifetz at home, Zubin was familiar with every recording of the maestro. In those days, the recording industry was characterized by a primitive reproduction of sound and there was music on only one side of the record. Zubin says that today he can accompany almost any violin concerto at a moment's notice, having known every single one since childhood. One of those recordings was the Beethoven Violin Concerto with Toscanini and, even today, when he conducts the piece, he remembers where the record changed because the first movement spanned three sides. It's a performance he still cannot get out of his ears.

Mehli returned somewhat reluctantly to India. 'He was very frustrated in Bombay,' recalled Dady Mehta, his cousin, a concert pianist and, before his retirement, a distinguished professor of piano at East Michigan University, near Ann Arbor. 'He felt he was not appreciated enough by the Parsi community for all of his incredible work in Western classical music.' (Mehli was the youngest of five sons, of whom Dady's father, Nariman, was the oldest. Dady's two sons, Bejun and Navi, are also musicians. Navi is a violinist and conductor in San Diego, and Bejun is a much sought-after countertenor who has also performed with Zubin on a few occasions.)

When Mehli returned from America in 1949, he had matured as a violinist. He focused his attention on the musical life in Bombay, giving concerts and organizing performances. As usual the Mehta house was where most of the rehearsals took place. Zubin recalls how his father taught him to read musical scores. He was a quick learner and was soon conversant with most of the important symphonies. Zubin harboured aspirations of becoming a conductor from the time he started helping his father with his orchestra. Zubin recalls: 'In any case I loved orchestral music and very early imagined becoming a conductor. In truth, deep down, I became a conductor because I had always wanted to conduct Brahms's four symphonies and Richard Strauss's tone poems . . .'[24]

When Mehli prepared at home for rehearsals, Zubin would conduct and he would play the violin. Later, Zubin used one of Mehli's broken batons and imagined himself in place of Toscanini, Weingartner or Furtwängler (he seems to have been an early favourite with the Mehtas). When Zubin received the Furtwängler Prize in 2011, he told an interviewer about how Mehli had rented a hall in 1953 and they had listened to a recording of Wagner's *Tristan und Isolde* conducted by Furtwängler. They did not have the score or the text but were overwhelmed by the music alone. 'But we listened and were swept away—by the music alone, since we did not understand but felt the Wagner revolution,'[25] he said. But Zubin had no exposure to opera in Bombay and it was only when he went to Vienna that his education in this form started.

By the time Mehli returned to India, the Bombay Symphony had disbanded. Craen had fallen foul of the authorities and the orchestra was stranded without a conductor. Mehli had no choice but to reform the orchestra, this time with himself as the conductor. Now he had to play as well as lead. As with the violin, Mehli was a self-taught conductor. Zubin notes in his autobiography that the ability to teach himself new musical skills was one of Mehli's special gifts. The British Navy Band had left India and their places in the brass and percussion sections were filled with members of the band of the Indian navy. Zubin called his father the 'Leonard Bernstein of Bombay'.

With such a quick turnover of musicians, Mehli found that he needed an assistant manager and a music librarian. Zubin filled both these posts. Mehli also sent him to study music theory on weekends under his old teacher, Savini, who had by then moved to Poona (now Pune). He also started him on the violin and continued his piano lessons. Tehmina recalled how Zubin would leave for Poona every Sunday at 8 a.m. for his three-hour lesson with Savini and return at 8 p.m. But Mehli found that Zubin needed to be coaxed into practising as he preferred to spend his time playing cricket.

If Zubin was passionate about music as a child, he was equally taken with cricket. Zubin's childhood friend Hamied, chairman of Cipla Ltd, one of India's pharmaceutical majors, recalls how they would meet every evening after school and play cricket in the compound. Hamied, a student of Cathedral School, lived at 25-A, Cuffe Parade, a stone's throw from the Mehtas. The two friends also played at the nearby Oval Maidan.

Many years later, Hamied bought a bat owned by Sir Don Bradman at an auction and presented it to his friend. Zubin had met the legendary batsman at the Adelaide Oval and called it one of the most memorable moments of his life (according to him as climactic as meeting Igor Stravinsky). Somebody who knew Sir Don said, 'Look, there's this young Indian conductor,' and they spent half an hour together. The next time he came to Australia, Zubin invited him to a concert. Sir Don sent a handwritten note saying he couldn't make it. Not many know that the batting legend was passionate about music. He was a pianist and used to be a soprano soloist as a boy. His granddaughter Greta Bradman is a promising soprano who grew up on her grandfather's LPs. She garnered praise from Zubin after auditioning for him in Vienna in March 2015 and performed with him on the Australian World Orchestra's tour of India in October 2015. Interacting with the media before the concert in New Delhi, she said, 'For my grandfather, maestro Mehta was the greatest hero and I have grown up listening to him. I wish that my grandfather could see me now. This is a most humbling and truly wonderful experience.' India's little master Sachin Tendulkar who, Bradman said, reminded him of himself the most, gifted Zubin two of his bats and both these maestros shared a stage at the 25 Global Living Legends Awards hosted by NDTV in December 2013.

Zubin has been passionately fond of the game since childhood and turns to it to unwind after a concert. Indeed, says a friend, he might have preferred to be a cricketer but, fortunately for music, he seemed not to possess an equal talent. In fact, Zubin's love for the game is such that he buys *The Times* of London wherever he goes because it is the only paper that provides all the cricket scores. His years in Vienna in the pre-Internet days, without access to scores, were the worst. He confesses that in one of his homes, he and his English and Australian friends filched cable so they could watch cricket. As Zubin has observed, 'Culturally, I'm a central European; sports wise I'm an Indian.'

Another childhood friend who has stayed in touch sporadically over the years is Ajit Hutheesing, son of Jawaharlal Nehru's sister Krishna. Zubin and he were in St Mary's together and have known each other since they were twelve. They also studied together for two years in St Xavier's College, Bombay. Hutheesing remembers him as a quiet child and adolescent who was socially uncomfortable with girls! Hutheesing used to host dance parties on the terrace of Anand Bhavan on Carmichael Road, where Zubin would be a 'reluctant participant'. Strangely, he never heard Zubin talk of his musical interests and, though they visited each other's homes, they met more often at Oomer Park, Breach Candy, in Suntook's home where Hutheesing's interest in Western classical music was seeded. He remembers Mehli and Tehmina, fondly calling them the nicest and most unassuming couple he had met as a child—or since. Mehli invited the Hutheesing family to his concerts and they always attended. Hutheesing, who became a highly successful investment banker in the US and later married the violinist Helen Armstrong, says that distance, disparate careers and Zubin's celebrity status served to keep them largely apart. 'As an old friend, I have found this difficult to accept—or to become part of a crowd trying to access "aapro Zubin".'[26]

Zubin had studied violin and piano but played both indifferently. By the time he was eleven, he had aspirations of becoming a conductor like his father and greats such as Rodziński, Walter and Stokowski whom he saw in the 1947 movie *Carnegie Hall*, a film he watched six times. Mehli's audience in Bombay remained sparse and the Bombay Symphony lost a good deal of money. As Tehmina recalled to Zubin's biographers Martin Bookspan and Ross Yockey, 'I watched my husband slave to make people understand and want to go to concerts, but it was a thankless task. I can't tell you how much of our own money we lost in making music.'[27]

This must have been a deciding factor in preparing Zubin for a career in medicine. After St Mary's, Zubin was admitted to the science stream of St Xavier's College with an eye on medicine as a future profession. At St Xavier's, Zubin was taught physics by a Jesuit priest called Father Ramon de Rafael. Father Rafael, it so happened, had been a music student in Barcelona under the renowned composer Enrique Granados before taking his holy vows. Zubin soon started taking lessons from him in music theory, especially counterpoint. They did not realize it then, but the family's dream of Zubin qualifying as a doctor was receding fast.

## MENUHIN'S VISIT TO INDIA

In 1951, a famine devastated India and the world community expressed alarm and compassion. The famous violinist Yehudi Menuhin contacted Prime Minister Jawaharlal Nehru, volunteering to perform throughout India in early 1952 to raise money for the famine victims. Before Menuhin, Western classical music was a rarity in India. Heifetz and Kubelík (father of the conductor Rafael Kubelík) were probably the only Western violinists who had visited India. Menuhin befriended the sitar player Ravi Shankar on his arrival in New Delhi. In Bombay, Mehli was given the job of arranging the tour for Menuhin, a task which he undertook with much pleasure and enthusiasm. (Assisting him in organizing the tour was none other than eminent scientist Bhabha, who was an accomplished piano and violin player. According to Prof. Gustav Born, son of the Nobel Prize–winning physicist Max Born, who was a friend, Bhabha played one of two violin parts in Johann Sebastian Bach's Double Violin Concerto in D Minor at a party in his own home. The other part, Prof. Gustav said, was played by 'the delightful leader of the Bombay Symphony Orchestra by the name of Mehli Mehta'.

Mehli, Menuhin and Menuhin's pianist travelled all over India. Mehli requested Menuhin to play a few benefit concerts with his orchestra and the maestro readily agreed. Mehli put together two programmes for Menuhin which included Mendelssohn's E Minor Violin Concerto, Édouard Lalo's *Symphonie Espagnole* and Bach's Double Violin Concerto.[28] The two violinists would duet on Bach's Double Violin Concerto, while Menuhin also performed as a soloist with the Bombay Symphony.

To cut down on rehearsal time, Mehli decided that he would play the violin solos himself as they practised. Seeing the orchestra struggle without a leader, Zubin picked up the baton and took his father's place in conducting Brahms's E Minor Violin Concerto. That experience changed his life. Lester recalled that the moment Zubin got on to the podium, he took command, gave them their correct cues and 'put us all under his spell'. The first step in what was destined to be a glittering international career had just been taken.

Zubin says that the first time he conducted in public was when he accompanied Mehli for a radio advertisement in Bombay, playing the Concerto in A Minor by Bach. He conducted a chamber orchestra from memory as he was fully acquainted with the music. Zubin called it a great experience: making music with his father was in itself special. In 1954, Menuhin returned to Bombay and once again Mehli's services as a musician were enlisted. Menuhin gave four concerts in Bombay with the Bombay Symphony Orchestra, all under the baton of Mehli.

Mehli also played a role in introducing Menuhin to yoga guru B.K.S. Iyengar of Poona.[29] Menuhin's chance discovery of yoga while sitting in a doctor's room in New Zealand had made him a convert and, when he visited New Delhi, he praised yoga as India's greatest contribution to the welfare of humanity. Before the welcome dinner, he and Prime Minister Nehru engaged in a contest to see who could execute the more perfect headstand, much to the amusement of those present. Menuhin in his autobiography says that when challenged by Pandit Nehru, he stood on his head in a somewhat rickety and unsatisfactory manner, watched by Nehru's daughter, Indira, and sister Vijaya Lakshmi Pandit.

Nehru thought he could do much better and elegantly upended himself on the drawing room carpet. Both Menuhin and Nehru were on their heads when the butler threw open the door to announce dinner.[30] Iyengar recalled that at first he had been allotted only two minutes to meet Menuhin at Bombay's Raj Bhavan. Considering that the journey from Poona took five hours in those days, he refused to come and it took all of Mehli's powers of persuasion to get him to agree. Those two minutes eventually ended up becoming forty-five, at the end of which Menuhin was hooked. His meeting with Iyengar made him a dedicated yoga practitioner for the rest of his life. He also wrote the Foreword to Iyengar's famous book, *Light on Yoga*. Iyengar's subsequent popularity in the West owed much to Menuhin's patronage. When I asked Zubin about Mehli introducing Iyengar to Menuhin, he said he too had heard of it but could not confirm it. Zubin had learned yoga from one of Iyengar's pupils (he could not recall his name) but gave it up when he went to Vienna at the age of eighteen.[31]

## A CAREER IN WESTERN CLASSICAL MUSIC

It was becoming increasingly obvious to Zubin that his future lay in music. Unsurprisingly, when his anatomy teacher asked him to cut up a dogfish in a practical class, Zubin left the room with the words: 'Cut it up yourself!' Zubin recalls, 'Every time I sat down to cut up a dogfish, there I was with a Brahms symphony running through my head.' It was clear to everyone that his medical career was ending even before it had started. Zubin told Mehli that he wanted to study music in Vienna where his cousin Dady—the only Mehta other than Mehli and Zubin interested in making music—was learning the piano under Bruno Seidlhofer at the Vienna Music Academy. Dady had initially been studying music in Paris but moved to Vienna when his teacher died. He used to write to Zubin about his experiences, musical and otherwise, only adding to the fire in Zubin's belly. Zubin too wanted to be a musician and tour the world.

Dady wrote in glowing terms about the marvellous opportunities to make music in Vienna. He also said that the city was affordable and it cost almost nothing to enjoy music there. But Zubin, even at that time, was clear in his mind that while his future lay in music, it would certainly not be as an instrumentalist. He had abandoned his violin when Mehli was in America and admits that he should have improved his piano playing but was often lured away by the charms of cricket. There is little doubt that Mehli was the primary musical influence on Zubin, especially after his return from America in 1949, until Zubin's departure for Vienna in 1954. Zubin told NDTV in September 2008, 'He introduced me to orchestral works, to the orchestra as an instrument, talked about his four years in America, about the things he had heard, all the conductors he had admired—so it was an ongoing twenty-four-hours-a-day education.'[32]

Zarin, who was the president and executive director of the New York Philharmonic, told Gilbert Kaplan in a radio interview in November 2005 that their father forbade them from making music their career. He had complied (only partially, opting out of accountancy to become a full-time music administrator), but was happy that Zubin had not followed that advice.[33]

Talking about it on the same radio show with Kaplan in February 2007, Zubin said: 'Well, it wasn't his advice; it was more a family decision. You know, the upper middle class, especially with my people, the Parsis, we have about five or six professions. We are doctors, lawyers, engineers and accountants. And the aptitude shown as a child prompts the family to choose your profession. So, I might have played with a thermometer as a three-year-old, and my mother decided that I should be a doctor. So I was sort of nurtured with that thought in my mind, brainwashed, and of course after leaving school, I went to university to do my pre-med studies, and that's where I decided, this is not for me.'[34]

More importantly, Mehli and Tehmina also agreed that music was Zubin's calling and it would be criminal to foist any other career on him. Mehli recalled how Zubin had come to talk to him about his future when he was praying. Since it was unusual for him to be disturbed at this time, he knew Zubin wanted to tell him something important. 'Daddy, I can't go on with medicine. I must quit because I'm a musician. I must go to Vienna and take up music.'[35] And so he did.

In October 1954, Zubin left for Vienna, a city that he calls his second home. The scene was now set for the first great chapter in the life of the eighteen-year-old. Vienna laid the musical foundation for his profession and, to this day, never fails to energize and inspire him. Zubin refers to the city as one of his spiritual homes, the other three being Los Angeles, Tel Aviv and Florence.

# Cuffe Parade *to* Vienna Woods

ZUBIN REACHED VIENNA IN November 1954. ('I arrived in Vienna at the Westbahnhof [Western Station] on a grey day in November 1954.'[1]) He had taken a ship to Genoa and then reached Vienna by train. On the ship he met many other young people like himself who wanted to go to Europe. Entirely on his own for the first time, he experienced a tremendous sense of freedom. His only wish at the time was that he be accepted as a student by the Music Academy in Vienna. Zubin says that they 'fooled around a little' in Genoa and 'obviously we had girls on our minds' but claims that it was a part of his 'emotional education or whatever'.[2]

Zubin could not help feeling the magic of the city. Vienna cast its spell over him and along with his musical discoveries came a growing awareness of Western civilization as reflected in the city which had once been its centre. On his third day in Vienna, Zubin saw snow for the first time. The vista of the Ringstrasse, the great horseshoe boulevard that encircles the inner city, took his breath away. He explored the tangle of cobbled alleys in the Altstadt, the old town, and Vienna soon had him in its thrall. 'Zubin followed streets like Sommerheidenweg and Haubenbiglstrasse, streets whose names he couldn't pronounce, into suburbs that dissolved into meadows, vineyards, and woods, and he began to understand the *Stimmung* of Vienna, the atmosphere that had inspired such dissimilar musical personalities as Brahms and Bruckner to create their masterworks.'[3]

When Mehli and Tehmina agreed to send Zubin to Vienna, they were reassured by the fact that his cousin Dady, then a veteran at living abroad, was already there. They felt that Dady, who was three years older, would guide and take care of Zubin in the new environment. Tehmina had even consulted a Parsi astrologer before Zubin's departure. Her anxiety was understandable since Zubin was about to exchange the solid certainties of his birthplace, Bombay, with a remote and alien city, Vienna. Not only was he going to live abroad, he was also embarking on something as unconventional (at the time for an Indian) as the study of Western classical music. She need not have worried. The astrologer prophesied future greatness for her son, saying that it was once in a lifetime that one came across such a chart. He said that Zubin was the reincarnation of a great Western artiste and he would be especially famous in the Western world.

He told Tehmina that the chart contained many powerful *rajayoga*s (planetary combinations for wealth, power and fame) and signified success in the arts, in addition to great personal charm. Such a combination only occurred in the rebirth of a highly evolved soul. However, this happy prophecy came with a word of warning: Zubin should not marry before the age of twenty-five. After that age, he would find his life partner and soulmate, with whom he would spend the rest of his life. Future events would prove the astrologer's predictions to be remarkably prescient.

## VIENNA

Music is Vienna's most important product and the city's chief cultural export is the Vienna Philharmonic. Vienna is music, a fact that is apparent the moment one steps out of the airport. There is a bust of Bruckner at the Stadtpark and, around the corner, a life-size gold statue of Johann Strauss, the waltz king. The Staatsoper, the city's famed opera house in the centre of the city, is a cultural landmark.

The city has furnished the sinews of musical creativity for many great musicians like Gluck and Schubert and, more particularly, the three classical masters Joseph Haydn, Mozart and Beethoven. Their work has created a pervasive cultural soundtrack in a city whose historic splendour is second only to Paris among European capitals. Vienna was one of the music centres of Europe during the classical period and Haydn, Mozart and Beethoven were all drawn to it. As the seat of the Holy Roman Empire (which included parts of modern Austria, Germany, Hungary and erstwhile Czechoslovakia) it was a busy commercial and cultural centre, with a cosmopolitan character. All three were born elsewhere but came to Vienna to study and further their musical fortunes. In Vienna, Haydn and Mozart became close friends and influenced each other's music. Beethoven travelled to Vienna at the age of sixteen to play for Mozart; at twenty-two he returned to study under Haydn.[4]

Vienna's rich musical life was encouraged by its rulers, and a universal interest in music ensured large audiences. There was also private patronage of music on a scale unmatched in the Hapsburg Empire. Music was an important part of the royal court and a good orchestra was a matter of great prestige. Many members of the nobility were excellent musicians. Emperor Joseph II was a competent cellist and Archduke Rudolf studied piano and composition under Beethoven. The nobility frequently hired servants who could double as musicians. There was also outdoor music which was light and popular in tone. Small street bands played at garden parties, and Haydn and Mozart wrote many outdoor pieces which they called divertimentos or serenades. It was the world's music capital, surrounded by music and the tradition of music. A successful musician in Vienna enjoyed a higher status than anywhere else in the world.

Towards the end of the nineteenth century, Richard and Johann Strauss, Mahler and Hugo Wolf treated the Viennese to their creative genius; later, Schoenberg, Alban Berg and Anton Webern sowed the seeds for a new kind of music. There are music makers of every sort in Vienna and the city is witness to more than 1500 musical performances every year. The Vienna Philharmonic Orchestra which started as the court orchestra to Emperor Leopold I is at the very centre of all the musical action. It is still considered one of the best orchestras in the world.

In the Vienna of the post-war years, both Furtwängler and Clemens Krauss had a powerful influence on the orchestra. Furtwängler's Nicolai Concerts in which Beethoven's Ninth was regularly played were eagerly awaited events, as were the New Year Concerts of Krauss with their inimitable performances of waltzes and polkas of the Strauss family. In the Vienna State Opera, Mozart's operas were still performed with great enthusiasm.

*The Vienna Philharmonic Orchestra*

The Vienna Philharmonic has been more closely associated with the history and tradition of European classical music than any other musical ensemble. It is one of the most unique musical institutions in the world. Its members are employees of the Austrian government working in the orchestra of the Vienna State Opera. They also form a self-governing symphonic orchestra, but have no music director and are not bound by any union rules. There is a unique symbiotic relationship between the Vienna State Opera Orchestra and the private association known as the Vienna Philharmonic, formed when the court opera musicians decided to present a 'Philharmonic' concert series independent of their work at the opera, at their own risk. It remains a democratically administered orchestra with only slight modifications over the course of one and a half centuries. The ruling body of the organization comprises the orchestra musicians themselves.

The origins of the Philharmonic can be traced to the Grand Concert led by Otto Nicolai on 28 March 1842, in the main auditorium of the Redouten Hall, organized by the entire personnel of the Royal Imperial Court Theatre. This Philharmonic Academy (the original title) marked the birth of the orchestra. The first of four subscription concerts was conducted by Karl Eckert. Since then the only change has been that instead of engaging conductors for an entire season, they have been inviting guest conductors.

In accordance with Philharmonic statutes, only a member of the Vienna State Opera Orchestra can become a part of the Vienna Philharmonic. A musician must first successfully audition for a position with the State Opera Orchestra and prove his mettle over a period of three years before he can apply for membership in the association of the Vienna Philharmonic. This arrangement provides the musicians with financial stability. In turn, the orchestra brings to its performances a higher level of expertise gained through its experience on the concert podium. Without the Vienna State Opera there would be no Vienna Philharmonic; and this symbiotic relationship has proved advantageous for both institutions, apart from greatly enriching Vienna's musical life. The Vienna Philharmonic, through its connections, facilitates the engagement of the world's best conductors for the Vienna State Opera.

The home of the Vienna Philharmonic is the Musikverein. It is considered to be one of the three finest concert halls in the world, along with Boston's Symphony Hall and Amsterdam's Concertgebouw. Redolent with history, this is where Haydn, Bruckner and Beethoven made appearances. This is where Mahler took the unprecedented decision to close all the doors of the hall during a performance and asked for the lights to be turned off. The aristocracy and the well-heeled who went there to be seen (and for many of whom such musical events were social rather than artistic events) were understandably displeased. The setting up of the Society of the Friends of Music ensured that admission prices to concerts became more affordable, thus making music, hitherto the preserve of the aristocracy, accessible to the common public. The interior is ornate and there is gold everywhere—gold plating and gold paint have been used to cover every inch of the hall, including the overhanging balconies. The ceiling is decorated with beautiful paintings of Apollo and the Muses.

The Vienna Philharmonic is an orchestral tradition and has long been associated with what is known as the 'Viennese sound',[5] the achievement of which became an ideal for Zubin in his conducting career. The very music sheets they play from have been marked by the likes of Brahms, Toscanini, Furtwängler and Richard Strauss. Many of the instruments are the age-old property of the orchestra. It has never had principal conductors. Each year a conductor used to be chosen for the whole season at the Musikverein. These conductors were called *abonnementdirigenten* (subscription conductors) as they were to conduct all the concerts included in the Philharmonic's subscription at the Musikverein. Some of the annual hiring contracts were renewed for many years; others lasted only for a few years. At the same time the Vienna Philharmonic also worked with other conductors, for example, at the Salzburg Festival, and for recordings or special occasions. With the widening of the Philharmonic's activities, the orchestra decided to abandon this system in 1933. From then on, guest conductors began to be hired for each concert, both in Vienna and elsewhere.

Since then, the orchestra has had a number of guest conductors, including many of the world's best known conductors—Richard Strauss, Toscanini, Furtwängler, Böhm, Barbirolli, Karajan, Solti, Bernstein, Abbado, Pierre Boulez, Barenboim and Zubin. After the Second World War, the orchestra continued with the policy it had begun in 1933 of working with every conductor of repute. Especially important in the history of the orchestra after 1945 were the artistic collaborations with its two honorary conductors, Böhm and Karajan, and with its honorary member Bernstein. (Zubin was made an honorary member of the Vienna State Opera in 1997. In 2001 he was made honorary conductor of the Vienna Philharmonic Orchestra.)

Every New Year's Day since 1 January 1941, the Vienna Philharmonic Orchestra has sponsored the Vienna New Year Concerts dedicated to the compositions of the Strauss family, particularly those of Johann Strauss Jr. Attending a concert of this orchestra is no mean feat. The subscription concert series of the Vienna Philharmonic are sold out years in advance. A single subscription consists of ten Saturday concerts, ten Sunday concerts, or a minimum of five soirée concerts which take place in the evening on weekdays. The waiting period for a Saturday or Sunday subscription runs into years.

Although the orchestra has moved with the times, it remains faithful to traditional principles: the emphasis on autonomy and the subscription concert series continue to form the artistic, organizational and financial basis of its work. In a break with 155 years of tradition, the Philharmonic decided in 1997 to offer women equal opportunities. Anna Lelkes, harpist, and a member of the

Vienna State Opera Orchestra became the first female member of the Philharmonic. The Vienna Philharmonic is not only Austria's most important 'cultural export', it is also an ambassador of peace. In 2005 it was named Goodwill Ambassador of the World Health Organization (WHO) and in 2006 the orchestra became an ambassador for the Phonak initiative, 'Hear the World'.

## WARM MUSIC, COLD CLIMATE

After the hustle and bustle of Bombay, Zubin found Vienna to be a much more orderly and peaceful city. Vienna had been subjected to severe bombardment by the Allies during the Second World War and had suffered serious damage. By March 1945, American and British aircraft had killed about 30,000 people and destroyed more than 12,000 buildings. The city was starved of electricity, gas and water. A quarter of a million people were rendered homeless. The biggest air raid took place on 12 March 1945 (the anniversary of the 'Anschluss') but the main target, the Floridsdorf refinery, escaped with no real damage. Instead, the centre of the city was ravaged.

The Vienna State Opera was gutted in the raid. The front, which included the foyer and the main stairways, remained intact, but the auditorium and stage were destroyed, and the entire decor and props for more than 120 operas perished in the fire. Its reconstruction began in 1948 and it reopened in 1955. Zubin recalls attending his first opera in the temporary premises in the Theater an der Wien.

Zubin, who arrived nine years after the war ended, was surprised to find that even then bombed houses dotted the cityscape. He calls it a city 'wounded by war' but says that it was the positive outlook of the people that made it a lively place. In Vienna there were four occupation zones. Zubin recalls seeing the Russian soldiers on walks. They looked alien to him—certainly not people with whom one could take liberties. The city was in the process of rebuilding itself from the ravages of war, but its magic soon became apparent to Zubin who soaked up as much music as possible.

Zubin found accommodation with his cousin Dady as a subtenant in a room in Vienna Woods (Wienerwald). It was a humble accommodation as he had to manage on the small allowance provided by his mother out of an inheritance from her father. Zubin was given a monthly allowance of $75 from the trust of $8000 shared equally with Zarin who was in London as an apprentice accountant. With care, Zubin could stretch his share to last four years. Money was tight and Zubin recalls that on occasion there was too much month left at the end of the money.

Vienna was dreadfully cold. In Bombay, Zubin never worried about switching off the lights when he left a room. In Vienna, the lights were put out—but so was the heat, a result of both inherent Viennese frugality and the city's need to remember the hardships faced during the Second World War. He realized that life in Vienna during the War had been very different from what they had witnessed in Bombay where rationed rice seemed to be the only hardship they had experienced. His room was freezing; there was only a tiny electric radiator for warmth and the bed sheets were as cold as ice. A desperate Zubin once set the little radiator on his bed and covered it with his goose-down quilt in the hope that the bed would become warm. He only succeeded in setting his bed ablaze and got a dressing-down from his landlady the next morning. Zubin is grateful that he knew very little German at the time.[6]

Hot water was a luxury that had to be paid for. For two schillings, he got five minutes of hot water. Thanks to his landlady even those five minutes were of variable duration and Zubin recalled how, without warning, he would be showering in ice-cold water! Some of Vienna's famous frugality had also rubbed off on Dady. He advised Zubin to ride a bicycle to the Music Academy to save money. But Zubin had not contended with the 10-mile journey over mostly cobbled streets which reduced him to shivering, trembling jelly. That was the last time he rode the bicycle, preferring to use the tram to commute.[7] Zubin and Dady stayed together for six months before Zubin left. Vienna Woods was just too far from the academy and he had to change two trams before he got there. Dady was not pleased to see him go but they attended many concerts together and remained close all through their time in Vienna.

Food was another worry: Zubin, who sorely missed Indian food and his mother's cooking, lost fifteen pounds in the first few weeks. He missed the spicy food he was accustomed to at home and was amused to find the other foreign students complaining about the heavy Viennese food. To an Indian, a deep-fried schnitzel meant nothing. Unable to resist the blandishment of flummery, he gorged on the desserts and developed a love for chocolate that continues to this day. A non-smoker and a teetotaller, he lapped up ice cream and orange juice in the cafes while other students had cigarettes and coffee or brandy. Alcohol and cigarettes are traditional strains on a student's purse and the fact that he did not drink or smoke (he still doesn't) meant that he had that much more money to spend.

His childhood friend Suntook, who visited him in Vienna, recalls staying with him at 93, Gumpendorfer Strasse. He narrates how he had set his alarm clock for a certain time in the morning. The shrill sound disturbed Zubin's landlady, who gave Suntook an earful. Only later did he realize that the sound had evoked memories of the war and that had been the reason for her discomposure.[8]

Zubin recalls that some crucial political developments took place in Austria during his first year there. In May 1955, an international treaty was signed in Vienna granting Austria full sovereignty and independence again. 'It was a great moment, even for a non-Austrian like me, as Foreign Minister Leopold Figl stepped out on to the balcony of the Belvedere, ten years after the end of the Second World War, with a peace treaty in his hands, and proclaimed: Austria is free.'[9] The occupying forces moved out of Vienna in accordance with the treaty. (Fifty years later, Zubin conducted a 'Concert for Peace' on the grounds of the Schönbrunn Palace for an audience of 90,000.)

♫

Above all, it was Vienna which was to shape Zubin musically. He is indelibly marked by the Viennese approach to music. 'Vienna taught me my whole concept of sound and Vienna taught me classical music. The music we perform is Germanic music—from Bach to Schoenberg.'[10] As a conductor he was destined to have a dizzying rise to fame and he has returned to conduct in Vienna every single year since 1961. In June 1961, he conducted the Vienna Philharmonic for the first time, becoming in the process the youngest conductor to ever lead that orchestra. But we are getting a little ahead of our story.

# *Der Inder*

THE INSTITUTION TO WHICH Zubin gained admission was the Akademie für Musik und Darstellende Kunst (Academy of Music and the Performing Arts). It traced its history back to 1817 when the Vienna Conservatory started with Antonio Salieri as its first director. Although the Vienna Conservatory was to be modelled on the Paris Conservatory, lack of funds meant that in 1817 only a singing school could be established. In 1819, violinist Böhm was taken on and, by 1827, courses in most orchestral instruments began.

Though tuition fees were introduced in 1829, the institution's finances proved to be unstable and it soon faced bankruptcy. The state eventually funded the conservatory from 1841 to 1844 and again from 1846 to 1848, when funding was discontinued for political reasons. Courses were stopped until 1851, after which support from the state and the city helped stabilize the finances again. The Society of the Friends of Music remained in control of the institution despite growing state subsidy. However, on 1 January 1909, the school was nationalized, becoming the Imperial Academy of Music and the Performing Arts. Its administration was assigned to a president (appointed by the state), an artistic director and a board of trustees.

After the Anschluss, many teachers and students were dismissed on racial grounds and, in 1941, the academy became a Reich university. After the end of the Second World War, the institution became a state academy again. In the process of denazification, fifty-nine teachers were dismissed, though a few were subsequently reinstated. By laws introduced in 1948 and 1949, the institution was granted the status of 'art academy'. Another law introduced in 1970 gave art academies a status equivalent to a university. In 1998 the title of art academy was changed to art university. It is now called the University of Music and Performing Arts, Vienna. Many of the musicians of the Vienna Philharmonic had been pupils at the academy.

## AT THE ACADEMY

In his first year at the academy, Zubin studied form, analysis, harmony and counterpoint along with other electives of his choice. He says that he had to study an instrument as well as learn theory. Only after two semesters of elementary music studies would he become eligible to join the conducting school, provided, of course, he passed the entrance examination. Though Zubin was struggling with a new language and unfamiliar surroundings, he felt that he was a step ahead of his class, being familiar with a far wider range of music than his classmates. He knew a whole lot more about chamber music thanks to Mehli who rehearsed practically every day at home. The music Zubin knew, he knew very well, since it was the result of studying entire orchestra scores rather than simply instrument parts. But though he had heard a varied range of music at home, Mehli had not been able to help him 'analytically', as Zubin puts it in his autobiography.

Whatever feeling of smugness Zubin might have had soon disappeared when he started theory class under Karl Schiske who discovered that his otherwise highly talented Indian student had problems with harmony. Zubin recalls his old teacher with much fondness and admiration. 'Hardly anybody else was as extraordinarily musical as he was. He played the piano fantastically. One could give him any theme and he would play it as a Bach fugue or in Brahms's style, as a [Frédéric] Chopin nocturne or as a Schubert waltz.'[1] Zubin says that he was a strict, harsh teacher, but taught his students all the musical basics in a most brilliant manner.

In an interview to *Los Angeles Times* after he became music director of the Los Angeles Philharmonic, Zubin recalled his days at the academy. 'Then I went to Vienna to study at the State Academy of Music—double bass, piano, composition. I went through the mill. At one time I had to take twelve courses at once. I graduated in 1957 with a diploma in conducting.' Zubin says that he would have had a diploma in composition too had he not quit in the last year. 'First we had to write strict fugues according to the rules. Then they made us write modern fugues in which everything was allowed. I decided if they were going to give me a diploma just for doing whatever I wanted to do, I didn't want that kind of diploma.'[2]

At the academy, Zubin was looked upon with both curiosity and affection and soon earned the nickname *der Inder*—'the Indian'. The term was used endearingly and Vienna embraced him enthusiastically. In an interview to *Opera* magazine's John Allison in June 2009, Zubin said, 'Now as soon as I set foot there, I feel at home. I learned the language on the streets, and still speak German with a Viennese accent. I cannot tell you one case of bias because I was Indian. They adopted me from the beginning.'[3] He voiced a similar sentiment when I asked him about his early days in Vienna. 'There was not the slightest bit of racial bias,' he said.[4]

The first time he felt a real sense of belonging was when one of his professors presented him with a ticket to a concert of the Vienna Philharmonic. Zubin's ticket was for a seat on the stage, almost within the ranks of the orchestra. They played Brahms's First, conducted by Böhm, and though he knew the symphony like the back of his hand, Zubin recalls that it sounded very different. It then dawned on him that, for the very first time in his life, he was hearing a professional orchestra play. What he had heard in the past were only pale imitations of real orchestras. 'Without question, the major turning point in my life was in 1954, the first time I heard Karl Böhm and the Vienna Philharmonic. I went into what I think is the finest concert hall in the world, the Musikverein of Vienna, and heard one of the great orchestras play Brahms. I didn't know such a sound existed.'[5]

Talking about it many years later in a radio show with Kaplan, Zubin said, 'You talk about a culture shock! This was a culture shock! I mean, then came the snow, which I never knew, and the food of Vienna, which, for me, was like a diet. You know, when Americans came to Vienna, they all gained weight because it was fatty food for them. For me, it was a diet compared to the Indian food! So there were a lot of shocks I encountered, but none as much as the first sound of the Brahms First Symphony in the Musikverein.'[6]

It was Zubin's first concert and it is hardly surprising that he told his early biographers Bookspan and Yockey that he felt he was hearing *music* for the first time. 'Suddenly I realized I had not simply come from a small town where I heard only a small orchestra. I had heard *no* orchestra.'[7] All he had heard before this point was the local, semi-professional orchestra in Bombay or records which, in the early 1950s, had serious limitations in producing high fidelity sound. Of particular importance that night was his discovery of the significance of the bass line in music. Zubin recalls that his seat was so close to the bass section that he was practically a member of it! He had never paid such close attention to the basses as he did that night.

This experience made him abandon the violin and take up the double bass. Also, Zubin had noticed that violinists in Vienna did not play the way he had been taught. Having no desire to unlearn and start afresh (as his father had done under Galamian), he opted for the bass which gave him the chance to start on a new instrument. That the academy was renowned for its instruction in the double bass was an added advantage.

Zubin also had a pragmatic reason for wanting to learn the double bass. It was an instrument he would be able to play in an orchestra very soon. Since conducting class was a future prospect, he reckoned that learning the bass was the easiest and quickest way in which he could be associated with an orchestra. He knew that he wanted to be a conductor but had no intention of going from the classroom to the podium. This way, he would get an idea of how a member of the orchestra felt.[8] Also, classical music, especially the Viennese school, is built on the bass line. The bass line assumes great importance because classical music is written vertically. As a student, it made a whole lot of sense to study the double bass. Zubin never hoped to be a professional double bass player. But he did occasionally play it among friends. (Notably, he played it in Schubert's *Trout* Quintet at a public concert in London with Barenboim, Perlman, Zukerman and Du Pré which led to the film *The Trout* by Christopher Nupen.)

Zubin's bass teacher was Otto Rühm, a brilliant player who was the solo bassist with the Vienna Philharmonic. This put Zubin in the enviable position of being able to attend practice sessions of the orchestra, something which opened a new and breathtaking world of music for him. Zubin recalled, 'Rühm was my bridge to the members of the Viennese Philharmonic, who soon became my friends.'[9] Zubin fondly remembers Rühm as the one who made him conscious of what beautiful sound was. Many years later, Rühm performed with Zubin on the podium. They played Mahler's First Symphony in which there was a bass solo and Rühm confessed that he was in fact quite nervous.[10]

## MUSICAL DISCOVERY

Zubin feels that the only real way to learn music is through a live performance. He says that one can learn theoretically and by listening to records but the best way to grasp music is a live performance. He is also emphatic about taking scores along to all rehearsals. He says that he was able to learn a lot because he always took the scores with him. He finds it strange to see young students without scores in his practice sessions since one must read together to be able to understand everything in detail, including the mistakes that are inevitable.

In his student days in Vienna, Zubin attended as many concerts as possible. Since standing room tickets cost only twenty cents, Zubin, with his modest allowance, was able to afford them. Sometimes, unable to choose, he would buy tickets for more than one performance, and he and his friends would rush from one concert to the other during the interval to witness the second half of another performance at a different hall. His experience was one of complete immersion in the musical life of the city, studying during the day and attending concerts and performances every other night. Vienna in the mid-1950s was an ideal place because artistes didn't travel much in those days. The Vienna Opera had an ensemble made up of legendary singers who were 'just living and singing every night'.

Zubin shares a particular musical experience from his first time in Vienna that is still fresh in his memory. One day, as he was walking past the Musikverein, on a whim (and driven by curiosity) he slipped in through the back door. He heard Tchaikovsky's Fourth Symphony being played. He was familiar with the piece, having heard a recording played by the Boston Symphony Orchestra under Koussevitzky. But as with Brahms's First, he thought that he was hearing something totally new. Running along the corridor he peeped through a keyhole and saw Karajan conducting. He had never seen him in real life but recognized him from his photos.

Zubin managed to get into the hall unnoticed and listened to the music, grateful that he had remained undiscovered. It was the first time he heard Karajan. Zubin says, 'The new sounds were very different from what I had in my head or ear. I felt like Columbus on a musical expedition. I set foot on a territory which was completely new to me, though I already knew its outlines. It was an enriching and wonderful time during which the foundation for everything that I later achieved was laid.'[11]

Alongside the course at the academy, the instrumental and theory training, Zubin joined the Singverein, the official chorus of the Musikverein. He was not yet proficient enough in bass to play in an orchestra, so the chorus was his best bet. He joined it a little after the course had begun, but found it to be relatively easy and experienced wonderful performances. He sang Mozart's *Requiem* conducted by Walter. Later, when Zubin met Walter in America, he told him about it. 'Naturally he did not remember me, but I have a photo of this performance, in which I am recognizable right at the edge of the picture.'[12]

Zubin's first concert, however, was when he sang under Karajan who was conducting Beethoven's Ninth Symphony. Zubin made his first recording not as a conductor, or even an instrumentalist, but as a singer. In the summer of 1955, Karajan, who was the director of the Vienna Symphony, the city's second orchestra, was making his first recordings of the complete Beethoven Symphonies with London's Philharmonia Orchestra. He brought the entire orchestra to Vienna to use the Singverein as his chorus for the Ninth Symphony. Zubin was paid fifty schillings for the recording and remembers treating himself to a hearty meal with the money. 'So I went to a good restaurant and treated myself to a real veal schnitzel, not the cheap kind made of pork.'[13] Zubin also recalls that he got a panic attack when Karajan insisted that all the members of the chorus should sing from memory. Even though Zubin was by now a little more familiar with German, Schiller's 'Ode to Joy' seemed to him more than he could handle and he spent half the night memorizing the piece. 'It worked out somehow. In any case, I don't remember embarrassing my choir members,' he recalls.[14]

Zubin was always running off to rehearsals, missing classes at the academy. Sometimes when there was a class on the history of music or on the theory of musical forms, it was quite likely that he would instead be listening to a Brahms symphony being rehearsed elsewhere.[15] He is never tired of reiterating that while theoretical analysis is important, nothing can replace the education gained through live performances. Kubelík, Böhm, Mitropoulos, Josef Krips and Hans Knappertsbusch all came to Vienna and Zubin attended as many of their concerts as he could. Just watching these great conductors showed him how much he still had to learn.

Zubin also discovered the music of Mozart in Vienna. The music he had listened to in Bombay had been dictated by Mehli's preferences and Mozart does not seem to have been a favourite. He also became acquainted with the music of Bach which, according to him, was largely ignored in Vienna. Though he studied the *St Matthew Passion* and the *Magnificat*, he always considered the music of Bach to be a gap in his musical education. He does conduct

Bach occasionally but prefers 'to leave this job to my other colleagues'.[16]

♫

Zubin had few friends among the Viennese students who lived with their families. His friends circle consisted of foreign students who lived in one-room apartments and ate out. This eating out was mostly at a place called Barry's Restaurant near the academy that served 'fast food'. The coffee houses served as the 'students' taverns and reading rooms, fraternity houses and sorority houses'. Before, after and between classes, they would frequent the nearby Liesingerkeller or Gösserkeller, with foreign students seated at a different table. Apart from Dady (who was the only other Asian at the academy), his friends were drawn from the English, American and Canadian students with an Egyptian Jew thrown in for good measure.

When the school year ended in summer, Zubin stayed behind in Vienna to prepare for the entrance examination for conducting school. In any case, given his budget, travelling was out of the question. He also moved out of his Thirteenth District Wienerwald apartment to a less expensive one in the Third District, nearer to the academy (which saved him some tram money). The owner of the building was a lady called Frau Mumb who raised chows at home. Zubin recalls how difficult it was to memorize scores because of the incessant yelping of the puppies. And, they never learned to recognize him in the eight months he lived there. 'Every night I would come home and one would start barking, and then all ten would bark at once. And they had blue tongues!'[17]

That September, a twenty-one-year-old Canadian singer-pianist named Carmen Lasky came to Vienna with two other Canadian girls. After two years at the local conservatory in Saskatoon, she had taught music to the people in the outlying villages. Terry Gabora, a Canadian violin student, and a part of Zubin's group, had told her of the unlimited musical potential of Vienna, of the endless concerts and musical events, and the high quality of teaching. Impressed with the stories, Carmen decided that she too would like to partake of the Viennese musical feast. 'I was a choral teacher in my home town for six- to seventeen-year-olds, but realized I had reached the saturation point in learning. So I decided to go to Vienna.'[18]

Since Gabora was part of Zubin's group, it was only a matter of time before Carmen was introduced to him. The first time she met him, he was ecstatic about having gained admission to the conducting class and wanted to tell everyone about it. It was not love at first sight. Zubin assumed the role of mentor and guide, and took it upon himself to show her round Vienna. He was also the leader when it came to deciding which concert to attend. Standing room tickets could be purchased on the day of the concert and sometimes they had to wait for hours in long queues in the snow for the privilege of standing for a few hours in the rear of an auditorium. Not a day passed when they did not hear at least one live performance. 'He seemed so much older than my fellow Canadian friends . . . He seemed already to know exactly what he wanted and didn't have to go through the growing pains of proving himself a man,' Carmen recalled.[19]

Zubin was very particular about reading what the important critics had to say about a concert. One of them was Joseph Marx, a composer himself, whose opinion Zubin valued greatly. Zubin's familiarity with the German language was growing and he was settling in well. It would be the start of a lifelong association with Vienna and its music.

## 'YOUR SON IS A BORN CONDUCTOR'

Zubin was admitted to the conducting class at the academy under the tutelage of the acclaimed Hans Swarowsky, who was celebrated both as a conductor and a teacher. Born in Hungary in 1899, Swarowsky studied composition in Vienna with Schoenberg and Webern, and conducting with Richard Strauss, Weingartner and Krauss. Even though he was an outstanding conductor, he owes his fame more to the fact that he was a gifted teacher who nurtured a whole generation of conductors. Apart from Zubin, his protégés include Abbado, Mariss Jansons, Giuseppe Sinopoli and Iván Fischer.

Swarowsky held positions in Stuttgart, Gera, Hamburg, Berlin, Zurich, Krakow, Graz and Vienna. He was chief conductor of the Royal Scottish National Orchestra from 1957 to 1959 and became the chief conductor of the Vienna Symphony Orchestra in 1959, also appearing as guest conductor of the Vienna State Opera. For many years Swarowsky held classes in conducting at the academy in Vienna, where he had been head of conducting since 1946. Today many aspiring young conductors compete in the Hans Swarowsky International Conductors Competition, held in Vienna.

There was an air of mystery surrounding his origins. It was rumoured that Swarowsky, who was adopted by a Viennese banker, was in reality the illegitimate son of one of the Hapsburg archdukes. It was Swarowsky himself who spread this tale and later, he even took to wearing a signet ring of the Hapsburg dynasty with a bend sinister to indicate illegitimacy. Zubin said, 'I do not know if this rumor was true, and eventually it is also unimportant.'[20] Swarowsky took a keen interest in art. He also spent a few years as a pupil-patient of Sigmund Freud trying to gain insight into why composers created their music the way they did, and its effects on listeners. He worked for the Nazis in Paul Goebbels's infamous ministry of propaganda and is said to have sent secret messages to the Allies by means of musical notations.

## 'THE ART OF THE LITTLE MOVEMENT'

Zubin says there are two methods by which one can be taught. One is the theoretical way and the other is where one meets a genuine master and is trained by him. Zubin recalls that Swarowsky passed on to his students a 'direct experience', one which involved a close relationship between master and pupil. He recalls, 'Who else could have told me how Richard Strauss conducted or about Schoenberg's ideas and thoughts in *Moses und Aron*?' Swarowsky was a personal friend of Schoenberg's, and used to play the harmonica at their meetings.[21]

Swarowsky was known to be a hard taskmaster, strict and relentless, and his tyranny was legendary at the academy. He advocated absolute loyalty towards the work of a composer and did not believe in experimentation. His emphasis on knowing the score thoroughly and following it scrupulously bred in Zubin the habit of familiarizing himself with a piece of music to the extent of memorizing it. Since the only way to face an orchestra is by being thoroughly proficient with the score, Zubin goes over the music till he understands it completely. Like many of his contemporaries on the podium, Zubin nearly always conducts without a score, relying on his capacity to ingest compositions in a few readings and retain them in his memory.

Though he was critical, Swarowsky was also supportive when the need arose. He saw to it that his students got opportunities to do concerts. Zubin had watched Swarowsky very carefully and studied the bash-beat-blow technique. Practice is one thing but to face an orchestra for a public performance is something else entirely. Zubin admits that he was nervous—in such a situation, it is very easy to forget all one has learned. He says that during that first public concert—a Mozart piano concerto—his conducting was a mixture of Böhm and Karajan, the two conductors he had seen and heard in Vienna and admired ardently. He brandished his baton wildly and came off the stage dripping with sweat. Swarowsky warned him against such overexertion and asked him how he would be able to keep up physically if he wanted to conduct Wagner for five or more hours.[22] 'If you allow yourself to get into this state during a Mozart "accompaniment", what will happen to you when you conduct *Tristan und Isolde*? You'll go crazy!' he said. Those words were prophetic, Zubin says. At the beginning of his career, he used to give 150 per cent to every performance. Later, he gave only 100 per cent but made better music.

The bushy-browed Swarowsky offered his students vintage Viennese musical heritage. A learned man who was familiar with Freudian psychiatry and art history as well as music, he had a classroom method that was unorthodox, strict and demanding. He believed that the trouble with conductors was that they were not sure of style. 'A Dürer is not a Rembrandt; a Bruckner symphony is not a Wagner opera. Each style needs its own realization.'[23]

To sharpen his students' sense of style, Swarowsky suppressed their personalities and dismissed their interpretive urges. Zubin recalls, 'You learn what the composer is doing and why, and how he entered the composition—through the back door, as it were. We never heard in Swarowsky's class what another conductor did. That is brainwashing.'[24] Swarowsky maintained that a complete analysis was necessary because the conductor must have the work in his head. He must know not only what kind of note there is, but also why it is there. 'A student should be able to determine by logic what follows next.'[25] (Zubin absorbed this advice very well, as an incident related by Jacob Druckman, composer-in-residence [1982–86] of the New York Philharmonic, shows. The staff of the Philharmonic was proposing an arrangement of *The Marseillaise* by Hector Berlioz which Zubin, then the music director, didn't know. The management had brought a recording for him to hear. Zubin listened to it for about ninety seconds and said, 'Sure, sure. I can see what he is going to do.' He then proceeded to give a detailed formal analysis of the rest of the piece and left the room. Druckman thought this a little presumptuous and stayed on to hear all of it. He says that what he heard was exactly what Zubin had predicted![26])

For Swarowsky, conducting was 'the art of the little movement', and the wrist—not the arm—was the key. Once, after a practice session with the Student Orchestra, Swarowsky stuck his fingers into Zubin's coat sleeves and pulled downwards, leaving only his wrists free. Zubin understood instantly that if the wrist movement could be mastered, there would be no need for his wild gesticulations. 'He told me I was a wild man, and one day he made me conduct the entire *Don Juan* of Strauss like that, with his fingers pulling down on my sleeves.'[27] In practice sessions with the academy's Student Orchestra, he made them stand still and beat time only with the right hand, keeping the arm tied to a chair or held out stiffly in front of them. The strictness of his regimen was intended as a counterbalance to the beginner's natural effusiveness and flamboyance. As he said, 'Once the student has learned the basic techniques, he is free to develop his genius.'[28] Zubin told the author that he could conduct an entire opera with his arm pinned down if necessary. Of course, the hands have a role to play, though both are not required all the time.[29]

He taught that the conductor is 'a necessary evil' who, while crucial to the rehearsal of a score, should be as unobtrusive as possible in performance. He was known to quote the ironical advice of his mentor Richard Strauss: 'Go up to the podium and don't disturb the orchestra.' In an interview, Swarowsky narrated how Strauss had taught him to give the orchestra all possible latitude and let it play by itself: 'A conductor can give only the spirit; the sound comes from the musicians.' According to Strauss, the best conductor is one who is superfluous after the second bar, and one who is never wet—meaning not soaked with perspiration from excess effort. 'When Strauss conducted Mozart, he hardly gave more than the downbeat. All the rest of the work was done at rehearsal. Today the tendency of conductors is to work harder in the performance than at the rehearsal.'[30]

Swarowsky said that Strauss also guided him on how to teach conducting. 'I try to teach what was in the composer's mind. I forbid students to hear a work until they have studied it thoroughly . . . In my youth there were no recordings. One had to learn a score directly from the notes. A conductor must build up an international technique. He must have the technique first, then he can put in the personality.'[31] Zubin credited Swarowsky with teaching him how to read a musical score. 'I learned from him how to look at a score and analyse what he called the "handwriting" of a composer, the thing that made one master's music different from every other's.'[32]

But he was a difficult customer. He subjected his students to a withering barrage of criticism. He gave them hell in German, which, Zubin says, is not the best language to get 'hell' in. His comments ranged from 'Stop boxing,' to 'Stop moving your fanny; I'm not teaching ballet.'[33] According to him such harshness strengthened character and taught the students how to gain the upper hand over the orchestra. Swarowsky was also a slightly eccentric man. He scowled and conducted to himself to avoid greeting passers-by on the streets of Vienna. He was forever trying to convince everybody about everything. His hottest public feud was with Böhm who he thought had an impossible technique and gave his singers too much freedom. These traits and the didacticism of his approach were the reasons for his never making it big as a practising conductor.[34] Nonetheless, he was one of the greatest teachers of all time.

Zubin feels that conducting with the wrist alone is not particularly motivating for the musicians. But he also adds, 'One does not always need two hands to conduct. Today I often leave my hand simply below; with that I also show that I am relaxed, and that also relaxes the orchestra.' Zubin says that though Swarowsky's style of teaching was a little unpleasant for some, he is thankful for the clarity he brought to his immature musical ideas with his strictness. He was always ready to mould the musical ideas of his students down to the last detail. Zubin idolized Swarowsky and admired him unreservedly.[35]

## FAMILY REUNION

In November 1955, Mehli, Tehmina and Zarin visited Zubin in Vienna. Mehli's sons had been prodding him to immigrate to a place where his talents and work would be better appreciated. He found an agent to book him on a recital tour in north Italy and Zubin used his influence to get a date for him at the Brahmssaal, the small auditorium in the Musikverein. Even though Mehli's violin recital in Vienna was only a minor event, it was the first such performance by an Indian and got wonderful reviews.

The autumn of 1955 was also important because the Vienna State Opera was opening for the first time since its almost total destruction in the Second World War. The opera house, with its grand staircase that soared in crimson splendour from a blue-and-ivory vestibule burnished with gold leaf, was a sight to behold. The nine Muses in marble looked down from their loggia on Mount Olympus. The Mehta family, unable to afford tickets for the opening night of Beethoven's *Fidelio* conducted by Böhm on 5 November 1955, witnessed the performance three nights later, buying standing room tickets. The next day Zubin heard *Don Giovanni* under Böhm and, a few days later, *Wozzeck*, again by the same conductor. Zubin also recalls a performance of Bruckner's *Te Deum* and the Ninth Symphony conducted by Walter, calling it unforgettable.

A little later Zubin discovered Wagner for the first time, being particularly impressed by *Die Walküre.* The night he heard it, he was standing with Carmen up near the ceiling and was captivated by the opera's opening bars. It is said that most opera lovers graduate to Wagner after exposure to Giuseppe Verdi and Puccini, but Zubin plunged headlong into the *Ring*. Zubin began reading all he could find on Wagner and his music. Along with this, he slowly started mastering German. According to Zubin, Wagner's tempi came out of the language. He knew he had a long way to go before he could conduct opera, let alone one of Wagner's works, but resolved that one day he would interpret the music of the great composer. (Five decades later, Zubin took part in the fifty-year celebrations of the reopening of the State Opera. The programme was divided into three parts and contained extracts from the six premieres performed in November 1955. Zubin's part was *Don Giovanni.* He recalls in his autobiography that someone who knew about his introduction to Wagner remarked that even fifty years on, Mehta is still *standing* at the State Opera albeit under different circumstances.)[36]

As the family reunion came to a close, Mehli sought out Swarowsky for an appraisal of Zubin's progress. Zubin was only a few weeks into the conducting class but Swarowsky's assessment was so complimentary that Mehli was taken aback. 'Your son is a born conductor. There is simply not much I can teach him. He knows everything already.'[37] Swarowsky was not exaggerating. When Zubin mounted the podium for the first time in Swarowsky's class to conduct (Beethoven's Fifth) it was a full ten measures before he received a reprimand from Swarowsky. In comparison, the others had been sent packing with a dismissive and peremptory '*Nein*' almost immediately. Zubin's performance impressed his fellow students as well. Ukrainian-born Eugene Husaruk recalled that Zubin's gestures were natural and there was tremendous energy in his conducting. The students often wondered what he was doing studying with them.[38] Zubin's relationship with Swarowsky became a close one. The maestro says that he was not only in his class but also in and out of his home. Later, he would visit him in Vienna even when he was no longer under his tutelage. They would talk and look at scores together.

A decade later, when Zubin was conductor of the Los Angeles Philharmonic, Swarowsky made his American debut guest conducting that orchestra. In an interview to Albert Goldberg of *Los Angeles Times*, he said: 'From the beginning I thought he would be exceptional. Now he is also becoming a fine opera conductor. I can only congratulate Los Angeles on having him. I think the time will come when he will be the dominant conductor in this country.'[39] Apart from his remarkable powers of concentration and conducting talent, Zubin's Oriental pedigree ensured that he attracted more attention than the average music academy student. The Viennese were very taken with anything faintly Oriental and made much of Zubin. This, and his warm, outgoing and gregarious personality, made a positive impact on everyone he met. His fame soon spread by word of mouth.

♫

Mehli left Vienna with Zarin, intending to look for work in England. After four weeks of searching, he got the job of first violinist with the Scottish National Orchestra in Glasgow. Unfortunately, there was a strong anti-Indian feeling in Scotland, and Mehli and Tehmina had trouble finding a decent place to live. The starting salary was low even for a back-chair first violinist, the equivalent of about $50 a week. Luckily after a few months, Sir John Barbirolli and the Hallé Orchestra in Manchester accepted Mehli as violinist. (Sir Charles Hallé founded the Hallé Orchestra in Manchester in 1858. It is Britain's oldest symphony orchestra. In 1943, Barbirolli took over the Hallé Orchestra, making it one of Europe's best. He was a conductor admired for his clear, well-proportioned, healthy and natural-sounding interpretation.)

Things improved thereafter and Barbirolli soon grew fond of Mehli. The pay was also better after a few months. More importantly, Zubin noticed that his father seemed to enjoy his work and was in high spirits. He joined the orchestra sitting at the back of the violin section. Within three years, he was moved up as assistant concertmaster.[40] Mehli considered this to be one of the greatest experiences of his conducting life. Many years later, talking about his father's decision to settle abroad, Zubin noted that the decision was forced on Mehli because it was becoming impossible to make ends meet. 'It was a purely economic decision, not a patriotic one,' he said.

Barbirolli was also a powerful influence—though at a slight geographical remove—on Zubin's early musical career. Zubin would go to visit Mehli in Manchester from Vienna once or twice a season and would also attend Barbirolli's rehearsals. He was a wonderful orchestra builder who had been offered positions in London orchestras but had stayed loyal to Manchester. This dedication to a place registers keenly with Zubin who today is proud of his loyalty to the orchestras he considers his own.

# Siena *and* After

IN THE SUMMER OF 1956 Zubin went to the Accademia Musicale Chigiana in Siena, Italy, to study conducting. He had missed out on going to Siena the previous summer as he had neither the time—he was studying to get into conducting school—nor the money. Many foreign students were in Siena at the time and Zubin too wanted to be a part of the musical action there. He sent a letter outlining his experience to Carlo Zecchi who was in charge of conducting classes, and was happy to be accepted by him. Zubin, Carmen and a few other friends were soon on their way to the picturesque Tuscan town.

The Accademia Musicale Chigiana was founded by Count Guido Chigi Saracini in 1932 with the aim of organizing master classes for the principal musical instruments. The count provided both the finances and the premises—a magnificent palace which he had restored for the purpose. He was successful in bringing to Siena a number of world-famous musicians as instructors. They included Pablo Casals, Antonio Guarnieri, Alfredo Casella, George Enescu, Andrés Segovia, Alfred Cortot, Jacques Thibaud, Nathan Milstein, Menuhin, Guido Agosti, Gino Bechi, Gina Cigna and André Navarra. Many well-known names in international music, apart from Zubin, have emerged from the classrooms in Siena: Carlo Maria Giulini, Daniel Oren, Roman Vlad, Nino Rota, Abbado, Salvatore Accardo, Uto Ughi, Barenboim and Alirio Díaz.

## FRIENDS IN MUSIC

At Siena, Zubin became friends with a young guitarist called John Williams, who helped him make it to the much sought-after class of the guitar maestro Segovia. At this point, his appetite for musical knowledge was insatiable. He even found time—and obtained permission—to listen in on the cello class of Navarra. Zubin had been admitted to Zecchi's conducting class and was in high spirits. He often dropped by at the Renaissance Theatre to see how the auditions of some of the other students were progressing. One day, as he entered the hall, he heard Schumann's Fourth Symphony being played almost perfectly. What was strange was that it seemed as though the orchestra was playing without a conductor! When his eyes grew accustomed to the darkness, he spied a tiny figure on the podium whose head barely reached the eye level of the seated musicians in the front row. Zubin initially thought that the conductor was a dwarf, but soon realized that he was a young boy. That boy was Barenboim and when Zubin and he met in a class sometime later, Zubin could not have guessed that this would be the start of a lifelong friendship.

The Argentine-born Israeli prodigy Daniel Barenboim at the time was only twelve but looked even younger. Barenboim had moved to Israel with his parents, Enrique and Aida, several years ago. Already a piano virtuoso of sorts, he had come to Siena to brush up on his not-so-inconsiderable conducting skills. Zubin and Barenboim took to each other and the former would often carry his young friend around on his shoulders. Zubin also befriended a young Italian conductor who too was destined to make it big as a conductor: Abbado. Unlike the effervescent Zubin, Abbado was shy, aloof and uncommunicative, even monosyllabic. But they say opposites attract. Zubin admits that Abbado was a man of few words. 'He was an introverted person all his life but not when he conducted. We were good friends.'[1] (When Abbado was conductor of the London Symphony Orchestra many years later, the story goes that he was asked to say a few words after dinner. All he said was, 'Thank you very much,' and that, according to cellist Clive Gillinson, was the longest speech Abbado had ever made!)

Barenboim, in his autobiography, narrates how Zecchi's classes marked the beginning of his friendship with Abbado and Zubin. He recalls gifting a poster to the Berlin Philharmonic of the last concert that summer of 1956, with the three of them conducting. He recalls that even though Abbado was ten years older and Zubin six, there was an endearing camaraderie between them and they 'played all kinds of silly games'. Barenboim looked upon Zubin as an elder brother who was much more experienced and adult, 'more experienced not only as far as conducting was concerned but also as regards life generally'.[2] He says that a special bond existed with Zubin right from the beginning, and he was 'probably the only person who became a soulmate of mine very early on and has remained one since'.[3]

Barenboim, Zubin and Abbado exchanged notes on music and, after listening to Zubin, Abbado became keenly interested in the academy at Vienna, believing that the Milan Conservatory where he had studied had little else to offer him. Zubin recalls that there was no professional jealousy between the three students—they shared a comradeship born out of their love for music.

Barenboim was fascinated by Zubin's 'facility in learning music and in translating musical ideas into gestures, and dealing with people in general and orchestral musicians in particular'.[4] Another reason for their continued closeness is the Israel connection. Zubin's affection for Israel and its people and, of course, its orchestra (of which he is music director for life) 'has remained a constant leitmotif both in his life and in the life of the Israel Philharmonic'.[5]

## GRABBING CHANCES

It was at the Accademia Chigiana that Zubin got an opportunity that figures prominently in his early career. This pattern was to continue: it was as if destiny was giving him one big break after another. When the student who was supposed to conduct Tchaikovsky's Fifth at a gala concert in the main piazza fell ill, Zecchi asked if anyone else was familiar with the piece and could fill his shoes. Zubin immediately volunteered, even though he had never even looked at the piece before.

'You must be ready to take a chance when it is presented to you. And when you get these chances, you had better do well or you may not get any others,'[6] was how he put it later.

Zubin feels that to make your way in a conducting career, it is not enough to simply get opportunities—you have to make them a success. He spent all afternoon and evening studying the piece despite the fact that his friend Husaruk was practising the violin just next to him—proof enough of his phenomenal powers of concentration. The concert proved to be a great success. Besides pursuing music, Zubin also played table tennis and learned some Italian. The summer months passed quickly and, before long, he was back in Vienna.

Zubin was always striving towards success even as a student. Another opportunity presented itself in October 1956 as the Hungarian Revolution erupted. A spontaneous nationwide revolt against the government of Hungary, it began as a student demonstration when they marched through central Budapest to the Parliament building. A group of students who entered the radio building in an attempt to broadcast their demands was arrested. When the demonstrators outside demanded the release of the students, they were fired upon by the police from within the building. The news spread quickly, and violence erupted throughout Budapest.

The revolt soon spread across Hungary and resulted in the fall of the government, bringing thousands of refugees to Austria. That was when a British army officer thought of organizing a concert to raise the spirits of the refugees and approached the academy. An orchestra of volunteers was put together with Zubin as conductor. They were taken by bus to the refugee camp about 50 miles from Vienna.

While Zubin was thrilled at the prospect of conducting his own orchestra, he found to his dismay that the soles of the two pairs of shoes he owned had worn out. Rather than conduct in boots, he preferred to wear a mismatched pair. At the camp, there was no stage and the orchestra played at the end of a long mess hall. The refugees were so taken by the idea that they sacrificed their evening meal to hear the students play. Zubin played pieces from memory and thus could dispense with a podium. They played the Overture from *Die Fledermaus*; a Mozart violin concerto, with Gabora as soloist; the first movement of Schubert's *Unfinished Symphony*; and finally Liszt's Hungarian Rhapsody No. 2. All the pieces elicited a warm and enthusiastic response but the biggest applause was reserved for the Hungarian Rhapsody at the end of which people were cheering and hugging each other; some were even crying.[7] Deeply moved, a Hungarian priest gave Zubin and his ensemble his blessings. Zubin recalls meeting a Hungarian couple in Los Angeles many decades later: they had been at the camp that day.[8]

## RETURN TO VIENNA

Back in Vienna, he was joined by Abbado who had also enrolled in Swarowsky's conducting class. Zubin made him join the Singverein, the Vienna choir. The two decided that they would attend rehearsals only by important conductors and not the routine sessions under chorus master Reinhardt Schmidt. They sang under Krips in Haydn's *Creation*, Erich Kleiber in Verdi's *Requiem* and Walter in the Mozart *Requiem*. Reiner and Karajan also conducted in the Singverein that season.[9] But Schmidt soon found out and was irritated enough to throw them out of one of Karajan's rehearsals, saying, 'Abbado, Mehta, out! You don't come to my rehearsals; you don't get the sugar either!'[10] That ended Zubin's career in the choir but his growing proficiency on the double bass ensured that he was a sought-after substitute in the secondary orchestras of Vienna. Apart from the valuable experience of watching other conductors at work, the extra money it brought was very welcome.

It was at a performance of Verdi's *Requiem* under Karajan that American soprano Leontyne Price met Zubin and Abbado for the first time. She recalled how two handsome young men in the bass section of the chorus introduced themselves to her. Little did she know that within a few years they would take the world of conducting by storm. When Zubin got an orchestra of his own (the Montreal

Symphony Orchestra), Price was one of the first soloists he contacted. She went on to appear with him in Los Angeles, Israel and New York, and in a highly acclaimed *Tosca* recording for the Radio Corporation of America.

Zubin's reputation as a quick learner had spread and he was a familiar sight at rehearsals of the Vienna Philharmonic. While all the others were turned out at the time of the final tuning up, Zubin was allowed to stay and learn. It helped that his bass professor was first bass and his chamber music professor one of the first violins. Zubin recalled, 'They had restrictions, but not for me. "The Indian can stay." So I stayed and I learned. I can't tell you how much I learned at those rehearsals.'[11] It was at this time that he began to bridge the gap between theory and practice. Training an orchestra is one of the essentials of a conductor's trade. Zubin observed that while Krips knew how to train an orchestra and put up polished and sparkling performances, Swarowsky, though he knew the score inside out, couldn't transmit that vision to the orchestra and get them to play it the way he wanted. Watching Karajan taught him about conducting style, something he could not pick up in Swarowsky's class. An admirer of Karajan, Zubin says that 'his movements made him *part* of the music, not merely the leader of musicians'.[12]

This hero worship inevitably led to Zubin imitating the great conductor. Later, when Zubin conducted the Tonkünstler Orchestra, Vienna's third-ranking orchestra, a critic said, 'Mr. Mehta suffers from Karajanitis.'[13] Zubin was stung at the time but later admitted that it was fair criticism. It was around this time that Zubin had to move out of Frau Mumb's apartment because she had caught him bringing a Jewish friend into the building, something the rules forbade. Zubin found accommodation with an old Russian lady who had no such objection to visitors.

Zubin and Carmen attended the annual Neujahrskonzert where the Philharmonic played Strauss waltzes, polkas and overtures. They saw the famous Willi Boskovsky, the concertmaster, conduct with his bow, the way Zubin had seen Mehli do in Bombay. Bookspan and Yockey observed:

> Zubin watched Boskovsky, swaying in three quarter time, his eyes closed, and knew that this must be the way to conduct Johann Strauss. Whether or not it was great music was academic. It was great Strauss.[14]

The concert ended with the 'Blue Danube', the ultimate encore. Zubin wondered if Vienna would ever invite anyone but a Viennese to conduct the New Year Concert, little guessing that he himself would conduct that concert five times (the last as recently as 2015).

Zubin had his own not-so-happy experience with Boskovsky when he conducted his first subscription concert in 1963 with the Vienna Philharmonic. They were to perform Schoenberg's *Five Pieces for Orchestra* and were rehearsing at the Brahmssaal at the Musikverein. Boskovsky was the concertmaster and he, after taking one look at the difficult score, decided that he didn't like it and would not play it. No amount of convincing had any effect and they had to make do with a replacement concertmaster. Later, Zubin and Boskovsky collaborated often and there was never any reference to this incident.[15]

Since the years in Vienna were formative ones for Zubin, it is not surprising that he developed a bias for the German repertory. He saw this as an advantage since the German repertoire makes up 60 per cent of a conductor's programmes over the years. While Mehli had inculcated in Zubin a liking for French music, exposing him to Maurice Ravel and Debussy, Zubin felt that these were not popular in Vienna because the Viennese conductors had never really learned to do justice to these composers.[16]

The spring of 1957 saw the end of Zubin's second year as a conducting student and the completion of his course at the academy. He, Abbado and four others were to conduct the Tonkünstler Orchestra in a public concert as their final examination. Zubin's piece was Tchaikovsky's *Romeo and Juliet*. But just a week before the concert, Carmen reminded Zubin that he did not possess a full dress suit. Unable to afford a set of tails and trousers, he asked the waiters of a fashionable restaurant where they had got theirs from and bought one at a throwaway price from the same store. The only hitch was that when he arrived for the concert, he realized the coat did not have pockets! His performance went well, the only negative being the lack of press coverage.

That summer saw Zubin and Abbado return to Siena feeling invincible. But unlike the gentle Zecchi who had imparted instruction to them the last time, the conducting professor was Alceo Galliera whose teaching technique brought the two quickly down to earth. Zubin recalls that Galliera was such a difficult man to please that he felt he couldn't do anything right. Carmen who had gone to visit her parents in Canada was not there to lift his sagging spirits but Zarin, then travelling in Europe, visited him. He told him that his grandfather Nowroji Mehta was shifting to Manchester from Bombay. Zubin was thrilled at the prospect of seeing his grandfather again.

# A Rising Star

WHEN ZARIN MET ZUBIN in Siena, he gave him a clipping from one of the British dailies. It announced a new competition for conductors in Liverpool to be held in May 1958. It was sponsored by the Royal Liverpool Philharmonic and was open to any conductor below the age of forty with a minimum of professional experience. The first prize was a season as assistant conductor at a salary of £800. Zubin sent in an application, but soon put the matter out of his mind. Little did he realize that it would be a milestone in his fledgling career.

## A BUDDING CONDUCTOR

At the end of the summer, Zubin returned to Vienna and became a bass player with the orchestra of the Jeunesses Musicales, an organization which aimed at fostering the love of music in young people. It was headed by Joachim Lieben who became a good friend of Zubin's. It was part of the Jeunesses Musicales International which originated in Belgium and was one of the world's largest music organizations for youth. Zubin had been introduced to the organization by Swarowsky. The Jeunesses Musicales was planning a programme for conductors but its initial interest in Zubin was as a bass player. (This organization was to play an important part in Zubin's first years as a struggling conductor. In 1958, he visited Belgrade as part of an exchange programme with Yugoslavia. Even after Zubin had 'arrived', he still made it a point to conduct at least once or twice with the Jeunesses later in his career.)

Zubin accompanied the orchestra to Paris, then left the group and visited Carmen and his parents in Manchester. His grandfather Nowroji who was ninety-one had shifted to Manchester from Bombay and Zubin was happy to meet him. But he was worried about how the old man would tolerate such a radical change in his life at such an advanced age, especially the wet, cold weather. (His fears were not unfounded. Nowroji passed away in March 1958, two days after he married Carmen).

On his return to Vienna, Zubin learned that he had been accepted in the Liverpool conducting competition. The competition was the brainchild of Royal Liverpool Philharmonic conductor John Pritchard, who wanted to test the talent of young conductors with a first-rate orchestra. He invited Cologne-born William Steinberg, conductor of both the Pittsburgh Symphony and the London Philharmonic orchestras, to help him judge the contest. The pair screened ninety applicants and finished with a list of nineteen competitors from nine countries. Each contestant had to prepare a repertory of twelve classical orchestral works, four works with soloists, and any two from a list of four modern works.

Zubin was familiar with most of them except Stravinsky's ballet *Petrouchka*, and he set about learning this new piece of music. He read whatever he could find on the piece, its composer and the historical background—the way Zubin studies any piece of music. As his knowledge of Petrouchka, the marionette with human feelings, grew, he became fascinated with it as a subject for music. In French, Petrouchka is called Pierrot. Soon Zubin became interested in Schoenberg's *Pierrot Lunaire*. This is one of Schoenberg's most important atonal pieces and one which is difficult for both vocal and instrumental soloists to execute. It also requires great concentration on the part of the conductor. Zubin's interest took a practical turn when the president of the Mahler Society, Erwin Ratz, who also taught at the academy, decided to sponsor a concert of the work. He agreed that the society would pay the rent for the hall as well as the musicians. He also said that Zubin should get paid for all his pains.

Once Zubin had recruited the musicians, he conducted it at the Brahmssaal where his father, Mehli, had given his violin recital in 1955. The programme was a pure Schoenberg evening and, among others, they played the Chamber Symphony No. 1 for fifteen solo instruments and *Pierrot Lunaire* for one vocal and five instrumental soloists. It was, Zubin says, a bold programme, and moreover, the pieces selected were difficult to play. The concert was a great success. According to the newspapers, no one had got to hear the piece since the time Schoenberg himself had conducted it fifty years ago. The concert earned Zubin and his ensemble much publicity and even attracted the attention of the government.

Ratz insisted that Zubin accept some form of payment. Since Ratz was the custodian of all the original Mahler scores (he kept them under his bed), Zubin asked for a copy of the score of *Kindertotenlieder* (*Songs on the Death of Children*), a song cycle for voice and orchestra by Mahler.[1] This was Zubin's first payment and he rates it as his most exciting remuneration till date. After the concert, Zubin called on Ruth Vasicek who worked in the office of the Konzerthausgesellschaft (Concert House Society) and was known to promote young artistes. It was the start of a happy relationship and Vasicek handled many contracts for Zubin in his career, the last being the signing of the contract with the Bavarian State Opera in Munich in 1996.[2]

As word about Zubin and his ad hoc ensemble spread, the Austrian government asked the young conductor and his group to go on a musical goodwill tour of Italy. They travelled to Milan and Rome and played a programme of Schoenberg, Webern and Stravinsky. Zubin took Carmen with him and also invited several of his musicians to bring their girlfriends along. That this raised a few Austrian eyebrows, in particular those of Egon Hilbert, head of the Austrian Cultural Institute in Rome, did not really trouble Zubin. His concerts in Milan and Rome were very well received. This was just as well, because Hilbert went on to become director of the Vienna Music Festival, and later, the Vienna Opera. In exchange, the Italian government sent a similar chamber ensemble from Milan to Austria. And conducting the Italian ensemble was none other than Abbado.

By 1958, Swarowsky had left Vienna to become the music director of the Scottish National Orchestra. It was his intention to hire Zubin as a bass player and assistant conductor once he found his feet there. Meanwhile, he had put Zubin in charge of a group, the Haydn Orchestra, which he had founded. He was in the process of promoting the recording of all 104 Haydn symphonies and Zubin was to rehearse the orchestra and also conduct its first public concert in March 1958. But Zubin soon had the orchestra rehearsing Romantic and post-Romantic compositions, with Haydn taking a back seat.

When Zubin sent Swarowsky a programme which contained just one Haydn piece, predictably he was called sharply to heel and had to restore Haydn to the primacy his teacher expected. The performance was well received. The pupil had not let his master down. But Swarowsky could only report failure from his side. When he had broached the subject of Zubin as assistant conductor, all that the board in Glasgow wanted to know was the colour of his skin. When Swarowsky said that he did not find Zubin particularly dark, they said, 'The father was very dark,'[3] and the matter ended there. It was also around this time that Zubin encountered religious persecution. Zubin had a Jewish friend, an Israeli singer by the name of Amnon Zalmonovitz, who used to visit him at his apartment. When Frau Mumb, his landlady, said that she would have no Jews in her house, Zubin decided to move out even though it was only a matter of a few weeks: he would be moving in with Carmen soon. While Zubin himself was never the victim of racial prejudice, the bias against Jews came as a rude shock. 'Coming from Bombay, I had never heard of such things. There were seven religions and we made fun of each other but there was never any animosity or hatred that I ever experienced,' he said.[4]

### *Marriage*

In March 1958, Zubin and Carmen were married in Vienna. As Carmen said, 'it more or less *happened*'.[5] Zubin had decided on a wedding in the spring and she said yes. The astrologer's predictions must have weighed on Tehmina's mind but who can deny destiny? Austrian law demanded a civil union, and Carmen's religious conviction a ceremony in church. Zubin encountered a good deal of red tape with the Viennese authorities but prevailed in the end with some plain-speaking. So there was a civil wedding as well as a church ceremony. Amid all the celebrations, Zubin forgot the ring and had to borrow a friend's! They then drove through a snowstorm to the Dominicanakirche, the parish to which Carmen belonged, where about thirty friends and professors were squeezed into the sacristy. Zubin named two best men, one for each ceremony: violist Eddie Kudlak and Zalmonovitz.

They could not be married at the altar since Zubin had no desire to become a Catholic. As it is, the brief ceremony in the sacristy was permitted because Zubin had promised to raise any children as Catholic. But he reserved the right to give them Parsi names. After that they walked to Carmen's one-room apartment which they planned to make their home. There were no gifts because their friends were as poor as they were. They celebrated with chocolate cake and sandwiches. Zubin and Carmen spent a one-night honeymoon in the old Imperial Hotel and Zubin purchased a phonograph with the $100 cheque his parents had given him.[6]

## NUMERO UNO

In May, Zubin reached Liverpool to participate in the music competition. Much to his delight, the judges chose *Petrouchka* for his first-round selection. He made it to the semi-final where he conducted the third movement of Schubert's Fifth. There, Zubin all but blew his chance. The third movement is a minuet followed by a trio. Schubert had marked his minuet *allegro molto*, and it is meant to be played at a lively pace but Zubin played it significantly slower. Pritchard thought that Zubin was nervous but the fact was that he had confused the piece he was playing with another composition, Mozart's Fortieth Symphony (which was also on the longlist of pieces to be prepared for the competition), and which also has a minuet third movement. While Schubert's is *allegro molto*, Mozart's is a much slower *allegretto*. Having started at the slow pace, Zubin had no choice but to continue till the judges asked him to stop and start again—something they did not do. Zubin was dismayed and wondered how he would tell Mehli about the mess he had made.

But the force, as always, was with Zubin. His name was among the three finalists. In the final round, he was given Beethoven's Fifth to play. Carmen, who was watching along with Tehmina, and Zarin, who had managed to make it just in time after writing his intermediate accounting examination, wondered why he had been given something as hackneyed as Beethoven's Fifth to conduct. When the results were declared, she was stunned to hear the judges declare her husband as one of the winners. After two weeks and fifty hours of music, Steinberg and Pritchard agreed on three 'equal merit' awards, signifying that no single contestant stood out sharply from the others. The winners: Zubin Mehta, 22; Detroit-born Haig Yaghjian, 33; and Norway's Sverre Bruland, 35.[7] Steinberg was a little disappointed but not particularly surprised that they did not find their boy wonder. He said that conducting is conveying experience and perhaps it was expecting too much from raw conductors who had too little of it.

Zubin says that he won because he had impressed Steinberg with his handling of the fermata in the first movement of Beethoven's Fifth. Steinberg told him later that it was his conducting of this piece which put him ahead of the other contestants. Steinberg too belonged to the Germanic school and fully agreed with Zubin's interpretation. A fermata is a symbol that indicates the prolongation (at the discretion of the performer) of a musical note, chord or rest beyond its assigned time value. In the opening *da dadadaa*s of Beethoven's Fifth, there is a fermata over each of the *daa*s. Without going into too much detail, it should suffice to say that it boils down to how long a conductor waits between a *daa* and the next *da*. Zubin attributed this to Swarowsky's training: he had played the piece just the way he had rehearsed it with Swarowsky.

Pritchard later said that he had spotted him as the winner right from the start as 'this boy had something special'. Zubin, however, disagrees. He says that it was thanks to Steinberg, who was head of the jury, that he won. When Mehli got the news in Prague, where he was with Barbirolli and the Hallé Orchestra, he was elated. Barbirolli waved Tehmina's telegram at the orchestra saying, 'Mehli's son is after my job.'[8] When Zubin spoke to Mehli, he gave him some more good news: Carmen was expecting their first child.

## TANGLEWOOD

After his success in Liverpool, Zubin and Abbado went to Massachusetts where they had been accepted as conducting students at the Berkshire Music Center at Tanglewood. Tanglewood is the summer home of the Boston Symphony Orchestra, located in the scenic Berkshire Hills of western Massachusetts. The Berkshire Music Festival was launched in 1934 by Henry Hadley. Its first orchestra was not the Boston Symphony Orchestra but the New York Philharmonic. Even today, it is New York that supplies the bulk of its crowds each year.

The foremost name associated with the Berkshire Music Festival is that of conductor Koussevitzky, a man who started out as a double bass player and earned legendary status with the Boston Symphony Orchestra. He studied conducting under Nikisch in Berlin and among his legacies was the Berkshire Music Festival. Koussevitzky took it over in 1936 and created a music school there in 1940. Both the festival and the school flourished: the festival became the most prestigious in America and some of the country's brightest young men came from the school. The star was of course Bernstein, who studied in Koussevitzky's conducting class.

When Zubin went to Tanglewood, he was one of eight conductors studying under Eleazar de Carvalho of Brazil. The music director of the Boston Symphony Orchestra, Charles Munch, also sat in on some of their rehearsals, once telling Zubin to place his feet together while conducting. Munch came to conducting late (aged forty-one) and was trained as a violinist; he was concertmaster of the Leipzig Gewandhaus Orchestra under Furtwängler for many years.

He appeared in 1932 with the Straram Orchestra and later formed his own Paris Philharmonic. He became music director of the Paris Conservatoire Orchestra in 1937, visited America in 1946 and succeeded Koussevitzky in Boston in 1949.

Zubin's six weeks in the Berkshire Hills were spent in working on interpretation, technique and theory with both students and professionals. At the end of the festival, when prizes were awarded, Zubin found he had been placed second in the conducting class, winning the Gertrude Robinson Smith Prize. In first place was his friend Abbado, who won the Koussevitzky Prize.[9] Two members of the faculty were particularly impressed with Zubin: conductor-pianist Seymour Lipkin and Lukas Foss of the Music Center's composition department. Foss, a composer, pianist, conductor and music professor, had been a member of the conducting class of 1940 under Koussevitzky, that had included Thor Johnson and the celebrated Bernstein. He had been impressed with the combination of enthusiasm, natural talent and technical skill that Zubin had exhibited.

After the awards ceremony, Zubin met Foss and asked for his help, hoping that Tanglewood would lead to bigger things. He told Foss, 'Lukas, what am I to do? Everybody says I am good and nobody *does* anything.'[10] Recognizing Zubin's talent, Foss, who also played a role in the early career of the American conductor Michael Tilson Thomas, recommended him to his German manager, Siegfried Hearst. Hearst specialized in managing conductors; among his other clients were big names like Klemperer, Stokowski and Solti. Hearst, after some convincing, agreed to meet Zubin. After the meeting in New York, Hearst was so impressed with Zubin that he asked the young conductor to 'go on to Liverpool and do your work there and you will be hearing from me'. Zubin remembers Hearst fondly, recalling how he had sat with him for hours telling him about the profession. Hearst was to be Zubin's only agent in the United States. He remembers him as being 'very kindly, fatherly almost'.[11] (Hearst had a roommate at the University of McGill in Montreal who went on to achieve great notoriety: Joachim von Ribbentrop, who went on to become Hitler's foreign minister. Zubin says he didn't know that till many years later.)

# Liverpool Let-down

ZUBIN LEFT FOR LIVERPOOL to take up his post as assistant to John Pritchard (later Sir) with a few misgivings. For one, he was unsure of how the orchestra would treat him. The musicians had been extremely aloof and patronizing when he had conducted them for the competition. Maybe that would change once he led them not as a contestant but as a professional. He hoped for the best. Another grey area was his contract: It did not specify how many concerts he would have to conduct. And would he be allowed to choose his own repertoire? From what he knew, Pritchard and he had widely divergent tastes in music.

## A LACK OF SUPPORT

From London Zubin took the train to Manchester, where he met Carmen. She was at the time staying with his parents. He then boarded a train to Liverpool, which is an hour's ride from Manchester. When Zubin met Pritchard initially, he thought that things would be fine. He was to conduct twenty concerts over the season, including some 'on tour'. Since the season was scheduled to begin in a few weeks' time, Pritchard asked Zubin to rehearse some pieces with the orchestra which he would conduct in the first series of concerts. Zubin thought that he would be given scores which were well worn, and which both the conductor and the orchestra were all too familiar with, and he worried about breathing new life into such musical compositions. But he needn't have worried. His problems were to be of an entirely different nature.

Zubin had never seen the three scores Pritchard handed him. Of the three, he was familiar with only one, Richard Strauss's tone poem *Ein Heldenleben*; the other two, Edward Elgar's First Symphony and Schoenberg's *Variations for Orchestra*, he had only heard of. Given that he had only a few days to rehearse, Zubin wondered what he was going to do. There was hardly any time for him to get familiar with the pieces, let alone teach them to the orchestra, especially the Schoenberg composition which is the first strictly twelve-tone composition ever written for orchestra. It would be some time before he himself knew the pieces well enough to conduct the way he wanted to. Also, it would require the full cooperation of the orchestra, something that Zubin soon learned he could not expect from the Royal Liverpool Philharmonic. The rehearsals were most unsatisfactory. Zubin says that it is good to be thrown into the deep end in some areas of your life so that you learn quickly but in music, it does not work that way.[1]

The orchestra disliked him and Zubin's own inexperience didn't help. He blames the inspirationally flaccid Pritchard for giving him a piece like Schoenberg's *Variations* to conduct. 'It's something you simply don't give to an assistant on such short notice.'[2] At the time he was just not ready to conduct the piece and his orchestra knew it. They treated him as their inferior, showing little of the respect owed to a conductor.

Zubin recalled: 'I never enjoyed real communication with John Pritchard. I learned a lot at his rehearsals, but he never properly prepared me to take over. He would just not feel like going one morning, and phone and ask me to rehearse Elgar's Second Symphony.'[3] Zubin was not familiar with Elgar's Second. He felt like a miserable failure and whenever things seemed particularly bleak, he would catch a train to Manchester and listen to Barbirolli. Zubin says that he has always been good to his assistants because of that experience. ('I never expect anything from an assistant for which he has not been able to prepare well in advance. More than anything else, I think one needs time to mature.'[4])

Another problem Zubin faced was that in most cases he was allowed only one rehearsal before a concert. Even today, after nearly six decades of experience, Zubin considers one rehearsal inadequate. For a greenhorn just starting his career, it was an almost impossible situation. He recalls his first programme in his autobiography. It comprised the *Forza* Overture, the adagio of Mahler's Fifth Symphony, Alexander Glazunov's Violin Concerto and Tchaikovsky's Sixth Symphony. The orchestra did not know Glazunov or Mahler and it was sheer chance that Zubin was familiar with the Glazunov composition, having heard Mehli play it in Bombay. There was dissatisfaction all around: for the orchestra, the conductor and the audience. Zubin felt the limitations of a solitary rehearsal even more keenly when he went to Belgrade to conduct an orchestra. They gave him four rehearsals, something which reinforced his belief that, given more time, he could produce better music.

Zubin travelled by bus with his orchestra to smaller towns like Bedford, Rochdale and Sheffield, performing in places with curious names he had never heard before, like Snake Inn and Ramsbottom. In the smaller centres, he was allowed to pick compositions that both he and the orchestra knew well, so even that one rehearsal could be dispensed with. Another problem was the orchestra manager who was fixated on timings. He wanted every concert to be exactly two hours and twenty minutes long. In case they fell short, he would stretch the concert by inserting one of his favourite pieces whether or not it fit the overall theme. Thus there would be something like *Eine Kleine Nachtmusik* at every concert.[5]

Zubin recalls an amusing incident that took place during the performance of the Orchestral Suite from Alban Berg's *Lulu*. In it, there is a piercing scream from the heroine in the end. Pritchard had hired a glamorous actress for the 'scream' and it was Zubin's job to give her the cue at the appropriate time. But Zubin started flirting with her backstage and, at the time of the climax, there was silence. The absence of the music and a glare from Pritchard made Zubin realize that it was time to end the backstage flirtation. He pushed her aside, hissing 'Scream!'[6]

Zubin's Liverpool experience was disappointing both for him and for the orchestra. On the Liverpool podium, Zubin quickly discovered that 'I was just unprepared to lead a professional orchestra. I learned at their expense but I learned.'[7] Since he received little by way of guidance from Pritchard, Zubin made trips to Glasgow to meet Swarowsky whenever he could. There, master and pupil would study scores and Zubin would clarify his doubts. Manchester was closer still and Zubin also spent a lot of time there. Barbirolli treated Mehli like a younger brother and immediately took young Zubin under his wing. Zubin says he learned more at Barbirolli's rehearsals than from 'my boss'.[8] As his disenchantment with Liverpool grew, so did his fondness for Barbirolli. Notwithstanding his relationship with Barbirolli, Mehli corresponded regularly with his old teacher Galamian in New York, requesting him to find a musical position for him in the United States.[9]

It was at this time that Zubin and Carmen became parents. Zarina, a daughter, was born in Manchester on 10 November 1958. Zubin received the news on the phone when he was rehearsing Tchaikovsky's Sixth Symphony, the *Pathetique*, with the Liverpool orchestra. He took the train to Manchester after completing his rehearsal. At the hospital, Zubin found Carmen in a huge room with about twenty other women. There was no sign of the baby. On frantically searching for the child, he found his firstborn all alone in a room, covered in blood, with the umbilical cord still attached. Since a child called Mehta would have to be an Indian, Zubin rates this as his first experience of discrimination. At least that was the way he saw it then.[10] The next day Zubin left for Liverpool. Given his frame of mind, it was no surprise that the concert that evening was a disaster. Zubin rates it as one of the worst in his entire career.

Sometime later, Carmen's parents came to visit her and Zubin in Liverpool. It was their first meeting with their son-in-law. Though Zubin charmed them, they had a feeling the marriage would not last. In fact, they were more impressed by Zarin, who had come to look at his niece and namesake. They also noticed the warm and comfortable relationship Carmen shared with her brother-in-law. Bookspan and Yockey tell us that Paul Lasky, Carmen's father, always maintained that she had married the wrong Mehta. (That wrong would be set right, as we shall see later.)

## RETURN TO VIENNA

If the environment in Liverpool was not to Zubin's liking, some good news came from an unexpected quarter. Just when Zubin had given up on Hearst, he received a cable asking him to conduct a radio concert of the Canadian Broadcasting Corporation (CBC) Orchestra in March 1959. The fee was $500 but Zubin would have to bear the expenses. Therein lay the rub because the fees would not even cover the expenses. On Mehli's advice, Zubin met Vijaya Lakshmi Pandit, the Indian high commissioner, in London. She was most helpful and the embassy paid for his entire trip, something that Zubin remembers gratefully to this day. They continued to be friends. (When Indira Gandhi was assassinated in 1984, Zubin remained by Vijaya Lakshmi's side during the funeral.) The Liverpool orchestra permitted him leave of absence for a week so that he could conduct in Toronto.

Since there was little time to prepare a programme, speed was of the essence. He decided to open with Brahms's *Tragic* Overture. He was delighted to find that *Petrouchka*, which he had conducted with some success at the Liverpool competition, was part of the CBC Orchestra's catalogue and plumped for it. By the time he conducted the CBC Orchestra from Toronto, his in-laws had returned to Saskatoon to hear him conduct on the radio. The musicians of the orchestra seemed impressed with the authority with which Zubin conducted and the concert was a success. In Montreal, his friends Husaruk and Kudlak, now both members of the Montreal Symphony Orchestra, heard the broadcast.

Zubin's performance with the CBC Orchestra in Toronto was one of the high points of what was otherwise a trying year. It appears that Zubin had stopped confiding in Carmen for she seemed largely unaware of his problems with the Liverpool orchestra. At the end of the year, Pritchard called Zubin and told him that much as he would have liked to, he could not invite him back for the following year. Looking back at that Liverpool season, Zubin and Pritchard saw things a little differently. Pritchard felt that someone as talented as Zubin did not need to spend that year with the Liverpool Philharmonic. Zubin, on the other hand, felt that he was just not good enough for some of the pieces Pritchard gave him. He took little or no interest in his concerts.

The musicians for their part had never liked Zubin and did not enjoy playing under him. Given the circumstances, there was no way the Liverpool Philharmonic would have called him back for a second season. Liverpool had proved to be a disappointment both for Zubin and the musicians. There was no choice but to return to Vienna. Almost two decades later, when Zubin had become an international celebrity, Pritchard said that it was the training in Liverpool as an assistant which had helped make Zubin what he was. But Pritchard's attempt to portray Zubin's Gethsemane as a training ground cut little ice with Zubin. 'How would he know anyway? I don't think he attended one of my concerts.'[11]

In the spring of 1959, the young parents found themselves back in Vienna. Zubin recalls how he spent his days studying Brahms's First Symphony and Piano Concerto in the City Park in Vienna with Zarina in the pram in front of him. Zubin contacted his old friends and professors in the hope of finding some work. The Jeunesses Musicales seemed to be his best bet and invited him to guest conduct one of their concerts. The fee was a pittance but Zubin was in no position to choose. He could no longer go back to his old job as a bass player because it would just not do to play last-chair bass one day and conduct the same orchestra the next. It was a difficult time, especially as Zubin now had a wife and child to look after. Mehli and Tehmina helped support the young couple.

In the summer of 1959 Zubin travelled to Salzburg for the music festival and ran into the pianist Lipkin whom he had befriended at Tanglewood. Lipkin had come to play with Bernstein and the New

York Philharmonic that was to perform in Salzburg. Zubin expressed a desire to meet Bernstein, and Lipkin arranged a meeting. The two established a good rapport on their first meeting and, when Zubin asked him if he would accept him as his assistant, the latter was most helpful and told him what letters to write and whom to address them to. But later Mitropoulos, the Greek conductor who had preceded Bernstein at the New York Philharmonic, and to whom Zubin had been introduced by his old professors, gave him some important advice: 'You may be starving now but don't you ever take a job as anybody's assistant again. If you do, you'll regret it later.'[12] However, given the dire financial straits he was in, Zubin doubted very much that he would be able to follow the advice.

Apart from the small assignments through the Jeunesses, there was nothing else. But those concerts got Zubin noticed and he received an invitation to a small tour independent of the Jeunesses, organized by one of his former classmates at the academy, which took him to Sarajevo, Ljubljana and Skopje. Zubin was also invited to conduct the orchestra of Trondheim, Norway, and was booked to conduct the Yugoslavian chapter of the Jeunesses Musicales in Belgrade in early 1960. He had also conducted a concert with the prestigious Lower Austrian Tonkünstler courtesy of the Jeunesses. They played Brahms's First and Piano Concerto No. 1. His soloist was Alfred Brendel, a student at the academy. Zubin had run into him at a bookstore and asked him if he would play with him; Brendel had immediately agreed.

Still, these conducting assignments were hardly likely to make Zubin famous or even financially secure. He had reached a difficult period in his life. After the years of self-discovery and recognition of his own genius, he had reached a point where visible symbols of success, which were slow in coming, assumed increasing importance. And it was unlikely that the busy Hearst would ever find time to help him. Or so it seemed.

# Destiny's Child

WHILE ZUBIN WAS GRATEFUL to Hearst for his Toronto sojourn, he still doubted if his agent could really catapult him into the big league. Hearst had realized by then that the charismatic Indian was special and had the potential to become a big star. Unknown to Zubin, he was plodding away on his behalf, canvassing for him to anyone who cared to listen. Hearst was also Stokowski's agent in the late 1950s, and both men (even though Stokowski had never met Zubin) felt that he was destined to make it big. What was remarkable about their support was that neither Hearst nor Stokowski had ever heard or seen Zubin conduct.

Harold C. Schonberg, music critic for the *New York Times* for thirty years, wrote in his book *The Great Conductors*:

> One other striking aspect of the period following World War II should be mentioned, and it involves the newer conductors. Two of them are Oriental—Zubin Mehta from India and Seiji Ozawa from Japan—and they are the first two in history to impress one as altogether major talents.[1]

Schonberg was spot on: both Zubin and Ozawa lived up to the potential he saw in them. In fact, Zubin went from jobless wunderkind in Vienna to international celebrity in the course of just a few years.

## A LUCKY BREAK

Stokowski was slated to conduct two concerts with the Philadelphia Orchestra during the summer season in Robin Hood Dell. The man in charge of the season in Robin Hood Dell was the industrialist–philanthropist Fredric R. Mann and Stokowski called him to advocate Zubin's case. When Mann said that there was no concert available, Stokowski asked him to give one of his to 'that fellow Mehta'. Behind all this was, of course, Hearst. 'Those were package deals of Siegfried's,' recalled Zubin. Both wanted Stokowski and he had to have a rest. So Hearst said, 'If you take this young Indian, you can have Stokowski.'[2] Zubin had grown up hearing Stokowski's records in Bombay. Now here was the great man himself helping Zubin get his big break in the United States. Talent without opportunity is impotent and opportunity without talent, sterile. Zubin had both talent and luck which explains his meteoric rise to international renown.

Mann, an industrialist and patron of the arts who helped finance music centres in Philadelphia and Tel Aviv, made his fortune founding and directing a company that made cardboard boxes. But since childhood, his principal interest was classical music and he used his wealth to support artistic endeavours throughout the country. Philadelphia's Fairmount Park used to host musical programmes in its outdoor amphitheatre since 1930. But by 1948, the Robin Hood Dell Concerts, as they were called, were in serious trouble. Mann, who had been a board member since 1941, took over the leadership completely. He devised a plan that called for joint support from contributors and from the city of Philadelphia, which provided free outdoor performances by the Philadelphia Orchestra. By the time he died in February 1987, music lovers of the city had been given an estimated 6 million free seats through this system. In 1976, a new concert hall was built in Fairmount Park, largely through Mann's support; it was renamed the Mann Music Center in 1979.[3]

Mann was also instrumental in the formation of the Israel Philharmonic. In 1936, the violinist Bronislaw Huberman asked Mann to help some Jewish musicians who had escaped from Nazi Germany to what was then the British protectorate of Palestine. With Mann's help, the ensemble now known as the Israel Philharmonic Orchestra was founded. He became a strong supporter, providing much of the financing for the orchestra's new hall, which was opened in 1957 and named the Fredric R. Mann Auditorium. (It was renamed the Charles Bronfman Hall in 2013, thanks to a bequest of $10 million for its renovation.)

When Mann died in 1987, Zubin said: 'He was my closest friend and mentor and supporter since my first days in the United States. It was through him that I made my debut in America, and we have been very close ever since. He was a unique person in that he was a friend to most of the world's greats. He never asked us for anything. He gave and gave and gave—if not money, then advice or support.'[4]

When Mann called Zubin to offer him one of Stokowski's concerts, Zubin confesses he did not know who he was. But when he heard the words 'Philadelphia Orchestra', he was all ears. The fee was again a paltry $500 but that made no difference to Zubin who knew a good chance when he saw one. So thanks to Stokowski and Mann, Zubin was all set to make his debut in the United States with one of the best orchestras in the world. But before that, Zubin was confronted with a familiar problem—he would have to fund his passage to the States. He decided to try the method that had worked in the past. He approached the Indian ambassador in Vienna. The ambassador, hardly as influential as Vijaya Lakshmi Pandit, asked him to wait a few weeks for a reply.

As he waited, there was more good news from Hearst. After Robin Hood Dell, Zubin would be required to conduct three of the Lewisohn Stadium Concerts with the New York Philharmonic. Stokowski, who was booked to conduct four concerts, had confirmed only one performance owing to health problems. The dates were in

July just after the Dell concerts in Philadelphia. Zubin realized at once that the whole thing had been set up by Hearst to help him. Hearst must certainly have been aware that Stokowski would be available for only one of the concerts but had nevertheless fixed dates for four performances knowing full well that he would ask Zubin to fill in for him. Zubin could hardly believe his luck: the Philadelphia and New York orchestras in the same summer! He dashed off a letter to Hearst thanking him and asking him for programme suggestions. In his autobiography, Zubin says: 'It is probably due to Siegfried Hearst's poker game that I had the fortunate opportunity to play with two such renowned and world-famous orchestras in Philadelphia and New York.'[5] Hearst was Zubin's only agent in the United States.

Zubin continued to conduct for the Jeunesses regularly and on 1 February 1960, after he conducted Stravinsky's *Pulcinella* in Brussels, he received news that a son had been born to Carmen in Vienna. Word went round in the orchestra quickly and throughout the next work, Paul Hindemith's *Der Schwanendreher*, every time he gave a musician his cue, he was greeted with a silently mouthed 'Congratulations'.[6] They called their son Mervon. The happy news was tempered with thoughts of their financial constraints and uncertain future. Carmen had her own set of problems: her life was one cycle after another of washing, feeding and clothing the children. She had no family to call on and no money to make the burden easier to bear.

Zubin and she were also drifting apart. Communication between them was poor. Zubin was unwilling to deny his own musical pleasures (something which Vienna had an abundance of) and Carmen now was unable to share them because of her maternal responsibilities. When Mervon was ten weeks old, Zubin asked Carmen to visit her parents with the children. Carmen readily agreed, no doubt physically and mentally exhausted from the responsibilities of being a mother. Carmen and the kids left for Canada on a ticket sent by the Laskys and Zubin watched them depart with regret. He would rejoin them in a few months. In the meantime, he resolved to get as much as he could out of Vienna's musical offering.

## MEETING BRUNO WALTER

The year 1960 was the Mahler Centennial and the German conductor Walter, who was a friend and disciple of Mahler, was rehearsing the Mahler Fourth Symphony at the Musikverein. Zubin, sitting behind his old double bass teacher Rühm, was present at that rehearsal and was entranced with what he heard. He was introduced to the octogenarian conductor (he was eighty-four) after the concert. As with Mitropoulos, a rapport was established between the future maestro and the aged conductor. Walter was not known to be particularly helpful to other conductors and Zubin was lucky to have got his advice on Mahler, whom Walter had known very well. Walter's advice was to have a profound effect on Zubin's musical career.

Mahler, though admired as a conductor, was often ridiculed in Vienna for his compositions. He was accused of stealing his musical ideas from other musicians and even working his own themes into new forms. As a student, Zubin had made a game of detecting Mahler's 'crimes'. A famous musicians' story at the time went as follows: Whenever Mahler's secretary went to the music library to get scores, it was said that Mahler was composing. But now, with Walter to guide him, he understood for the first time his genius for orchestration. Zubin recalls, 'He recounted for me the details of past performances, both his and Mahler's, and he analysed the scores for me, but apart from that Bruno Walter gave me so many of those terribly important details that one can never find in the printed score, details that a young conductor treasures for the rest of his life.' Mahler was known to borrow harmonic progressions and tonalities, but his genius, according to Swarowsky, lay in what he ultimately did with them. Zubin says there are motifs from *Carmen* in Mahler's Third Symphony and a little harmonic progression in the third movement of the Sixth Symphony that is pure Sergei Rachmaninoff but this in no way makes Mahler less of a genius.

Zubin met Walter again in Los Angeles later that year, when he requested permission to be present at one of his recordings with the Los Angeles Philharmonic. He seemed to know who Zubin was and told the young conductor that he had read a review in a Viennese newspaper of his conducting the Brahms Third Symphony. On Zubin's request, they went through Mahler's First Symphony together and Zubin recalls how Walter 'brought it to life' for him. Zubin found him kind and helpful and the two shared many heart-to-heart conversations. He told Zubin that he overcame his homesickness for Vienna by playing Boskovsky's recordings of waltzes with the Vienna Philharmonic. That was the last time Zubin met Walter—he died in February 1962, a little more than a year after that meeting.

Zubin also had a memorable meeting with Alma Mahler Werfel, Mahler's wife, in New York. A Viennese-born socialite, she was married to Mahler, architect Walter Gropius and novelist Franz Werfel, and was the consort of several other prominent men. One of her serious liaisons was with the Austrian artist Oskar Kokoschka. In later years, she became part of the artistic scene in Vienna, and subsequently in Los Angeles where she settled. She had moved to New York when Zubin met her surrounded by Kokoschka's fans and Gropius's plans, living, as he puts it, with 'all her genius about her'.

He recalls that she had enormous charisma and held his hand throughout the visit. Whenever he tried to leave, she made him stay, recounting something new which he was only too eager to hear. Zubin was so much under her spell that he lost track of the time and missed his flight to Paris. When he praised her granddaughter's beauty, the grand dame told him that she thought that the young lady had 'too big a bottom'! (Schoenberg's widow, Gertrud, also lived in Los Angeles and Zubin was very friendly with her and her two sons. He also occasionally met her daughter, Nuria, who was married to the avant-garde composer of classical music, Luigi Nono, considered one of the most prominent composers of the twentieth century.)

When Zubin returned to Vienna after conducting the Jeunesses in Yugoslavia and Norway, he found a letter from the Indian embassy informing him that his request for money had been granted. In addition to these glad tidings was an offer from Bernstein for Zubin to go to New York and work as his assistant for the 1960–61 season. Mehli too had some good news of his own. Thanks to Galamian, he had earned a chance to serve on the faculty of the New School of Music in Philadelphia as well as the position of second violinist in the Curtis Quintet.

Mehli continued to share a close relationship with Barbirolli, who would sometimes invite him and Tehmina for a home-cooked Italian meal. In those days Mehli had to work especially hard. The orchestra played nearly 300 concerts a year and the remuneration was a paltry £20 a week. 'Sir John said he wanted to die on the podium, but we told him that we preferred not to go with him,'[7] Mehli told John Rockwell of the *Los Angeles Times* in an interview in 1972. Even for a man of Mehli's energy, the schedule was too taxing. Mehli and Tehmina were also sick of the cold. Tehmina was perhaps the hardest hit. Her retinue of servants was a thing of the past. Among her household chores, she had to carry coal from the cellar and the only time she was warm was when she was next to the stove. At the time there was no central heating as we know it today. Thus, when the twin Philadelphia openings came his way, Mehli lost no time in accepting the offers. Mehli, despite his great affection for Barbirolli, was only too pleased to leave Manchester. Now the Mehtas were all set to conquer America!

## ROBIN HOOD DELL AND THE LEWISOHN CONCERTS

Zubin's American debut at Robin Hood Dell was a sensational success. He struck up an instant rapport with the orchestra and they even applauded him after he had conducted the Overture to Verdi's *La Forza del Destino*. His rehearsal of the Brahms First Symphony and Beethoven's C Minor Piano Concerto also went off smoothly. The soloist for the Beethoven composition was Rudolf Firkušný, whom Zubin had heard in Vienna but never met. The understanding between the conductor and the soloist was perfect.

The Philadelphia Orchestra had become one of the finest in the world under the stewardship of Stokowski and Ormandy. Zubin's programme consisted of familiar music which the knowledgeable audience knew well and it was therefore that much more risky for a fresh face to conduct. Philadelphia made Zubin that night but it could just as well have ended in disaster. He was cheered not only by the audience who called him back for bow after bow, but also by the orchestra. While Zubin drank in the spontaneous adulation, Mehli and Tehmina, who would later grow accustomed to their son's prodigies, spent the next day collecting clippings of the rave reviews from the newspapers. Praise from one particular quarter meant a lot: Max de Schauensee, the doyen of music critics, prophesied that 'the sky might be the limit' for Zubin.

After Philadelphia, Zubin was slated to conduct three concerts at the Lewisohn Stadium in New York. Lewisohn Stadium, an amphitheatre and athletic facility built on the campus of the City College of New York, had opened in 1915. Adolph Lewisohn, after whom the stadium was named, was a financier and philanthropist who had funded its construction. The stadium hosted many athletic, musical and theatrical events and was one of New York's public landmarks. Though it was demolished in 1973, the stadium remained in the memory of people who paid a nominal sum to sit under the stars on summer nights and listen to great orchestras and performers.

The concerts at the stadium were started by wealthy arts patron Minnie Guggenheimer in 1918 and served the dual purpose of bringing top-class music to the people at low prices and providing work in the summer for the musicians of the New York Philharmonic. Only the musicians got paid reasonably well—soloists and conductors were paid a pittance and turned up more for the publicity and prestige which ultimately came to be attached with performing there.

Guggenheimer, who organized concerts at the stadium for forty years, became something of a legend. She hired the artistes, handled negotiations and worried about everything, even the weather. Since Lewisohn Stadium was an open arena, she once called the weather bureau for a prediction for the night of a concert about two months later. The forecaster told her, 'Lady, you want to talk to God.' During the interval she always made speeches about current and forthcoming events. She prefaced her remarks with 'Hello, everybody!' and the audience would respond with 'Hello, Minnie!' If for some reason she was absent or late for the customary intermission speech, the audience would set up a chant of 'We want Minnie!' She was always mispronouncing names and words much to the amusement of her audience. Her greatest contribution was that she made it possible for a large number of people to hear good music at low prices, apart from providing a platform for young performers to be introduced to the public.

For over fifty years, Lewisohn Stadium featured prominently in the cultural life of New York City, allowing hundreds of thousands of concertgoers to hear the world's leading symphonies, conductors and soloists. Ella Fitzgerald sang with the Metropolitan Opera and Marian Anderson and Ormandy gave their first concerts here. George Gershwin played his *Rhapsody in Blue* for the first time and Van Cliburn repeated two concerti that he had played to win the first prize in Moscow's International Tchaikovsky Competition in 1958. Performers ranged from Heifetz and Menuhin to Price, Pete Seeger and Jack Benny.

## NEW YORK

If Zubin was flying high in Philadelphia, he would soon be brought rudely down to earth in New York. For starters, Giuseppe Di Stefano, the soloist who was to perform with Zubin, backed out. Obviously he had assumed that he would be singing with the venerable Stokowski and not an unknown conductor called Zubin Mehta. Roberta Peters, who was asked to fill in, also declined, no doubt for the same reasons. Finally, Risë Stevens was prevailed upon to accept. By all accounts, even the members of the New York Philharmonic were a choosy lot and made no secret of their disapproval if they found that a conductor was below par. Zubin, however, had no problems with the orchestra when he walked in to conduct his first rehearsal on 25 July 1960. He succeeded in winning the fussy players over with his winning personality. The problem was that the reviews the next day were unfavourable. At best they were mixed.

Zubin had played pieces like Béla Bartók's Concerto for Orchestra, Richard Strauss's *Till Eulenspiegel's Merry Pranks*, Tchaikovsky's Fifth

Symphony and various operatic arias. Rain cancelled the second concert scheduled for 27 July and most of that programme got added on to the next day's fixtures, so that the New York audience got a musical bargain at least in quantity. Zubin recalls that the operatic arias went badly since he did not know how to accompany them but thought that the Bartók and *Till Eulenspiegel* went well.

The reviewers thought otherwise. They were critical of his interpretation of Bartók and Tchaikovsky. One reviewer called his ideas 'expansive and romantic' but frequently 'excessive and uncomfortably saccharine'. However, at the same time, they also praised his control over the orchestra, his fluent technique and his ability to impress his ideas on the players. 'His faults result, perhaps, from overzealousness for he worried the music almost constantly,' wrote Allen Hughes in the *New York Times*. He went on to add:

> Mr. Mehta did achieve clarity in the music nearly all the time, but it was so labored that it counted for little artistically. He obviously knows the scores inside and out; indeed, he seems to have X-rayed them. But the skeletal structures of musical scores are not very attractive to the listener.[8]

The criticism must have had more than a germ of truth since that is the way Zubin studies a score. 'Basically, I study the structure of a piece of music first—the ironwork before you put the bricks on. After you know the large scheme, then you can fit in the parts. Assuming, of course, that I know the notes first of all. First I learn the notes, then the structure.' No mental photography is involved according to Zubin. 'Memorization comes with the study of structure,' he said. 'I have a definite system.'[9]

But in each review there were the seeds of what many critics were later to proclaim as the essence of Zubin's greatness: his ability to bring out something new and revealing from a piece of music. However, the tone of the reviews in New York set an unfortunate trend which dogged Zubin throughout his subsequent stint as conductor of the New York Philharmonic, a story which is told later in the book.

## A WINDOW OF OPPORTUNITY

After the concerts, Zubin spoke to Hearst about his career. When Hearst heard that Zubin was going to Saskatoon to meet his family, he asked him to stop in Montreal and meet Pierre Béique who was in charge of the Montreal Symphony Orchestra. Béique had been appointed administrator of the orchestra in 1939 and, in that capacity, directed the destinies of the Montreal Symphony Orchestra until his retirement in 1970. As special adviser to the president of the orchestra (1970–75), musical adviser to the managing director in 1977, special assistant to the artistic director (1978–80), special adviser to the artistic director (1981–87), and general director emeritus since 1987, Béique was the main architect of the Montreal Symphony Orchestra as we know it today.

It was through his efforts that the likes of Walter, Klemperer, Munch, Szell, Igor Markevitch and Pierre Monteux came to Montreal. Later Bernstein, Leinsdorf, Abbado, Ozawa and Zubin too performed there, ensuring that the Montrealers were able to enjoy and appreciate their prodigious talents at almost the same time as the American and European musical cognoscenti. Considering that the Montreal orchestra was a second-rung orchestra with a limited budget, this was no mean achievement. During the early years of the orchestra, Béique's private enterprise, Les Concerts Pierre Béique (1940–45), presented a large number of world-famous artistes, among them Vladimir Horowitz, Rudolf Serkin, Robert Casadesus and Lauritz Melchior. By the time he died in February 2003, Béique was, to use a cliché, a legend in the musical world of Montreal.

Béique was always on the lookout for fresh talent. His music director, Markevitch, who was in demand as a guest conductor with superior ensembles, could not be relied upon to conduct the whole season. Out of sheer necessity, Béique kept track of young performers, both soloists and conductors. He had been following Zubin's career ever since he won the Liverpool competition. Hearst had also mentioned Zubin to Béique, and Munch, his old friend, had recommended him in glowing terms. So when he came across the review by Schauensee, he already had a good idea of Zubin's abilities and potential.

When Zubin called on Béique, he welcomed him warmly and asked him about the New York concerts and the season in Liverpool. Béique, a confirmed Wagnerian, was obsessed with music. He was impressed with the self-assurance of the young conductor and realized that he was meeting a future star. After an hour, Zubin left for Saskatoon to meet his family and was overjoyed to see his kids. After two weeks in Saskatoon, they decided to visit Mehli and Tehmina in Philadelphia so that the fond grandparents could see their grandchildren again. They drove down in an old black Plymouth belonging to a priest who was a friend of the Laskys and who wanted to visit the Rodin Museum in Philadelphia. After 2000 miles and eight days on the road, they finally made it to Philadelphia.

Zubin planned to stay on in Philadelphia. He had concerts in Linz which were slated for mid-October, after which he was to conduct a series of provincial concerts in Graz. Since the season of the Philadelphia Orchestra was about to start, Zubin, never one to miss out on any kind of music, decided to attend some of Ormandy's concerts. Carmen had assumed that she would be accompanying her husband back to Vienna, but Zubin had other plans. There was no point, he thought, in dragging the family back to Vienna when they were so much better looked after in Canada. Carmen was unhappy about it and it took a telephone call from Béique to convince her that if she stayed behind, they would soon be united. It proved to be one of the most important telephone calls in Zubin's entire career.

# Montreal

THE EVENTUALITY THAT NECESSITATED Béique's call to Zubin in Philadelphia would have come as no surprise to him. Markevitch had cancelled his first series of concerts with the Montreal Symphony Orchestra ostensibly owing to a severe ear infection. This meant that Béique had to find a substitute for the first six weeks of the season. He prevailed upon an old acquaintance, Vladimir Golschmann, to take up the assignment for at least part of the time. But what was he going to do for the first two weeks for which Golschmann was unavailable? He also needed someone to open the season. The first concert was to be held in the Montreal Forum, an indoor arena which was home to the Montreal Canadiens, a professional ice hockey team based in Montreal, and more than 11,000 tickets had already been sold. Finding a replacement, and that too at such short notice, was a difficult task because the beginning of the season in Montreal coincided with the opening season of almost every other orchestra. That the orchestra could afford only a modest fee was an added disadvantage.

## A FORTUITOUS REPLACEMENT

Since a big name was out of the question, Béique thought that a newcomer with flair and audience appeal was the only answer. And who better than Zubin whom Béique had met recently and been very impressed with! Béique who was in London en route to Montreal from Bayreuth wasted no time in calling Zubin and offering him the concerts in Montreal. This was in itself fortuitous because, had Béique waited to get to Montreal to contact Zubin, he would have discovered that Zubin had already left for Europe. A message would have reached Zubin much later, by which time Béique would have been forced to find someone else.

When Zubin received the call in Philadelphia, he was slated to conduct a concert in Linz. He told Béique that he would need to reschedule his concerts in Linz and, provided the management agreed, he would be available for two weeks in Montreal. The management in Linz agreed to postpone Zubin's concerts for a few days so that he could include Montreal in his conducting itinerary. It was decided that after his three concerts in Montreal, he would fly back to Austria to conduct in Linz. Carmen and the kids would join him in Montreal and they would all return to Vienna after that.

As these plans fell into place, Zubin's mind went back to Bernstein's offer of making him assistant conductor. He had not responded to him yet. Mitropoulos's advice of not getting into an assistant's position again was playing on his mind. With the assignments in Montreal and Linz, money was no longer a problem. There was also an upcoming tour of Yugoslavia thanks to his success with the Jeunesses in Belgrade. What would an assistantship achieve? What would he do once the initial glamour wore off? These were the doubts which assailed Zubin when he met Bernstein in Carnegie Hall. They took a walk in nearby Central Park where Bernstein told him that he did not want three assistants, but only one Zubin Mehta. Sanguine about the future, he said, 'There is tremendous opportunity here in New York, and you and I are going to accomplish great things together.'[1] Realizing that it was a crucial decision for Zubin, Bernstein gave him till after the Montreal concerts to respond to his offer.

Béique had offered the Forum concert to Zubin but he still had some persuading to do. The sponsors of the Forum series needed convincing that the unknown twenty-four-year-old was indeed their man. John McConnell, the principal sponsor and publisher of the

*Montreal Star*, had his doubts and could well have pulled the plug on Zubin's Canadian debut. But as always, Zubin's luck held and McConnell did not veto the idea. Béique also strengthened Zubin's case by stating the obvious: they just didn't have a choice.

But if Béique stuck his neck out, Zubin didn't let him down. Fifteen minutes into Zubin's first rehearsal with the orchestra, Béique knew that he had picked a winner. After a lifetime of music, of which twenty-five years had been spent listening to some of the world's best conductors, Béique's finely honed sixth sense told him that he had made the right choice. He immediately saw that the musicians had taken to Zubin and that he could communicate well with them. Things were going to be fine after all. Zubin's control over the orchestra was obvious when he played Berlioz's *Symphonie Fantastique*, generally considered to be a severe test of a conductor's skill. Zubin had never played it before save at a rehearsal in Liverpool.

Zubin had charmed his orchestra within a few rehearsals. The views of the musicians echoed those of Béique. The appreciative players wanted to know if Zubin was going to stay permanently. After the second and third rehearsals, their interest, if anything, was heightened. It was unusual for the Montreal musicians to take so much interest in a conductor.

Zubin's concert at the Forum on 25 October 1960, a one-time-only 'dollar concert', received rave reviews. He also received an overwhelming ovation from the audience. Béique's faith in Zubin now had the seal of both critical and popular acclaim. Understandably, Béique was thrilled with his find. What did not please him at all was his discovery that his music director Markevitch, who was supposedly convalescing from an ear infection, was conducting a concert in Paris. An extremely miffed Béique decided that he and the orchestra had suffered enough condescension from Markevitch: he decided to give Markevitch's job as music director of the Montreal Symphony Orchestra to Zubin.

Zubin himself was astonished at the enthusiasm his performance at the Forum had generated. The next two concerts on 1 and 2 November were to be in the orchestra's regular hall, a high-school auditorium which could accommodate 1200 people. These two concerts left, in the words of the *Musical America* critic, 'an overwhelming impression'. Zubin conducted Rossini's *Barber of Seville*, Ravel's *La Valse,* Mozart's *Sinfonia Concertante* and Bartók's Concerto for Orchestra. Known to be cool to unfamiliar conductors, the Montreal audience warmed to Zubin from the start, even applauding him as he first walked on to the stage. Zubin recalls that he never had any problems with that orchestra. 'They all became my friends. Remember, I was a young man. They had many experienced musicians from whom I learned a lot. There was an "Italian mafia" of six Masella brothers who were very fine musicians.'[2]

## MUSIC DIRECTOR AT MONTREAL

The morning after the second concert, Béique contacted each member of the executive board seeking permission to appoint Zubin as music director. Having received the permission, Béique waited for the final concert and then made Zubin the offer. Zubin, who had been waiting for just such a lucky break, accepted without hesitation and was named music director of the Montreal Symphony Orchestra for the 1961–62 season.

Béique remarked later that 'when a comet passes through your life, you don't have to be a genius to realize it! I was immediately impressed by this young man who was personable, who was willing to work and who needed an Orchestra . . . Maybe in the beginning the diamond was rough, but it was still a diamond, and I could see that later on it would become more and more polished. The talent was unlimited.'[3]

Zubin recalls Béique with great affection. 'He was very kindly. He had heard of my success in Philadelphia and recognized the potential.'[4]

Hutheesing relates an amusing anecdote about the period preceding his appointment as music director. Apparently, Zubin had been invited to audition for the post of chief conductor of the Havana Symphony Orchestra and stayed with Hutheesing and his new bride in their one-bedroom apartment in New York. Zubin slept on the living room sofa. However, Fidel Castro was in the process of abolishing the *ancien regime* and it soon became obvious that there would be no Havana Symphony Orchestra. Zubin, it seems, stayed on for longer than anticipated.[5]

Carmen and Zubin celebrated his sudden rise in the musical world till late in the night. Zubin also had an important phone call to make. He had to keep Hearst abreast of the latest developments in his career. There was another reason for speaking to Hearst. He had phoned to say that the Hungarian conductor Georg Solti (later Sir) who had just been designated music director of the Los Angeles Philharmonic had shown interest in Zubin as an assistant. Solti also had engagements with the Royal Opera at Covent Garden, London. Could he fly down after the concerts in Montreal and audition for Solti? Every American conductor appointed an assistant who directed youth concerts, gave outstation performances and stood in for the main conductor if the need arose. As Zubin said, 'In short, all those supposed trifles that the boss has little time for.'[6]

Hearst, who also represented Solti, cajoled a reluctant Zubin into agreeing. Now with the music directorship of the Montreal orchestra in his hands, Zubin thought the audition unnecessary. But the shrewd Hearst had other ideas. 'Just let them come and know you,' he told Zubin.[7] When Zubin worried about the ethics of auditioning for Solti after having accepted the offer in Montreal, Hearst, ever the pragmatist, responded, 'Nobody knows about your appointment here. It hasn't made the front page of *The Times* yet.'[8] He told Zubin that it would do him no harm to make the acquaintance of a veteran conductor like Solti. In the final analysis, Hearst's words provided great opportunity. Little did Zubin guess that the audition with Solti would open up doors which would ultimately lead to the podium of the Los Angeles Philharmonic. Instead of assisting Solti, he would take his place. But more about that later.

Zubin landed in Los Angeles and Hearst was there to help him settle into his hotel room. He also tried to put to rest his qualms of conscience about auditioning for Solti. He told him that he just wanted Solti and some of the Los Angeles management to hear him conduct. The audition was to be held during one of Solti's rehearsals and Hearst had suggested Brahms's First and Mozart's *Prague* Symphony, both compositions with which Zubin was familiar. Zubin played Brahms's First and was stopped by Solti when he had played the first movement of the *Prague* Symphony. Apparently, he had heard enough to be impressed by Zubin's skills as a conductor.

Solti offered Zubin the post of assistant. The moment of truth had arrived. He was then told how, just the day before, Zubin had been offered the music directorship of the Montreal Symphony Orchestra and had accepted. Since Zubin had already arrived in Los Angeles at his own expense, he saw no reason to cancel the audition. (Zubin was a little guilty at this bald-faced misstatement of the truth but there really was no choice.) Solti said that he understood. After giving Zubin some advice on his choice of tempi for the Mozart symphony, he wished him well and bade him goodbye. In his autobiography, Zubin says, 'Solti understood, and I was happy that we at least got to meet each other. This had also been Hearst's deeper intention in playing this not quite honest game.'[9]

On his way back to Europe, Zubin contacted Bernstein between flights and told him of the Montreal offer. Bernstein congratulated him and expressed regret that they would not be able to work together. Bernstein had offered Zubin the post of assistant—his only assistant. Zubin would often go to him for advice when he was music director of the New York Philharmonic, and the two grew quite close.

A lot had happened in the space of a few months. But this was just the beginning.

# Annus Mirabilis

THE WEEK BEFORE CHRISTMAS of 1960, Zubin was back in Vienna. His Yugoslavian tour had been well received by audiences but he was a bit dissatisfied with the performances of some of the local outfits. On returning to his hotel one evening, he found a cable waiting for him. It was from George Kuyper, manager of the Los Angeles Philharmonic. Kuyper wanted to know if Zubin was available for rehearsals starting 15 January as conductor Reiner had cancelled suddenly owing to ill health. The Los Angeles management that had recently met Zubin and been impressed with his skills as a conductor, had no hesitation in inviting him to take Reiner's place. Hearst's insistence that he meet Solti and present himself to the management in Los Angeles had been justified after all!

Zubin cabled back promptly, saying he would be delighted to accept the offer. Within a week, he received the dates of the four concerts, along with Reiner's programmes. The featured works, none of which Zubin had conducted before, were Schumann's Second Symphony, Beethoven's Seventh, *Le Rossignol* by Stravinsky and Richard Strauss's *Don Quixote.* He substituted Schumann's Second Symphony with the Fourth because even though he had not conducted it before, he was familiar with it. Beethoven's Seventh stayed because he had always wanted to conduct it. He studied the scores of *Le Rossignol* and *Don Quixote,* both new pieces. Later, he replaced *Le Rossignol* with his old favourite *Petrouchka* which had served him admirably on more than one occasion. He added the *Coriolanus* Overture and Webern's *Six Pieces* to round out the programme.

## THE ASCENT TO FAME

Zubin returned to Los Angeles on 15 January 1961, a young artiste on the threshold of a glittering international career. So much had happened in the last two years—he had zoomed up from the rank of apprentice to the status of an international artiste. The trajectory of his career had been one of uninterrupted upward progression from novice to superstar, as continuous and soaring as a Richard Strauss melody. He arrived onstage for the first rehearsal with a score of *Don Quixote*, which he put down on the music stand but never opened. He smiled at the orchestra and gave the downbeat. All at once, the orchestra seemed electrified. Zubin sensed it too and was happy that he was an instant hit with the musicians.

Zubin made his debut in the old Philharmonic Hall on the evening of 19 January 1961, with a programme of *Don Quixote* and Schumann's Fourth. It was a resounding success. After the first concert, he obliged autograph seekers backstage. In the audience was Heifetz, the man Mehli called 'God'. And when Heifetz came to congratulate him, it was the ultimate compliment for Zubin. The twenty-four-year-old conductor was riding the crest of a phenomenal wave of success and popularity. As soon as he could find the time, he phoned Mehli to tell him about it. 'You'll never believe this, but "God" was at my concert tonight,' he said.

The orchestra too seemed to like him and his style of conducting. As one philharmonic pro said, 'He's not like many big-time conductors who force their orchestras into submission. Look at that young man up there. Don't you get the feeling they're making music together, he and they? There are few great conductors like that. One day he's going to be one of the greatest.'[1]

William Severns, who was on the Philharmonic staff at the time and later became chief administrator of the Southern California

Symphony Association, sponsor of the Los Angeles Philharmonic and the Hollywood Bowl Association, recalled how, having missed Zubin's debut performance, he attended the repeat programme the next afternoon for a predominantly female audience. Even though he was backstage he could sense the great enthusiasm of the audience. 'I thought that Siegfried had hired a claque,' he recalled.[2] According to music critic and author Philip Hart, it is the night of 19 January 1961—Zubin's Los Angeles debut—that marks the dramatic emergence of a new generation before the public.[3]

There was another important person in the audience that night—one who would have a hand in moulding not only Zubin's immediate future but also his entire career: Dorothy Chandler. As the wife of Norman Chandler, publisher of the city's leading newspaper, *Los Angeles Times*, Chandler or 'Buff' as she was known in social circles, was active on the Los Angeles cultural scene. Her aim was to build a performing arts centre for Los Angeles. In 1955 she collected $4,00,000 at a benefit concert, which began a nine-year crusade that raised almost $20 million of the estimated total cost of $35 million.

She was featured on the cover of the 18 December 1964 issue of *Time* magazine, where her fundraising efforts were hailed as 'perhaps the most impressive display of virtuoso money-raising and civic citizenship in the history of US womanhood'. By the time Zubin had completed his second series of concerts on 26 and 27 January he was well on his way to becoming a hero in Los Angeles. The concerts of *Petrouchka*, Webern's *Six Pieces* and Beethoven's Seventh were magical nights and Zubin himself agreed that 'everything had gelled'. Chandler was greatly impressed by the young Zubin. But there was another opportunity in store for Zubin. And it came from a familiar source: Markevitch. Once again, Markevitch's ill health—pretended or real—was to play catalyst to Zubin's fortune. Markevitch had cancelled his concerts with the Los Angeles Philharmonic and Zubin was invited to take his place. His programme consisted of Bartók's Concerto for Orchestra and Tchaikovsky's Piano Concerto No. 1 which Zubin had heard often but never conducted. His soloist was to be Byron Janis.

By now the press too had warmed to Zubin and was treating him like a celebrity. There were articles in newspapers and interviews on radio and television. There were also rumours of how the good-looking Indian was a playboy and a ladies' man cavorting with female celebrities. Los Angeles feasted on rumour. While 'Zubi Baby' (supposedly his nickname in Los Angeles, though Zubin insists no one ever called him that) was being projected as a relentless discharger of libido, he was in reality busy studying scores over the weekend. When Zubin opened the programme on 2 February 1961, with the Overture to Verdi's *La Forza del Destino*, the pianist, the players and the audience all knew that it was going to be a special evening. The Tchaikovsky Piano Concerto No. 1 which followed was also a stupendous success. The collaboration between conductor and soloist was flawless and when Zubin finished, the audience exploded into a frenzy of applause. The orchestra members too started to applaud. He was called back for bow after bow. As an encore Zubin decided to repeat the last movement.

**OFFERS GALORE**

In her box Chandler had all but decided that she was not going to let the enormously talented and charismatic young Indian get away. The next morning, she contacted the other board members and secured their approval for what was termed an 'associate conductorship' for Zubin with a compulsory attendance of six weeks per season. The conductor Solti was to spend only twelve weeks per season with the orchestra since his engagements with the Royal Opera at Covent Garden and his guest conducting assignments would keep him busy the rest of the year. Chandler asked Zubin if he could come for eight weeks so that he could fill the gap left by Solti. Since Zubin was contractually bound to be in Montreal for sixteen weeks, he could spare himself for eight weeks with the Los Angeles Philharmonic.

Zubin agreed but expressed doubts about Solti's response: he was concerned about how the maestro would react to what was clearly a unilateral appointment. He was told, 'That side will be taken care of.' Future events showed things in a different light. Zubin had every reason to be slightly uncomfortable with the arrangement: he had just turned down Solti's offer to be his assistant and was now about to rub shoulders with him on the same podium as a near equal. Thinking that the Los Angeles management would take care of Solti, Zubin left for Vienna after three eventful and rewarding weeks in Los Angeles. All going well, he would return to conduct his concerts in the Hollywood Bowl that summer.

On his arrival in Vienna, Zubin received a telegram from Hilbert, director of the Vienna Festival, asking him to guest conduct the Vienna Philharmonic because Ormandy had cancelled his concerts. It was an offer that seemed too good to be true. Since the dates were prior to the start of the Hollywood Bowl season, Zubin indicated his availability. Never in his wildest dreams had he thought that he would be conducting the venerated Vienna Philharmonic at twenty-five!

### *'Palphilorc'*

Close on the heels of this offer came another which baffled Zubin. He received a cable from something called 'Palphilorc'. 'I did not know who the orchestra was,' said Zubin. 'I had to ask around.' It turned out to be the Israel Philharmonic Orchestra. Apparently, the telegraphic service had not updated its name from Palestine Philharmonic Orchestra in the thirteen years since Israel had become a nation. Ormandy, who had been slated to conduct in Israel before his concerts in Vienna, had cancelled the whole tour. Zubin said: 'The orchestra had heard about me—I don't know how. I'd just started my career that year in Montreal and would be performing for the first time in Los Angeles in 1962. But at that point I was jobless. I was sitting in Vienna doing nothing, except an odd concert here and there. So, I said, "Yes, I am available." I was available for anything. Then I said, "By the way, who are you?"'

Abe Cohen, who was managing director of the Israel Philharmonic at the time, told the story behind the cable to Peter Marck, double bassist with the orchestra for nearly four decades. Zvi Haftel, the concertmaster and orchestra manager, had gone to Europe to look for a replacement. He first asked Barbirolli, who declined as he had prior commitments, but suggested Zubin's name. Haftel and Cohen were aware of Zubin winning the Liverpool conducting competition and knew that the conductor Steinberg thought highly of him. After consulting with the orchestra committee, Haftel said, 'Let's try him,' and asked Cohen to send the now-famous telegram. They were worried about the reception Zubin would get in Israel and decided to promote him by emphasizing the Indian side—that is, as a talented conductor from the East.[4]

No one could have guessed that it was the start of an association that would last a lifetime. In December 2006, at the seventieth anniversary celebrations of the Israel Philharmonic Orchestra, Zubin paid homage to Haftel calling him 'a fireball' and acknowledged his role in founding the orchestra along with Huberman.

At about the same time, another light appeared on Zubin's rapidly expanding musical horizon. He received an offer from Lies Askonas, a British agent who had heard him conduct in the final of the Liverpool competition. Askonas promised a concert with the Royal Philharmonic provided he could be available immediately. Naturally, Zubin accepted. On 8 March 1961, Zubin rehearsed with the Royal Philharmonic which had been founded by Sir Thomas Beecham (with whom Zubin shares his birthday). Zarin, then an accountant in London, was also present. It took Zubin some time to win the complete confidence of the orchestra, but in the end he thought that they had established a fairly good rapport. Another dimension was added to this natal connection when the orchestra received the news that Sir Thomas had passed away during the performance.

After his successful debut with the Royal Philharmonic in London, Zubin and Carmen travelled together to Tel Aviv where Zubin was to fill in for Ormandy. By now both realized that the magic had gone out of their marriage and they hoped that the time spent together would help get some of it back. They were met at the airport by Barenboim's parents, Enrique and Aida. For Zubin, the crowded streets of Tel Aviv and Jerusalem evoked memories of the homeland he'd left behind. 'I loved Israel right from the start,' he recalled with affection. 'After seven years in Europe, I felt like I was home again because, in many ways, it's just like Bombay: the way everybody's in the streets, everybody talking, giving you advice. It's very Asian. So, I felt right at home. I also had friends there, the Barenboims. And they sort of adopted me. That was in 1961. By 1969 the orchestra made me music director.'

The Israel Philharmonic consisted mainly of emigrants who had fled Austria and Eastern Europe before and after the Holocaust. This meant that Zubin was greeted by sounds which were very European in tone and with which he was familiar. At the second rehearsal, the Israel Philharmonic cheered the young conductor as he walked into the room. Zubin says, 'I could tell they meant it from their hearts. This was for a young man a very great boost.' But the concert on 23 May 1961, as Zubin himself admitted, could have been much better. It was a difficult programme: *Dances of Galanta* by Zoltán Kodály, Stravinsky's *Symphony in Three Movements* and Antonín Dvořák's Seventh Symphony in D Minor. 'I don't think the concerts were that good. I wasn't the greatest rehearser of all time. But we got to like each other. And two seasons later, they called me back.'

Zubin had chosen completely new pieces for his programme, compositions which neither he nor the orchestra had played before. It was an experiment which proved to be only partially successful. They had four rehearsals but were still quite unprepared at the time of the concert. They played the same programme thirteen times and the Stravinsky went well, but the Dvořák was much more difficult. Zubin worked hard on the Stravinsky because he was also slated to conduct it in Vienna, where mistakes could prove to be costlier than in Israel. However, both Zubin and the orchestra had a good time together and he says that he learned that music should come from the heart as much as from the mastery of technique. He was impressed with the fortitude of the Israel Philharmonic and said that making music in Tel Aviv and other parts of Israel meant spreading hope for peace.

*Vienna*

Back in Vienna, Zubin was supposed to conduct the Vienna Philharmonic in a concert in June that year. Ormandy had cancelled his concerts at the Vienna Festival and, as we have noted before, Hilbert, the artistic director of the festival, had invited Zubin to take his place. It was a great honour for the young conductor and Zubin acknowledged that he was overwhelmed by the offer. His old ties with the Vienna Philharmonic only made it more special. But his first rehearsal was one of the worst of his career. He was facing many of his old professors as their conductor. Among the players were young musicians with whom he had spent time joking barely a year ago. To make matters worse, the Stravinsky was a difficult piece and largely incomprehensible to the Vienna orchestra. A disconsolate Zubin bumped into conductor Krips after the rehearsal and confided his fears of never being called back for another concert. The senior maestro did his best to allay his fears but Zubin expected the worst.

However, the programme of 11 June 1961, the ninety-seventh birth anniversary of Richard Strauss, was a success. After the Stravinsky, he played Beethoven's Piano Concerto No. 3 with Friedrich Gulda as the soloist, followed by *Don Quixote* by Richard Strauss, which he had thoroughly studied while in America. At that time it was rather unusual for the Viennese to play Stravinsky since the Vienna Philharmonic was nurtured in the Viennese tradition by the likes of Furtwängler, Knappertsbusch and Krauss. Today, however, Zubin says, things are totally different and the Vienna Philharmonic has a large and diverse repertoire. The press hailed the return of 'Vienna's own Indian' and prophesied a great career for him. Zubin took the praise with caution but there was no doubt that he had made a mark in Vienna. The Vienna management was talking about asking him back for the regular season and he was also on their radar for the Salzburg Festival.

Zubin made his debut in Salzburg in 1962 in a programme of Mozart's *Prague* Symphony, Bartók's Second Piano Concerto (with Hungarian pianist Géza Anda) and Dvořák's Seventh Symphony. He says that the Salzburg invitation happened largely on the insistence of the members of the Vienna Philharmonic who wanted to play under his baton at Salzburg. They told the Salzburg Festival, which had Karajan at its helm, that in case they did not agree, they would play under Zubin at Lucerne. Zubin says that his relationship with Karajan was a warm one; the maestro had always been kind to him and they had spent many hours together discussing the scores of *Otello* and *Tristan und Isolde*.

## L'AFFAIRE SOLTI

At the time that Zubin had been appointed associate at the Los Angeles Philharmonic, Solti, the music director, was away at the music festival at Lucerne and could not be reached on the telephone. There is no unanimity on what Zubin calls 'a dirty business' to this day. Solti said that he knew nothing of the appointment until American newspapers reached him in Lucerne. The board and Chandler, however, maintained that they had immediately cabled Solti seeking his approval. According to an orchestra member with access to board files, Chandler sent Solti a telegram: 'Congratulations! We have hired your choice, Zubin Mehta, to be associate conductor.' They said that they even waited three weeks before releasing the news to the press. Zubin believes that no one had asked Solti if he approved of the offer made to him; that no one had told him that Zubin would be conducting for eight weeks to his twelve. He was obviously upset when he came to know that the man who had recently turned down the offer of becoming his assistant was taking up a position that was nearly his equal in the orchestra, and that too in a manner that must have appeared to him as nothing short of deceitful.

Solti, since he had stumbled upon the news in the press, thought it appropriate to respond through the same medium. He blamed the board for making an appointment without consulting him, conveying his sense of outrage at what he called an 'unconscionable act' of the board. The matter escalated in the press and Zubin first read the story in the European edition of *Time* magazine. Events soon acquired a fateful momentum.

Solti protested that as music director, such decisions were 'his' to make. No one could blame him for thinking that his directorial prerogatives had been compromised. He demanded a withdrawal of the offer to Zubin, but Chandler did not back down. Citing a 'serious breach of contract', a furious Solti submitted his resignation by cable from Germany, clearing the way for Zubin to assume his place at the helm of the Los Angeles Philharmonic. In an attempt to pacify the angry Solti, Zubin suggested that he would reduce the time he would spend with the orchestra. But Solti, who viewed the affair through the distorting medium of a personal grievance, insisted on quitting. Because Zubin was busy elsewhere (as head of the Montreal Symphony Orchestra), Solti suggested that he only be a guest conductor, and for a short period, to leave more time for other guests.

It was a shabby affair that left a poor taste in the mouth for both Zubin and Solti. Solti said he had nothing against Zubin, but that it was a matter of principle. While Solti was aware that the main actor in the whole drama was Chandler, he can be forgiven for thinking that Zubin must have been complicit. What was at stake, he argued, was not merely a few weeks more or less of Zubin's conducting stints, but whether he himself was to be boss of his own orchestra. 'If I had given in on this one point, it would never have been the same. I wasn't happy then at all. No, not a bit. But today I am grateful. Because if I'd stayed on at Los Angeles, I wouldn't have Chicago, and where would I be then?'[5] Solti became director of England's Royal Opera at Covent Garden in 1961 and this served to soothe much of the humiliation he had suffered.

While Solti fumed, calling the situation 'grotesque', Chandler, California's 'first citizen of music' maintained a studied silence. Chandler usually got her way. She was a director of the San Francisco Opera, lifetime honorary chairman of the Hollywood Bowl, a committee chairman for the Los Angeles Music Center and president of the Southern California Symphony Association. With the Chandler fortune (oil, ranching, television, insurance), she dictated terms on the cultural scene in Southern California. Her notable contributions to culture included saving the Hollywood Bowl through a vigorous fundraising campaign in 1951 and the launch of the new music centre. Her detractors accused her of 'ignoring better-informed musical opinion than her own and of alienating, before Solti, such talented musicians as the Dutchman Eduard van Beinum and the cellist and conductor Alfred Wallenstein'.[6]

The resignation created a furore in Los Angeles and Zubin was unhappy with the way things had gone. There were questions raised yet again about Chandler's style of functioning. A music critic wrote:

> Once more Los Angeles has been tumbled from possible artistic eminence to obvious artistic disgrace. Why? Is the Philharmonic Orchestra a civic enterprise . . . or is it a private enterprise, dictatorially controlled?[7]

There never had been any intention on Zubin's part to outsmart Solti (though it is possible Solti thought otherwise) or to do anything behind his back. It was a set of strange circumstances which led to the contretemps. A lot of misunderstanding had led to the mess which could quite easily have been cleared, had either Zubin or Solti spoken to each other on the phone. Today, with the twenty-twenty vision which hindsight allows, Zubin regrets that he did not deal with the issue with more care and finesse. Long-distance communication was hardly what it is today. Since in those days Zubin did not have a telephone at home and had to go to the post office to make a long-distance call, it did not occur to him to discuss it with Solti on the telephone.

When Zubin's name was announced as music director of the Los Angeles Philharmonic, Murray Schumach, the Los Angeles correspondent of the *New York Times*, filed a story titled 'Feuds and Confusion Preceded Appointment of Coast Conductor'. The story said that Solti had resigned from the position to which Zubin had been appointed because the latter had been engaged as a guest conductor without consulting him. Chandler was quoted as saying that she thought jealousy might have coloured Solti's motives in resigning. The news report also spoke of how an advisory committee of five, including Heifetz and Gregor Piatigorsky, had been formed to offer suggestions on Solti's successor and this committee, after much struggling, had submitted 'three' recommendations to the orchestra's board.[8]

Heifetz and Piatigorsky responded in the press through their spokesman William Judd that the name of only one conductor had been submitted and that there had been no 'struggle' as the recommendation was unanimous.[9] More importantly, Hearst, who was manager to both Solti and Zubin, wrote to the *New York Times* seeking to clarify certain issues, noting that Schumach's articles contained a number of false assertions. He said that it was Solti who first invited Zubin to appear with the Los Angeles Philharmonic in November 1960, and it was his enthusiastic report about Zubin to both Chandler, president of the board, and Kuyper that had made possible Zubin's guest engagement for three weeks in January in the first place.[10]

Hearst clarified that during negotiations, Solti asked for an assurance that there would be no future infringement of his rights as music director. As a token adjustment, he asked the management to invite Zubin to guest conduct for seven rather than eight weeks. Since Solti was to come to Los Angeles as guest conductor in April, Chandler had hoped to clarify any misunderstandings at that time. 'However, Solti wished that such misunderstandings should be straightened out before his return in April. When no action was taken by the end of March, Solti cancelled his April appearances and resigned as music director.'[11] At that time, given the controversy, Zubin thought that his career in Los Angeles would be a non-starter. But Chandler had other ideas. When Heifetz, Piatigorsky and John Vincent of the music department of the University of California, Los Angeles, suggested Zubin's name, she promptly recommended that he take Solti's place as the permanent music director.

Chandler told *Time* magazine: 'I'm a great one for getting all the expert opinion I can. Then after everybody has registered his view, somebody has got to say "That's it—let's go." This is my job.'[12] Chandler also denied that any conductors named for the post had refused to take it because of the circumstances surrounding Solti's resignation. Zubin's choice, she asserted, was the most popular one that could have been made.[13] In a rare, if officially meaningless display of unity, the orchestra itself voted for Zubin unanimously.[14]

After all the brouhaha, Zubin was naturally circumspect about the offer. And given what had happened to Solti, who would shield him from Chandler's alleged capriciousness? He aired his fears to Hearst, who must have been wondering how a seemingly harmless audition he had orchestrated could provide such tremendous opportunity as well as make so much mischief. Hearst worked out a contract that gave Zubin independence from the board in all artistic matters. Feeling more secure, Zubin accepted, and was named music director of the Los Angeles Philharmonic. Hearst died two years later. In his autobiography, Zubin expresses his heartfelt gratitude to him for everything that he had done for him.

On 9 November 1961, Chandler announced Zubin's appointment as music director at the opening concert of the orchestra's forty-third season. The audience cheered and members of the orchestra gave a standing ovation to their new leader, rapping their instruments in the custom of musicians. Zubin was unable to be present for the announcement as he was in Montreal.

He had to break the news of the Los Angeles offer to the Montreal Symphony Orchestra. Understandably, they were not thrilled, but they could not prevent Zubin from accepting, considering they had only twelve weeks to offer him. Zubin now had two major assignments in his bag: good fortune had promoted him far beyond his immediate ambitions. He was now only twenty-five, but it was as if he had lived a lifetime.

Whatever the reasons behind the manner in which Zubin was appointed, this affected his and Solti's relationship for twenty years. Solti never forgave Zubin and the latter's efforts to mend fences met with only partial success. Zubin extended the peace pipe but Solti refused to take a puff. Both were under contract with the recording company Decca and Zubin did not mind his senior colleague getting precedence when it came to the recordings. The ice did not break for a long time but after twenty years it started to thaw. Only in Solti's final year with the Chicago Symphony Orchestra did the breach heal substantially when Zubin conducted both the piano concertos of Brahms, with Barenboim as the soloist. 'In the end we became quite close,' Zubin said.[15]

## 'YOU HAVE TO BE CALLED BACK'

His achievements that year had been unprecedented but Zubin still had one more important feather to add to his cap: on 18 September 1961, Zubin conducted the Berlin Philharmonic. At twenty-five, he was its youngest conductor. The performance had been made possible thanks to the good offices of Hearst and Wolfgang Stresemann of the Berlin Philharmonic (son of the former chancellor of Germany Gustav Stresemann). In this context, Zubin narrates an amusing anecdote involving Enrico Mainardi who was playing Schumann's Cello Concerto. Throughout the performance, Mainardi tried to tell Zubin something, but the conductor did not catch on. At the end of the concerto, when Zubin saw that his fly was open, he realized what Mainardi's whispered *'Pantaloni son aperti . . .'* had meant. During the interval, members of the orchestra told him the same thing in hushed tones. But his brilliant rendition of Mahler's First Symphony soon made them forget the faux pas of the first half. The choice of Mahler's First now appears to Zubin, with the wisdom of hindsight, both courageous and foolhardy. He had never conducted the piece before and was far from being a master on Mahler. To top it all, he was conducting a new orchestra. It was, according to Zubin, nothing short of a mixture of 'courage and megalomania'.

If ever there was an annus mirabilis, this was it. It was a busy time indeed, and just trying to keep up with Zubin on paper makes one short of breath. In exactly one year, Zubin had conducted seven major orchestras of five nations. Four important conductors had cancelled appearances and bequeathed him a total of eighteen important concerts—all in the space of nine months. He was now the master of two orchestras. Several years later, Zubin observed: 'I made half my career by jumping in at the last moment. Sometimes I think my success was due almost entirely to the misfortunes of my elderly colleagues.'[16] Zubin acknowledges that 1961 was a watershed in his career since much of what was going to be decisive for the rest of his life fell into his lap that year. ('For me 1961 represented a chain of coincidences and strange and unforeseeable events that did not want to seem to end. A benevolent angel seemed to be watching over me, repeatedly bringing me in contact with people who were apparently interested in my well-being.'[17])

'I had a lot of lucky breaks when I was a young man,' Zubin recalls, referring to these concerts. 'But the lucky break is not enough; you have to be called back. I got called back to every single orchestra.'[18] Many of his chances may have resulted from the incidental kindness of strangers, but Zubin hardly lacks chutzpah. After an important concert in Brussels which was a success with both the orchestra and the audience, he was so sure that he would be called back that he went to the manager's office and demanded dates for the next season. The manager said they would like him to taste some more success in Paris before he came back to Brussels. Zubin never saw the man again. He later said he had been so confident because he had left Vienna well prepared. 'I had things to say. I wasn't bluffing. I was confident because I knew my stuff.'[19] Zubin is right. The proof of the pudding in the world of music is not in the first performance but in the return invitation. Zubin was invited to return to world capitals and major music festivals on numerous occasions. The fires burned in him with a rare passion and you could always see that glow.

Zubin notes in his autobiography that from August 1960 to September 1961 he had conducted all the orchestras which constitute his 'musical homeland'. He adds that by nature he is a loyal person and this trait extends to his profession as well. He does not believe in doing one-off concerts with unfamiliar orchestras. Doing a concert after a few rehearsals with new musicians is simply not his style and it is for this reason that he has never conducted certain orchestras even when invited time and again. He must feel at home with the musicians and be able to bank on them, and they, in turn, on him.

And so, Zubin has never conducted the Boston Symphony Orchestra, the Cleveland Orchestra or the San Francisco Orchestra, while on the other hand, he has conducted the Vienna and Berlin philharmonics every year since 1961. He believes that even though the musicians have the score, they must know '*what and how* the conductor means something'. This is something that cannot be achieved in a few rehearsals no matter how good the orchestra is. At any rate, Zubin feels that he cannot do it. Nor does he want to try. However, he made an exception for the first time when he conducted the Royal Concertgebouw Orchestra of Amsterdam in 2005, with a repertoire which included Bruckner's Eighth Symphony. He said that a mixture of sentiment and nostalgia was responsible for this violation of his own rule since he had heard this orchestra as a student in Vienna. I asked Zubin if he ever felt apprehensive before a performance. He said that since most of the time he was performing with musicians whom he knew well, and whose abilities he was confident of, the question of feeling nervous did not arise.[20]

♫

In the autumn of 1961 Zubin relocated to Canada with Carmen and the children. They made the transatlantic journey by ship from Cherbourg and were welcomed fondly at Montreal by Béique. Still financially insecure, Zubin says that Béique helped them in any way he could, even buying a house for them through the Montreal Symphony Orchestra. Carmen was happy to be back in the land of her birth and Zubin was looking forward to taking up his first big assignment as music director of the Montreal orchestra.

Only three at the start of the Second World War, Zubin emerged in a period where the effects of that conflict resulted in stunting the development of men twenty years his senior. But this is only part of the explanation for his swift and acutely vertical career. He was quick to learn, dedicated and assiduous in his work habits, and it would be fair to say that his meteoric rise was as much the result of his own labours as the lucky breaks he fully exploited.

# The Next Toscanini?

THE ORCHESTRA ZUBIN ENCOUNTERED in Montreal was, in his own words, 'a good orchestra of the second class'. He rated the lead hornist and concertmaster Calvin Sieb as outstanding. The Italian Masella brothers were also superb. But it had a few musicians who lowered the general standard of the orchestra. Since the orchestra was woefully short of funds, the musicians had neither the best instruments nor sufficient pay. And the Old Plateau Hall, the East End high school auditorium the orchestra had used since 1934, had terrible acoustics, and could accommodate only 1300 people. That the orchestra had survived and come this far was almost entirely due to the efforts of the indefatigable Béique. He had joined the orchestra as managing director in 1939 when it was called Les Concerts Symphoniques de Montreal. A graduate in commerce from McGill University, Béique had been employed in a perfume and pharmaceutical company before his love of music got the better of him. Since there could be no salary on a budget of $17,000, Béique's father agreed to bankroll his son for the three years it took him to turn the orchestra's finances around and give himself his first pay cheque.

Béique also contacted Hearst, a former resident of Montreal, who now managed big stars such as Arthur Rubinstein and Mischa Elman. Hearst allowed some of his biggest stars to play in Montreal for ludicrous sums of money. Almost immediately, the poor orchestra became a forum for international artistes. Béique was also responsible for unifying the French and the English factions of the arts community in Montreal. In 1952 the grand-sounding Les Concerts Symphoniques de Montreal, became the Montreal Symphony Orchestra. (The French called it L'Orchestra Symphonique de Montreal).

## BUILDING A REPUTATION

Montreal had no wealthy benefactors and little or no corporate support to finance the arts. While the orchestra received funds from federal, provincial and local governments, most of the money went into financing the construction of a new civic centre and arts complex. The only way Zubin could help his musicians earn more was by extending the season. He extracted a promise from the management in Montreal that over the next few years, the season would be expanded from twelve to twenty-six weeks. He also instituted a pension fund for the musicians. There was nothing more he could do to raise the standard of the music since he did not have the power to hire or fire musicians as he pleased. The rules imposed by the Montreal Musicians' Union were so strict that he could not even hire musicians from outside the province of Quebec.

Zubin now had to wait until the new arts complex, the Place des Arts, opened in 1963. First envisaged in 1958, it ultimately became a complex of three theatres, seating 3000, 1500 and 850 people respectively. La Grande Salle was planned as a multipurpose venue for all kinds of events such as opera, ballet, symphonic concerts and even rock 'n' roll concerts. Its principal tenant was to be the Montreal Symphony Orchestra. (Since 1966 it has been called the Salle Wilfrid-Pelletier in honour of its former music director. Today, in addition to the Montreal Symphony Orchestra, the Salle Wilfrid-Pelletier accommodates two resident companies: the Opera de Montreal and the Great Canadian Ballet.)

But before the Place des Arts could open its doors, an opportunity from an unexpected quarter presented itself. It was the height of the

Cold War and the United States Congress had refused permission to the Red Army Chorus to tour America. Nothing daunted, the Russians responded by sending the chorus to Canada, where it was received with open arms. Since the chorus had been flown in on a special Aeroflot plane to Montreal, it seemed a real waste to send the plane back empty. Thus it was that Zubin found himself and his orchestra winging their way to the Soviet Union in the spring of 1962. There were sell-out concerts in Moscow, Kiev and Leningrad. Zubin even managed to learn enough Russian by the end of the tour to give a short speech at the concerts. (Carmen had accompanied her husband to Russia, but they were drifting apart. Zubin felt that a split was imminent and he told me that it was he who started divorce proceedings.)

Zubin and the Montreal orchestra also played in Vienna. As soon as the Russian tour was announced, the Viennese impresario Rudolf Gamsjaeger invited Zubin to perform. It was a new high for young Zubin to conduct his own orchestra in front of an audience which comprised his old professors, colleagues and friends. Like everything Zubin had touched in the recent past, these concerts too proved to be successful. There was no denying he had the Midas touch.

Zubin had to work hard in Montreal to build a repertoire, bringing in changes and trying out new things. He had only limited time at his disposal, given the fact that from the autumn of 1962 his assignment with the Los Angeles Philharmonic would commence. One of his earliest concerts in Montreal was the Piano Concerto No. 1 by Brahms in which his friend Brendel was the soloist. Barenboim, who had already emerged as a brilliant soloist in his early youth, also visited him. Zubin tried to infuse some glamour into Montreal by arranging for guest conductors. Those who accepted his invitation included his guru Swarowsky, his friend Abbado, and Munch who loved the French atmosphere in Montreal.

During his years with the Montreal orchestra, Zubin had to memorize practically an entire new programme every week, often while en route between engagements. One of his solutions was to stage rehearsals of an operatic score while studying an orchestral score placed on the floor next to him. This method inevitably involved some lapses and tended to make for slightly ragged first performances but these were smoothed out with practice.

When the Place des Arts opened in September 1963, it was Zubin and his orchestra who had the honour of playing on the opening night. It almost didn't happen because a grand gala 'festival week' of opera had been planned for the opening and since Montreal had no opera company of its own, the Royal Opera House at Covent Garden was supposed to do the honours. When the press got to know about it, it questioned the need to pay large sums of money to British singers when the honour of opening La Grande Salle should rightly belong to the Montreal Symphony Orchestra. The idea of inviting the Royal Opera House was dropped and it was Zubin and his orchestra who played on the first night, with the opening selection being guest conducted by former music director Wilfrid Pelletier. The opening festival was to continue with a variety of performances, including one by Munch conducting pianist Serkin as soloist. Zubin was closely associated with Serkin later in his career and described him as 'shy, quiet and always very kind'.[1] He had survived the horrors of the Third Reich by fleeing to Austria in the nick of time. He celebrated his 100th performance with the New York Philharmonic in 1972, an unusual achievement by any standard.

Munch was with Béique in his box when Zubin played his opening concert. Ever since he had first heard Zubin in Tanglewood, Munch had formed a high opinion of his abilities. He had discussed Zubin with Hearst on several occasions, and had also suggested him to Béique. A little-known fact is that when Munch announced his retirement as the music director of the Boston Symphony Orchestra in the winter of 1960–61, he proposed Zubin as his successor. Zubin was simultaneously being considered for the assignments in Montreal and Los Angeles. But Boston was not yet ready for a twenty-four-year-old upstart from Bombay and offered the job to Viennese-born Leinsdorf, a successful guest conductor and the music adviser of the Metropolitan Opera.

What Munch heard on the opening night in Béique's box more than confirmed his high opinion of Zubin's musical talent. His treatment of Mahler's First was simply wonderful—and it was not just the superior acoustics which made it so. After the performance, Munch turned to his friend Béique and told him in French, 'Pierre, when Toscanini died, we all thought now the brightest light of our profession has gone out forever. But you have found Toscanini's successor.' It is perhaps the highest praise Zubin has received in his entire career. What made it even better was that it came from someone who really knew his music.

*A Concert in Prague*

In the spring of 1963, Zubin received an invitation from the Czech Philharmonic to conduct Beethoven's Ninth Symphony. There is a tradition that the annual Spring Festival in Prague ends with Beethoven's Ninth in the Cathedral of St Vitus in Prague Castle. An excellent example of Gothic architecture, the fourteenth-century masterpiece dominates the Prague skyline.

Things started off on the wrong note for Zubin. His flight from Frankfurt was delayed by an hour and, as a result, he arrived thirty minutes late for the rehearsal. In the chancel arranged around the central altar were the members of the Czech Philharmonic and an enormous choir. Since the chorus and the soloist would not be needed till the final movement of the symphony, he asked them to leave. But this did not go down too well with them because they were used to rehearsing the finale first. Zubin's popularity plummeted further when he told them that he always rehearsed a piece from beginning to end. The chorus departed, but not before voicing its resentment. Thankfully, Zubin could not understand what was being said but the severe glances in his direction told him that he was already unpopular.

In retrospect Zubin feels that maybe he should have gone along with their wishes and started with the finale but since he was conducting the piece for the first time, he wanted to build himself up to the incredible climax. The rehearsals were terrible and Zubin was extremely low on confidence. 'If ever an orchestra has drained me of my confidence, it was that one. From the minute I stepped on to the podium, I had such bad vibes I wanted to go home.'[2] To make matters worse, the festival directors told him on the day of the performance that the audience would not applaud as it is against tradition to do so in church. In the audience were high-ranking officials of the Czech government and members of the diplomatic corps. Behind the seated dignitaries were some 8000 people, all of whom were standing.

Maintaining his calm that night was most difficult but at the end of the performance, he knew that he had pulled it off. By the time he had spurred the orchestra into the prestissimo coda, he was beginning to enjoy himself. It would have been nice to have received spontaneous applause but he knew that was ruled out. He left the cathedral through a side door to a waiting car. As the car rounded the cobblestone street to the front of the cathedral, Zubin was greeted by an amazing sight. The 8000-strong audience was lined up on either side of the street that curved down the hill and when his car came into sight they began to applaud and cheer. Zubin, like a visiting monarch, waved to the crowds. Later, overcome with emotion, he started sobbing.[3] In the 1970s Zubin returned to Prague to play pieces like Stravinsky's *Le Sacre du Printemps*, Bruckner's Eighth Symphony and Mahler's *Resurrection* Symphony. But he says that after that first experience, he was not surprised that it took eight years for them to call him back.

## THE WORLD OF OPERA

Zubin's first exposure to opera had been in Vienna when Dady invited him to Beethoven's *Fidelio* in 1955. He believed that Beethoven's Ninth was in some ways a necessary preliminary step to the task of managing a full-scale opera. When he returned from Prague in May 1963, he put forward his plans for a season-ending *Tosca* in Montreal. He also entered into negotiations with the Maggio

Musicale Festival in Florence to do a *La Traviata* there. Béique, who was an opera buff, agreed, but since finances were a perpetual problem, it had to be produced on a shoestring budget. Zubin's early musical experience did not include opera because, as he notes in his autobiography, Mehli 'was miles away from this musical genre'.

While he had been exposed to it in Vienna, he had hardly studied any opera with Swarowsky. He had witnessed a performance of *Tosca* long ago but that counted for nothing when it came to conducting it. Unsurprisingly, opera for Zubin meant Vienna. He says that he had to put in a lot of effort to first learn the work and then get the desired effect. He also worked with the set and costume designers, and told the director and the stage designer exactly how he wanted the performance to be staged. Opera is an organic unity of music and drama. The task of both the conductor and the producer is to recapture the creative vision that lies behind it.

This urge to take control of every aspect of the production had its origins in the way Karajan did opera. He wanted to take care of anything and everything, and Zubin—who was initially so taken with his style of conducting that he unconsciously started imitating him—also appeared to nurture the Karajan complex with regard to opera. Zubin says that he does not know if his overarching approach found favour with the others but he was happy to handle as far as possible all aspects of his first opera. Zubin also had some brilliant singers for his opera: American soprano Ella Lee as Tosca, Richard Verreau as Cavaradossi and George London in the role of Scarpia.

The opening performance of *Tosca* in Montreal went off without a hitch (which is rare in the case of opera) and the next morning's papers were full of Zubin's bravura performance. A member of the Montreal Symphony Orchestra was so impressed that he telephoned Rudolf Bing (later Sir), the general manager of the Metropolitan Opera (Met) in New York, to tell him about Montreal's great find and to invite him to witness the spectacle in person. Impressed by the vicarious account and curious to judge for himself the musical prowess of the young man in the middle of all the fuss, Bing flew down from New York to attend Zubin's second performance.

He was sufficiently impressed to go backstage and compliment Zubin on his performance. Bing was, according to Zubin, one of two Austrians who significantly improved the musical life of America. He was actually an Austrian but introduced himself as an Englishman. The other was the conductor and administrator Kurt Adler, who transformed the San Francisco Opera into one of the nation's leading opera companies. 'I was quite close to Bing—remember he was Viennese. With me he didn't pretend to be English, but with everyone else it was "Sir Rudolf".'[4] Bing recalls that 'it was very funny'. He told *Time* magazine in 1968, 'There were many mistakes. He was totally inexperienced. But it was all overshadowed by his personality and talent. Experience anyone can get.'[5] (Bing,[6] the acerbic general manager of the Met from 1950 to 1972, ushered the company into the modern era and established it as not only the biggest, but also in many ways the most prominent, company on the world stage today.)

The operas in February 1964 were standout performances and bred nostalgia for many years. It was the orchestra's first sally into anything as extravagant, and the glittering audiences were treated to some special evenings. Buoyed with the success of *Tosca*, Zubin convinced the management in Montreal to agree to two operas for the 1964–65 season, *La Traviata* and *Carmen*, along with *Aida* the following autumn. Zubin also received an invitation from Bing asking him to conduct nine *Aida*s in the winter of 1965–66 at the Met soon after his performances of the same opera in Montreal. Returning to Montreal in subsequent years, Zubin performed *La Traviata*, *Aida*, *Otello*, *Carmen* and *Tristan und Isolde*.

In 1964 Zubin was invited to Florence for the first time to conduct *La Traviata* (a detailed account of his time in Florence appears in Chapter 21). The director of the Maggio Musicale Fiorentino had invited Zubin on other occasions but that was as concert conductor. This time, he would be making his opera debut in Europe. Zubin recalls in his autobiography that he was '. . . An enterprising combination': an Indian trained in Vienna who was at the head of two orchestras in North America, conducting an Italian opera in Italy! Zubin says that they were reasonably satisfied with his performance (and he with theirs). Their relationship continued after a couple of years and now conductor and orchestra share a close musical and personal bond. Zubin proudly recalls that he conducted the Italian operas from memory, something he still continues to do. He, however, has not been able to conduct Wagner from memory because the composer's language, with all its alliterations, is too difficult for that. He attributes this to the fact that he did not grow up from early adolescence on Wagner but says that the same holds true for Italian as well. Zubin finds the Italian much easier than Wagner's German, and the text of, say, a Puccini opera, is just like the Italian spoken on the streets.

What really kick-started Zubin's career in opera was the rousing ovation his performance of Mozart's *Abduction from the Seraglio* received at the Salzburg Festival in the summer of 1965. The opera had been commissioned by Emperor Joseph II who, on hearing it, made the remark famously attributed to him: 'Far too beautiful for our ears, my dear Mozart, and a monstrous quantity of notes.' Mozart is said to have replied, 'There are just as many notes as there should be.' Zubin was no stranger to the festival, having first received an invitation in 1962. After acquitting himself creditably, he received another invitation the following year. Now the Salzburg management did him the signal honour of inviting him to open the festival with a new production of *The Abduction* by Giorgio Strehler, starring Fritz Wunderlich, Reri Grist and Anneliese Rothenberger. Zubin says that he had been invited by Karajan to conduct at the Viennese Opera in 1962, but refused because he had not conducted a single opera till then and would certainly have failed. The great Karajan promised to take Zubin under his wing but the latter told him that he first wanted some experience with opera before he could accept such an assignment.[7]

When I asked him about his relationship with Karajan, he described him as 'friendly but distant'. Zubin often went to him for advice. 'I didn't want anything from him. People of that station in life run away from young talent because there is always somebody who wants something. I didn't want anything. I was very satisfied with what I had in my life. I sat with him in his home in Salzburg and we went over the score of *Otello*. In Vienna, he once came to my hotel room and we went over the score of *Tristan und Isolde*.'[8]

His performance drew appreciation from Karajan who said that he liked Zubin's musical interpretation—he praised his composure and agreed with his tempi. But conductor Szell had a radically different opinion. He was highly critical of Zubin's performance, telling him that he did not like his interpretation at all. However, the performance was a stunning success both with the audience and the critics. A critic from the *Chicago Tribune*, unfamiliar with Zubin's success in Montreal and Los Angeles, declared that he was 'the most promising young Mozart man the festival has found in seasons'.

Reviewing the opening performance, Karl Lobl wrote in the *Vienna Express*:

> Mehta does Mozart with exemplary relaxation, clarity and balance. Not since Krips have I heard an *Abduction* so soaring in the interplay of rhythm and melody, in musical flexibility, and so convincing in stylish nuance . . . With this work whose deceptive simplicity lures so many conductors into superficiality, Mehta has proved himself to be a first rate opera conductor of personality and instinct . . .[9]

Lobl also said that this was unexpected because Zubin, in the last couple of years, had been seen to be an exhibitionist of his own talent but in *Abduction* he had found himself and also rediscovered music.

The European music critic for *Time* magazine was so impressed that rather than running a story on the entire festival, he did a full-page piece on Zubin, headlined, 'The Next Toscanini?' The article quoted Krips as declaring, 'The Next Toscanini has been born.' It praised his 'clean precise beat' and called his performance 'the height of Mehta's career to date'. Zubin continued to conduct this opera for the next six seasons. By the start of 1966, Zubin would be recognized as an emerging star among opera conductors in both America and

Europe. Confirmation of this came when he was invited to conduct *Abduction* again at the Salzburg Festival that year. The summer of 1966 was also special for another reason. He had a concert with the Vienna Philharmonic, with Barenboim as soloist. Barenboim played Mozart's Piano Concerto in C Minor and Zubin conducted Strauss's *Ein Heldenleben*.

# Allegro Con Brio

THOUGH ZUBIN HAD BEEN appointed music director of the Los Angeles Philharmonic, he still had to wait a whole season before taking charge. Since he had conducted the orchestra a number of times, he was acquainted with its strengths and weaknesses. He called it 'a good orchestra without much character'. After the death of its sixth conductor, Beinum, in 1959, the orchestra had no permanent conductor and it was left to a succession of guest conductors which included Walter, Stravinsky, Stokowski and Ormandy to guide the fortunes of the musical orphan. As in Montreal, the hall in Los Angeles left much to be desired by way of acoustics. The auditorium was a barn-like structure which belonged to a Baptist parish. Zubin described its acoustics as 'simply dreadful'.

In the summer the orchestra played at the Hollywood Bowl, a natural amphitheatre in the Hollywood Hills with a capacity of 17,000 people and which four orchestras would find difficult to fill with sound. Still, there was never any dearth of audiences and the only fear after Beinum's demise was of indifferent performances and a fall in the artistic standards of the orchestra. The morale of the musicians soared the moment Chandler announced Solti's acceptance. As a distinguished conductor of international repute, he was expected to raise the level of the orchestra to that of a world-class one.

The only problem with Solti's appointment was that he had

agreed to spend just twelve weeks of the year with the orchestra—the remainder would be given over to guest conductors. Zubin's appointment as 'associate conductor' was Chandler's brainwave to provide continuity during Solti's absence. Of course, no one could envisage the ugly turn things would later take. Zubin says that some people presumed that the glamour of Los Angeles and the charm of the film world attracted him to Los Angeles. Nothing could have been more absurd, given the unusual circumstances which led to his appointment.

## A QUEST FOR EXCELLENCE

When Zubin took over at the Los Angeles Philharmonic in 1962, the demoralized orchestra had been without a permanent conductor for nearly four years. He recalls that though 'it could play anything, it had no style, no sound, and was undisciplined musically'.[1] Zubin quickly took charge. He began by holding sectional rehearsals for the strings, the weakest part of the orchestra. Then he fostered healthy competition within the orchestra by introducing a system of shifting assignments, giving promotions and changing seating arrangements as he saw fit. It was not his aim to merely rest content with the music directorship of a semi-prestigious orchestra—it was his desire to build the orchestra into something better. Zubin says, 'Since my earliest days with my father, I was brought up on orchestra *building* . . . That's what I wanted to do in Montreal and Los Angeles.' Los Angeles Philharmonic cellist Kurt Reher recalled that at Zubin's first rehearsal with the orchestra, 'within two beats we were entranced. It seemed this young man had the ability, the musical knowledge of a man of fifty or fifty-five.'[2] Concertmaster David Frisina said that it was great to have a boss again and another musician said that 'with Mehta there's no discipline problem'.

Zubin was enthusiastic about the possibilities of the Los Angeles Philharmonic: 'I have seldom come across a group of musicians who are so warm and adaptable. They can change their whole attitude. This is impossible in Europe, where every orchestra has its own rigid style.' He said his first objective was to get the musicians to think alike technically and musically. He did not want to change every violinist's style, but only wanted them to share his concept of the beauty of sound. 'In short we want to achieve a definite personality . . . I have achieved that goal in Montreal. It was the first North American orchestra to receive sensational reviews in Vienna, because we had the Viennese style of playing.'[3]

His first concert as music director was on 15 November 1962, when he conducted the Overture to Mozart's opera *Don Giovanni*, excerpts from Hindemith's *Mathis der Maler* and *Dvořák*'s Seventh Symphony. Commenting on the Dvořák piece, Albert Goldberg of *Los Angeles Times* wrote:

> The orchestral sound was rich, the details were aptly revealed, and like the other works on the programme it was conducted from memory, with unobtrusive authority. The whole programme was an auspicious beginning to Mehta's regime, and at the conclusion of the symphony the public gave him and the players a standing ovation.[4]

At the end of the year, the same critic wrote that while it was too early to comment on Zubin's achievements as a music director, it was obvious that he had the talent and enterprise to meet the challenge of the future. (Fifty years later, at the anniversary concerts in Los Angeles in December 2012, Zubin conducted the same programme.)

Zubin's approach was a relaxed one. He called his musicians by first name, joked with them and sometimes refused social invitations unless the entire orchestra was included. The resulting esprit de corps in the orchestra made for better music. 'With the old tyrants, the rehearsal was the high point, the performance a let-down,' Zubin said. He told his orchestra that it would be different in performances before the public where he made music on the spot. 'In rehearsals, I am the doctor with the stethoscope. In performances, I am the gypsy.'

On the podium he conducted with graceful gestures. 'I can feel the audience through my back as if I were facing them,' he told *Time* magazine. 'For a cymbal crash, the player will come in anyway, but if I give a big gesture, it just adds to the high point. Or in the development section of Beethoven's *Eroica* Symphony, I am not sure the audience is hearing everything ... The different modulations, the canonic effects. I point to the orchestra as if to say, "Look who is playing. Now the theme is in the first violins, now it is in the basses."'[5]

Zubin's concept of a musical ideal was the Vienna Philharmonic and he wanted to shape the Los Angeles orchestra in the same mould. There were no harsh sounds with the Vienna Philharmonic, so the harshness of, say, Stravinsky, was foreign to them. On the other hand, Zubin found that the Los Angeles Philharmonic could play Stravinsky well. It was for German music that Zubin wanted to inculcate the Viennese sound in his new orchestra. He selected the music of Bruckner as a bridge to mastery of the post-Romantic German repertory. Impressed with the way the orchestra had played the difficult *Six Pieces* by Webern, Zubin had told the Los Angeles management that he would introduce as much modern music as he could. This was despite their having indicated to Zubin that he would do well to avoid such music in future.

## 'MARRIAGE PROBLEMS'

While Zubin had compassion for the orchestra members as individuals, he knew that inadequate musicians would have to be sacrificed for the sake of the ensemble. He drew up a list of nine players who were to face the axe. Joseph Fishman, who had until then played second oboe and was past his prime, was appointed as the new personnel manager. Zubin hoped that this step would pave the way for a smooth and graceful exit of musicians. His greatest difficulty was with the wind players, many of whom had lost their lung power to advancing age. The strings were only marginally better, with many musicians playing in the first row when they should have been in the fourth.

While choice of music was one thing, getting rid of the deadwood was far more tricky and threatened to destroy Zubin's warm relationship with the musicians of the orchestra. Zubin called these his 'marriage problems'. An inexperienced Zubin failed to realize that this was bound to be a touchy topic with the musicians and that he would have to exercise caution. He also counted on the assurance of Kuyper, the orchestra manager—whom Zubin describes as a 'great administrator and a lovely man'—who told him that it would not create any problems. He couldn't have been more wrong. When the musicians learned of Zubin's 'hit-list', they were understandably alarmed. The ensuing commotion could only be quelled with the intervention of the orchestra committee. With time, the players eventually left the orchestra through a process of natural attrition. Zubin was only trying to get on with his job as fast as he could, but his inexperience in such matters stood exposed. He had erred in not having taken the advice of other senior conductors who must certainly have faced a similar situation in their careers.

'I was badly advised by management and well-meaning players of whom to get rid of in order to improve the orchestra and I signed a request to get rid of nine musicians. I couldn't have made a worse tactical mistake. There was a storm, of course, and the nine musicians were not fired.'[6] It was not a very happy state, though it cooled down later. 'Some of my earlier rehearsals were not very comfortable because of this,' he said.[7] In those days good string players were a rarity. And since the unions did not allow national auditions, it became even more difficult. Unsurprisingly, not many musicians were fired. Zubin recalls that he engaged eighty-six musicians and fired very few in his sixteen years with the orchestra. Others were retired on a pension plan he helped introduce during his first years at Los Angeles.

One of Zubin's more prominent recruits was Glenn Dicterow, who had joined as associate concertmaster. His father was principal second violin and Dicterow himself had trained under Galamian as a soloist. Zubin asked him to audition for the post and Dicterow, attracted by the steady income of an orchestral position, soon found himself playing in an ensemble for the first time, alongside his father. Commenting on Zubin's conducting style, Dicterow said that the learning curve was a steep one. 'He would interpret every performance a little bit differently, so you basically had to memorize the chart in order to see what he was going to do next.'[8] Dicterow managed well enough, eventually winning the concertmaster's seat when it opened a few years later. (He remained with the orchestra for ten years before deciding to pursue a solo career full-time. But within a year he received a call from Zubin—who by then had moved to the New York Philharmonic—and he ended up becoming concertmaster in New York, where he stayed for more than three decades, leaving after the 2013–14 season.)

Zubin's attempts, unpopular as they were, were the initial steps towards instilling a sense of pride in the orchestra. As Fishman put it, 'It used to be we were just happy to fill a chair. Now we have a choice of the best.' Still, Zubin was a bit of a softie when it came to firing musicians. It was always a difficult job, especially since the vast majority of musicians thought that they still had it in them to go on. 'I think firing musicians has taken years out of my life,' Zubin says.

The case which caused Zubin the most heartache was that of concertmaster Frisina. He was not only a great concertmaster but also a valued friend. He had joined the orchestra in 1937 and had been serving as concertmaster since 1942. In 1972, Zubin thought that it was time for him to step down from the concertmaster's chair. He convinced him to play second stand, first violin. The decision took a lot of heartache to implement and Zubin said that he hoped he would never have to experience that kind of anguish again.[9] His rapport with the musicians extended to talking about music all day and often visiting their homes.

After Kuyper retired, Zubin was assisted by Jaye Rubanoff, the orchestra manager, whom he described as 'my absolute breath, my conscience'. A great personal friend, Rubanoff drove Zubin to all his concerts until the latter started driving. Zubin recalls, 'It was hard in those days in Los Angeles. We not only played two concerts a week in Los Angeles but also played six concerts a season in Long Beach, Santa Barbara, Santa Monica and Pasadena.' But between them, they found that they weren't strong enough to take some unpalatable decisions. And that's when Zubin invited Ernest Fleischmann, former general manager of the London Symphony Orchestra, to join him in Los Angeles in 1969. Fleischmann was born in Frankfurt and grew up in South Africa, where he started his career as a conductor, and then became a successful impresario of the Johannesburg Festival. Before his stint in Los Angeles, he was manager of the London Symphony and Fleischmann seemed proud of the fact that he had been fired from his old job with that orchestra. He said, 'The musicians felt I was usurping some of their powers and they were absolutely right.'[10] He was just the man Zubin needed.

Zubin recalls, 'I told Ernest, "Come, let's do this job together."' Zubin assured him that they would not sit on separate pedestals and communicate through memos as most managers and conductors do.[11] The main people to be replaced were some woodwind soloists and there was an unhappy mood in the orchestra. The contract stipulated a year and a half's notice to any player who was to be fired and Zubin says that that period was 'murder—murder for both' (i.e. musician and conductor). Zubin also had to answer to an arbitration board but Fleischmann stood solidly behind him. Thanks to Fleischmann's deft handling of personnel matters, the orchestra enjoyed particularly good labour relations. Contracts which were usually negotiated till the eleventh hour were now finalized months in advance of their effective date.

Zubin not only respected Fleischmann's musical scholarship and ability with ledgers and schedules, but also realized that he was capable enough to keep things going while he was jetting around the world. It was observed, and quite justifiably, that Zubin could not have held down two jobs—at Los Angeles and with the Israel Philharmonic—without leaning heavily on Fleischmann.[12] The working relationship between the two was extremely close and each had great respect and affection for the other.

Fleischmann positioned himself as a buffer between the orchestra and the board of directors. He bargained for—and won—important areas of participation in orchestra affairs for the musicians, everything from programming suggestions to evaluation of conductors.[13] Since one of the touchiest areas is the weeding out of musicians who are past their prime, Fleischmann instituted a system whereby an orchestra committee could vote out a musician after a series of warnings and probationary periods. This method ensured that it was impossible to blame the conductor or a personality conflict. In a notable victory, Fleischmann also managed to banish outside arbitration in the matter of a dismissed player. This was both revolutionary and unprecedented. Fleischmann argued that it was impossible for a 'neutral' lawyer to comprehend the conditions that had led to a player being shown the door.

Fleischmann also made another important contribution to the orchestra. Ever since Hearst's death, Zubin had no manager or press agent in the United States. Had he been affiliated with an influential manager, he might have had more success in getting top conductors and soloists to appear with the orchestra. Rubanoff too did not know the world's best artistes, the ones Zubin wanted to invite to Los Angeles. Fleischmann's connections in the music world ensured that this was no longer a problem. Zubin observed: 'The best thing for any music director is to get absolutely top-notch guests to take care of your orchestra. It is no fun to come back and find the orchestra full of bad habits, believe me.'[14] Zubin says that the three of them managed excellently but there were many arguments with Fleischmann. 'We argued about music from morning to night,' Zubin said. But this creative tension resulted in some of the more ambitious and innovative ventures with which the Los Angeles Philharmonic was associated: a twelve-hour Beethoven Marathon to mark the composer's 200th birth anniversary (in which Dady and Mehli also performed) and the *Star Wars* concert at the Hollywood Bowl.[15]

When Fleischmann first came to Los Angeles, season ticket sales were running at about 56 per cent of capacity. A few years after he took over, 96 per cent of the tickets were sold out before the first concert. The musicians also had much to thank Fleischmann for. The average player's salary before Fleischmann came in was $8000 a year. In 1977, after the new contract, each would make about $20,000, with some principal players making $30,000.[16]

In 1970 Zubin stirred up quite a storm in feminist circles when he questioned the place of women players in orchestras. 'They become men,' he was quoted as saying. 'Men treat them as equals; they even change their pants in front of them. I think it's terrible.'[17] Despite the undeniable excellence of the ladies, some of the male musicians and conductors were wary of them. They subscribed to Sir Thomas Beecham's dictum: 'If she is attractive, I can't perform with her; if she is not, then I won't.' Zubin says that initially he had a bias against women because there were none in the orchestra in Vienna, but insists that he never rejected a woman musician who had 'won an audition'. His subsequent tenure with the New York Philharmonic also proved that there was no gender bias. There were twenty-seven women orchestra members in New York, the highest percentage of women musicians in any major US orchestra, and of them, eighteen had been brought into the orchestra by Zubin himself.[18] When asked about it, he said, 'When I first started, I was very young, and in Vienna there were no women in the orchestra. But I completely changed and, in a few years, I engaged more women than ever before.'[19]

Zubin was also always aware that he faced a challenge when conducting musicians who were vastly more experienced than he was. In his autobiography, he says that he came across a lead bassoonist who, as an eighteen-year-old, had played under Nikisch. He also encountered musicians who had played Beethoven with fifty different conductors! Zubin soon came to appreciate that every orchestra has a distinct musical memory and every conductor should exploit it to his best advantage.

The musicians had yet another reason to thank Zubin. It was during his tenure that the orchestra could get some of the most valuable Italian instruments for its players, especially for the strings section. Thanks to the generosity of the Michael J. Connell Foundation, his prizes included a $75,000 Stradivarius violin for the concertmaster and a $50,000 Stradivarius for the principal cellist. Zubin and Frisina went to Europe on a buying spree. The total expenditure for the collection was $2,21,499. The instruments were the property of the Southern California Symphony Association. The only restrictions imposed were that the instruments be used for the purpose intended; they could not be sold and would have to be protected by insurance. The instruments included two famous Stradivarius violins, the Earl of Plymouth of 1711 and the ex-Perkin of 1728, and the General Kyd Stradivarius cello of 1684.[20]

Zubin's ambition was always to create a velvety Viennese sound and he takes particular pride in the instruments he obtained to help make that happen. He inspired the clarinettist Michele Zukovsky to change to a Viennese clarinet. 'The beautiful sound she makes,' Zubin enthused, 'that's Vienna.'[21] Zubin encountered opposition from a most unlikely source for his acquisitions: Heifetz told the orchestra board members that the musicians would not take care of the instruments. The musicians, however, proved him wrong. The instruments are still in top condition and now in the hands of a third generation. 'In other words, musicians have come and gone but the voice is still there,' says Zubin.[22] The instruments are now worth over $35 million, according to Zubin.

Zubin worked to burnish the overall sound of his orchestra after the model of the Vienna Philharmonic. He systematically set to work with every section, especially the strings, which he describes as the proletariat of any orchestra because they do most of the work, and persuaded the board in Los Angeles to get new, darker-toned German trumpets with special mouthpieces, capable of producing the kind of pianissimo he wanted from the brass section.

He imported trumpets from Vienna because he thought that they had a warmer tone than the ones in America which tended to be sharper. He was also responsible for being the first to bring German trumpets with their rotary valves and a distinct sound to the orchestra. Viennese trumpets can be played loud without compromising warmth. The technique is fundamentally different and musicians get paid more when they play Viennese trumpets. In the case of the double bass, there is a distinction between the French bow (used in France, Italy and the US) and the German one. The former is larger and heavier, and the player needs less force to play with it while the sound is correspondingly lighter. The two bows are shaped differently and have to be held in different ways. It is common for German orchestras to play exclusively with the German bow and Zubin too had attempted to make his musicians in Los Angeles use the German bow but could not entirely succeed, having to settle for a compromise solution.

'I smuggled a mouthpiece out from Vienna,' Zubin said. 'It was like a state secret.'[23] Helmut Wobisch, the legendary trumpeter of the Viennese Philharmonic, gave his trumpet to Zubin, who got others made to the same specifications. He was obsessed with the 'Viennese tone' and pestered the Los Angeles Philharmonic for sixteen years to reproduce the sound of the Viennese Philharmonic which, for him, was the 'true sound'.

Zubin was distressed by the fact that there was no money for sectional rehearsals which he thought the orchestra badly needed. He also set up a revolving fund from which musicians could buy instruments free of interest and then pay the money back in instalments.

Zubin had no complaints about the artistic freedom he enjoyed in Los Angeles. When he had taken over, there was talk about how the dominating Chandler would also want to dictate the music. If there was ever any such fear in Zubin's mind, it proved to be entirely unfounded. 'I don't think there are many conductors in America who enjoy the authority I have. In five years, I have never been told what programmes to do. All they ever do is to ask me to smile a little,' he told the *New York Times* in 1967.[24] Zubin was famous for scowling during conducting. His wife, Nancy, called it her husband's 'Beethoven scowl'. When I asked him about the scowl he said that much of the music was serious music and it was not as if he scowled all the time or didn't smile at all.[25]

## THE MUSIC CENTER

In December 1964, Los Angeles finally got a decent home for serious music with the opening of the Music Center (officially the Performing Arts Center of Los Angeles County), the brainchild of the energetic and dynamic Chandler. Her relentless nine-year campaign had raised more than $18.5 million. After having successfully saved the Hollywood Bowl in 1951, Chandler decided that if she kept up the pressure, she could realize her dream of a new music centre for Los Angeles. The fundraising started in 1955 and, by 1960, the fund had grown to $4 million—all private donations for a public building.

In 1960, Chandler was provided a site for the music centre by the County of Los Angeles and the services of Welton Becket as architect.

Initially there were plans only for a stately auditorium, the Music Pavilion, but a visit to London convinced the grand dame that Los Angeles should cater to drama as well, and the plans were changed to include two theatres, one big and one small. The extra cost of another $7 million was obviously not going to deter a person like Chandler. She assured the County of Los Angeles that she would raise additional funds and got them to agree to her plans for an augmented music centre. By November 1961, the plans had been approved, and in March 1962 construction started. All through the construction, gifts poured in. Contributors included President Kennedy and his wife, Hollywood actor Cary Grant and singer Nat King Cole. *Cleopatra* had its gala opening night as a fundraiser and brought in $1 million.

The Dorothy Chandler Pavilion (widely known as the Parthenon), the first building of the Music Center, became the first public building in California named in honour of a person who was still alive. The Pavilion was furnished extravagantly and was steeped in luxury. There were bespoke carpets woven in Hong Kong and Bavarian chandeliers, including three massive ones dominating the Grand Hall, each consisting of 24,000 individual pieces of hand-polished crystals. 'The Grand Hall with its honey coloured onyx walls, massive chandeliers and two graceful balconies, was a masterful combination of warmth and tasteful luxury.'[26]

The interiors had Mexican onyx, white Byzantine tiles from Italy, black bean wood panelling from Australia and beige silk curtains from Japan. Concertgoers mounted an elegant cantilevered marble stairway that stretched across a pool filled with white azaleas set in the lobby floor. In contrast to the sharp edges and cool-toned decor of the Philharmonic Hall at Lincoln Center, the Pavilion was all curves and warm shades of gold, coral and beige. The auditorium was also wider and shorter than most others, giving a sense of intimacy which is rare in a major concert hall. Ninety per cent of the seats were within 105 feet of the stage, each with clear sight lines.[27] There were busts of Klemperer, Wallenstein and Gregor 'Grischa' Piatigorsky. In the Founders Room, there were portraits of Chandler and Zubin. The Pavilion also boasted of a custom-built carillon to tell the audience when the concert was about to begin.

Zubin also did his bit: he contributed $1000 towards endowing a seat in the new hall.[28] But his contribution to the fundraising was immeasurably more. There is no question that his intensely masculine magnetism and youth greatly contributed to the enthusiasm of Chandler's helpers. It was also the beginning of the glamorization of Zubin, a process which continued all through his sixteen years in Los Angeles.

The 3250-seat Pavilion opened on 6 December 1964. There were floodlights and cameras everywhere; everybody who was anybody in the worlds of entertainment, culture and finance was there, to say nothing of the many socialites who attended. The previous morning, Zubin had rehearsed for the first time in the new hall. After the 'Star Spangled Banner', Zubin had decided to play *Festfanfare* by Richard Strauss. On the day of the opening, Zubin was surprised to find the ushers dressed in red silk sherwanis and Nehru caps, something which would attract disapproval later and be cited as proof by the critics of the culture of adulation which he enjoyed in Los Angeles. 'I was surprised. He was a fine designer who was inspired by my Indian background but the people who gossip said I was behind that,' he said.[29] Nobody had consulted him on this but he put this at the back of his mind as he stepped on to the stage in what was a hugely emotional moment for all assembled there.

It was also a tense time for Chandler and architect Becket because the success of the new hall depended on how good its acoustics were. Just two years ago, critics had mercilessly panned the new Philharmonic Hall in New York as being unfit for human ears declaring that no 'multipurpose hall can have fine acoustics'. Zubin too, was aware of the threat irresponsible critics posed. He notes in his autobiography that the management in Los Angeles was very nervous about the reaction to the new hall since they feared that the New York critics would carp about it, possibly out of envy.

Immediately after the opening number, Zubin acknowledged the applause of the audience and said, 'This is the most unique city in the twentieth century. I do not think it is too late now in mid-century, to begin a new cultural life. This evening we are going to usher in a new era.'[30] Then, after the Strauss piece, Zubin turned to the audience and said simply: 'Ladies and gentlemen, we *like* the acoustics.' Zubin's one-liner recorded an elegant transition from the accomplishments of the past to the commitments of the future. He observed later that he deliberately wanted to forestall possible criticism with this statement. In any case, the acoustics were certainly much better than in New York. Zubin purposely chose Ottorino Respighi's *Feste Romane*, to show the acoustics off. It is a composition 'which includes the most delicate pianissimos as well as the most plangent brass'.[31]

Zubin naturally also acknowledged the lady who had made the evening possible: 'Buff' Chandler who sat shyly in her seat while the applause rose around her. Only when her son Otis tugged her to her feet did she rise and smile at the applauding audience. Zubin said: 'I would like you all to join me in paying homage to the one person who is most responsible for the creation of this edifice. Unlike the princes of Florence and the Pharaohs of Egypt, she is a dignified, simple lady.'[32] There was no doubt that the ovation was only her personal due. Not only had she conceived the idea for the Music Center, she had almost single-handedly raised $18.5 million to build it and then set up a company to float another $13.7 million in bonds to complete the venture. *Time* magazine described it as 'perhaps the most impressive display of virtuoso money-raising and civic citizenship in the history of US womanhood'.

Zubin says that his choice of music for the evening, *Festfanfare* and *Feste Romane* were supposed to demonstrate the jubilation over the orchestra's new home. Also on the programme was a performance with Heifetz playing Beethoven's Concerto in D Major. This was the first and only time Zubin ever made music with Heifetz and he still remembers this experience as being a slightly unnerving one. Heifetz had his own idea of different tempi which Zubin did not share. This inevitably led to some confusion. During the first movement, when the orchestra was playing the four beats, and before the solo was to start, Heifetz started playing his solo. His reason: 'My four bars are already over.' Apparently he found Zubin's tempo to be too slow.

Heifetz also proved to be a little temperamental. When he came for the first rehearsals, he was constantly finding fault with something or the other. He refused photo requests and did not want to be addressed as 'maestro'. He also wanted Zubin's podium to be a little lower and did not want him to conduct the piece from memory, something which was conveyed to Zubin in a most roundabout fashion. Olive Behrendt, president of the board of directors, Los Angeles Philharmonic, made a lunch appointment with Mehli and told him that Heifetz did not want Zubin to conduct from memory. Naturally, Zubin agreed: it was a small request from a giant of the musical world. In fact, before the concert, Heifetz invited Zubin to his Los Angeles home and played the entire Violin Concerto for him in private.[33] At the concert, Heifetz played with 'monumental mastery' and at the close, the audience stood and cheered, a prolonged demonstration he shared with Zubin and the orchestra for an accompaniment of 'splendid incisiveness and flexibility'.[34]

Zubin paid him a fine tribute when he died in December 1987. 'Not since Paganini has an artist evolved as completely as Heifetz. I know that he only wants to be remembered for his music. Thank God we have his entire recorded repertory, so that he will never leave us.'[35] But Zubin bemoaned the fact that there was no video or radio recording of the concert. 'We were so myopic in those days. Today it would be a coast-to-coast special.'[36]

The reaction of the press to the new hall was in general highly favourable. Music critic Schonberg's pat on the back must have meant the most to both patron and architect. Schonberg wrote:

> Mr. Mehta purposely chose for one of his pieces the Respighi *Feste Romane*, a dreadful piece of music but one that is overwhelmingly orchestrated, with everything from the wispiest pianissimos to the most shattering fortissimos. The Pavilion handled both elements of the dynamic scale with ease.[37]

Zubin's performance also attracted praise from Schonberg:

> Mr. Mehta is one of those dynamic leaders, all in motion, strongly rhythmic, with a flair for the dramatic . . . he conducted with brilliance and technical surety.[38]

Menuhin in his autobiography noted how Zubin had been associated with the new hall right from the planning stages. He bemoaned the fact that when the Lincoln Center was being planned, his attempts to influence the acoustics had come to nothing. Menuhin says that he sent the plans of Stuttgart's Liederhalle to John D. Rockefeller III (who was promoting the Lincoln Center) but received no response. 'In contrast, Zubin Mehta, advising at every stage of the planning of Los Angeles' Dorothy Chandler Pavilion, ensured a rich, appealing sound, sufficiently median for lone singer or full orchestra.'[39] Zubin had also donned a construction worker's helmet for a tour of the building he would one day fill with music. 'I like it. It's very intimate. Now I'm more impatient than ever.'[40]

The opening of the Pavilion got both Chandler and Zubin a fair share of publicity. *Time* magazine put Chandler on its cover and ran a fourteen-page colour story. Stories on Zubin appeared in magazines such as *Newsweek* and *Vogue*. The *New York Times* also did a full story on him. The new Pavilion worked wonders for revenues and attendance. During the 1964–65 season, the Los Angeles Philharmonic doubled not just its highest previous gross, but also the previous season's attendance record and the number of its season ticket holders. Some 11,000 sets of season tickets were mailed to subscribers for 1964–65, the highest season sales in the forty-six-year history of the orchestra. The credit was divided equally between the new auditorium and the new conductor.

When I asked Zubin about Chandler, he described her as being 'formal, distant but kindly'. 'She never interfered with my programmes and always came to my concerts,' he said.[41] When she died in 1997, Zubin was heartbroken that the Chandler family did not want a memorial for her in the Chandler Pavilion. He said that nothing, to his mind, would have pleased her more and that he would have cancelled anything in Europe to do it. 'I did not know her intimately, there was always a distance that she kept, that I kept . . . Sometimes people whose names are on buildings are given too much credit. It is not true of Mrs Chandler, not true.'[42]

## WELTON BECKET'S BOMBAY CONNECTION

Becket could well have been responsible for designing the National Centre for the Performing Arts' Tata Theatre in Bombay had it not been for his death in January 1969. Jamshed Bhabha, the man responsible for giving Bombay its first modern hall, had met architect Edward Durrell Stone, the designer of the Kennedy Center for the Performing Arts at Washington DC, at the American embassy in Paris. Bhabha was in Paris to attend a meeting of the International Fund for the Promotion of Culture, a UNESCO body. There was a model of the Kennedy Center there and Stone saw Bhabha admiring its design. They got talking and one thing led to another. Stone agreed to give his plans free of charge for a similar complex in Bombay, provided the Board of Trustees of the Kennedy Center agreed.

A few days later, Bhabha met Zubin at the Lincoln Center in New York where he was conducting a performance of Puccini's *Turandot*. When he recounted all that had happened, Zubin made him promise to visit them at the Dorothy Chandler Pavilion. On his next visit to the United States, Bhabha visited Los Angeles and was introduced to both Chandler and Becket. He even attended a concert with Becket and experienced the fine acoustics of the Pavilion for himself. After consulting Zubin, he invited Becket to Bombay.[43]

When Becket came to Bombay, Bhabha introduced him to Sir Dinshaw 'Fali' Petit, Third Baronet at 'Petit Hall' where Becket saw its magnificent Carrara marble staircase and four antique chandeliers. He remarked how beautiful it would be to locate the staircase in the entrance foyer of a theatre and the chandeliers in its extended foyer. Becket too had promised his plans free of charge to Bhabha but unfortunately passed away soon after he returned from Bombay. His partners pleaded complete ignorance about his wanting to donate the plans and there this episode which showed much promise ended.[44]

The fan-shaped Tata Theatre which was ultimately designed by Philip Johnson, one of the three principal architects of the Lincoln Center, with acoustics by Cyril Harris, opened in 1980. The marble staircase and the chandeliers found their way into the hall, named after Jamshed Bhabha, which opened at the NCPA complex in November 1999. Sir Dinshaw had donated them in memory of his wife, Sylla, J.R.D. Tata's elder sister. The marble staircase was resurrected in all its pristine glory; each stone was numbered, polished and reassembled in the foyer according to the original plan. Petit's benefaction remains the cynosure of all eyes at the Jamshed Bhabha Theatre. The Tata Theatre does not have a classical proscenium and a stage curtain. Former prime minister Indira Gandhi, who had inaugurated the Tata Theatre in October 1980, too had remarked that it was a pity the theatre did not have an orchestra pit. On her last visit to Bombay in 1984, she had attended a special Indo-Italian performance of Rossini's *Barber of Seville*. Since there was no orchestra pit, 100 seats had to be removed to accommodate the orchestra. She voiced the need for a hall in which opera could also be performed, and Jamshed Bhabha vowed to her to collect the funds and build such a theatre in a decade. It took five years longer, but he kept his word.[45] The new theatre addressed both these deficiencies and became Zubin's venue for his performances in the city.

♫

The week after the opening of the Music Center, Zubin began recording Respighi's *Feste Romane* and Strauss's *Don Juan* for RCA Records. RCA Records had decided to use the debut of the new hall as a demonstration for their new Dynagroove recording process. Both works were meant to exploit the rich sound of the new hall and the orchestra. Zubin told the engineers from RCA that he wanted 'a warm expansive tone'. After several alterations, adjustments and innovations, the recording started and the test tapes were pronounced to be satisfactory both by the engineers and by Zubin. The record did not sell particularly well and it was Zubin's last recording with the Los Angeles Philharmonic in the Music Center though it was by no means his last with the orchestra.

The record also served as confirmation to music critics that Zubin's repertoire consisted solely of compositions in a narrow, Romantic range that included Mahler and Strauss. Zubin himself is alive to this criticism and, in his autobiography, denies that he specializes in any particular music. He blames his repertoire of music records for the tag of post-Romantic specialist. The fact that he has recorded more of Strauss and Mahler also have to do with pragmatic considerations. For, say, a Mozart composition only fifty players would be required but the entire orchestra would have to be paid. If the record company wanted a Mahler or a Strauss then at least all the players would be needed.

In August 1965, Zubin conducted at the Hollywood Bowl after a hectic past few months where he fulfilled extensive conducting engagements in Europe. All of June he had led concerts in Prague, Milan, Zurich, Paris and Florence. The highlight of the summer was of course *The Abduction* at the Salzburg Festival, which we have already noted in the preceding chapter.

In October 1965, Zubin returned to Philadelphia for the first time since his Robin Hood Dell concerts. There were four concerts on consecutive days from 28 October to 1 November, followed by the opening of the Philadelphia Philharmonic's Carnegie Hall engagement in New York City. He had chosen a difficult programme: the *Coriolanus* Overture of Beethoven, Schoenberg's *Five Pieces for Orchestra* and Bruckner's Ninth Symphony. The Bruckner Ninth had been Zubin's first recording for London/Decca with the Vienna Philharmonic in 1966 and was considered a successful interpretation. But he seemed to have given some thought to his previous interpretation in the intervening years and his performance of the Ninth this time was different from the recording, prompting one critic to observe that Zubin at twenty-nine was 'enormously gifted, but still in the process of trying things out'. The same critic said that Zubin's growth in the coming years would be 'a tremendous thing to watch'. And part of that musical development was to come in the near future when Zubin would conduct a series of *Aida*s at the Metropolitan Opera at the end of the year, thanks to Bing's invitation.

## OPERA AT THE METROPOLITAN

At the Metropolitan, Zubin enjoyed working with the orchestra but found that there was inadequate rehearsal time. He also encountered criticism from his peer group for the first time. Zubin recalls that barring Bernstein, the other Met conductors would sit behind him at rehearsals and criticize his performance. It was a new experience for Zubin, considering that all through his formative years his colleagues, especially the senior ones, were supportive and ready to clarify any doubts he had.

His opening night on 29 December 1965 had an added tingle of tension since he arrived just minutes before curtain time. A nervous Carmen, Zarin and Béique waited for him to show up not only so that the performance could start but also because Zubin had their tickets. As for Bing, he was in a frenzy of nervous excitement as he fretted and fumed outside the orchestra pit waiting for his boy wonder to show up. 'Don't worry, Mr Bing,' said one of the musicians with a grin, 'there are at least two dozen fiddlers out there in the pit with batons in their cases ready to conduct, just waiting for an opportunity like this.' 'What about me?' replied Bing, pretending to feel insulted because his own candidature had been ignored.[46]

But whatever irritation Bing may have felt at Zubin's late arrival vanished after the prolonged ovation following the first act. It was obvious to all that Zubin was the find of the season. The critics too, barring a few voices of dissent, were full of praise. They commended Zubin's mastery over all elements of the opera. One critic called his performance 'one of rare completeness'. His pacing of the opera and adjustments of balance and control over all elements of the production found special mention. Winthrop Sargeant, writing in *New Yorker* magazine, called Zubin 'probably the most important find among conductors that Mr Bing had made during his career here'. He observed, 'And beyond everything else I have mentioned Mr Mehta has a degree of authority—an ability to rouse the eighty or hundred men under him to special effects—that is found only in born maestros.'[47]

*Los Angeles Times* wrote:

> In the simplest terms possible, Mehta's debut . . . was a sensational event. Conducting the season's first *Aida* from memory, he showed himself to be a complete original, and a baton technician of consummate skill. He wowed the audience and New York critics as well.[48]

This was high praise for a man who had conducted his first opera only two years ago.

Bing had engaged Zubin to conduct all nine performances of the opera that season. It was as if he knew the young man would be a runaway success. William Bender, writing in *Los Angeles Times* observed:

> His *Aida*, dazzling, exciting, and different as it was, would be virtually impossible for another conductor to take over on short notice. But Rudolf Bing, general manager of the company, has solved the problem very neatly by engaging Mehta to conduct all nine performances of the opera this season—as though he knew what he was in for.[49]

Zubin was called back to the Met and in four seasons, from 1965 to 1969, he conducted seven operas. Apart from *Aida*, he did *Carmen*, the world premiere of Marvin David Levy's *Mourning Becomes Electra*, *Otello*, *Tosca*, *Il Trovatore* and *Turandot*. Zubin was unhappy with his performance in some of the others, especially *Otello*, which he did for the first time at the Met with minimal rehearsal. He says that he was tempted to do it because of a near-perfect cast but didn't have the orchestral preparation for it. The Hungarian-born American conductor Szell, whose name is synonymous with the Cleveland

Orchestra, told Zubin after the performance what his conducting had lacked. Zubin kept returning to the Met till 1971.

At Zubin's first performance of *Il Trovatore* at the Met in 1969, he conducted the acclaimed tenor Domingo who came as a replacement for Franco Corelli. It was not the first time since Zubin had engaged the very young Domingo in a concert performance of *Carmen* in Israel in 1968. The two had also come together in Verdi's *Requiem* at the Pablo Casals Festival. In his memoirs Domingo recalls that he worked with Zubin many times since:

> I have since worked many times with Zubin who has a fine sense of humour and is a good friend. I find him an extremely gifted conductor, and I greatly admire his fine memory and musical intuition. Apart from being charismatic, he has great facility in absorbing scores . . . He is exuberant and spontaneous, and he enjoys working with singers, which contributes to the confidence we feel when we work with him.[50]

Domingo, whose voice has been described as 'molten chocolate', and Zubin remain good friends to this day.

On 16 September 1966, Thomas Schippers conducted the world premiere of Samuel Barber's *Anthony and Cleopatra* to mark the opening of the new Metropolitan Opera House at the Lincoln Center. Zubin was slated to conduct Puccini's *Turandot* the next day. The singers included Teresa Stratas, Birgit Nilsson and Corelli. The stage, which Zubin described as fantastic, was designed by Cecil Beaton. Zubin also did Levy's *Mourning Becomes Electra* that same season but according to him, it was not a success.

Similarly, *Carmen* too proved to be an unhappy birth. Zubin blames Bing for offering him everything except a German opera. 'I had to learn Italian operas for him, whereas I had grown up with Mozart and Wagner in Vienna and he wouldn't let me do them. I would have been on much better footing at the Met had I done the operas that I grew up with.'[51] Zubin recalled how he used to negotiate his own contracts since he did not have a manager. This used to annoy Bing, who once told him, 'Why don't you have a manager I can fight with!'[52] In a world where every word is devised by consultants and weighed by spin doctors, Zubin was unique in not having anyone to represent him on a full-time basis. Sharing a fact which was never made public, Zubin told me that Bing wanted him to be his successor at the Met. 'Till I'm around I cannot have a music director, but after me, I think you should take over,' Bing told him. Zubin, who was too young and inexperienced, naturally refused. 'Just let's be friends,' he told Bing, and the matter was dropped.[53]

## FRENETIC PACE

In June 1966, Zubin conducted the Israel Philharmonic Orchestra in a series of concerts, shuttling from Tel Aviv to Haifa to Jerusalem. The orchestra was supposed to go to Russia but the Russians abruptly cancelled the concerts. Sometime after conducting these concerts, Zubin received a telegram from Israel asking if he was free to conduct the orchestra again, on their tour of Australia, New Zealand and Hong Kong. The orchestra had planned to visit these countries with two conductors—Antal Doráti and Giulini—but the latter unfortunately had to cancel for health reasons.

Zubin was being asked to fill in for an indisposed colleague yet again and it did not require much persuasion to get him to accept. Zubin says that he was pleased to go since this way he could spend his time a little differently till his New York premiere of *Turandot* at the new Met in mid-September. He boarded a plane at Munich en route to Adelaide where he met the Israeli musicians. There were numerous programmes and therefore many rehearsals. Zubin and the musicians of the Israel Philharmonic grew close during this long tour. As Zubin puts it, '. . . I blended in completely for the first time with the orchestra during this long trip.'[54] Zubin especially loved the way the Israelis played Mahler. He thought they brought out the Jewish half of the composer's personality the way no other orchestra could. Their virtuosity was surprising because even after thirty years, they had never worked under a permanent conductor. While the experience with a never-ending list of guest conductors made them versatile, it left them without any characteristic sound that could be identified as that of the Israel Philharmonic.

In 1967 Zubin and the Los Angeles Philharmonic signed a four-year exclusive contract with Decca in London. The record company had been pleased with the success of Bruckner's Ninth. Zubin had also done an album of opera preludes by Wagner and Liszt's *Les Preludes*. With Vladimir Ashkenazy and the London Symphony Orchestra, he had recorded Brahms's Piano Concerto No. 2. All the recordings were artistic successes. Such a contract had been high on Zubin's list of priorities since he felt strongly that quality recordings on a good label would boost their international reputation. It was a historic event because it was the first exclusive contract ever signed between an American orchestra and a major European recording house.

Zubin recounted this deal with great pleasure. 'The orchestra released three or four LPs a year for a decade. Showpieces were favoured, and the sound quality was so glorious that the original LPs have become collector's items.'[55] The idea had been to get the city of Los Angeles to underwrite the recordings, and Zubin recalls that Chandler asked Mayor Sam Yorty for funding. *Los Angeles Times* had lampooned Yorty in numerous cartoons and he wanted to make a deal with her: he would fund the recording provided the offending cartoons stopped. Chandler naturally declined. Ultimately the orchestra reached an agreement with Decca that the $52 cost per player per session would be split between the Philharmonic and Decca equally.[56]

While no one had called the Los Angeles Philharmonic second-rate, no one ever really claimed that it was superior to the so-called Big Five[57] either. It was well known that an orchestra which did not record with a major label was not considered an orchestra of the first rank. This contract put the Los Angeles Philharmonic in the big league and it was with some justification that Zubin later made his famous remark of how he was not interested in the New York Philharmonic since his orchestra was much better.[58]

The recording took place not at the Music Center but at the

1. Zubin's grandparents Nowroji and Piroja Mehta.

2. His parents, Tehmina and Mehli Mehta.

3. A young Mehli playing the violin.

4. (From left) Zarin, Tehmina, Mehli and Zubin

5. (From left) Mehli, Zubin, Tehmina and Zarin.

6. Yusuf Hamied and Zubin in Bombay as children.

7. Yusuf Hamied and Zubin many decades later.

8. The young conductor, 1958.

9. Zubin playing the double bass, 1966.

10. Zubin with the Shah of Iran and his wife, Farah Diba, on the occasion of their coronation, 1967.

11. With Indira Gandhi.

Photograph by Ilan Brunner

12. Zubin with Golda Meir.

13. Zubin and Nancy on their wedding day.

14. Zubin and Nancy.

15. With Tehmina in the Fire Temple on his wedding day.

Photograph by Itzhak Berez

16. With Vladimir Ashkenazy.

Photograph by Jacob Aviram

17. With Arthur Rubinstein.

18. With Frederic Mann, 1970.

19. With Radu Lupu.

Photograph by Bert Bial

20. With Carlos Moseley.

21. Zubin in Masada.

22. Zubin with Teddy Kollek (second from right).

23. With Jan Peerce and Daniel Barenboim.

24. Conducting at the Good Fence.

Photograph by Jacob Aviram

25. With Isaac Stern.

Photograph by Bert Bial

26. With Woody Allen (extreme right).

Photograph by Bert Bial

27. With Glenn Dicterow.

28. Zubin being made conductor for life of the Israel Philharmonic Orchestra as Avi Shoshani (extreme left) looks on.

Photograph by Jacob Aviram

29. Zubin being conferred honorary citizenship of Tel Aviv, 1986.

Photograph by Roni Na'aman

30. Zubin receiving the Israel Prize, 1991.

Photograph by Bert Bial

31. With German baritone Dietrich Fischer-Dieskau in Berlin, 1980.

Photograph by Bert Bial

32. Zubin and Nancy in Edinburgh, 1980.

33. With the author's family at Siri Fort, New Delhi, 1984.

University of California at Los Angeles' Royce Hall which had been declared better for recording. A new stage was erected and members of the American Youth Symphony which had recently come under the direction of Mehli provided the music so that the recording engineers could place their mikes. Zubin also insisted that the university's music students be allowed to attend. At the end of ten days of recording, they had done the Modest Mussorgsky/Ravel *Pictures at an Exhibition*, *Petrouchka* and *Circus* Overture by Stravinsky, Alexander Scriabin's *Poem of Ecstasy*, Schoenberg's *Verklärte Nacht* and Tchaikovsky's Fourth Symphony.

Zubin's aquiline features and energy gave him the appeal of a movie star and made him a kind of cultural icon. Eagerly sought after by the wealthy and famous, he was unsurprisingly also a big hit with women. Zubin's interest in Los Angeles apart from his parents and the orchestra, included, in the words of one of his friends, 'girls, girls, girls'.

Zubin was a little embarrassed by the oversized portrait of himself painted by Marion Pike that was displayed in the lobby of the Dorothy Chandler Pavilion near the bar. He was known to have remarked, 'Well, I'll say one thing: the bar makes a lot of money since that portrait was put up.' Bernheimer, music critic of the *Los Angeles Times*, deplored the 'climate of adulation'. But even if the glamorization was misguided, it was still a tribute to the impact of his charismatic personality and galvanizing performances. 'Who gave me that glamour image—you people did,' Zubin once told the *New York Times* in an interview. 'To you people, anybody with any kind of charisma is looked upon as a sinner. What am I to do—paint my tooth black? Or shave my hair, which is going anyway, goddammit.'[59] He actively argued against this image. 'I have it practically written into my contract in Los Angeles that there are to be no parties. I work so hard, I don't have time to do all this stuff I'm accused of.'[60]

Zubin's life at the time was akin to that of a gypsy. He lived in hotels, had no secretary or manager and entertained at restaurants. He drove a green Jaguar 3.8 sedan and counted among his friends Hollywood personalities, like Edward G. Robinson and Vincente Minnelli. (In later years Zubin got himself a Bentley with a vanity number plate: M8A which, when said aloud, sounds like 'Mehta'. Zubin told me that the number was Nancy's idea). 'He fenced with film composer Bronislau Kaper, enjoyed jazz at drummer Shelley Manne's club, and sang all the parts in impromptu living-room opera performances with musical friends such as Israeli violinist Ivry Gitlis and Daniel Barenboim.'[61]

He was also known to have a predilection for drenching his food with Tabasco sauce, something which invited comment. (He no longer likes Tabasco and said that he used it then only because there was no choice.) Zubin is known for carrying a small silver box with red chillies in it. He was forced in those days to cook for himself since, as he puts it, 'every Indian as soon as he gets out of India starts cooking because one can't get anything'. The situation now is vastly different with Indian restaurants everywhere, but in Zubin's time this was not the case. He had once said, 'In America you must cook on the table.'[62] 'In those days I used to cook. Now it's not necessary. Now we get it everywhere. I carry my chillies when I travel. I grow my own chillies and carry them in my pocket. I don't mix them with Indian food though.' There was then a lone Indian restaurant in New York called Kashmir and it was run by a Bangladeshi. During the 1971 Indo-Pakistan war, the owner refused to serve Zubin who told him that this was surprising in the light of the fact that an Indian general was giving them their freedom. (The reference was to Field Marshal Sam Manekshaw, who was a four-star general then.)

Zubin had once complained: 'I can't go to American restaurants because I feel I'm in a hospital.'[63] When he enters some restaurants, the maître d'hôtel offers a plate on which Zubin places the chillies for inclusion in whatever dish he orders. Zubin takes his chillies with him even to the best restaurants and has joked about how some Michelin-star restaurants would love to throw him out because of what he does to their gastronomic creations. 'I keep ready a jar of dried chilli peppers at all times,' said Sirio Maccioni of the upmarket Le Cirque restaurant in New York. Zubin grew his own peppers in the garden of his Los Angeles home and passed them around to such chilli freaks as actor Gregory Peck and King Juan Carlos of Spain. Zubin used their mutual tailor as his chilli courier to the king.[64] Zubin's box of chillies once helped him have a conversation with former prime minister Atal Behari Vajpayee. Zubin was seated quite close to Vajpayee at a banquet in Munich but the latter took no notice of him as he had not been introduced to him. When the main dish arrived, out came Zubin's box, and he started distributing red chillies to his neighbours, including Vajpayee. It was only then that Vajpayee noticed Zubin and the two had an animated conversation.[65]

♫

In 1967 the Los Angeles Philharmonic travelled East in a tour that included Washington DC, Detroit, Fort Wayne and other Midwestern cities. It began in New York with the orchestra's Carnegie Hall debut. Washington proved to be a personal high for Zubin. 'As he led music from Barber's score for *Medea* and the Eighth Symphony of Dvořák, his baton was as often a whip as it was a guide.'[66] The Indian ambassador B.K. Nehru presented Zubin with the Padma Bhushan, India's third highest civilian award. It was a gratifying feeling for Zubin who had seen his father struggle just to get people back home to listen to his music.

In a display of amazing energy, Zubin also found time to conduct the Metropolitan Opera's production of *Otello* between stops on the orchestra's tour. Monday nights were free and Zubin led the Met on its opening night in Atlanta, Dallas, Detroit and Cleveland. After the Cleveland performance, Zubin hired a private plane to Montreal where he rejoined the Los Angeles Philharmonic for the gala opening of Expo 67. The Montreal Symphony Orchestra and the Los Angeles Philharmonic played Berlioz's *Symphonie Fantastique*, Ravel's *La Valse* and Respighi's *Pines of Rome* together. (Zubin's tenure with the Montreal Symphony Orchestra ended in 1967 and his successor was Rafael Frühbeck de Burgos. He said that the Montreal stint did him a lot of good and he looks back upon his time there with gratitude.)

As if all this was not enough, Zubin then set off to San Juan,

Puerto Rico, in May to conduct at a Pablo Casals Festival. Also at the festival was the cellist Piatigorsky, like Zubin, a resident of Los Angeles, and his friend and ally. Both were a little disappointed they did not have any concerts together. To remedy this, Zubin substituted the Bruckner he was supposed to conduct with Strauss's *Don Quixote* for cello and orchestra. Hearing them perform was none other than the aged maestro Pablo Casals himself, who enjoyed the distinction of being the first to play this piece in America, one which Richard Strauss himself conducted.

Zubin's days of jet-setting were hardly over. The day after the concert, he read that President Nasser of Egypt had moved troops into the Sinai. The news became grimmer in the days that followed when Nasser closed the Gulf of Aqaba. In Israel, they were preparing for war. Zubin, who had been conducting in Israel for the past five years and had developed a deep affection for the country and its people, knew that he had to do something to help. Just as he was mulling over how he could help, he was told that the conductor Leinsdorf who was scheduled to conduct concerts in Tel Aviv, Haifa and Jerusalem during this period had cancelled in the middle of his tour. Hearing of this, Zubin sent a telegram offering his services to the orchestra that was stranded without a conductor. It was to be the start of a lifelong love affair with not only the Israel Philharmonic but also the country and its people.

# The Love *of* Zion

ZUBIN HAD PLANNED ON going to Israel but for that he needed a visa. Along with Zubin, violinist Isaac Stern was also a guest at the Pablo Casals Festival. Stern's wife, Vera, had a close connection with the Israeli consulate in New York. Zubin prevailed upon her to use her good offices to speed up his visa. At the same time he called his European agent, Ruth Böttcher, to cancel his guest appearances in Budapest and Paris—the first cancellations of his career.

Vera Stern's contacts worked and Zubin was soon aboard a TWA flight to Tel Aviv. Zubin knew that Barenboim and Du Pré were already there and he was eager to join them. Zubin's association with the Israel Philharmonic Orchestra resulted in an even closer bond with Barenboim. His parents looked after Zubin when he was in Israel. But beyond the personal friendship, he and Barenboim also have a great deal in common as far as music goes. Since their engagements in various parts of the globe made it difficult for them to meet often, Zubin and he talked regularly on the phone. On one occasion, he played recordings by Furtwängler over the phone to Barenboim. They have even performed in a few noteworthy concerts together, one of them being the November 1964 concert with the Berlin Philharmonic Orchestra to mark the tenth death anniversary of Furtwängler. They performed the Symphonic Concerto for Piano and Orchestra in B Minor by Furtwängler, which, at seventy minutes, is a long and difficult piece. But Barenboim, playing the entire piece from memory, pulled it off with aplomb.

In mid-air, while Zubin was flying over the Mediterranean Sea, the pilot announced that they would be unable to land at Tel Aviv since war had broken out; instead, they would be landing in Rome. Getting to Israel was not going to be so easy after all! Zubin was a little uneasy about landing in Rome since he did not have a visa. He immediately contacted the Israeli ambassador, who told him that he was powerless to assist since all commercial flights had been cancelled and only military planes were being allowed to land at Israeli airports. The ambassador invited him to dinner and Zubin pestered him throughout the evening, requesting a fast passage to Tel Aviv.

The next morning, Zubin received a call asking him to be at the airport at 5 a.m. to board an El Al flight for Tel Aviv. Though Zubin does not mention it in his memoirs, apparently the Israeli premier Levi Eshkol personally intervened and ordered an Israeli aircraft to fly to Rome.[1] The ambassador also told him that it would be an uncomfortable flight. This proved to be a gross understatement. The seats of the aircraft had been removed, and Zubin and his co-passengers sat on the unmarked crates and boxes that filled the cabin.

The aircraft was full of Israelis, all of whom wanted to go to their families or who had been called up to do military service. Also travelling with him was Curtis Pepper, the Rome bureau chief of *Newsweek* magazine; an Israeli member of Parliament; and the governor of the Bank of Israel. Shortly before landing, a member of the crew asked them casually if they knew what the crates they were sitting on contained. When they replied in the negative, they were informed just as casually, that the crates contained weapons and ammunition. Zubin recalls, 'I do not even dare to think about what could have happened to us if a stray bullet would have hit the plane.'[2] Obviously, the Israeli army thought that an El Al aircraft had a better chance of getting through with arms and ammunition than a military transport plane.

We have already noted Zubin's first encounter with the Israel Philharmonic when he was asked to fill in for Ormandy in 1961. For fifty years now, Zubin has regarded the Israel Philharmonic and Israel as his second home. Zubin's attachment to Israel and all things Jewish is even closer than his bond with Vienna. 'I would convert to Judaism,' he once quipped, 'if the operation didn't hurt so much'—but he claims that he follows his own faith devoutly.[3] He has never hesitated to interrupt his manifold activities and fly to Israel, with no advance notice, in times of war and crisis, in order to conduct the orchestra and stand by the Israeli people in their tribulations.

No other orchestra in the world has been so moulded by emergency. Beyond its customary growing pains, it has weathered the ravages of war, offering visiting conductors such inducements as 'the largest and most luxurious air-raid shelter in the Near East, with excellent acoustics'.[4] Sir Malcolm Sargent nearly got picked off by an Arab sniper while travelling to a performance in Jerusalem in 1937, and Bernstein conducted during an attack by Egyptian bombers in 1948. The orchestra often travelled in armoured cars and on one occasion even played a series of concerts without a conductor. All this did not prevent it from having the largest number of subscribers and one of the longest seasons of any orchestra in the world.

After Zubin's first experience with the orchestra in May 1961 when he substituted for Ormandy, he was invited back two years later. He recalls that he played some unorthodox compositions that were not part of the standard repertoire of the orchestra: *Six Pieces for the Orchestra* by Webern and Bruckner's Ninth Symphony. At that time Webern was not very popular anywhere, and certainly not in Israel. It was the same with Bruckner.

Zeev Steinberg who was assistant viola when Zubin first came to Israel, said in an interview that it was that second visit which really won over the orchestra. Bruckner's Ninth had never been played in Israel before and he recalls that Zubin came to the first rehearsal and said, 'Let's just read it.' He didn't open the score, closed his eyes and conducted the first movement from start to finish. The first violins were flabbergasted: 'So young, conducting from memory, so musical!' He didn't need to look—all eyes were on him and it was simply the strength of his personality that shone through.[5]

In June 1966, Zubin led the Israel orchestra through a schedule of twenty-one concerts over a period of twenty-four days, playing concerts in Tel Aviv, Jerusalem and Haifa. The conservative audience received his reading of Bartók's First Piano Concerto with Barenboim enthusiastically. He was equally successful with Ravel's *Daphnis et Chloé*, a piece that until a few years ago the orchestra could barely manage because of weak brass and woodwind sections.

## THE ISRAEL PHILHARMONIC ORCHESTRA

The Israel Philharmonic Orchestra is a distinguished institution that is among Israel's most beloved cultural symbols. It is at the centre of Israeli cultural life and has been a part of the state from the beginning. In fact, the Jews of Palestine had an orchestra before they had a state. Vienna had been around for a millennium before its philharmonic was founded. In Berlin, Bilse's Band turned into that city's orchestra only a decade after German unification in 1871. The Israel Philharmonic Orchestra, on the other hand, is older than the nation it represents.

It was founded in 1936 as a self-governing ensemble of European émigrés. The founder, Polish violinist Huberman, foresaw the Holocaust and persuaded seventy-five Jewish musicians from major European orchestras to immigrate to Palestine—then a British protectorate—to create what he called the 'materialization of the Zionist culture in the fatherland'. The Nazis helped strengthen the ensemble by throwing many talented musicians out of work and the players were predominantly German, Polish, Hungarian and Austrian. Huberman's orchestra building also became a kind of rescue mission from Nazi Germany. Among the original seventy-five musicians was Haftel, who became concertmaster and later took over the orchestra in 1946. (A 2013 documentary, *Orchestra of Exiles*, by Josh I. Aronson tells the story of Huberman and the orchestra he founded, using a combination of archival photographs, letters and recreations to shine light on a little-known chapter of musical history. In it, Zubin says, 'Huberman had a calling and we are very grateful to him that he followed that calling.')

Toscanini, the most famous conductor of his time, led the first concert in Tel Aviv on 26 December 1936. Toscanini, who had fled fascist Italy, refused to accept payment saying, 'I am doing this for humanity.' The legendary sixty-nine-year-old Italian maestro stood on the stage of a pavilion of the Tel Aviv Levant Fair and conducted a group of musicians who had been forced to flee Nazi Europe in search of a homeland.

Calling it the happiest day of his life, Toscanini lit the musical flame in Palestine, and went on to appear with the orchestra for another twenty-one concerts in Jerusalem, Haifa, Cairo and Alexandria. (On 15 February 2007, with Toscanini's granddaughter Donna Emanuela di Castelbarco in attendance, the Israel Philharmonic Orchestra conducted by Riccardo Muti, and with pianists Itamar Golan and Saleem Abboud Ashkar, gave a commemorative concert on the fiftieth anniversary of Toscanini's death to express its eternal gratitude to the man who came to Palestine to defy the Nazi regime.) Today, the orchestra depends greatly on the Jewish diaspora whose sympathy and support remain all-important not only to the musicians but also to Israel.

After Huberman, Haftel took charge. In the years that followed, Haftel brought virtually all of the world's top soloists to Israel, apart from starting a highly successful opera and ballet programme, and launched the orchestra on world tours. He was also responsible for raising the players' average salary manifold. Functioning as a board of directors, chaplain, negotiator, booking agent and benevolent dictator, he was jokingly referred to as the musicians' 'Jimmy Hoffa'. His duty, as he saw it, was to remain as the orchestra's *shamas* (synagogue caretaker) till the right conductor came along.[6] In 1968 the orchestra finally found Mr Right—Zubin Mehta—a story which is told later in the narrative.

After Toscanini, there were several local conductors, notably Michael Taube and George Singer, who led the orchestra during the war years. When there was no conductor available, the orchestra appeared in public performing on its own. In 1947 guest conductors began to arrive. Bernardino Molinari, who orchestrated the music for *Hatikva*, was followed by Munch and Bernstein.

When on 14 May 1948, David Ben-Gurion, Israel's first prime minister, gave orders for the ceremony to mark the birth of the Jewish state at Tel Aviv's Municipal Museum, the orchestra was also instructed to be present. By 1948 the orchestra had become so identified with the Jewish people that an occasion of such historic significance would have been unthinkable without it. Unfortunately the orchestra missed its cue and failed to play *Hatikva* when Ben-Gurion was about to declare the new state of Israel. But it made its presence felt by bringing the proceedings to a close with a rendition of *Hatikva*, something which also converted the Palestine Philharmonic Orchestra into the Israel Philharmonic Orchestra—the title they have borne ever since. A moving concert on Be'er Sheva's dunes in November 1948, when the young Bernstein conducted Mozart's piano concerto before 5000 soldiers, is now part of the orchestra's folklore. Bernstein convinced his famous teachers Koussevitzky and Mitropoulos to visit Israel, and in 1951 the orchestra went on its first North American tour under Koussevitzky. A world tour followed in 1960, with Giulini and Krips.

Two towering figures in its history—Bernstein and Zubin—share equal credit for forging the unique symbiosis between the orchestra and the people of Israel, which is the outstanding characteristic of the ensemble. No other top-flight orchestra in the world is so closely identified with its constituency or so woven into the very fabric of its audience's lives as the Israel Philharmonic. Wherever the Israeli people have gone, there has been the orchestra, giving musical expression to the great events in the nation's story.

While the fledgling orchestra had excellent players, they had diverse styles and thus, in the early period, the musical unity of the ensemble was a concern. The main languages spoken in the orchestra were German, Polish, Hungarian, Russian and a bit of Hebrew. Some of the world's most renowned artistes showed their solidarity with the orchestra, and through it, with the new state of Israel: conductors Koussevitzky, Markevitch, Sergiu Celibidache, Paul Kletzki, Paul Paray, Ferenc Fricsay and Giulini; violinists Heifetz, Menuhin, Elman, Milstein, Stern and Zino Francescatti; pianists Rubinstein and Claudio Arrau; cellist Paul Tortelier; singers such as

Jan Peerce and Jennie Tourel and many others. But the parade of guest conductors turned the players into musical chameleons, denying them a distinctive style that could be considered a distinguishing characteristic of the orchestra.

The orchestra is a cooperative, with the musicians deciding on their own salary. They also owned the guest house for visiting artistes and a half interest in what was till recently called the Mann Auditorium in Tel Aviv. All this and the freedom from the discipline of a permanent conductor resulted in a strong streak of independence. Zubin spoke of a 'tendency towards musical anarchy' among the orchestra members. 'At rehearsals you suddenly find yourself in the middle of a brain trust over how a phrase should be played. Everyone has a suggestion, and everyone thinks that the way he played it back in Poland is the only way.'[7] With a group of musicians whose rehearsals have been known to evolve into debating societies, Zubin has not only managed to get things done but also earned the respect of his players in the process. All Israelis are passionate about their music. Listening to music with an Israeli audience is listening to music with people who care.

In October 1957, the orchestra's new home, the Fredric R. Mann Auditorium, was inaugurated in Tel Aviv. The initiator and principal benefactor was Fredric R. Mann who, as we have seen, also helped in the formation of the orchestra. The Mann Auditorium began with a $4,00,000 contribution by Mann. The 2800-seat auditorium cost $2.8 million and the first piece performed at the opening concert was 'The Star Spangled Banner', in acknowledgement of American contributions.

The programme consisted of the *Consecration of the House* Overture by Beethoven, *Festival Prelude* by Noam Sheriff, *Schelomo* by Ernest Bloch, Mendelssohn's Violin Concerto and Beethoven's Piano Concerto No. 5 (*Emperor*). The conductor was Bernstein and the soloists were Rubinstein (*Emperor* Concerto), violinist Stern (Violin Concerto) and cellist Tortelier (*Schelomo*). Sheriff was then an unknown twenty-year-old and his *Festival Prelude* had been selected by Bernstein himself for the opening concert from a contest to find the best new piece. The evening was a great success despite Ben-Gurion's gaffe in referring to the guest conductor as Arthur Bernstein.[8] His wife, Paula, was also guilty of her own blooper. She mistook Sheriff for the late Bloch, the composer of *Schelomo* and, since then, Sheriff was known in the orchestra as Mr Bloch.

Yaacov Mishori who was principal hornist at the orchestra for many years narrates another amusing anecdote about the inauguration. Along with Ben-Gurion, President Yitzhak Ben-Zvi was also present at the opening ceremony. During the concert, Paula Ben-Gurion nudged her husband and said: 'Look David, the President has fallen asleep.' Ben-Gurion answered angrily: 'So what, you had to wake me up for that?'[9]

We have already noted Mann's role in giving Zubin his first chance to conduct in the United States. It was the joint vision of Mann and Zubin which created an endowment fund in the United States to ensure the Israel orchestra's future. Since the Israeli government could not provide the funds needed, the American Friends of the Israel Philharmonic Orchestra (AFIPO) was set up in 1981 to secure the ensemble's financial future.

The orchestra, which until then had been performing before thousands of subscribers in the shoddy Ohel Shem Hall, with a capacity to seat only 920 people, moved into the new auditorium. This greatly increased the number of its subscribers—a loyal audience that forms the orchestra's backbone till today. The Mann Auditorium became a focal point for a sophisticated and knowledgeable musical culture and a continuing love affair between musicians and their audience. (At the close of the concert, the audience could rush to the edge of the stage—it was only waist-high—and show its approval.) The Israel Philharmonic is an ensemble that serves the entire country. There are subscription series in Haifa and Jerusalem too, and playing seven concerts a week is routine.

Artistes from Russia too managed to cross the Iron Curtain: the violinist David Oistrakh and cellist Mstislav Rostropovich were warmly received; and conductors such as Krips, Jean Martinon, Solti, Doráti, Celibidache, Ormandy and Mitropoulos visited Israel. It was also in the late 1950s that young and promising artistes like Barenboim made their successful debuts. At the same time, the orchestra continued to record with conductors such as Solti and Lorin Maazel.

The great pianist Rubinstein was a true friend of the orchestra and often accompanied it on tours. He also made it a point to visit Israel once a year. He enjoyed playing with Barenboim and would often perform with him outside Israel. Zubin says that apart from being technically perfect, he also remained faithful to the score, playing the work as it had been composed.[10] The first time he performed with Zubin was when the latter had been enlisted as a last-minute replacement for Reiner in Los Angeles. It did not bother him that he would be playing Brahms's First Piano Concerto with an unknown conductor from India. Unlike some soloists who master only their own part leaving everything else to the conductor and the orchestra, Rubinstein was also interested in orchestral details and was only satisfied when he was convinced that everything was in perfect balance. Zubin says that he played Brahms like no other pianist of his generation. The cigar-smoking maestro was also an accomplished raconteur and his stories and jokes were legendary.

Towards the end of his life, when Rubinstein was rehearsing the same Brahms concerto with Zubin and the Israel Philharmonic, he expressed a wish to conduct the orchestra. Since there was no question of denying him, the orchestra prepared itself to read through Brahms's Third Symphony, the piece which Rubinstein had chosen to conduct. His joy knew no bounds and the exhausted musicians too were happy to have granted his wish. As to the experiment of him being a conductor, 'both sides rated the effort as less than a hundred per cent successful'.[11]

Since Zubin and Rubinstein were under contract with different record labels they could not make any recordings together, save for one. Shortly before he died, Rubinstein insisted on making a recording with the Israel Philharmonic and Zubin. His record company RCA released him from his contract for this one occasion. They made a recording of Brahms's First Piano Concerto for Decca, the label Zubin was under contract with. It proved to be Rubinstein's last recording. (In 1987, Barenboim and Zubin came together in Tel Aviv along with some of the best pianists in the world to honour Rubinstein's memory on his birth centenary. Barenboim played two concertos long associated with the master—the Fifth Beethoven and First Tchaikovsky. Calling it an extraordinary night of music, a critic said that Zubin and Barenboim's interaction with one another resulted in a level of excitement that neither could hope to produce alone.)

## MUSIC AND THE SIX-DAY WAR

Tel Aviv was under a total blackout when Zubin arrived there. Thirty miles to the north-east, Israeli soldiers were crossing the Jordanian border into the West Bank. Zubin and his co-passengers were taken into town by military transport. There, Zubin met Haftel, head of the orchestra committee, who told him that Barenboim and Du Pré had arrived two days before him. He also told him that the two planned to marry soon. Met stars Richard Tucker and Roberta Peters, who were soloists for the same series which conductor Leinsdorf had cancelled, remained in Israel and were busy singing arias and duets in the front lines.

Zubin was taken to Orchestra House, the guest house for visiting artistes, where Barenboim and his parents, Du Pré, and Sergiu Comissiona, the Romanian-born conductor and former director of the Haifa Symphony Orchestra, was there with his wife. They all were living in the cellar of the house, which served as a sort of makeshift air-raid shelter. Zubin recalls that they talked and joked but the undercurrent of fear and uncertainty was ever present. They made Comissiona the target of their jokes. On one occasion, when he went out to get a glass of water, Zubin climbed on to the mattress with his wife. When Comissiona returned, he was surprised to find that there was already someone in his bed! Zubin admits that it was juvenile stuff but since the tense atmosphere was almost unendurable, the silly jokes helped to keep up their spirits.

Despite the suspense, Zubin and Barenboim were confident that Israel would win the war and were planning a 'victory concert'. Since one of the principal Israeli objectives of the war was the reunification of the divided city of Jerusalem, it was decided to hold the concert there. There was no knowing when it would happen but events were unfolding in a manner that made it seem as though their optimism was not misplaced. They even had a programme ready: Zubin would conduct Beethoven's Fifth and after that Barenboim would play Beethoven's Piano Concerto No. 5 and Du Pré the Cello Concerto by Schumann.

After rehearsing Beethoven's Fifth with the orchestra, Zubin borrowed a car and drove to Jerusalem with the aim of making preparations for the concert. Zubin's destination was the old King David Hotel and it was dusk when he reached the city. Suddenly, he found himself surrounded by tanks and jeeps filled with soldiers who were singing and cheering. The Israeli soldiers had taken the Old City: Jerusalem was reunited. The people too were cheering and waving flags in the streets celebrating the event.

Zubin met Theodor 'Teddy' Kollek, the mayor of New Jerusalem—now the mayor of a united Jerusalem—in his office and was given a hearty welcome. Kollek was mayor of Jerusalem from 1965 to 1993, having been re-elected five times. During his tenure, Jerusalem developed into a modern city, especially after its reunification. He was once called 'the greatest builder of Jerusalem since Herod'. Zubin narrates in his autobiography that he and Teddy shared a close relationship, adding that he looked on Barenboim, Bernstein, Stern and Zubin as his children. Originally a resident of Austria, he also shared with Zubin his love of Vienna. Teddy was famous the world over for his ability to 'bind politics and humanity together'. He was a lover of music and art, and Zubin recalls that they understood each other right from the beginning.

Zubin has always had a knack for grabbing headlines with his orchestra, both as a cultural peacemaker and as a morale booster during crises. One such event, which was a milestone, was the open-air concert in Manger Square in front of the Nativity Church in Bethlehem which was the brainchild of Kollek. The orchestra played on a makeshift stage and there were seats for several hundred Arab notables, Christian religious leaders and Israeli officials, both civilian and military. The concert was held on 21 July 1968, a year after the Six-Day War. Here Arab and Jew sat together and heard Verdi's *Requiem*. The singers included Martina Arroyo, Shirley Verrett, Tucker and Bonaldo Giaiotti. They ended with *Liberame*. It was not only an altogether moving experience but also a unique night in the annals of music.

However, the stark reality of their situation could not be ignored. Kollek warned Zubin of a possible attack by the Al Fatah and advised him to be calm in case there was one. There have been many moments in Zubin's career which, while charged with much excitement, have also been fraught with danger. Zubin recalls that it was not a particularly reassuring thought and that a couple of times during the concert, he had the uneasy feeling that danger was very near. But he adds that he feels relatively safe in such situations because he considers himself to be on the side of truth and justice. (Zubin visited Kollek at an old age home in Jerusalem in 2004. He was mentally alert but physically decrepit and depressed with old age. Zubin recalls that it was a touching reunion and the two took a nostalgic walk down memory lane.)

Zubin and the orchestra have lived with fears of terrorism during their tours abroad. He recalls how his first violin once sat on stage with a pistol in his pocket to shoot back. He says that in those days there were bomb threats on almost every tour; sometimes they told the orchestra and sometimes they didn't. In 1972, when news broke of the massacre of eleven Israeli athletes at the Munich Olympics, Zubin and the Israel Philharmonic were playing in Brazil where some of the former Nazis were known to have settled. They were a frightened bunch of musicians very far from home, but they played Mahler's First Symphony, which symbolizes the victory of the spirit. 'Just try and touch us. That's what they were saying,' Zubin said.[12]

That night Zubin was the only guest in the King David Hotel and he has an interesting tale to tell. Sometime after midnight, he was awakened by what sounded like a gunshot from close range. Zubin ignored the sound and was soon fast asleep. When he awoke the next morning, he noticed that the painting above his head had an unnatural slant to it. As he straightened it, he discovered a splintered hole in the frame and a bullet lodged in the wall behind it. The painting had caught a stray bullet from the sporadic fighting still going on with the remnants of the Jordanian army!

In the morning, Zubin accompanied his friend Memi De-Shalit, head of the Israeli tourism ministry, to the New City. They walked through the Mandelbaum Gate, symbol of the city's division, and were told by a soldier on the Arab side that they were the first civilians to come through that gate. They walked to the nearby Ambassador Hotel, which the occupying forces of the newly appointed military governor Major General Chaim Herzog (who went on to become the sixth President of Israel in 1983), had made a command post. The general was pleased to see them and invited them to breakfast. He also arranged a car for them in which Zubin and his friend drove to Mount Scopus, north-east of Jerusalem. There they discovered a naturally formed amphitheatre which they felt could make a wonderful setting for the victory concert. The hill, which overlooks Jerusalem, has been strategically important as a base from which to attack the city since antiquity. Today, Mount Scopus lies within the municipal boundaries of the city of Jerusalem. They walked up the hill to an amphitheatre built as part of the old Hebrew University of Jerusalem. Long neglected, it was overgrown with weeds but, at 2700 feet above sea level, it commanded a great view of the surrounding hills and the Dead Sea.

Two days later, the Jordanian army was in full retreat and the Egyptian army was tending to their wounded on the other side of the Suez Canal. When it became clear that the war was ending, it was decided that the victory concert would be held on Mount Scopus. De-Shalit had arranged for a gang of boys and girls to clean the amphitheatre for the programme. The orchestra and soloists were summoned from Tel Aviv. But when Zubin, De-Shalit and his party arrived, they were greeted by the army who told them that the area was out of bounds since the Arabs had mined the area before pulling out. It was divine protection which had prevented Zubin and De-Shalit from being blown up on their first visit!

The concert was ultimately held at Jerusalem's Binyanei Ha'Ooma

Convention Centre, with half the audience wearing khaki. While the music was not exactly top drawer, its emotional appeal was undeniable. Zubin vividly remembers Ben-Gurion's warm embrace after the concert. The next day Zubin accompanied De-Shalit and some other Israeli officials, including foreign minister Abba Eban (who happened to be Chaim Herzog's brother-in-law), to the Wailing Wall. Zubin narrates how the war got its name that day. When a journalist asked Eban what they were going to call the war, he smiled and said, 'I guess we'll have to call it the Six-Day War, won't we?'

Zubin was a little miffed when Bernstein gave a concert at the same location on 9 July 1967, which is now part of orchestra folklore. It is this concert which has gone down in history as the 'Victory Concert'. He conducted the full orchestra and chorus in a programme of Mendelssohn and Mahler. The Mahler Second had a special significance since Bernstein had played his *Resurrection* Symphony in 1948 in the midst of the Israeli war of independence and it had become a national favourite ever since. Stern was the soloist at the concert.

Funnily, music was seen by the Arabs as Israel's 'secret weapon'. In fact, an Arab newspaper had even blamed the defeat on Israel's tricky use of music. When Arab intelligence agencies tuned in to Israeli radio broadcasts, there was nothing but classical music on every station. This lulled them into a false sense of complacency as they erroneously believed that the Israelis were relaxing at home listening to music.[13]

Since the war began, the Israel Philharmonic Orchestra had been playing endlessly with Zubin and Barbirolli, including a dozen performances of Beethoven's Ninth. It had been on call continuously, playing at all military outposts and battlefields, and the inspiration for Bernstein's commemorative concert brought them all together again with a renewed freshness and joy.[14] In February 1968, Zubin was presented the State of Israel Freedom Medal at a reception in Henry Mancini's home in recognition of his 'demonstration of friendship for the people of Israel' during the Israel-Arab hostilities.

The orchestra also played at the ancient Roman amphitheatre in Caesarea, which was one of the biggest ports in ancient times. Zubin says that they performed many unforgettable concerts and operas in this amphitheatre built by Herod the Great. The production of *Fidelio* was particularly impressive since the Roman theatre is suited to the dungeon scene like no other.

## A WEDDING

In the middle of all the confusion, Barenboim and Du Pré set a date for their wedding. In 1970, Du Pré told *Time* magazine about how she first met him at a party in London in 1966. 'Instead of saying "Good evening,"' she recalled, 'we sat down and played Brahms.'[15] The first thing he and Du Pré had in common was glandular fever and they used to call each other up and compare swellings. They finally met at the home of Fou Ts'song, the Chinese pianist who was married to Menuhin's daughter. 'When I met him,' Du Pré said, 'I was huge; I weighed 180 pounds and I felt like a great lump. We were all drinking coffee when this dynamic small thing burst into the room. Being a very shy and somewhat insecure person at that time, the only thing I could do was get up and play.'[16]

Two weeks later, Barenboim decided that he wanted to marry the twenty-one-year-old big, tall girl with blue eyes, a broad forehead and long, wavy, fair hair, who was already Britain's leading cellist. He tried to rearrange his performance schedule and when that was not possible, ran up astronomical telephone bills as he conducted a courtship across two continents. In the spring of 1967, they announced their engagement, with a marriage planned for the following September—the earliest that their respective schedules would allow. However, when the war broke out, 'Pear Tree' (Barenboim's nickname, since Barenboim is the Yiddish version of Birnbaum or pear tree) and 'Smiley' (Du Pré's name given to her by Barenboim since she smiled so much) cancelled their previous engagements and hastened to play for the troops in Israel.

Du Pré was born in Oxford and, like Barenboim, grew up in a musical household: her mother was a musician, conductor and composer at the Royal Academy. Her father, an accountant, used to play the piano accordion but with no great distinction. She started playing the cello from the age of five, when she received the instrument as a birthday gift after she evinced interest in it on hearing a radio programme called 'Children's Hour'. In London, her principal teacher was William Pleeth, but she also worked with Tortelier in Paris and Rostropovich in Moscow. Barenboim says that she had a gift for making one feel that she was actually composing the music as she played. There was a feeling of pure abandon when she played. She never knew what it was to have technical difficulties, or what it meant to play safe.[17]

Du Pré had decided to convert to Judaism. In fact, she said she had wanted to be Jewish since she was a child. As music was her life and 90 per cent of musicians were Jewish, she felt that Israel was the right time and place to set about the conversion. She read material, passed oral exams and was given a Hebrew name as part of the process. Her conversion had to be thoroughly orthodox for any offspring from the marriage to be considered Jewish.

Zubin recalls that only orthodox Jews could witness the marriage. Since he was determined to be a part of his best friend's wedding, they all gladly connived in the fiction that he was Moshe Cohen, a Persian Jew who had just immigrated. Thus it was that 'Moshe Cohen' found himself holding one of the poles of the chuppah, the wedding canopy, at the ceremony on 15 June. The officiating rabbi became suspicious because Zubin did not speak Hebrew. Never short of chutzpah, Zubin explained: 'I'm a Persian Jew, and we don't speak Hebrew.'

Among the guests at the wedding were Ben-Gurion and his wife. Ben-Gurion had heard Barenboim play in the early 1950s and was keen that he should change to a Hebrew name. He tried to persuade Barenboim's parents to change to the Hebrew Agassi, meaning pear. The suggestion was met with little enthusiasm and Ben-Gurion joked that it would be better to make the change before Barenboim became famous because the name Agassi would be easier to remember and even had an Italian ring to it. (It is just as well that Barenboim did not make the change or else he might have been mistaken for a tennis player: Andre Agassi.)

While Ben-Gurion did not really care for music he was a

great admirer of Du Pré. He was also quick to realize the political significance of an English girl, and a Gentile at that, who had converted to Judaism when the country was at war. 'She became a sort of symbol in Israel and Ben-Gurion was very aware of that,' said Barenboim.[18]

After the other guests had chanted Hasidic songs for the couple, Zubin sang themes from Dvořák's Cello Concerto and Beethoven's *Hammerklavier* Sonata with Hebrew inflections. Later, Zubin told the rabbi they were old Persian Jewish hymns.[19] Zubin gifted Du Pré a fur hat to match the mink coat her husband had given her. After the ceremony, they had lunch together at the restaurant of the King David Hotel.

The courtship and marriage quickly captured the fancy of the music world and the public. It marked the beginning of one of the most remarkable relationships that music has known since the days of Clara and Robert Schumann. The 'musical romance of the century' as it was dubbed, received more than its share of media attention. Singly they drew crowds; together, as the Barenboims, they packed halls. The attention outstripped that which the close-knit group called the Kosher Nostra got. Apart from the Barenboims, the others in this group were Zukerman (Pinky) and his wife, Genie; Perlman and his wife, Toby; Vladimir (Vova) Ashkenazy; Stern and of course Zubin. They met four or five times a year to play chamber music. 'We are more than friends,' remarked Zubin. 'If there could be something like a family outside a family, that's what we have.'[20]

That night they appeared in Tel Aviv with the Israel Philharmonic. The bride played the Schumann Cello Concerto conducted by the groom. Barenboim then played a Mozart concerto conducted by Zubin. As Du Pré told an interviewer a few years later, 'So you see it was a conversion, a wedding, a rehearsal, a concert and a party—all in one day.'[21] The Israel Philharmonic Orchestra was planning a goodwill tour to the United States and Canada to raise funds for the new nation's depleted treasury, and they wanted Zubin, Barenboim and Du Pré to kick off the tour in New York with a repeat performance of the victory concert. Calls were also being made to other conductors and soloists who might volunteer their services.

## ON TOUR

The three of them flew to New York from where the tour was to start. There, Zubin's interview with a reporter from Pittsburgh led to some very amusing scenes. The reporter had some questions for Barenboim, and since Barenboim thought that his suite was a little crowded, he requested Zubin for the use of his for the interview. The reporter showed up at Zubin's suite and began to speak before Zubin could tell him who he was. He obviously thought that he was speaking to Barenboim, and Zubin—who is partial to practical jokes—decided to play along. The subreption was easily accomplished since he knew enough about Barenboim's life and career to easily answer any question put to him.

When Du Pré entered the room and was about to apologize for Barenboim's late arrival, Zubin promptly made her a partner in the fun. She played along, even holding Zubin's hand as they spoke about their recent marriage and their musical careers. When Barenboim arrived, he caught on almost immediately and went along with the joke, watching Zubin's sterling performance with increasing mirth. Zubin then introduced Barenboim as himself and the unsuspecting and somewhat star-struck reporter faithfully noted everything 'Zubin' had to say. The joke lasted until the moment Barenboim walked on to the stage in Pittsburgh (this time as his real self).

The Israel Philharmonic Orchestra played twenty concerts in fifteen cities in the United States and Canada, with a number of famous conductors and soloists volunteering their services to raise money for the Israel Emergency Fund. They included Arrau, Heifetz, Menuhin, Perlman, Leon Fleisher, Serkin, André Watts, Robert Merrill and Ormandy among others. It is fair to say that without Zubin, Barenboim and Du Pré, the tour would not have been possible at that scale, nor would it have met with the success it did.

Wolfgang Levy, horn player and acting manager of the orchestra at the time, said that the four-week tour beginning at the end of July 1967 was organized in just three weeks and came as a surprise to the musicians who were preparing to leave for their vacation. But when the opportunity came to serve their country, they simply could not say no. 'Technically we were all mobilized but we remained as a musical unit because the government considered the activities of the orchestra as important as military activities,' Levy said. According to him the victory concert conducted by Zubin was the orchestra's most stirring experience. 'There was an enthusiasm as I have never witnessed in my life,' he said, recalling the ovation from government officials, Israeli troops and the residents of Jerusalem.[22]

The orchestra's main support in the United States came from the American-Israel Cultural Foundation of which violinist Stern was president. Music is one of the most active spiritual forces in Israel, as important to its daily life as food and shelter. Stern narrated a story to illustrate how the public regarded the Philharmonic. In 1948, Jerusalem had been cut off from the rest of Israel for three weeks until an Israeli column broke through with a convoy of supplies. When the people were asked what else they needed, they replied, 'Send us our Philharmonic.'[23]

♫

Zubin, within a decade of finishing his conservatory training, pushed so far ahead that Ormandy remarked, 'In spite of his youth, he has very much arrived. I consider him the finest of the young conductors.'[24] Zubin's success at so young an age illustrated the striking departure from the pattern of a generation ago when conductors rose through an arduous apprenticeship with provincial orchestras, making it to the international arena only in their forties and fifties. The aeroplane also catapulted careers into the global orbit and made possible widespread guest conducting which spanned continents. Zubin became a jet-age conductor who hopped between continents when just in his twenties. Conducting, it appeared, was increasingly becoming a field for younger, more vibrant men (inspired no doubt by Bernstein, whose projection and box-office appeal made him the model for conductors of his era). Among the younger conductors, Zubin was seen to have something of Bernstein's forceful personality—dashing, vigorous and glamorous—even as he eschewed the latter's choreographic antics on the podium.

An idea of just how busy Zubin was can be had from his booking for 1968: Twenty-two weeks with the Los Angeles Philharmonic, three operas at the Met, one opera on Italian television, five recording sessions, and guest appearances at five festivals with five other orchestras. Some older observers viewed this torrent of activities with disquiet. Karajan, warning the younger lot against moving too precipitately for their own good, remarked that they had jumped from elementary school to university without going to high school, hinting that at some point the gap in musical experience would show. But Zubin had already done enough to silence the doubting voices of tradition.[25]

Barenboim said that for him Zubin was the first and best example of someone who had 'internationalized' music. Before the Second World War, it was generally accepted that German musicians played German music, French musicians played French music and the Italians played Puccini and Verdi. And then suddenly, a Parsi from India who had happened to study in Vienna came to be identified with Western classical music. Eclectic in his choice of music, as much at home with Wagner and Strauss as with Puccini and Verdi, to say nothing of his vast symphonic repertoire, there was barely any area of music he was unfamiliar with. Zubin in this sense, says Barenboim, became a role model for many younger conductors of later generations. He also credits Zubin with getting him interested in a great deal of music which he did not know, especially opera, and Strauss and Bruckner. He recalls a headline of a review after Zubin had conducted Bruckner's Ninth Symphony with the Vienna Philharmonic in Linz in the 1960s: 'From Bombay to Linz Is Not So Far.'[26]

Zubin was not the only star in the conducting firmament at that time. Among the young talent, there was a crack cadre of gifted conductors in their thirties and forties, all of whom lived up to their early promise in their riper years: Bernard Haitink, André Previn, Schippers, Colin Davis, István Kertész, Boulez, Maazel, Ozawa and Abbado.

# A Busy Conductor

AFTER THE NORTH AMERICAN tour with Barenboim and Du Pré, Zubin returned to Los Angeles for a series of concerts at the Hollywood Bowl, which would serve as practice sessions for the international concerts the Los Angeles Philharmonic would be undertaking from mid-September. The whirlwind tour of 1967, which was to include forty-one concerts in nine weeks, would take the Los Angeles Philharmonic to Belgium, Luxemburg, Germany, Austria, Yugoslavia, Romania, Hungary, Turkey, Greece, Cyprus, Italy and France with concerts in Iran and India rounding it off. This would be Zubin's first visit to India since 1954 when he left. As it was being sponsored by the American State Department, it was fittingly, if somewhat unimaginatively, called the 'State Department Tour'. It has been Zubin's longest tour till date. There is now an unwritten rule (with the Israel Philharmonic Orchestra) that they will not do tours longer than five weeks at a time. The orchestra members don't want to tour for longer because their spouses don't like it.

## TAKING THE WORLD BY STORM

Zubin joined the orchestra for the start of the tour in Antwerp. He had flown in from Kenya where he had accompanied his friends Ted and Jarma Bensinger on a shooting safari. As there was a gap of about ten days between the Hollywood Bowl concerts and the commencement of the tour, he had accepted the invitation which saw him bring down four animals, including a zebra, a Grant's gazelle, an antelope and an impala.[1] Zubin told me that he went on a tiger hunt outside Nagpur in 1968. He did not, however, bag a trophy, and became an avowed supporter of the anti-hunting movement soon after. (The Mehta property in Florence is home to a large number of wild boars; Nancy has put up signs prohibiting hunting on the premises.)

The programmes consisted of Barber's *Medea's Meditation and Dance of Vengeance*, Beethoven's *Eroica* Symphony, Bruckner's Seventh Symphony, Dvořák's Eighth Symphony, William Kraft's Concerto for Percussion, Mahler's First Symphony, the Mussorgsky/Ravel *Pictures at an Exhibition* and Richard Strauss's *Ein Heldenleben*. The soloist for the piano concertos by Brahms and Liszt was to be Watts.

Zubin and the orchestra received a fabulous reception wherever they went. In Belgrade, they played four encores. This was despite the slight unpleasantness that had resulted from a television crew setting up a glaring light without consulting the orchestra. Zubin refused to go on stage and the programme was delayed by twenty minutes. In Bucharest, Zubin and his orchestra had competition. Kirill Kondrashin had brought his Moscow Philharmonic, one of Europe's best, to play in the triennial Georges Enescu Festival. But Zubin and his parvenu Los Angeles Philharmonic need not have worried. The Romanians disliked the Russians far too much to bother about attending the concert. The concerts of the two orchestras were scheduled only twenty-four hours apart, and the two Los Angeles Philharmonic concerts that preceded the Russians' not only swept the box office clean of tickets but also created a thriving black market. At one concert 600 crashers forced their way in.

The Angelenos were greeted with cheers, flowers and demands for encores. The Romanians rushed to the stage to hug and kiss Zubin and the musicians at the end of the concert. The next night when the Russians played, a near empty hall greeted them, with the crowd dwindling further after the intermission. It was not that conductor

Kondrashin had given a poor concert: it was just that Zubin's performance, along with the Watts rendition of the Liszt concerto, was a hard act to follow. (To think that the festival officials had even asked Zubin to remove the scheduled Tchaikovsky Fourth from his programme 'because Russian music belonged to Russian orchestras'!) However, Zubin had no problems with Kondrashin and the two joked and discussed politics together. Kondrashin was generous enough to tell Zubin after the Californians' debut: 'Maestro, it was beautiful.'[2]

Concerts followed in Istanbul (where the President of Turkey fell asleep during *Pictures at an Exhibition* but awoke to present Zubin with a Golden Palm award); Athens (where the Queen Mother, a devoted Indophile, prepared some Indian curries for Zubin) and Cyprus. From Cyprus, Zubin flew to Paris to meet French actor-director Jean-Louis Barrault with whom he would be conducting a new production of *Carmen* at the Met the next season. After Paris, Zubin flew to Rome to meet a United States Information Agency crew from California who wanted footage of him conducting in Tehran and India.

The concerts in Tehran in the middle of Coronation Week marked the opening of a newly built opera house. Zubin decided to play a Persian composition that was well received. The unnerving things, however, were the encores. Iranian protocol demanded that when the Shah left, everybody left. So when after only one encore the Shah and his Queen left, the entire audience also started to file out. But the Queen came back and the people took their seats again. Then the Queen left and the Shah returned. After the fourth encore the royal couple left, and so did Zubin.

### *Homecoming*

The next stop on the itinerary in November 1967 was a special one: Bombay. A lot had happened in the intervening thirteen years and Zubin was now an international celebrity. The hero's welcome he received reflected this, with all the Parsis claiming him as their own. Hoardings all over the city welcomed him and the orchestra.

He was welcomed by Mrs H.P. Mody, wife of industrialist Sir Homi Mody, who put a tika on his forehead. He met Prime Minister Indira Gandhi and other Indian notables. (Thanks to the airline losing his luggage, he was forced to meet the prime minister in the casual attire he had worn on the plane.) Tehmina had flown in from the United States and several relatives were also present. Missing were Mehli and Zarin. Zubin says that Mehli felt so strongly about leaving India that he just couldn't make the trip back. In 1972 Mehli told *Los Angeles Times*: 'I am not an Indian in any sense of the word now, except for my passport. One of these days I'll study up and go to city hall and become an American citizen. I have nothing to do with India any more.'[3] It was obvious that the rancour of having been ignored and unappreciated remained. Zarin, too, took a long time to visit the country of his birth.

Zubin had, in his words, come to 'make music' but for Bombay it became the cultural event of the year. At the old Shanmukhananda Hall, Bombay's Western classical music cognoscenti were treated for the first time to live performances of Strauss's *Ein Heldenleben* and Mahler's First Symphony. Added to this was the fact that it was the very first time that they saw Zubin conducting. Zubin recalls, 'After the rambunctious welcome, I went alone for a walk on the streets where I grew up, and I felt as if I had never left.'[4] The die-hard cricket fan that Zubin is, he had gone to Brabourne Stadium to watch a match before the performance and made it back in the nick of time. He changed into his tails only during the interval. The atmosphere was all the more festive because it coincided with Diwali and Zubin recalls that they could hear firecrackers all through Mahler's First.

Zubin also found the time to visit his old home at 21, Cuffe Parade. Jal Billimoria, who stayed there and whose family had been landlord to the Mehtas, pointed to the long, narrow garden beneath the window and reminded Zubin of how his cricket shots had broken the windows of his car three days in a row.[5] Silloo Billimoria, Jal's sister-in-law, now ninety-four, recalled vividly how Tehmina would come to apologize for the damage inflicted by her son. 'It doesn't matter whose children break the glass. We are all one big family,' Silloo told her. They remained in touch after the Mehtas emigrated and Silloo received long letters from Tehmina, many of which contained a description of Zubin's growing list of achievements and accolades.[6]

Zubin's celebrity status had not gone to his head. Hamied says that he did not go to meet him since he was unsure how Zubin would respond. He need not have worried. Zubin was the one who called, inquiring why he had not come to see him. Hamied and his wife then went to meet Zubin at the Rajput suite of the Taj Mahal hotel where he normally stays when he visits the city. It was the same old unassuming Zubin. Hamied admitted that meeting Zubin was difficult. This is not surprising since he gives about 150 concerts a year, and way back in 2001, had given concert dates till 2009! Still, they kept in touch on the phone and fixed dates in advance so that Hamied could co-ordinate his trips with Zubin's concerts. It was also on this trip that he met Nusli Wadia for the first time, and it was the start of a long friendship. The Mehtas and the Wadias (Nusli and his wife, Maureen) remain fast friends.

On their return, Zubin and the orchestra were received by a welcoming party of friends and family, including Mehli. The 122 musicians had travelled some 20,000 miles and given forty-one concerts in twenty-three major cities of Europe and Asia.

In December 1967, Zubin was featured on the *Bell Telephone Hour*'s examination of the impact of Indian culture on Western music. They invaded the Music Center to film Zubin rehearsing, eating, talking to the camera and playing a concert. They also visited Tehmina and Mehli's Los Angeles home. The highlights included Zubin guest conducting the Rome Opera Orchestra and conducting at Los Angeles' Music Center. While some saw the Ed Spiegel documentary as 'essentially an hour of adulation', it did introduce the mass audiences to a man in the news in the world of music. At thirty-one, Zubin brought to the podium 'the undeniable vigor of rugged youth and a chemistry of commanding virility'.[7] But more international publicity was in store for him. In January 1968, *Time* magazine put Zubin on its cover. It was an extraordinary feat for a conductor of any age, let alone one who was only thirty-one.

## ROCK CONCERT FIASCOS

As conductor of the Los Angeles Philharmonic, Zubin earned a reputation for doing the unconventional; rushing in, as *Time* magazine described it, 'where many Angelenos fear to tread' and also 'getting away with it musically'. In April 1968, at a regular concert of the Los Angeles Philharmonic, Zubin showed the audience motion pictures while following the score of *Contextures*, a new multimedia orchestral work which he commissioned from Kraft, who also happened to be his principal timpanist.

Zubin tried two experiments, mixing the classics with rock music. Both generated much controversy, bringing the odium of the musical literati on Zubin. The first, in March 1970, was an NBC television special called *The Switched On Symphony* in which Zubin and the Los Angeles Philharmonic appeared with such rock performers as The Who and Jethro Tull, and soul singer Ray Charles. The aim was ostensibly to show the connection between rock music and the classics.

A more practical aim was to enthuse the younger generations to take to classical music by associating rock with orchestras. That this was attempted by trying to forge a non-existent link between the two did not particularly worry anyone. It did not really fool anyone, however. An observation in the *New York Times* provides a flavour of what the critics thought about it. 'Maestro Mehta insisted on viewing this silly piece of camp as a vital link joining the world of the symphony with that of the rockers. What absurdities men are persuaded to utter on television!'[8]

The second experiment, and one in which Zubin broke new ground, was when he collaborated with the American composer, guitarist, singer and director Frank Zappa in May 1970. It was a decision he would regret. Throughout the autumn of 1969, Zappa had been finishing an orchestral piece and in the spring he finally heard it performed. He met Zubin at KPFA-FM during a radio interview and mentioned it. Zubin was impressed by his knowledge of the music of Edgar Varese and Stravinsky. Zappa told him that he would go to libraries when on tour and look through their scores. Zubin was too busy to read what Zappa had given him but his orchestra manager liked the score and persuaded him to read it.

After three months of talks, it was announced that on 15 May 1970, Zappa's *200 Motels* written for his band, The Mothers of Invention, and the orchestra would be performed in concert with the Los Angeles Philharmonic at Pauley Pavilion, University of California, conducted by Zubin. It was to be part of 'Contempo '70–20th Century Music', a series of four concerts of twentieth-century music with Zubin conducting the first three and Boulez the final one. Fleischmann and Zubin had been stressing the need for a wider variety of contemporary orchestral music performances in Los Angeles. Zappa's inclusion was part of a broader effort to expose the orchestra and its audiences to the most vital trends in the music of the day. But both Zubin and Fleischmann were clear that this was not another attempt to wed symphonic music to rock.[9]

In the first half, Zubin conducted Varese and Stravinsky and in the second, *200 Motels*. Zappa's *200 Motels* required the musicians to perform, to put it mildly, in an unconventional way. Attired in yellow-striped pants, a ponytailed Zappa prefaced the performance with a short speech and then turned to Zubin and said, 'All right, Zubin, hit it.'[10] The players were required to snort, grunt and throw confetti; the bass horn player had to twirl like a drunken elephant and at one point the entire 104-member orchestra stood up and walked into the audience, improvising their own music. The players had to do fey finger snaps over their heads and also belch (literally). Percussionist Kraft, dutifully following the score, fired a popgun as the Mothers, on a platform six feet above the orchestra, performed some of their greatest hits.[11] Zappa used the occasion for a parody of Jim Morrison's stage act, reworking Morrison's 'The End' with its theme of incest and patricide.

Zubin, despite his remark about how 'most rock groups could not do this sort of thing because they cannot read music', was pretty disgusted with the goings-on and, despite Zappa's protests, cut out the entire second part of *200 Motels*. This was just as well because part two called for a chorus to blow bubbles through straws and the soprano soloist to sing 'Munchkins get me hot'. Zubin may just have forgotten that he was teaming up with a man whose main goal in life was to zap the musical establishment. All that the concert before 11,000 rock fans at the basketball arena proved was that any marriage between rock and classical music was likely to be a mismatch. As the Mothers' bassist Jeff Simmons remarked on the orchestra: 'Those dudes are really out of it, man. It's like working with people from another planet.'[12] No doubt the orchestra players must have felt the same way. There were no complaints from the management of the Los Angeles Philharmonic, though, which was happy with the $33,000 the box office brought in. Zappa wanted to record the concert but the union insisted on the Los Angeles Philharmonic being paid full-scale even if the recording was not released, which, for ninety-six players, was just too much. They tried to sell it to the networks but without success.

Zubin described in strong language the piece Zappa composed: 'It was the worst piece of music I have ever heard. But I'd given him my word, so we performed it. During the concert we were playing on two levels: his band would strike up something and keep quiet, and then we would strike up; it was really most boring. But when we were playing he would attract the audience with the most vulgar gyrations on stage. I really got very upset by the end of the concert. And I never spoke to him again.' Zubin says it was his curiosity that made him do it. It was also consciously done to entice young people.[13] When Zubin left the Los Angeles Philharmonic in 1978 to assume the music directorship of the New York Philharmonic, *Time* magazine referred to this unfortunate experiment. 'In his sixteen-year tenure there, Mehta made a few memorable mistakes, one an embarrassing rock-classical concert.' When I asked him about the collaboration, he said, 'It was not a happy one. I never saw him again.'[14]

In a reference to this performance, the Frank Zappa song 'Billy the Mountain' includes a character who 'some folks say he looked like Zubin Mehta'. Zubin's other pop culture reference is that of the Muppet, Zubin Beckmesser. The second part of the name (Beckmesser) is a character from Wagner's opera *The Mastersingers of Nuremberg*. The Muppet Beckmesser is a conductor who gets electrocuted when he absent-mindedly inserts his baton into an electrical outlet. According to doctors, he would have died instantly had he not been such a poor conductor!

## MORE MUSIC AND SOME CONTROVERSY

In October 1970, Zubin led the Los Angeles Philharmonic in a concert to celebrate the twenty-fifth anniversary of the founding of the United Nations at New York. There is a story behind this performance. Zubin discovered that the hall where he was supposed to conduct was unavailable for practice sessions since President Richard Nixon was slated to give his speech there. At a dinner before the performance, Zubin took the opportunity to bring this fact to Nixon's notice. Nixon was most cooperative and asked Henry Kissinger to postpone his speech and ensure that the hall was put at Zubin's disposal. Kissinger, Zubin recalls, was 'more than angry' and told Zubin that he did not appreciate what he had done.

Nixon's speech was postponed, but Kissinger had his revenge. He changed the venue of Nixon's address to the heads of state to Washington. As a result, only undersecretaries and other administrative staff of various countries were present at Zubin's concert. Indira Gandhi wrote to him later saying that she would have loved to attend his concert but was unavoidably detained. Zubin and Kissinger eventually made up and were able to laugh at the incident in later years.

Speaking his mind publicly is a well-known trait of Zubin's as is his inability to resist a smart one-liner. In 1976, the Los Angeles Philharmonic and Zubin were to tour Eastern Europe (including the Soviet Union), coinciding with the bicentenary celebrations of the founding of the United States. A Russian official came to Los Angeles to discuss the details with them. On first being introduced to Vladimir Golovin, then deputy director of Gosconcert, the state concert agency of the Soviet Union, Zubin beamed mischievously and said, 'In the name of Israel, I want to thank you for sending us so much talent.' Blood draining from his face, Golovin politely held his tongue.[15] Zubin narrates this in his autobiography where he tells us that Golovin (he does not name him, though) pretended he could not understand and then just stopped talking. The next day, a furious Golovin called Fleischmann and said that the orchestra could perform in the Soviet Union but not under 'this Mehta'. Fleischmann politely told him that it was either the full package (with Zubin leading the orchestra) or nothing at all. The USSR part of the tour was cancelled, and later Zubin came to know that Golovin was a prominent KGB man.

In November 1977, Zubin took part in another musical experiment. He played excerpts from English composer Gustav Holst's orchestral suite *The Planets* and Richard Strauss's *Thus Spake Zarathustra*, better known as the theme from *2001: A Space Odyssey* with the Los Angeles Philharmonic in 'Music from Outer Space—a Star Wars Concert' at the Hollywood Bowl. He also led the orchestra in music from the films *Star Wars* and *Close Encounters of the Third Kind*. For special effects, each instrument's stand in the orchestra had been hooked up to a microphone controlled by sound engineers, and stabbing rays of laser light began criss-crossing the bowl. As the music varied in intensity, the shape of the laser beams changed.

The 17,500-strong crowd erupted in uncontrolled frenzy and gave Zubin a nine-minute ovation. The success of the concert prompted Decca/London to make a crash recording of the *Star Wars* and *Close Encounters* suites that were soon at the top of the charts. Zubin told *Time* magazine: 'This was an adventure. I wouldn't do a Beethoven symphony this way, but surely other music could be enhanced with electronics.' Though many thought that such experiments largely resulted from Zubin's insatiable musical curiosity, it was not generally known that it was the irrepressible Fleischmann who encouraged and promoted some of the more unconventional performances associated with Zubin, the *Star Wars* concert being one of the best known. Fleischmann came up with the *Stars Wars* concert when the orchestra had to vacate the Dorothy Chandler Pavilion for the Academy Awards ceremony. It started a trend and such concerts began to be held all over America, and then the world. That event kicked off the kind of movie-score concerts that are popular even today.[16]

There may have been another reason for Zubin's frequent experimentation: the need to find ways of bringing the younger generation to concerts and opera halls, where the audience is getting progressively older. Zubin feels it is the duty of music directors and managers to think about ways of rekindling public interest so that this wonderful legacy is successfully passed on to future generations. Zubin makes this very clear in his memoirs:

> This is why I believe that we should allow a lot of innovation or 'gimmicks' so that people are enticed to attend concerts and operas. Ceremonious solemnity alone is not enough to win over the younger generation. The valuable musical heritage that we are responsible for merits careful consideration. We simply have to come up with new ways of awakening our interest in classical music.[17]

# 'I Do'

WHILE ZUBIN'S CONDUCTING CAREER seemed unstoppable, his marriage had not been a success. Even though Carmen and he divorced in 1964, the cracks were apparent if one read between the lines of an interview Carmen gave to *Los Angeles Times* in January 1962: 'He just lives . . . lives for his work.' Carmen could not recount a schedule for their life. 'You see, we haven't had a chance to develop a routine. It's like following an orchestral score. It depends on the music.' With a touch of sadness in her voice, she also said: 'I don't like the separations from Zubin but they are inevitable . . . He works and lives at such a high pitch, I just feel exhausted for a week after he goes.'[1]

As noted before, when Carmen and Zubin returned to Montreal from Russia in 1962, he began divorce proceedings. The immediate provocation appears to have been the soprano Stratas. 'It just happened.' Carmen said, 'I never did anything nasty to him, and he never did anything nasty to me.' There was a separation, a Mexican divorce, followed by an annulment in Ottawa. There was no rancour in the break-up, no pettiness. Carmen said that she always thought of him as a musician and not as her former husband. He was, above all, Zubin the conductor.

By 1964 the divorce was complete. After his divorce, Zubin led the life of a bachelor once again and appears to have had a pretty busy life as far as women were concerned. It seemed he always had a pretty girl in tow. The image of 'playboy conductor' grew, thanks in no small measure to his most trenchant critic, Bernheimer of *Los Angeles Times*. But he never made false promises to his numerous conquests who offered little resistance to the combination of good looks and musical deification. Women found his tousled hair, piercing eyes and magnetic personality difficult to resist. Alexandra, his daughter, was born in Los Angeles in 1967, the offspring of an affair Zubin had between his marriages. (Zubin has also fathered a son, Ori, now in his twenties, who was the result of a casual liaison in Israel after he had married Nancy. He has completed his army training and now studies in an agricultural college in Rehovot.)

## 'BABY CALLAS'

Zubin's affair with Stratas which started on their trip with the Montreal Symphony Orchestra to Russia was the final straw for Zubin's marriage. Stratas[2] who was called 'Baby Callas' (a reference to her diminutive physical stature) is today regarded as one of the foremost talents of the last century. She was a 'lirico spinto', a soprano whose range encompassed the light and the dramatic. The affair was serious enough for marriage to be discussed and the couple was engaged to be wed. Zubin told a newspaper in February 1965 that he planned to marry the soprano 'next summer'.[3] Speaking to *Los Angeles Times* from Montreal, Zubin said that no date had been fixed for the wedding because 'we are both professionals and neither of us can be at our beck and call'.[4]

But things started to sour after the initial infatuation. Both were devoted to their careers and one of them would have to give it up. It was not going to be Zubin. And, as Zubin discovered, it was not going to be Stratas either. She told the press that Zubin had asked her to give up singing. 'I just couldn't see myself going through life as Mrs Conductor,' she said.[5] They split sometime in 1967. When I asked Zubin about the relationship, he said, 'She didn't want to marry. I was in Los Angeles and she was at the Metropolitan in New York.'[6] Stratas continued with her highly successful career but ended up as a recluse. (In the 1980s, Stratas travelled to Calcutta and worked with

Mother Teresa. In the 1990s she cared for sick and dying orphans in a hospital in Romania.)

## 'THE CHILDREN HAVEN'T CALLED ME UNCLE'

After the divorce, Zubin asked Zarin, who had by then immigrated to Montreal via England, to look in on Carmen and the children whenever he could. Zarin did look in occasionally, and then more often. In 1966 Zubin, who was rehearsing the Israel Philharmonic in Haifa, suddenly announced that he wanted to dedicate the concert to his brother, who was 'getting married to a very nice girl'. When asked to whom, Zubin replied, 'To my former wife.' Zarin had moved to Montreal just as Zubin's marriage was in the final stages of dissolution. Carmen showed Zarin around Montreal and he escorted her to the company box at the Montreal Symphony concerts. They were soon married and, a year later, they had Rohanna, their first child. Rustom was born a year later.

The situation was a little odd at first but things soon settled down. They were one big happy family. 'At first, my mother thought it was incest, but I explained it to her,' he once said.[7] One of Zubin's favourite lines was: 'I must remember that my ex-wife is now my sister-in-law. But so far, the children haven't called me uncle.'[8] Many years later, Mervon told an interviewer: 'After my parents divorced, my mother married Zarin. It was like *Hamlet,* only no one got killed. I adored my uncle so it didn't feel strange when he moved in.' When Silloo Billimoria asked Tehmina if they did not find the situation a little odd, she said, 'We were always very fond of her and are very glad that she will remain in the family.'[9]

Zubin says that he was grateful to Carmen for not having married a stranger and to his brother for bringing up his (Zubin's) children the way he has. Zarin became a partner in Coopers and Lybrand and later became vice president of the Montreal Symphony board of directors. He went on to become the president and executive director of the New York Philharmonic till his retirement in 2012. Carmen became one of Montreal's best known voice instructors.

## MEETING NANCY

In the autumn of 1968, Zubin was invited to a dinner party by Vincente Minnelli (father of Liza Minnelli) and his then wife, Denise. At the party he met an actress, Nancy Kovack, daughter of a Polish-born mother and a Czech immigrant father. A liberal arts graduate from the University of Michigan, radio deejay and winner of beauty pageants, Nancy had auditioned for TV comedy giant Jackie Gleason and was selected out of 1567 hopefuls as one of the Glee Girls. Her selection has an amusing story connected with it. A hundred of these girls were re-auditioned and Nancy was not chosen. In what proved to be a master stroke, Nancy went to the back of the line and, this time, she was selected! Nancy said she was the only girl Gleason did not know at the time. After her first appearance as a Glee Girl, she featured more prominently in *The Dave Garroway Show, The Today Show* and *Beat the Clock*.

While shooting for TV shows during the day and doing a Broadway show at night, she was spotted by a Columbia Pictures executive in Broadway and signed a five-year Hollywood contract. Nancy, a brunette, had to turn blonde when she played Annie Oakley and has since remained so. She appeared in twelve films, including *Strangers When We Meet* (1960), *The Wild Westerners* (1962), *Jason and the Argonauts* (1963), *The Great Sioux Massacre* (1965) and *Frankie and Johnny* (1966) which starred Elvis Presley as a riverboat singer with a weakness for gambling. She later became a star on television as well, and her most famous roles were as Sheila Sommers in the smash hit *Bewitched* and Nona in *Star Trek*. Her final film role was in *Marooned* where she played an astronaut's wife. Gregory Peck also starred in the film.

While shooting for Columbia in a lonely region in South Italy, Nancy read an article on Iran in a magazine. From then on, she developed a fascination for Iran and everything Persian. She had a strong desire to travel to that country at least once. In 1965, her dream came true when she received an offer to shoot for a film in Iran. After 100 episodes of a TV series and an Emmy nomination, she left

California to go to Iran. She even hired a teacher to learn Farsi. She was to spend a good deal of time in Iran—a total of nearly three years.

Soon after, Nancy was invited to a Thanksgiving dinner by the American embassy in Afghanistan. On the plane, she read about Zubin in the *Time* magazine issue which had him on the cover. She was a little put off by the man in the article and decided that she would have nothing to do with him. It was this bias which made her turn down Denise and Vincente Minnelli's invitation to the opening night of the Los Angeles Philharmonic and a pasta party afterwards, once she knew that she would be meeting Zubin. Finally, she accepted a dinner invitation in November 1968 to The Bistro, where Zubin was placed in front of her intentionally.

At the dinner Nancy and Zubin got talking about Iran. Zubin's own experience and knowledge about the country was restricted to his attendance of the crowning of the Shah of Iran. In contrast, Nancy had lived in Iran for a few years and was far more knowledgeable about the place. Zubin made a few observations on how many Iranians could not read the ancient Kufic inscriptions on the mosque's dome. He also aired his views on the language and other aspects of Iran in general. Nancy opposed most of his views as she knew Iran much better than Zubin did. She has written about this first meeting in Zubin's autobiography. She says that even though Zubin's impressions were those of a single day, he seemed to have a decided opinion on everything. Their first meeting ended when Zubin got up and headed for the airport, en route to New York to conduct at the Met.

Zubin called Nancy after a month and the subject of the Kufic inscriptions was resumed. There was, of course, also an invitation to meet again. This was the beginning of their romance. Zubin invited Nancy to one of his concerts in Los Angeles, where she remembers discovering on this first date that she shared Zubin's addiction for orange juice, later learning that he didn't drink either. It soon became obvious to Nancy that Zubin was interested in her and the two became involved in a long-distance courtship conducted over the telephone. Nancy recalls that his telephone bills during that period were between $5000 and $7000 each month, an astronomical sum of money at the time. (Zubin has thought nothing of spending absurd sums on telephone bills. He ran up bills of $1500 a month just to keep in touch with distant friends. Sleepless in New York City at 5 a.m., a day before New Year's, he suddenly realized that in Vienna, where it was 11 a.m., the Vienna Philharmonic would be playing one of its traditional New Year's Johann Strauss concerts. Zubin put in a call to the concert hall, had the manager hold the phone up to a backstage loudspeaker for a while, and then dozed off.)

## EXCHANGING VOWS

In early April 1969, Mehli, who was recovering from his second heart attack in Los Angeles, received a phone call from Zubin asking his permission to marry Nancy. Father and son had always been close and the fact that Zubin, at thirty-three, and a celebrity to boot, asked for permission only reflects this closeness. Mehli gave his assent and the date was set for 19 July 1969, the first date that was free in Zubin's calendar.

There were two ceremonies slated for the same day. The first, to which only about 100 guests comprising family and friends were invited, was an early afternoon ceremony in Westwood Methodist Church. It was performed by the Rev. F. Harold Essert, associate minister. Waiting at the altar with Zubin was Barenboim, who served as best man. The couple, who repeated vows in a traditional double ring ceremony, exchanged simple gold wedding bands. Among the guests were the Minnellis whose perseverance had culminated in a wedding.[10] (Nancy is an ardent and devoted Christian Scientist. Zubin is not, and neither is he a practising Zoroastrian. He does not wear the sacred *sudreh* and *kusti* worn by Parsis. But he did act in a docudrama on his religious faith and its roots in 1985, as we shall see in a later chapter.)

The second ceremony which took place four hours later at the Bel Air Hotel was a Zoroastrian ceremony witnessed by nearly 300 people. Officiating at the wedding was Framroze A. Bode, a Parsi priest who the papers reported had also presided over Mehli and Tehmina's nuptials. Writing about the two ceremonies, Nancy has observed, 'I do not recommend two weddings in one day.'[11] Zubin and Nancy then flew to Hawaii for a short honeymoon; Zubin of course, took his scores along to study.

## THE *TROUT*

After their honeymoon Zubin and Nancy flew to London. Zubin was to participate in a concert of Schubert's *Trout* Quintet as a bass player. Playing with him would be Barenboim (piano), Du Pré (cello), and the violinists Zukerman (viola) and Perlman (violin), all of whom were good friends and who were known affectionately as the 'musical mafia'. The concert had been put together by Barenboim who had been invited to organize the South Bank Summer Music Festival by the Greater London Council, a festival mainly devoted to chamber music.

At that time the famous promenade concerts at the Royal Albert Hall were already in existence but the Festival Hall and the Queen Elizabeth Hall were unused in summer. Barenboim was engaged to fill this gap and the concerts took place under his direction from 1968–70. What made the festival unique was that it was mostly chamber music with young artistes keen to work with one another. There was an unmistakable freshness of approach and the programmes and artistes were chosen by Barenboim with these qualities in mind. The spirit of the whole festival was epitomized by the *Trout*, a piano quintet in A minor written by Schubert in 1819.

Zubin recalls the concert at Queen Elizabeth Hall in August 1969 which was part of the second season of the South Bank Summer Music Festival, and which ultimately became the famous film *The Trout* by Nupen. Zubin told me that after the interval he conducted Schoenberg's *Pierrot Lunaire* which is a combination of spoken text and instrumental accompaniment. Actress Vanessa Redgrave read the poems in English before the performance. Not only was the entire concert filmed by using a special kind of camera that worked soundlessly but Nupen filmed the five of them from the time of their first rehearsal till they left the stage after their performance. In fact, there were shots of them arriving at the airport as well. What emerged was a rare documentary and Zubin says that they all enjoyed the experience thoroughly. The film, now considered a classic, was telecast countless times, distributed on video, and is now on DVD. It is also extremely popular on YouTube.

After their wedding, they made their home in a charming little cottage in Bel Air. In 1974 they bought a house in the Brentwood area west of Beverly Hills, once the home of actor Steve McQueen. Now married to Zubin for nearly forty-seven years, Nancy says that she has never involved herself in nor interfered with Zubin's professional life. His musical decisions are not within her purview and she sees her role as one of protecting their private life and keeping their relationship alive. She says that the continuous travelling which she does with Zubin has taken a lot out of her.

Nancy has made many sacrifices for the marriage to work. It became obvious from the beginning that if she were to work, there would be no marriage. Zubin was on tour for nine months of the year and their time alone together was between 1 a.m. and 2 a.m. where they continued a long-running backgammon game in bed. Nancy told an interviewer nine years after marriage, 'I don't know of one exception in my business. Did you ever hear of Mrs Toscanini or Mrs Barbirolli?' She also proceeded to justify Zubin's absorption with himself and his music saying that great people in any field are 'basically self-oriented'.

As for the extent of music in her life, she observed: 'I would never have expected or desired to have this much of anything. It is all-consuming. We see only musicians and people connected with music. In the nine years we've been married, we've had maybe five evenings that were not musically connected.' She added later, 'I can't think of a way this life isn't a sacrifice. It is total sacrifice.'[12] She realized that music for Zubin was his life. 'But it has been very important not to try and change him, because that's a comment that there is something wrong. And a person who has reached our age and continues at this pace must love it. We are both here because we choose to be.'[13] In Zubin's memoirs, she wrote, 'It takes uninterrupted attention to protect our personal time. Basically it's difficult to describe a life determined by other people.'[14]

The two have no children of their own but Nancy and Zubin support Darla Motley and her two children (without formally adopting) and this has given them great joy. The marriage has not been without its ups and downs—no marriage is—and there have been rumours from time to time about strains in the relationship. Possibly one of the toughest periods came in the 1990s, coinciding with the case of embezzlement the Mehtas brought against Nancy's former bookkeeper and assistant Susan McDougal. Nancy ran a lucrative rental business in California. The Mehtas had acquired five properties in Brentwood and Malibu and rented them for up to $16,000 a month to tenants who included Hollywood actors Tom Hanks and Marsha Mason, and media mogul Ted Field. In 1991, it was estimated that the properties generated more than $3,00,000 a year. Nancy ran the business out of their Brentwood home. Since she travelled a lot with Zubin she had trouble keeping up with the accounts and decided to take an assistant. The first was Pat Harris (in 1988), and then McDougal in 1989, who worked with Nancy until 1992.[15]

In 1993, Nancy accused McDougal of embezzling some $1,50,000 during her employment from 1989–92, allegedly using her credit cards and cheques for travel, clothing and other luxuries. The case which went to court turned a little ugly and ended with McDougal being acquitted in November 1998. Nearly a year after her acquittal, McDougal sued the Mehtas for malicious prosecution, slander and libel. The case was ultimately settled out of court.

# The Israel Philharmonic Orchestra

THE ISRAEL PHILHARMONIC ORCHESTRA accepted advice and assistance from many famous conductors but did not officially tie itself to any single music director. After Zubin's first visit in 1961, his name too was added to this illustrious list. In fact, it was decided that the orchestra would invite Zubin to conduct every year till both their fiftieth birthdays. Both orchestra and conductor were twenty-five at the time. The friendship between Zubin and the orchestra grew through the early and mid-1960s but it was only when Zubin flew to be with the Israel Philharmonic during the Six-Day War that the musicians realized just how much he cared for them. The following year, in September 1968, the musicians voted to appoint a music director (he was called 'adviser' as the contract in Los Angeles did not allow him to take up the music directorship of any other orchestra) for the first time in the orchestra's history and offered the job to Zubin.

The Israel Philharmonic Orchestra, as we have noted earlier, is a self-governing cooperative and the players have a say in programme content, artistes, salaries, marketing, administration and fundraising. After Zubin's second visit in 1963, when he impressed the players by conducting Bruckner's Ninth from memory, the entire orchestra wanted him as music director. Orchestra manager Haftel was set on getting him to Israel from the start and flew to the United States when the contract was being prepared to ensure that Zubin could hold both positions. Since the Los Angeles contract was an exclusive one, Zubin became 'artistic adviser'.

After 1963, it became obvious that Zubin could build the orchestra. There were other conductors of course, but he was young and had the energy to do it. In those days there were no young people in the orchestra but Zubin got on very well with all the players. The audience and the orchestra loved him. And Zubin knew what he wanted: good players with a strong self-identity who were willing to give up that identity for the orchestra's benefit. More importantly, he always 'kept his ears open to constructive criticism'. Zubin treated his musicians as colleagues and human beings, unlike other conductors who thought of them as mere music-making machines. His closest friends in those days were Haftel, Uri Töplitz (principal flute) and concertmasters Josef Kaminski and Chaim Taub.

Zubin became the lord of two castles ever since he assumed the music directorship of both the Montreal Symphony Orchestra and the Los Angeles Philharmonic. Zubin was given a free hand in all matters by the Los Angeles management; in return, all they asked was to have Zubin exclusively for themselves. The Montreal orchestra, with its small budget and short season, was no threat and the management did not object to Zubin's activities in Montreal. In any case, he was there first. But the Israel Philharmonic Orchestra was a different matter. John Connell, one of the trustees of the Michael J. Connell Foundation, was against it. But they had not reckoned with Zubin's strong affinity for the Israel Philharmonic and Israel. After a great deal of arguing, the Los Angeles management overruled Connell and allowed Zubin to accept the Israel Philharmonic offer. Connell later remarked that he was sorry he didn't make a bigger issue out of it.

Unlike Los Angeles, Zubin found that the Israel orchestra suffered from a lack of financial support. There were competing claims on the finances of the government: the Jerusalem Symphony Orchestra, the Batsheva Dance Company and the Habima Theatre Company, to name a few. After becoming music adviser, Zubin made some important contributions to the Israel Philharmonic Orchestra. The percussion section which had been weak was strengthened; the brass too was considerably tightened, and the strings became uniformly good (previously the lower strings had been seen to be a little weak).

More importantly, it was at his insistence that the wages of the players were raised: 'Believe it or not the Israel Philharmonic used to be in the black. But the players were getting $300 and $400 a month. The orchestra was losing musicians to symphonies in other countries. I said we had to raise salaries if we wanted to keep building the orchestra.'[1] When asked, Zubin did not comment on his own remuneration but with his constant international phone calls to Tel Aviv to discuss plans and programmes, many felt that he spent more on the orchestra than what he earned from it.

Zubin also took steps to introduce contemporary music to Israeli audiences whose musical tastes favoured the lush and the familiar. The orchestra didn't play contemporary music because the audience didn't like it. And the audience never had a chance to like it because the orchestra never played it. Zubin's solution to this vicious cycle was the Musica Viva, a series of instructional programmes outside the regular season to expose the audiences to contemporary music. These achieved limited success and were allowed to die a natural death owing to poor response and financial constraints. Till today, Zubin tries to stage a premiere of an indigenous composer or a contemporary work, guided by his belief that it is the responsibility of a conductor to also perform something apart from the well-known classics which, in any case, most music lovers possess as CDs.

## MISCHIEF IN MUSIC

Zubin's wit and prankish ways are well known in the music world. There are countless anecdotes to show that the Bombay-born Parsi also has a Jewish sense of humour. There is the story of a young Zubin's tour to Vienna with the Israel Philharmonic in 1968, where his orchestra was to play under both his baton and that of the legendary Krips. The night after Zubin's concert—a triumph—he took his musicians out to Grinzing on the outskirts of Vienna famous for its sparkling wine. It was 3 a.m. when the very happy, if not completely inebriated musicians, reached their hotel. Only half turned up at next morning's rehearsal with Krips and, when they all finally assembled, they played terribly. A visibly upset Krips wanted to know what was happening. When he was told about the previous night's outing, he fumed with a heavy German accent, '*Das ist sabotage*,' and left the stage. The orchestra had a difficult time convincing him to return.[2] In the end, the orchestra overcame its collective hangover and performed well enough to keep its and Zubin's reputation intact.

There is also the tale of a particular concert on Purim (a Jewish holiday that commemorates the deliverance of the Jewish people of ancient Persia), in which the orchestra's concertmaster Uri Pianka was to play Tchaikovsky's Violin Concerto. The night of the concert, according to former principal French horn player Mishori, Zubin had the orchestra play the beginning of the Mendelssohn Violin Concerto instead. The surprised soloist did his best to join in, until Zubin stopped the music and told the audience, 'That was a Purim prank. Now we will play Tchaikovsky.'[3] Zubin also likes to imitate other people on the phone (mimicking in any one of seven languages) and once threw an entire hotel into chaos during a concert tour by sneaking around the corridors early in the morning and changing all the breakfast orders. Once, on leaving a concert hall in a Communist country, he incited a host of fans in a dark alley to 'Revolt.'

Perhaps the funniest moment came on one of his tours of Japan with the Los Angeles Philharmonic. He was so amused by the natives' confusion over the letter 'L' that he changed the billboards to 'Ros Angeres Phirharmonic'. After one concert, the Japanese manager of the hall came and said, 'Please play an encore because the whorehouse is shouting.' The side-splitting laughter which followed ensured that there was no encore.[4]

Mishori, who joined the Israel Philharmonic in 1965, reveals insider stories—moments that form the essence of the ensemble's orchestral lore—in his book *Smiles, Pranks and Coughs of the Israel Philharmonic Orchestra*. He narrates an incident when the orchestra had some fun at Zubin's expense. In the old Mann Auditorium, the front of the stage had an elevator that descended into the basement and was used for raising and lowering a piano. On one occasion, the orchestra decided to have some fun at the expense of Zubin and the two concertmasters. The conductor's podium and the two chairs of the violinists were placed on the part of the stage which normally had the piano. They agreed that when Zubin conducted Johann Strauss's *Perpetuum Mobile*, the stage manager would lower the elevator. As Zubin played this fast and merry piece, he and the two leading violinists appeared to be swallowed by the earth. The audience joined the orchestra in the ensuing mirth and the piece was concluded with the conductor 'buried' in the basement. Zubin took it all sportingly. In fact, he was so amused by the prank that he asked for it to be repeated on other occasions.[5]

Another incident which inadvertently resulted in amusement was when the soprano Jessye Norman came to Israel. After her arias from Georges Bizet's *Carmen* and Camille Saint-Saëns's *Samson et Delilah*, it was only natural that the audience would clamour for an encore. Zubin knew that she had performed a 'spiritual' without an accompanist as an encore in one of the concerts with the New York Philharmonic, and reminded her about it. She also thought it a good idea but ended up singing 'Were you there when they crucified my Lord' before an audience of a few thousand Jews. Nobody took offence and Norman said that it was the only thing that came to her mind at that moment.[6]

## HISTORIC CONCERTS

Zubin has been part of and witnessed milestones in not only Israel's orchestral, but also Jewish, history. It was Zubin who conducted the Israel Philharmonic Orchestra in its first concert in Berlin in 1971 after a lively debate and vote by the ensemble. Zubin recalls that only two of the 115 musicians in the orchestra refused to play—a personal decision which Zubin respected. It was the opening of the Berlin Festival and the concert, given only metres away from the ruin of the Reichstag, consisted of pieces by Mahler and Mendelssohn. Dietrich Fischer-Dieskau sang Mahler's *Kindertotenlieder* in a moving performance. He was familiar with the Israeli orchestra since he visited Israel often. After *Kindertotenlieder*, they played Mahler's First Symphony to a standing ovation and Barenboim played Beethoven's *Emperor* Concerto.

As an encore, the orchestra played the Jewish anthem *Hatikva* which most people in the audience did not know. Zubin says that he decided this at short notice. He recalls, 'If we had played it at the beginning of the concert, we would have had to play the German anthem, and we were not going to do that. So we played it as an encore. It was very emotional. In the audience, they were crying.' Mishori, while remembering the event, said that it felt like revenge. 'We, the members of the Israel Philharmonic, who are survivors of European anti-Semitism, playing so close to the Reichstag, playing pieces by Jewish composers and our national anthem—who would have thought that twenty-five years earlier?' The two conductors who most left their stamp on the orchestra are Bernstein and Zubin. Mishori said that Bernstein who was involved with the orchestra since its inception was like Moses, and Zubin who has led the orchestra to so many victories, like Joshua.

It was the Berlin concert that Zubin mentioned when in 1996 the *New York Times* asked him about his most memorable performance. 'Sometimes you remember a concert because you've finally achieved what you've dreamed of with a particular work, and sometimes it is because of the occasion.' Zubin says that he still gets goose pimples when he remembers the *Hatikva* they played as an encore. The Israel Philharmonic's first tour of Germany also took them to Bonn where they were chaperoned by Johannes Wasmuth, the famous impresario who had turned the Rolandseck railway station outside Bonn into a Mecca for chamber musicians. Members of the Israel Philharmonic later performed there on several occasions. The orchestra also received an invitation in 1971 to participate in the festival concerts in Salzburg for the first time. It was the beginning of a long series of guest performances with acclaimed soloists, including Zukerman, Perlman and Maxim Vengerov.

Then there was the Israel Philharmonic Orchestra's concert under Zubin during the Yom Kippur War of October 1973. Zubin was already in Israel when the war broke out and, with Stern and

Barenboim, he took the orchestra to military outposts on both fronts. Danny Kaye, an old friend of Zubin's, put in an unexpected appearance. Zubin had been leading concerts every night since the third day of the war. One concert in Jerusalem had to be cancelled because of an electricity blackout. To make up for lost time, there were as many as three concerts on each of the holidays of Sukkot and Simchat Torah, with proceeds benefiting the soldiers' welfare fund. The orchestra had lost 'five or six' players in the call-up. Zubin recalled that the assistant first bassoon was a tank commander and they were all praying that he would come back. The orchestra also played one programme at an air force base in the north. The commander of the base had apologized in advance for the noise made by the Phantoms and Mirages taking off and landing during the concert.[7]

Zubin related an anecdote about the time when he had crossed the border into Syria with an NBC crew, some 10 km from the front line. They encountered a troop carrier with a tired Israeli officer, and Zubin asked him if he could bring him some water. He refused the offer but, in reply, said: 'What you can tell me is why you changed the programme last week at Binyanei Ha'Ooma (the Jerusalem International Convention Centre).'[8]

It was déjà vu for Zubin and Barenboim with one big difference—Du Pré was absent. She was suffering from multiple sclerosis, that incurable degenerative disease of neural deterioration, to which she ultimately succumbed in 1987. When Barenboim was first told that his wife had been diagnosed with multiple sclerosis, he did not know what it implied. Neither did Zubin, who phoned a doctor friend to enlighten them. Barenboim put his head next to Zubin's so that he could hear what was being said. Both were devastated by what they heard. Zubin recalls, 'It was over the telephone, from a doctor he didn't even know, that my friend learned that his wife was crippled with a deadly nerve disease. We cried there together.' Aghast sadness followed this levelling discovery. The best medical advice on two continents brought no cheer. There was nothing anybody could do to arrest the progression of the disease. New living quarters were found in London with the help of Margot Fonteyn, whose husband was a paraplegic. Du Pré progressed enough under therapy and expert medical care to a point when, in the autumn of 1977, she started teaching.

In the summer of 1977, when there was a slight thaw in relations, Zubin took the Israel Philharmonic Orchestra to the Good Fence at the Israel–Lebanon border, conducting a concert for an audience of Christian Arabs and Jews, some of whom attended in their uniforms. Zubin became friendly with a Lebanese army captain who had been assigned to liaise with the orchestra. Their friendship made headlines but with disastrous consequences for the army captain. A few weeks later, Zubin received the news that he had been killed by the Palestine Liberation Organization who had branded him a 'traitor' and a 'collaborator with the Zionists'.

The Israel Philharmonic Orchestra has also contributed at each anniversary of the Jewish nation by playing a musical tribute suitable for the occasion. One such memorable concert was held at the Sultan's Pool, the square between Old and New Jerusalem, in 1978, on the thirtieth anniversary of Israel's founding. It was Kollek's idea to organize the concert at this historic site and it inspired world-class soloists to perform there: Price, Rostropovich, Jean-Pierre Rampal and Stern.

Zubin and the Israel Philharmonic have performed across Israel, in halls and auditoria of a poor standard both acoustically and aesthetically, without complaint. The entire orchestra travels by bus to the south and north of the country and brings music to people who travel long distances to hear them play. 'We have been in regions where a big philharmonic orchestra normally does not stray,' says Zubin. As an example, he cites the concert held in January 1982 at the border of Israel and Lebanon in the middle of a tobacco field. It was arranged by Zvi Bar, the commander of the border police, and a close friend and keen music lover. He had erected a temporary stage surrounded with the army's sunblock shields. They played light music (what Zubin calls 'lollipops') to entertain the audience which consisted primarily of Lebanese people sitting in the open. After the concert, they came and embraced the members of the orchestra. In June of the same year, Zubin even went all the way to Beirut with Bar and with Vidal Sassoon and Rafi Eitan (who had arrested Nazi criminal Adolf Eichmann from Buenos Aires).

## AMERICAN FRIENDS OF THE ISRAEL PHILHARMONIC ORCHESTRA

In October 1981, Eban and Zubin invited a select group of people to an evening of music to benefit the Endowment Fund of the Israel Philharmonic Orchestra. It was sometime in 1980 that Fredric Mann and Zubin got the idea of setting up an endowment for the Israel Philharmonic, the American Friends of the Israel Philharmonic Orchestra (AFIPO), something which was necessitated by the lack of substantial Israeli government subsidy, and to ensure the future of the orchestra they both loved so much. Mann and James D. Wolfensohn, who later became president of the World Bank, were the first major contributors.

Mann wrote a letter in May 1982 to the AFIPO, where he said that he was enormously pleased that Zubin Mehta had joined their effort as honorary chairman of the American Friends. Twenty-five years ago, his name and talent were known only to a select few but today, Mann said, he was one of the towering figures on the world music scene. Zubin was not a 'fair-weather' friend of the orchestra and had stood with it—and in front of it—in good times and bad, always providing the inspired musical leadership without which no combination of musicians could ever be called an orchestra. Noting that the orchestra had recently elected him music director for life, thereby guaranteeing a long association, he raised the question of the fate of the ensemble. 'Will it continue to be one of the great symphony orchestras of the world? Will it become even greater? Our new Endowment Fund can provide an answer. It can be the cornerstone for years of growth and development for a unique institution. Once again, the Israel Philharmonic's future is in our hands.'

Since 1981, contributions from thousands in the United States and Canada have generated millions of dollars, helping to secure the orchestra's financial future while providing general operating support. Americans with ties to Israel have recognized the importance of the Israel Philharmonic Orchestra as the foremost cultural representative of an embattled nation and have proved to be the institution's most committed constituency over the years. Numerous events, concerts and fundraisers have contributed to the resources of the fund. The American Friends travel to all parts of the world to hear Zubin and the orchestra make music.

## THE CASE FOR RICHARD WAGNER

Zubin is an outspoken person who speaks his mind freely on any subject. His very vocal advocacy of performing Wagner's music is therefore hardly surprising. In the 1960s, there was a public debate in which Gideon Hausner (the main prosecutor in the trial of Nazi criminal Eichmann) and Zubin held two contrary points of view. There is no official ban on playing Wagner in Israel but, unofficially, his music is anathema to a certain part of the Israeli population that has suffered the horrors of the Holocaust. The Wagner question was not simply an academic one: the composer was not only an anti-Semite but was also idolized by Hitler. He wrote a treatise called *Jewry in Music* which espoused anti-Semitic postures, and survivors of concentration camps said his music was often played there. However, the fact that Wagner's music transcends time and space has escaped many of the old guard. The fact that art can be separated from its creator, however evil he may be, has thus far not convinced the Holocaust survivors in Israel. Nor have they been persuaded by the argument that censorship and artistic suppression, regardless of the source, are dangerously myopic.

Zubin was one of the first to bring up this sensitive subject when, in June 1974, he expressed his intent to conduct the Israel Philharmonic Orchestra in a programme of music by Wagner. The concert was cancelled at the last minute in keeping with the unofficial ban on music by the Romantic genius who had been idolized by the Nazis. The last time a Wagner programme had been allowed on Israeli soil was in

April 1938, when Toscanini conducted what was then the Palestine Philharmonic. Another Wagner programme had been scheduled for 12 November 1938, but conductor Eugen Schenker decided to delete the Overture to Wagner's opera *Lohengrin* as a protest against the infamous German rampage against Jews called Kristallnacht (the Night of Broken Glass) that had occurred three days earlier.

On 15 October 1981, Zubin broke the unwritten taboo and conducted Wagner's 'Prelude' and 'Liebestod' from *Tristan und Isolde* as an encore. There was chaos but Zubin didn't stop the concert. He knew that the powerful crescendo of the 'Prelude' would drown out the commotion. He says that the pianissimo of the 'Liebestod' completely calmed everyone and the performance ended in triumph.

Zubin had told the audience beforehand that he intended to play Wagner so that those who found it offensive could leave. Nobody left. The next night, an organized group of protestors prevented a repetition. Zubin says they conducted a poll among their subscribers and 86 per cent voted for playing Wagner. However, he respects the need to be sensitive to the issue as Holocaust survivors with numbers tattooed on their arms, who are considered holy in Israel, are still alive. The matter generated much passion and public discussion. Zubin was accused of being insensitive and callous. He recalls how a traffic policeman who had stopped him for jumping a red light in the wee hours of the morning gave him a tongue-lashing on the subject. He, however, did not give him a traffic ticket.[9]

Zubin observed: 'Only afterwards did I understand that it was too soon to play Wagner in Israel. I understood that I had offended people. I was not unaware of the fact that there are too many people with a number tattooed on their arms, survivors of the concentration camps, who love hearing classical music. Some of them have no problem driving a Mercedes, but Wagner takes them back to the time of the Holocaust.'[10] Zubin explained that he acted out of his love for Wagner's music. If Zubin the musical idealist came out a loser in this confrontation, he did manage to spark a debate on the question of music as an extension of politics. Israeli politician Dov Shilansky, a Holocaust survivor himself, was so incensed that he suggested that

Zubin 'go home'. Zubin, ever the man of spontaneous phrase, riposted with, 'But I am home. So where is he telling me to go? Home is everywhere. America, Israel and India.'[11] The then prime minister, Menachem Begin, attempted to apply salve to Zubin's wounds. He dismissed Shilansky's comments and praised Zubin as 'a great maestro and friend of Israel'.[12] When Zubin received the Israel Prize in 1991 (the only non-Israeli to receive the prize), Shilansky, whom Zubin does not name but calls a 'notorious politician' in his autobiography, was also present. Zubin says that they did not even look at each other, to say nothing of shaking hands.[13] When I asked Zubin about it, he recalled Shilansky saying, 'We have done enough for Mr Mehta and his career.'[14]

Avi Shoshani, the secretary general of the Israel Philharmonic Orchestra, said, 'After meeting with Holocaust survivors, we understood that as long as there are survivors around, we will not play Wagner. Yet, we play composers like Richard Strauss and Carl Orff. But it is Wagner who has become a symbol of a nightmare. And music is about human beings, about being a mensch.'[15] But Zubin believes that not playing Wagner is a hole in their musical experience. 'Wagner was a musical revolutionary who started an entire world. For my orchestra to not play Wagner is a tragedy. It is like for a pianist not to play Chopin. We play the music of Wagner's children—all the composers who carried on this tradition. Wagner is Queen Victoria. She has children all over Europe: [Edvard] Grieg, Mahler, Bruckner and Schoenberg. One day we have to play the trunk of the tree, the fruits of which we enjoy all the time.'[16]

Zubin had been asked to 'go home', wherever that meant; the orchestra thumbed its nose at his detractors by asking him to stay forever. At the conclusion of a concert sometime after this episode, one of the representatives of the orchestra's governing board, Daniel Benyamini, the principal viola, invited Zubin to become music director for life. Zubin was delighted, and agreed. There is no formal lifetime contract. He says that every five or six years, he asks the orchestra if they still want him and so far the answer has always been in the affirmative. Zubin, who has developed a soul that is as Jewish as it is

Indian, and sprinkles his conversation with Yiddish, explained that his contract with the orchestra was a '*mazel* and a *brocha*—just a handshake'. Bernstein sent a telegram of support. There was also talk of inviting him to conduct music by Wagner to overcome Israeli resistance to the Nazis' favourite composer.

Ten years after Zubin's attempt to play Wagner, his good friend Barenboim also tried to break the five-decade-old ban. In December 1991, members of the Israel Philharmonic Orchestra voted by a large majority to set aside the unofficial ban and to hold a special event in Tel Aviv on 27 December 1991, featuring portions of *Tristan und Isolde*, *The Flying Dutchman* and other works by Wagner. The vote was thirty-nine to twelve, with nine abstentions. Barenboim, who was to lead the concert, had long argued that even though Wagner was a notorious anti-Semite, his music is a critical element in the repertory of any major orchestra. A week after its musicians voted to perform the concert, the orchestra decided to postpone the programme and ask its constituency of 36,000 subscribers if they agreed with ending the ban on Wagner. Finally, the orchestra decided against the concert.

Inevitably, there were arguments both for and against. Mishori cited the example of Richard Strauss who, as a Nazi sympathizer, had faced a similar ban for decades but whose music was now being played in Israel. There was no reason why this latitude could not be extended to Wagner, given the importance of his music. But Shilansky, now the Speaker of the Knesset, could not 'understand this pressure to play Wagner and thereby cause pain to people who have suffered more than a little'.[17] His feelings were echoed by Avraham Melamed, a violinist who as a teenager had survived the Transnistria camp in Ukraine. Melamed, an outspoken supporter of retaining the ban on Wagner, refused to play. He had been one of the musicians who had walked out when Zubin had tried to play Wagner as an encore in 1981.

Barenboim, who had urged that the ban be dropped, said he fully understood the agony felt by concentration camp survivors and, for that reason, had made it a special event and not part of the Philharmonic's subscription series. Those who felt that they could not stand Wagner's music could miss the concert, Barenboim said. But it had become a principle of democracy for him and he saw no reason why anybody should stop other people from artistic expression in a democratic society.

Anguished memories of the Nazi Holocaust came alive once more, and so did appeals for artistic freedom, as Israelis debated the decision. Hitler had ordered that Wagner operas be played at Nazi functions and Holocaust survivors have spoken of hearing Wagner's overtures played by Nazi camp commanders. Some Israeli critics said that the popular mood had changed and the emotions were not as raw as they were a decade ago. But the fact remains that Israel then had 3,00,000 concentration camp survivors, about 6 per cent of the population. Acceptance of Wagner's music has been growing, however. The Symphony of Rishon Lezion, a Tel Aviv suburb, was the first in Israel, to remove the ban in 1990 without repercussions. It was also pointed out that Israel's state-run radio played Wagner and television dramas used his works as background music. One can buy Wagner's music in Israel, watch videos of his works on television, and cellular phones even had the *Ride of the Valkyries* as a ringtone. Apart from Shilansky, the anti-Wagner ranks also had other powerful allies. They included former prime minister Begin, the directors of Yad Vashem, the Holocaust memorial in Jerusalem, and also American donors whose contributions were an important source of income for the Philharmonic.

The issues at stake are hardly clear-cut. Wagner's prejudice was shared by many intellectuals of his time and, in contrast to Richard Strauss who actually worked under the Nazi regime, Wagner died six years before Hitler was born. Nor was he responsible when his English daughter-in-law, Winifred, married the Bayreuth Festival to the Third Reich. While for some, Wagner's music still retains the full weight of Nazi aggression, others think that it is time to grant the composer his place in music history.

In fact, the point has often been made that without Wagner, the achievements of Mahler and Schoenberg, both Jews, become incomprehensible. The claim that Wagner was played in the background as Jews were led to the gas chambers is apparently an urban legend, though there are many who still believe its authenticity. On the other hand, sympathizers of the many Holocaust survivors feel that it is still too soon to abandon this particular symbol. But what many Israelis do not know is that Wagner was also a great favourite of Theodor Herzl, the founder of modern political Zionism who, more than many others, was responsible for the creation of Israel. Herzl attended numerous performances of Wagner's *Tannhäuser* at the Paris Opera when he was writing *Der Judenstaat*. He viewed this opera as a lesson in propaganda: how to manipulate people through art.

In January 1994, the Knesset's Education and Culture Committee, recognizing the supremacy of freedom of expression, said that it did not intend to intervene in artistic content and directed an emotional appeal to avoid playing Wagner if this hurt people's feelings. Thus while there is no official ban, orchestras that receive public financing are expected to refrain from playing Wagner. In June 1998, Israeli musicians and conductors told the committee that the time had come to lift the embargo on Wagner. One lawmaker spoke for many when he said that they should wait for the next generation for any change in the ban.

In July 2001, Barenboim led the Berlin Staatskapelle in a performance of music from Wagner's opera *Tristan und Isolde* as an encore at the Israel Festival, the country's most prestigious arts forum. The concert with the Staatskapelle took place in Jerusalem on 7 July, with a programme of music by Schumann and Stravinsky, and an encore by Tchaikovsky. Afterwards, Barenboim turned to the audience and proposed the 'Prelude' and 'Liebestod' from Wagner's *Tristan und Isolde* as a further encore. Since he did not want to play Wagner for an unprepared audience, he asked the audience if they wanted him to play it—a question that drew applause, angry shouts and a forty-minute debate. He performed the piece despite promising the festival management beforehand that he would not play Wagner. Some twenty or thirty people left but those who remained gave him a standing ovation. The protests that followed had nothing to do with those who had witnessed the performance. Barenboim noted in his autobiography, 'It was only the next day that the scandal really erupted, which means that it was organized by people . . . who had some political agenda, which greatly saddens me.'[18] 'I do not believe that someone who sits at home in Tel Aviv or Jerusalem suffers because he knows that in another city someone is playing Wagner,' he said.[19]

In 2011, the Israel Chamber Orchestra under conductor Roberto Paternostro played a piece by Wagner at the Bayreuth Festival for the first time. Even the rehearsals for this concert took place in Bayreuth. Zubin observed, 'I don't agree with that. I told the conductor, my friend Roberto Paternostro: "If you really want to play Wagner now at long last, which I wholeheartedly support, then play him in Israel. Don't do it secretly abroad." That seems sanctimonious to me.'[20]

While conceding the need for Israelis to have a sense of history, Barenboim says that a constant harking back to the Jewish identity of the 1930s and 1940s will not help them establish a fruitful dialogue with non-Jews. This is why he believes that there is a connection between Wagner and the relationship with Palestine. In fact, the aggressive posture adopted by some of the Holocaust survivors does not reflect the feelings of all of them, many of whom admired Wagner's music. The grieving memories will persist but the Israel Philharmonic hopes it will one day join the community of orchestras and play *Ride of the Valkyries*. The cumulative ripples caused by the pebbles thrown by the Mehtas and Barenboims of this world may eventually wash away the anti-Wagnerian shore. Till then the Holocaust survivors will continue to negotiate with a seventy-year-old memory without any pretence of definitive closure. Does Zubin think that he will be able to play Wagner in his lifetime? 'Perhaps I'll get to the age of 120, and then I'll be able to play Wagner in Tel Aviv,'[21] he told an interviewer in April 2015. When I asked him, he simply said, 'I'm still waiting.'[22]

Marck says that when they discussed performing Wagner in 2006, only four musicians wanted to play his music. He says, 'I don't think it is linked to the direct survivors of the Holocaust, I think that there will always be people who call themselves and think of themselves as "survivors". The Israel Philharmonic Orchestra will one day perform Wagner, and the sky will not fall, but in most likelihood it will be with an Israeli music director and the initiative will come from the orchestra.'[23] Marck's observation is ample testimony of how involved the members of the Israel Philharmonic are in all facets of music-making and in their orchestra. This is apparent not only with Zubin but also with all the other conductors and soloists of the ensemble.

Every musician in the Israel Philharmonic Orchestra wears several hats. Marck, the principal bass, is also the head of the players' committee, writes the blog for the orchestra on tour, serves on audition committees and edits material for the Jeans concerts. The second trombone is chairman of the management committee responsible for the livelihood of 150 families. The concertmaster plays in the Israel Philharmonic Orchestra's string quartet, sits in on all auditions and also has a solo career on the side. In Marck's words, 'The Israel Philharmonic invites involvement and that is a unique setting for making music.'[24]

# 'The Maestro of Our Hearts'

RALPH WALDO EMERSON ONCE said that an institution is the lengthened shadow of one man. The Israel Philharmonic Orchestra has a character that has been moulded by Zubin in the course of five decades. Over the years, the composition of the Israel Philharmonic, as well as its quality, government support and financial solvency have changed dramatically. The population of Israel has also changed over the years, with an influx from the erstwhile Soviet Union. While nobody knows the exact number of Russian musicians who have come to Israel in recent decades, there is some truth to the old joke about a plane-load of Russian immigrants, half of whom walked down the metal staircase carrying violins, while the other half were pianists.

Another joke was that the unofficial language of the strings section is Russian.[1] Shoshani says that the Israel Philharmonic Orchestra received a significant influx of Russian musicians starting in the 1970s and they quickly moved into key positions in the string section, paving the way for a steady stream of their countrymen over the next twenty years. At one point, Russian musicians held over half the string positions in the orchestra. The Russian immigration proved to be a twin blessing: it provided a large pool of talented players and, later, an enthusiastic and well-educated audience.[2]

Zubin tried hard to keep demographic trends from affecting aesthetic traditions. When he took over, it was still an orchestra of the

Hapsburg Empire. There were Poles, Hungarians and Austrians as well as Sabras—Israelis born in Israel. Most players spoke German. It then became an orchestra of the ex-Soviet bloc: Russians, Latvians and Lithuanians. Now the positions in the orchestra have been filled almost entirely by Israeli-born musicians returning after their studies in Europe and the United States, and many of the vacant positions in strings are exactly those which Russian immigrants filled in the 1970s. Today only a third of the orchestra is of Russian extraction and well over 60 per cent of the entire ensemble is born and trained in Israel.

Because their schooling was different, Zubin says, they were in a completely different world stylistically. His task was to maintain the Central European sound—the Viennese sound—that the strings had before. It was a constant effort to make them play mellow. It is ironic that Zubin was trying to preserve the sound of the same region that expelled the Israel Philharmonic Orchestra's founders. In fact, the ironies were numerous: a Parsi conductor born in Bombay, trained in Vienna, and now a resident of Los Angeles, Florence and Valencia, remarking on the diversity of a Jewish orchestra.

Zubin says that he inherited a Polish orchestra and converted it into a Russian one. In the 1960s, the Israel Philharmonic Orchestra was very much a Central European ensemble. In those days 20 per cent were Sabras and most were from Eastern Europe. They even have a musician from Kyrgyzstan. But since Zubin can't speak Russian, language is sometimes a barrier. He is certain that the Israel Philharmonic Orchestra today is a much stronger ensemble than what it was when he began his tenure. 'It used to be that the strings were great and the winds were second-rate. It is not the case any more. Now there are really no low points. The musicians are also much younger.' Marck says that one of the conditions of Zubin becoming music adviser and then music director was the 'final say' in the hiring of new players. By 2000, all the players in the orchestra were musicians hired by Zubin. He recalls how Zubin recently reminisced about the wonderful sound of the first violins when he first came to Tel Aviv and how it reminded him of Vienna, but how some of the other sections were terrible. Whichever orchestra Zubin has led, he has always ensured a vastly improved level of players by the time he left. Marck feels this is due to his conscientious hiring policies and his ability to see potential over long periods of time. 'Mistakes are sometimes made, but ultimately one can see an almost linear improvement over the years.'[3]

The jet age no longer knows the narrow identification of conductor and orchestra that produced, for example, the 'Philadelphia sound' widely admired during Ormandy's many decades with that orchestra. Yet those who know the Israel Philharmonic Orchestra immediately recognize a character that is distinctive. To most ears the Israel Philharmonic is a decidedly 'Western' orchestra; it has more in common with European and American ensembles than with their Russian counterparts.

Rockwell, writing in the *New York Times* in March 1991, said the Israel Philharmonic Orchestra sounded like a warm Central European ensemble without the flashy brilliance of the best American orchestras, but with considerable heart and soul. This, despite the fact that over the decades there were nearly forty musicians from the former Soviet Union. The distinctiveness is explained in part by the influence of Zubin and Bernstein, both of whom played a significant role in defining the character of the Israel Philharmonic Orchestra. We have already noted that with the Soviet immigration, there was an incredible cultural injection in the orchestra. They had to pass a difficult audition and the selection committee did not know who was playing because the musicians would be behind a curtain (so that personal bias and extra-musical criteria are kept out of the process of selection). Also, these musicians entered the orchestra one by one over a long period of time. It is not as if the Israel Philharmonic Orchestra absorbed thirty or forty Russians overnight. At rehearsals which were conducted almost entirely in English, one heard more Russian than Hebrew.

Zubin's association with the Israel Philharmonic Orchestra as music director is more than four decades old and the symbiosis between the two is stronger than ever. Zubin's English is peppered with Hebrew and Yiddish, and the food at orchestra outings with the hot chillies he is famously fond of. Among the musicians, the most frequently heard tribute is 'he is one of us'. And they don't mean that he is primus inter pares in an orchestra that is one of the few true cooperatives in the world of Western classical music. 'One of us' means: he is an Israeli.[4] Zubin has himself said, 'You do not know how many people call me "Rubin" because they are convinced I must be Jewish.'[5] (In 2005 the Israeli news website Ynet conducted a vote to determine whom the Israeli public considers the 200 greatest Israelis of all time. Zubin was ranked 117). 'He is not a guest or a visitor any more,' said Zeev Dorman. 'Ask any taxi driver in Israel who is Zubin Mehta and he will tell you.' Some writers have tried to explain Zubin's affection for Israel in terms of the shared experience of persecution among Parsis and Jews. Zubin denies this, saying that he does it because he likes Israel so much.

Zubin and the Israel Philharmonic Orchestra act as Israel's cultural ambassadors. Over the years, Zubin has used the orchestra in what might be called philharmonic diplomacy. He has taken the orchestra to India, China and Poland; it has been a window opener to many places where, politically, Israel was not welcome. And the orchestra is all too conscious of its diplomatic mission which in a sense started within a week of its existence, when it travelled to Cairo for concerts with Toscanini.

The Israel Philharmonic is a unique orchestra with almost all of its seventy-two original members being refugees from the Nazis. It has played through blackouts and air raids, in club rooms, in the world's famed concert halls and even in the Vatican for the Pope. Although the Israel Philharmonic dwells largely outside Israel's political sphere, the impact of daily events upon the life of the orchestra is inevitable. In late October 1994, twenty-three people were killed in the bombing of a bus near Mann Auditorium. In March 1996, a bomb exploded 500 metres from Mann Auditorium and the orchestra could not enter the building because the entire area was blocked. The orchestra was already rehearsing and heard sirens all morning. Bombings and violence affect morale but they realize that the peace process has to go forward despite difficulties.

But there are still bridges to be built. The bridge with the Arabs—that is one thing Zubin has not been able to build. In 1978, after the Camp David Accord, he asked Begin for permission to take the orchestra to Cairo as a gesture of goodwill. He was told, 'First I have to think of settlements.'[6] Zubin is still waiting for an Israeli government to send him and his orchestra to Egypt. But he has done his bit for Arab-Jew peace. He was instrumental in founding and finding funding for a Jewish-Arab educational programme in Israel. He supports the orchestra's Jewish-Arab ensemble where players of traditional Arab instruments join Israel Philharmonic soloists in concert.

Zubin has said, 'I can't wait to come here when I am away. I just feel at home here. I feel free with the orchestra. I have absolutely no nerves going in front of this orchestra. They are all home-picked people: how many musicians did I not engage myself? It is a family and of course as in any family there is sometimes tension.' The Israel Philharmonic Orchestra is famous for being argumentative. Bernstein was once quoted as saying that rehearsing the Israel Philharmonic was like negotiating in an oriental marketplace. There were conductors who wouldn't work with the Israel Philharmonic Orchestra because of their reputation for arguing. Szell, it is said, wanted to add a clause in his contract that if anybody talked during a rehearsal he would have to leave.[7] Is the orchestra a democracy or a dictatorship? Zubin says that when a soloist's opinion of how to play a piece matches his overall conception of the piece, he allows him freedom of interpretation. But with the tutti one cannot allow sixteen violins to do their own thing, so one has to be a little autocratic with the strings.

The players, argumentative, passionate and with ferocious loyalties, are not individuals who give up their personalities for the common good; they compete as well as egg one another on. 'This is not so much a collective of complaisant artists in a peaceable kingdom as a musical army on a mission.'[8] And many feel that Zubin is exactly what the orchestra needs. He gives them enough room to be their passionate selves when that is appropriate, but also knows how to marshal their forces and exploit their collective power.

Zubin says that unlike other orchestras where the musicians perform as if they are obeying orders, the Israelis enjoy themselves, playing with their heart, something which infects him as well. 'I have already come to terms with the endless arguments, especially since this is an Israeli phenomenon and not an orchestra one . . . I prefer to work in Israel because my conditions here are much more flexible. I don't work according to the clock and do not have to use a whip. I don't mind if the rehearsal begins ten minutes late, and they don't send the union secretary when the rehearsal runs ten minutes overtime.'[9] The cooperative structure of the orchestra, in which the players themselves are partners in the orchestra's management, contributes to the orchestra's flexibility. Mishori believes that without this structure, the body would fall apart. This motivates the players and gives them a sense of partnership.

In rehearsals, the conductor concentrates first on practical aspects: is the orchestra playing together, is it playing in time? In an orchestra like the Israel Philharmonic, 90 per cent can be taken for granted but they have to work on the remaining 10 per cent. Zubin calls his relationship with his orchestra a benevolent dictatorship. 'My position is to make the orchestra feel comfortable in interpreting my vision of the piece. The overall picture is mine. The details I leave very often to the individual musicians playing their little solos,' he says. Zubin also has a reputation as a shrewd talent scout, transforming the Israel Philharmonic Orchestra, known primarily for its violins, into a well-balanced group. As of today, Zubin has hired every single member of the orchestra.

Zubin has the ability to immerse himself in the music intensely and tell the musicians a great deal about how he wants it played. Haftel, who was chief concertmaster of the Israel Philharmonic, said, 'He is more than just a gifted conductor. To change from Bruckner, which he conducts like a saint or an Indian priest, to Webern, and then to Stravinsky with a burning fire and conviction—and transmit it to the orchestra—that is genius.' Zubin does not take liberties with the score. But he does believe that despite the composer's instructions, there is something called reading between the notes. A conductor's reading of a piece also changes over time.

## MUSIC WITHOUT BOUNDARIES

Zubin has conducted more than 3500 concerts with the Israel Philharmonic Orchestra and led the musicians on tour around the world. Some of the highlights of these concerts over the years appear in the following account. Zubin is known to use the force of music to heal wounds and deploy the orchestra in philharmonic diplomacy. In November 1987, the Israel Philharmonic's first trip to Poland helped the cause of reconciliation between Poles and Jews. Zubin noted that many of the musicians were children of Polish Jews.

### *Masada*

In October 1988, Zubin conducted the Israel Philharmonic to close the fortieth anniversary celebrations of Israel's founding. The hosts for the evening were Gregory Peck and Yves Montand, both friends of Zubin, and the setting was the rock fortress of Masada, the last holdout of the Jewish zealots against the Roman legions, which finally fell in AD73 after a seven-year siege. The 960 defenders committed suicide, preferring death to slavery. Today, Masada has become a symbol of resistance to the bitter end and is a revered shrine of modern-day Israel. Bar mitzvahs and army induction ceremonies take place regularly and mass suicide is seen as the epitome of Jewish courage when facing the enemy. Zubin played Mahler's Second Symphony (*Resurrection*) in the desert fortress. Hundreds of choir members were led by soloists Florence Quiver (mezzo-soprano) and Sylvia Greenberg (soprano). The eighty-minute symphony is physically exhausting for the conductor and musicians but Zubin, whom Shimon Peres had called the 'maestro of our hearts', conducted passionately and got a standing ovation. As the music soared, lights played on Masada and flares were launched at especially dramatic moments. At the end of the symphony, a fireworks and laser show lit up the sky.[10]

The symbolic setting had its share of technical challenges since Masada is in the middle of the Judean desert. The stage and acoustic shell were built just for this one evening and dismantled after the concert.[11]

The climax of the evening was a telephone link between Masada and Leningrad. A young violinist in the orchestra, Anna Rosnovsky, had not seen her sister Lena Kuskuna for fourteen years. Kuskuna had been refused an exit visa and, with her son being drafted into the Soviet army soon, any chance of getting one would disappear since he would be privy to state secrets, the favourite excuse for denying exit visas. The two spoke in Russian and then switched to English. It did have a practical use as well. The Soviet authorities who had listened to this conversation ensured that Kuskuna and her son were given a visa and they reached Israel in fifteen days.[12]

### *Historic Tour of the Soviet Union*

In April 1990, Zubin proved that music knows no boundaries when he took the Israel Philharmonic Orchestra on its first tour of Moscow, Riga and Leningrad despite the absence of diplomatic ties with the Soviet Union over the 1967 Arab–Israeli war. Zubin said, 'You know we can't change boundaries. Musicians can't talk about that. But we can make people smile at each other and today, God knows, that is important. Since nearly one-fourth of the musicians are former Soviet citizens—a quarter of the orchestra won't need interpreters. That gives the Russians something to think about.'[13] At the final concert of this tour, Perlman played Tchaikovsky's Violin Concerto in the same Concert Hall where the Russian composer had conducted its first performance 150 years ago. During this time Perlman filmed 'Perlman in Russia', depicting the Israel Philharmonic Orchestra's historic trip and, in 1992, the PBS documentary of this tour won an Emmy Award for best music documentary.

### *The Gulf War*

In January 1991 when the Gulf War broke out, Zubin was in Austria conducting the Vienna Philharmonic. He then drove to Munich from where he caught a flight to Paris. There, he was to board the Concorde and return to New York where he was music director of the New

York Philharmonic, a story which is told in a later chapter. In Paris, he changed his plans and headed for Tel Aviv since he felt that it was not possible for him to be anywhere else but Israel at such a time. He was replaced by his assistant in New York, Samuel Wong. Zubin cancelled his performances with the New York Philharmonic, giving no date for his return. This did not go down well with Nancy who was of the opinion that her husband should not try to play the hero.[14] Zubin went up and down the busy Dizengoff Street in Tel Aviv with Mayor Shlomo Lahat to build confidence in the people. But there was reason to fear since Saddam Hussein's scud missiles were aimed at Israel and no one knew their target or level of precision.[15]

In February 1991, minutes before the deadline for leaving Kuwait, Saddam's forces fired a scud missile at Israel. When the sirens wailed their warning, Zubin was conducting the Israel Philharmonic with the violinist Stern at the Jerusalem Theatre. The audience donned gas masks and the orchestra left the stage. But Stern, with admirable courage, returned to play a saraband for solo violin by Bach. When the all-clear sounded, the concert resumed. An old Jewish custom holds that if a guest at a wedding is stricken or dies, the service should continue nonetheless to affirm the primacy of life. In the same spirit, Stern affirmed the primacy of art and civilization, even as Saddam's missiles were seen soaring through the sky.[16] After the war ended, Zubin brought the Israel Philharmonic Orchestra to New York and Carnegie Hall, and a glamorous audience made it a festive occasion for reasons that went far beyond mere music. They played Dvořák's Seventh Symphony and Beethoven's Violin Concerto, with Perlman as soloist.

### *Asian Tour*

In 1994, Zubin and the Israel Philharmonic Orchestra undertook a tour of Asia which included India for the first time. After performances in Tokyo, Beijing and Shanghai, in November 1994, Zubin's dream of bringing the Israel Philharmonic to India was finally fulfilled when the ensemble landed in the country of his birth for a performance on 27 November in New Delhi and four concerts in Bombay from 30 November to 3 December. Most of the concerts had Perlman as the violin soloist who, like the orchestra, played without a fee. The concerts were sponsored by the Government of India, besides private parties. The five concerts broke a political taboo after India and Israel opened embassies in 1992 and embarked on a rapid expansion in economic and cultural ties.

Welcoming Zubin at the Indira Gandhi Stadium was another famous Parsi, Field Marshal Manekshaw, in his capacity as president of the Delhi Symphony Society.[17] It was little surprise that Zubin got the reception he did, for no Israeli orchestra had performed in India before, and an audience of 7000 cheered Zubin and the musicians. 'I have waited for more than thirty years to bring this famed orchestra to my own country,' Zubin said. The show was billed as a 'Concert for Peace' to commemorate the 125th birth anniversary of Mohandas K. Gandhi. The concerts in New Delhi included Beethoven's Seventh Symphony and Tchaikovsky's Violin Concerto with Perlman as soloist.

Zubin's concert at Brabourne Stadium ended with a rousing encore of Johann Strauss Sr's *Radetzky March* that brought the 14,000-strong crowd to its feet. Doordarshan carried live broadcasts of the final concert. After the concert, there was an open-air dinner for a smaller gathering in which Zubin was named an honorary life member of the Cricket Club of India. As Raj Singh Dungarpur, the president of the Cricket Club of India, listed the legendary cricketers who had preceded Zubin in the honours list, he dabbed his eyes. Zubin recalled how, as a child, he would save to witness the Pentangular matches at Brabourne Stadium in the 1940s. Costs for the final concert in Bombay soared when Zubin opted to improve acoustics in Brabourne Stadium by flying in the specially constructed band shell used in Los Angeles for the Three Tenors concert in Dodger Stadium.

In coming back to play for Indian audiences Zubin said that he did not think of himself as establishing a new beachhead for Western classical music which has had little influence outside Bombay, Calcutta, New Delhi and Madras. 'India does not need Western music as Japan and China do,' he said, 'because unlike the Japanese and the Chinese, Indians have maintained a passion for their own classical music. Every nook and cranny in India has its own music, so Western classical music in India will always be for a relatively small number of aficionados.'

The concert was attended by top political leaders, and the then prime minister, P.V. Narasimha Rao, wrote a note of apology for not attending, explaining that electioneering had kept him away. During the performance of Beethoven's Seventh in New Delhi, Zubin and the Israel Philharmonic Orchestra had to compete with the crackle of walkie-talkies held by policemen near the stage and the crunch of peanuts being snacked on by dignitaries. Zubin showed no sign that he noticed.

## CELEBRATIONS AND MUSIC

In April 1996, Zubin and the Israel Philharmonic Orchestra travelled to the United States to celebrate both their sixtieth anniversaries in nine programmes across the country. Soloists included Gil Shaham, Perlman, Zukerman and Barenboim. Yo-Yo Ma and Emanuel Ax also played on tour with the ensemble. The climax came on 29 April, Zubin's sixtieth birthday, when he and the Israel Philharmonic Orchestra were joined by the Los Angeles Philharmonic to celebrate the occasion in a Dorothy Chandler Pavilion gala benefit. Barenboim, Perlman and Zukerman also took part. Strauss's *Don Quixote* was on four of the nine programmes. The eight-city US tour started off with a concert in Chicago. In fact, in those last three months, Zubin had appeared before the Chicago audiences on numerous occasions. He had guest conducted the Chicago Symphony Orchestra in January and in March he was in the Civic Opera House pit for Lyric Opera's highly successful cycles of Wagner's *The Ring of the Nibelung*.

The Israel Philharmonic concert featured Strauss's *Don Quixote* and Beethoven's Seventh Symphony. The performances at Carnegie Hall, New York, were as much political as musical events. Security personnel milled around, discreetly encircling a handsome black-tie audience. The programme consisted of Beethoven's compositions the *Leonore*, the Seventh Symphony and the Triple Concerto, with Perlman, Ma and Ax playing the violin, the cello and the piano respectively. On the heels of the Triple Concerto came Opus 54, Beethoven's piano sonata. Bernard Holland of the *New York Times* noted that the music was all Beethoven but seemed all-Israel as well. A musical identity, the message went, defends a country too. After the concert, which was a benefit for the orchestra, there was a dinner at the Plaza Hotel a few blocks down the street. Limousines lined 57th Street for nearly the entire stretch between the Avenue of the Americas and Seventh Avenue. There was a smaller party afterwards for Zubin's sixtieth birthday.

In December 1996, five of the world's leading violinists, Perlman, Zukerman, Midori, Shlomo Mintz and Shaham, appeared with Zubin and the Israel Philharmonic Orchestra at the International Convention Centre in Jerusalem to mark the conclusion of the fifteen-month-long 'Jerusalem 3000' celebration—a homage to King David who had designated the city as the capital of the kingdom of Israel 3000 years ago.[18]

That same month AFIPO played principal sponsor of the Israel Philharmonic Orchestra's sixtieth anniversary gala in Israel, which was nationally telecast on PBS. An extraordinary assemblage of musical talent performed with Zubin and the orchestra, and included Stern, Yefim Bronfman, Midori, Perlman and Shaham among others. Over the years, Midori has come to be a valued friend to the AFIPO, performing at numerous special events and family programmes. Midori, made her concert debut under Zubin and the New York Philharmonic as an eleven-year-old in 1982 and was musically chaperoned by Zubin, who paved the way for her meteoric career. She first came to Israel when she was seventeen and has returned almost every other year, usually playing under Zubin's baton. 'Israel is one of my favourite countries to visit. The people are so emotional. I feel quite at home here. And it is so wonderful to play with Zubin. He is energetic and very romantic and full of fire. I feel very secure with him, much more than with other conductors.'[19]

## MUSIC FOR PEACE

Zubin's use of music to heal wounds is well known. He did this to telling effect in August 1999 with the Israel Philharmonic Orchestra's first concert on German soil, playing alongside a German orchestra. In a setting beneath the hill where Buchenwald once disgorged its daily horror (50,000 people died here between 1937 and 1945), Zubin conducted 170 musicians from the Bavarian State Orchestra and the Israel Philharmonic just hours after accompanying many of them on a visit to the former Nazi camp. Initially a little apprehensive about how the Israelis and Germans would sit side by side and make music, Zubin said that he detected no feelings of resistance. And Zubin, as eager to promote peace as he is to make music, said that if Jews and Germans could be together near Buchenwald after fifty years, one day there would be reconciliation with Arabs too.[20]

The German and Israeli musicians played Mahler's Second Symphony, the *Resurrection*, whose passage from a first movement that is virtually a death march to the soaring finale in which the victory of the spirit is affirmed, reflected the themes of the evening. Though Mahler's performance was thrilling, it was less than perfect: a sharp drop in temperature as dusk gave way to night affected the pitch of the wind instruments. But no one seemed to mind. The director of the year-long Weimar festival said that the concert was about showing that even the past symbolized by Buchenwald could be overcome, and the Germans whose forbears murdered Jews could sit together with the Israelis and play the music of a Jewish-Austrian-German composer.[21]

Zubin's close friend Barenboim also did his bit for peace. He spent much of his time in Weimar directing a workshop of young musicians drawn largely from Arab countries and Israel. Driven by the conviction that the Middle East is a small area and that political solutions based on separateness can never fully resolve the conflict of the region, he brought together some seventy musicians to ponder their problems of identity while exploring their shared passion for music. This meeting of musicians, most of them in their early twenties, was a huge success and led to the formation of the West-

Eastern Divan Orchestra. The name is taken from Goethe's book *The West-Eastern Divan*, in which, late in life, he explored aspects of Arab and Islamic culture, their relationship to Western ideas and the need for tolerance. This humanism of Goethe gave way during the nineteenth century to an expression of Romantic cultural nationalism that the Nazis would later distort.[22]

Helping Barenboim was Edward Said, the Palestinian writer and intellectual who joined the discussions after rehearsals. Said was invaluable in explaining that an understanding of Jewish history was essential, whatever problems might exist between Arabs and Jews. The idea was to provide a forum for the young generation of musicians in the Middle East, not so they could forget their differences but so they could learn from making music. 'When you make music you have to express yourself to the utmost and simultaneously listen to what the other is playing. From that point of view, it is a wonderful school of life. Imagine if politicians could express themselves and listen to what others were saying,' Barenboim told *Newsweek* in an interview in December 2008.

In August 2005, Barenboim brought together Israeli and Arab musicians for a concert in Ramallah. Though Barenboim had often appeared there, this was the first time that his orchestra, the West-Eastern Divan, whose 100 members hail from Israel, Palestine, Syria, Lebanon, Egypt and Jordan, performed there. The 700-seat Ramallah concert hall had only standing room and a spillover crowd watched the performance on closed-circuit television in a nearby hall. The concert was in memory of Edward Said, who died in 2003. But there were hurdles. For one, it is illegal for Israelis to go to Ramallah. And since the Syrians and the Lebanese had to pass through Israel, it was illegal for them too. The whole orchestra was given Spanish diplomatic passports to overcome this problem. (The orchestra is based in Seville, the capital of Spain's southern region of Andalusia, where Muslims, Christians and Jews lived amicably during the Middle Ages.)

♫

A noteworthy event took place in January 2003, when the Israel Philharmonic Orchestra and the New York Philharmonic performed together on the same stage under Zubin and Maazel. Zubin conducted Tchaikovsky's Symphony No. 4, while Maazel conducted Mahler's Symphony No. 1. The evening raised a total of $1.6 million, equally benefiting both orchestras. Later that year, the Israel Philharmonic performed in St Petersburg to celebrate the city's 300th anniversary. One of the most memorable experiences of this excursion was the Israel Philharmonic's performance at the Grand Choral Synagogue. In December of that year, sold-out performances at the Walt Disney Hall in Los Angeles, Kennedy Center in Washington DC and Carnegie Hall in New York made the Israel Philharmonic Orchestra's United States tour one of the most successful ever.

## MUSICAL EDUCATION AND THE ORCHESTRA

In 1999, the Israel Philharmonic Orchestra founded the KeyNote Programme for Music Education and Community Outreach with the support of the AFIPO. Originally founded to solve the problem of a shrinking audience for classical music, it soon became apparent that the programme was filling a cultural and social vacuum in the school system and in Israeli society.

The year before, Zubin had been approached by the Middle East Children's Association with the idea of performing for an audience of Palestinian and Israeli children. The offer found immediate acceptance from Zubin. At the time there was great hope for a lasting agreement between the Palestinian Authority and Israel. Shoshani called Marck and asked him to suggest a programme that would prepare a culturally mixed audience for a symphony concert and to execute it with Palestinian partners.[23]

Over the next sixteen months, Israel Philharmonic Orchestra ensembles travelled in the Israeli development town of Beit Shemesh and Beit Jala on the West Bank for concerts with Palestinian children from the Deheishe Refugee Camp. Arab-Israeli actress Chaula Dibsi presented the concerts first in Hebrew and then in Arabic. Marck arranged the ensembles for the concert series and prepared material for the presenter. They also brought an ensemble of Arab musicians with a programme of Eastern music. The finale took place at the YMCA in Jerusalem when Zubin conducted the Israel Philharmonic for an audience of 600 Israeli and Palestinian children. It was this programme which was the trigger for the creation of KeyNote. The AFIPO provided the seed money and KeyNote soon became an integral part of the Philharmonic.[24]

Reaching out to the community and visiting schools has now become an integral part of the orchestra's activity. Over 20,000 children and adults of all ages take part in diverse activities and get acquainted with classical music through personal sessions with Israel Philharmonic musicians and the orchestra's concerts across Israel. In addition to thirteen mornings of concerts, which the orchestra has added to its schedule, seventy musicians of the ensemble regularly take part in the in-school classroom presentations. The programme serves all Israelis—Jewish, Christian and Muslim—and uses music to provide a common language to unite them.

Marck, who has participated in these efforts from the beginning, says that it is difficult to imagine the Philharmonic before KeyNote. He feels that the biggest winner in all this has been the orchestra itself. As one of his colleagues told him after a morning spent in the classroom, 'I don't know how to say it but I come out of these sessions with a feeling of [a] "mission".'

Shesh-Besh,[25] the Arab-Jewish ensemble under the auspices of the Israel Philharmonic Orchestra, brings together players from the orchestra and the finest musicians from the Arab community in northern Israel. The ensemble was founded in 2000 by KeyNote in its first year of activity. As part of the KeyNote programme, Shesh-Besh appears regularly in schools both in the intimate setting of the classroom and in concerts. It also tours outside Israel regularly and has performed at the Tanglewood Festival, Germany, Hungary and Switzerland.

The AFIPO is a major underwriter of the KeyNote programme. In 2001, tragedy struck the AFIPO when board president Herman

S. Sandler died in the 11 September bombing of the World Trade Center in New York. To honour his memory, the AFIPO Endowment Fund was renamed the Herman S. Sandler Endowment Fund. An ensemble of eight musicians from the Israel Philharmonic Orchestra and the Arab community performed at St Bartholomew's Church in Manhattan in June 2002. In 2007 the KeyNote programme and the ensemble was awarded the European Tolerance Award.

In March 2005, Zubin forged another lifelong link with Israel, with the inauguration of the Buchmann–Mehta School of Music. In 2002, the Rubin Academy of Music at Tel Aviv University faced the threat of closure due to lack of funds. With the establishment of the Buchmann–Mehta School of Music, the moribund academy got a new lease of life. The finances of the university were inadequate and the music academy would have been the first to be shut down because educating musicians is a costly process, especially in terms of the professor–student ratio. Rather than one professor lecturing to 100 students, it is a one-on-one relationship with only one professor and one student.

Josef Buchmann, a millionaire philanthropist, stepped in with a generous donation, and Zubin agreed to lend his name to the institution. Buchmann and Zubin have been friends since the mid-1980s and Zubin says that he has always been generous with his help, including donating two Steinway pianos. The school is helmed by Tomer Lev, with Zubin as a lifelong honorary president. One of the principal aims of the school is to ensure the development of Israel's best musical talent at home, rather than lose them to foreign music schools. Buchmann's donations ensure the academy's future, for at least the next generation.

Sulamot, a music education programme for children with limited resources in underprivileged communities, was created as a joint endeavour of the Israel Philharmonic Orchestra and the Buchmann–Mehta School in 2010. Its mission is to promote music as a fundamental tool for the education of new generations and as a means of social development. Players from the Israel Philharmonic visit the children, who are also invited to attend the concerts of the orchestra. The

Buchmann–Mehta School trains the young teachers who participate in the programme. In December 2013, as part of the Sulamot programme, 600 children met Zubin at the Charles Bronfman Auditorium and played before him. In addition, four young soloists were chosen to play for the maestro.

In Nazareth and Shfaram there are 250 children studying music supervised by the Israel Philharmonic Orchestra. It is Zubin's dream that one day an Israeli Arab will sit among Israeli Jews and make music. In 2009, he announced the establishment of Mifneh (which aptly means 'change'), a programme aiming to change musical education for Israel's Arab citizens. In addition to Zubin and the Israel Philharmonic Orchestra, Bank Leumi and the Arab-Israel Bank committed to supporting the project for five years, as did an anonymous Jewish donor from Europe. In 2010, he visited the Beit al-Musika conservatory in Shfaram, one of the three schools in the pilot project. The other two are the Jezreel Valley Center for the Arts and the al-Mutran school in Nazareth. The Buchmann–Mehta School of Music is also a partner in the project.

The school has thrown up some technically sound, talented students. A handful of graduates from the Mifneh programme are now pursuing advanced instrumental studies at the school and Zubin says, 'So one of these days we'll move the curtain at the end of an audition, and there will be an Arab boy or girl there. It's my dream.'

Zubin cherishes the memory of how, in 1978, he urged the then prime minister, Begin, to send the orchestra to Cairo as a gesture of goodwill after the peace accords had been signed. 'He didn't react at all,' Zubin said. 'But that would have been the time to do it.' He also remembers a personal invitation from King Hussein to bring the orchestra to Jordan. But Queen Noor subsequently retracted the invitation when the right-wing Likud Party under Benjamin Netanyahu came to power in Israel in 1996. 'She had her own festival at the time at the Dead Sea, and she said, "I would love for you to play there, but since you have a new government, with Netanyahu, my husband would like to see how things are going."'[26] And they never heard from them again.

Unlike his players, Zubin who holds an Indian passport, is able to travel to Palestine and often visits Ramallah on the West Bank. He says his encounters with Palestinian intellectuals confirm his faith in the need for a continuing peace process. Despite such a belief, his appearances with the Israel Philharmonic Orchestra continue to get picketed by pro-Palestinian protestors, the most disturbing incident being the shouting and singing during the London Proms in 2011.

Zubin has consistently supported dialogue with the Arab world through music. His performances in Bethlehem and the Good Fence, and his support of the Israel Philharmonic's activities with Arab musicians and children bear ample testimony to his commitment which is absolute, lasting and unselfish. Many of his contributions go unknown and his endeavours continue quietly out of the spotlight of the media. Marck says that Zubin's love of Israel includes his hope of a just and lasting peace between Palestine and Israel.[27]

♫

Apart from the Israel Philharmonic Orchestra, Zubin's association with the Tel Aviv Hilton (TAH) also goes back four decades. When the hotel was under construction, he left his imprint in the wet concrete and, once it opened, it became a home away from home for him. The hotel has a permanent Zubin Mehta Suite with his name inscribed at the entrance. The TAH has also been a sponsor of the annual Israel Philharmonic Orchestra fundraiser for several years and, in 2003, it also served as a concert hall. More than 640 guests paid NIS 1000 to sit twelve to a table in the TAH ballroom to hear Zubin conduct the Israel Philharmonic. Zubin, whose oratory does not fall very short of his musical talents, and who knows how best to exploit the charismatic moment, told the audience: 'This orchestra travels a lot bringing the positive word of Israel—and it's helping. It is your duty as Israelis to support that which is the best in Israel—and this is the best.'[28]

Another old association of Zubin's is with restaurateur Reena Pushkarna. Born in New Delhi to a Jewish mother and a Sikh father,

Pushkarna is known as Israel's curry queen and is yet another example of how the great Indian diaspora is playing a role in diplomacy and trade. She and her husband, Vinod, own a chain of seven prominent restaurants in Israel, including Tandoori, where the famous peace talks with former Israeli prime minister Yitzhak Rabin and Palestinian leader Yasser Arafat were reported to have first started. Pushkarna also sells Indian and Thai ethnic food under the brand name 'Reena' to a 170-strong supermarket chain in Israel. When she opened her first restaurant along with her sea-captain husband, it was dubbed Ichikdana since that was the only thing Israelis knew about India from the Raj Kapoor film *Shri 420*.

Zubin loves tandoori cuisine, particularly the specialities he sampled regularly at Pushkarna's restaurant, Tandoori. In fact, one way of knowing that Zubin was in town was by looking out for the Tandoori catering van outside Mann Auditorium! No wonder Nancy thought that the most appropriate gift for her husband's sixtieth birthday would be a tandoori feast, and invited Pushkarna to come over and cook. She had to decline because her mother was unwell but promptly dispatched her executive chef to Los Angeles where he spent five days in hiding so as not to spoil the surprise. When Zubin walked into his celebrity-studded party, it hit a high note the moment he saw the food! Nancy reported to Pushkarna that 'it was the best surprise of all'.

Pushkarna related how once, many years ago, Zubin had come over for dinner when her basmati rice reserves were nearly exhausted. She told him that she was on her last sack of basmati because the Israeli government had stopped the import of rice from India. On Zubin's suggestion, they invited Ariel Sharon, the then minister of trade, to dinner at Tandoori after an Israel Philharmonic concert. Sharon was very fond of lamb and rice, and they stuffed him with different kinds of rice. When Sharon appreciated the rice, Zubin promptly remarked: 'Well, she is on her last sack of this special rice and she invested it in entertaining you.' A week later, Pushkarna could bring her rice in. Fifteen years later, when Sharon was prime minister, he reminded her of this incident when they were flying together on a diplomatic mission to India. He joked that if she did not have sufficient stocks, she could fill up the aircraft and bring back the rice.[29]

## THE ISRAEL PHILHARMONIC TURNS SEVENTY

The Israel Philharmonic Orchestra turned seventy in 2006, with a two-week festival to mark the milestone. The anniversary festival was opened by Zubin on 17 December at the International Convention Centre in Jerusalem. Pianist Evgeny Kissin, and violinist Julian Rachlin and cellist Mischa Maisky played Brahms's Concerto for Violin and Cello. The rest of the programme consisted of Schumann's Piano Concerto and Mozart's *Jupiter* Symphony. In the days that followed, there were concerts conducted by Gustavo Dudamel and Valery Gergiev at the Mann Auditorium. One chamber music concert was dedicated to works by Brahms, with Bronfman, Shaham, Rachlin and Maisky, and Yigal Tuneh.

On 22 December, Zubin conducted a programme of Dvořák and Rachmaninoff at Haifa Auditorium; Maazel conducted a concert of Beethoven and Mussorgsky, and Barenboim gave a piano recital, both at the Mann Auditorium. At the seventieth anniversary gala concert on 26 December, the programme Zubin conducted consisted of Max Bruch's Violin Concerto No. 1, Ravel's *La Valse* and Beethoven's *Emperor* Piano Concerto, with Barenboim on the piano and Zukerman on the violin. Ravel's *La Valse*, a symphonic poem that employed the entire orchestra, showed the ensemble at its most controlled, colourful and precise, highlighting Zubin's superb technique and command of his musicians.

The gala concert brought together three of the Israel Philharmonic Orchestra's closest friends. Like the other guests of the concert series, the three appeared free of charge, lending their expertise in honour of the orchestra's seven decades. The concert was broadcast live all over Europe on the French/German Arte network. (The only shortcoming of the evening was that there was no intermission due to the broadcasters' demands and this challenged many of the patrons' bladders.)

After another chamber music concert and a programme in which

Barenboim conducted pianist Radu Lupu in Mozart's Concerto for Two Pianos and Beethoven's Piano Concerto No. 3, the two-week musical extravaganza ended with honorary guest conductor Kurt Masur wielding the baton for a programme of Schoenberg's *A Survivor in Warsaw* and Beethoven's Choral Symphony.

Earlier that year, in April, Sophia Loren, a good friend of Zubin's, came to Tel Aviv to attend his seventieth birthday celebrations. Carlo Ponti Jr, Loren's son by her movie-producer husband of the same name, is also a conductor who has studied privately under both Zubin and Mehli. Loren met Zubin when she took her son to him for music lessons as a teenager. (Ponti Jr who started his musical studies as a pianist in Paris was the music director and chief conductor of the San Bernardino Symphony Orchestra in California from 2001 to 2012. He has rapidly established himself on the international scene as one of the most imaginative conductors of his generation. In 2013, he founded the Los Angeles Virtuosi Orchestra—an ensemble emphasizing the educational value of music—of which he is music director and principal conductor.)

In 2006, Zubin was honoured by the orchestra at a gala concert and the evening included Mozart's Concerto No. 5, conducted by Zukerman as a tribute to Zubin, and a ten-minute film featuring highlights from Zubin's life by Dalia Meroz, the head of public relations of the ensemble. As a grand finale, 180 musicians performed Berlioz's *Symphonie Fantastique*.[30]

The anniversary celebrations in the United States included a five-city tour starting with New York. The first two performances of the tour were at Carnegie Hall. On 30 January 2007, Maazel led the Israel Philharmonic Orchestra and guest violinist Vengerov in a concert and, on 1 February, Zubin conducted an AFIPO benefit performance, with guest baritone Thomas Hampson. In San Francisco, Zubin and the orchestra performed at Davies Symphony Hall at a sold-out concert on 4 February, despite it being Super Bowl Sunday. In Los Angeles, the orchestra performed two concerts at the Walt Disney Hall. A concert at the Dorothy Chandler Pavilion on 6 February was once again led by Maazel.

The year 2009 marked Zubin's fortieth year as music director. 'I've enjoyed every minute. I wouldn't exchange it with any other conductor. I think I learned more from the musicians than they learned from me. We've grown up together, and achieved everything together,' Zubin said at a press conference.[31] In July of that year, the Israel Philharmonic Orchestra released a box set of twelve CDs to celebrate Zubin's 3000 appearances with the orchestra (now over 3500) under its new label, Helicon Classics. It featured live performances with Zubin leading the orchestra and world-class soloists. Zubin said that he was grateful that this was documented, calling it a little drop in the ocean.

Two years later, in 2011, the Israel Philharmonic Orchestra celebrated its seventy-fifth anniversary and Zubin his seventy-fifth birthday. In July, President Peres hosted a concert in honour of Zubin and the orchestra, which coincided with the fifth anniversary of the Second Lebanon War and was dedicated to the Israeli Defence Forces. Peres credited Zubin with being a builder of Israel's culture and a carrier of its hope. 'In the five decades, you became part of us, and we became part of your inspiration,' he said. Peres said that Zubin had made music tear down many walls and had stood by the country when others were hesitant to support it. 'Your music became a message, a light upon all audiences all around the world.'[32] In 2010, Zubin conducted a short concert near the Gaza border, adding his voice to the growing chorus for the release of Sgt Gilad Shalit, an Israeli soldier held by Hamas militants in the Gaza strip for the last four years. He said that he hoped the concert would inspire Gazans to pressure the Hamas government to allow the Red Cross to visit the soldier for the first time.

It is this care and involvement which has made Zubin the beloved of all Israelis. In October 2012, President Peres conferred Israel's Presidential Medal of Distinction on Zubin for his contribution to Israeli society. He said, 'Israel used to be a drama, you made us into a dramatic symphony without compromising one for the other. You harmonized us.' Zubin, who has always advocated peace through his music, said that 'if you can sing together, you can live together.'[33]

♫

The Israel Philharmonic Orchestra today faces the same problems that plague other orchestras: an ageing audience, a stagnant repertory and decreased support from the state. The old European emigrants, many of them German, are still a large part of the audience and so it is not surprising that the choice of musical works is conservative. The Israel Philharmonic makes an effort to encourage and support Israel's many composers and, when on tour, it usually includes a contemporary work by a countryman.

Zubin acknowledges that Wagner aside, the audience has a conservative choice. He conceded once that if he had scheduled Schoenberg's *Variations for Orchestra* after the intermission, the hall would have been empty. At the same time, he knows that since the population has lived in a state of terror and anxiety for the last fifty years, they do not want to come to a concert hall and have to concentrate on contemporary music and pay attention. Instead, they want to sit back and listen to their favourites.

The Israel Philharmonic Orchestra has made every effort to attract a young audience but, as Marck puts it, a good product will attract all ages, with the older generation in a better position to actually pay for the tickets. The Jeans Concert Series, in which listeners of all ages enjoy a glass of beer before a late evening concert, is a success, as is Intermezzo (coffee and cake before a matinee lecture concert), which, though intended to attract students, turned out to be the perfect hour of day for an older, less mobile audience. Life expectancy has improved and people live noticeably longer and better than they did forty years ago. Marck feels that this has been a wonderful boost for the orchestra and for culture in general.[34]

But inevitably, there is criticism as well. Leon Botstein, the music director of the Jerusalem Symphony Orchestra, which is less celebrated but bolder in its repertory, calls the conservative concert culture a carry-over from the Central European audience, of which the Israel Philharmonic Orchestra is the best example. Much harsher criticism came from Noam Ben Zeev. Writing in the newspaper *Haaretz* in December 2006, he urged Zubin to resign, saying the orchestra had failed in the genuinely important missions: nurturing Israeli soloists, producing young conductors and in-house composers, introducing a daring new repertoire and recruiting a new audience. He complained that works composed by Israelis made up barely 1 per cent of the CD collection released by the orchestra to commemorate its seventieth anniversary. When I drew the maestro's attention to the criticism, he said: 'He has always been complaining about how little Israeli music we play. He writes without doing his homework. I point to facts which prove the contrary but he still writes. He is like a broken record.'[35]

Even if some of the criticism is true, the difficulty of selling innovation to older audiences is a common complaint among most of the world's orchestras, including those with much higher public subsidies than the Israel Philharmonic. For many years the Israel Philharmonic Orchestra was the country's dominant institution. As a result, it enjoyed substantial government support. This is no longer the case. Middle Eastern politics, the Intifada and the collapse of the Soviet Union changed all that. Until 1969, the Israel Philharmonic Orchestra was the only show in town. There was hardly any television. Nor was there much sports going on. Today there are more than 200 cable channels and every little village has its own Russian chamber orchestra. When Shoshani went to the minister of education and culture, Limor Livnat, to protest a cut in government funding in 2003, he was rudely told that there would be no more money from the government. With a deficit, the Israel Philharmonic Orchestra had to constantly beg artistes to reduce their fees, which they invariably did.

The Israel Philharmonic pays for half of its approximately $20-million annual budget through ticket sales and some 25,000 subscribers. Only 12 per cent of the budget comes from the state; private donors make up the difference. This is in stark contrast to Europe, where orchestra budgets are typically subsidized by governments at 80 per cent or more. Most of the balance comes from individual donors, many of them American. Israeli law allows for few tax breaks for charitable giving and corporate sponsorship is relatively new here. A rare deal with Bank Hapoalim, Israel's biggest bank, resulted in contributions of $1.5 million spread over five years.

The Israel Philharmonic also has self-generated income, which includes crossover style concerts of Israeli music, guest artistes from pop music and surplus income from touring. The orchestra is very dependent on (and grateful for) support from the Israel Philharmonic Foundation and the AFIPO.

In 2008, the government allotted only $2.3 million, about 1.5 million less than in the previous year, to the Israel Philharmonic Orchestra. Shoshani blamed the cuts on the fact that while the number of cultural bodies in Israel is growing, the state budget is not. In a country full of classical musicians, the competition for funds is becoming increasingly bitter. The same year the Israel Philharmonic Orchestra launched a public campaign to shame the government into giving it more funds but the state has to dole out money to seventeen different musical ensembles. Zubin called the cuts in government funding not just 'culturally unwise but also politically short-sighted', given the fact that the orchestra boosts Israel's image abroad, countering headlines of violent confrontation with beautiful music.

In addition, the orchestra now competes with a plethora of other sources of entertainment from local opera and chamber music groups to movies and satellite television. Marck feels that television and other electronic media do not actually compare with the excitement of a live performance. The audience wants to enjoy and be stimulated by a great piece of music, and a charismatic artiste or an enthusiastic performance provides that. In its first season, the Israel Philharmonic Orchestra had 6000 subscribers out of a population of 3,50,000—an incredibly high percentage. In the 1980s the subscribers peaked to a high of 36,000 and they played twenty concerts a month. Today there are about 25,000 subscribers with thousands of single tickets constantly on demand.[36]

The orchestra has also had to cope with a wave of no-shows by big-ticket artistes over the years, owing to security problems. Some are honest about acknowledging security fears, others cite sudden scheduling conflicts—excuses which orchestra officials suspect are motivated by political reasons. In 2003, Marck, who was on the orchestra's management team, said they had become like an island. 'We used to be the last stop in Europe. Now, many soloists and many conductors don't want to touch us.'[37] Cancellations elicit different responses, depending on who is cancelling. Zubin goes along with his Israeli colleagues in this matter. If a Jewish player refuses to come to Israel, they don't take it too well, but with others they have no choice since they cannot guarantee their safety. In fact, the orchestra's own safety while abroad has been another concern and a drain on its resources. That the orchestra has played in many tense situations before—indeed, it has become a point of pride to do so—is a different matter.

Not everything Zubin and the Israel Philharmonic Orchestra have done together has attracted praise. Writing about a concert at Avery Fisher Hall in February 1995, Alex Ross of the *New York Times* wrote:

> Neither conductor nor orchestra has achieved a consistently high level of musicianship, but both are capable of great things when the spirit moves them.[38]

In the same review, he went on to add:

> The Israel Philharmonic Orchestra digs into music with great enthusiasm, but it does not possess a polished or precisely unified sound; it needs the task-masterly attention of an orchestra builder . . . He gets his best results with virtuoso European groups like the Vienna Philharmonic or the Berlin Philharmonic, with whom details tend to take care of themselves.[39]

Similarly, Holland observed that the Israel Philharmonic would sound more like other orchestras if its members played together, which they didn't:

> Articulation even in broad passages is rarely consensual; rapid ones produce a voluptuous haze. Mr Mehta conducted with furious precision, but no one seemed to pay much attention. I suspect he has long since learned just to keep the traffic moving and otherwise stand out of the way.[40]

But critics also noted that the orchestra's concerts are always welcome not because it is a brilliant virtuoso ensemble at the absolutely top international level but because when at its best, it offers 'deeply musical, songful performances that evince a spirit and personality more important than mere virtuosity'.[41] Holland observed that an enormous amount of work might get the orchestra playing as tightly as others, but then it would no longer be the Israel Philharmonic.'The messiness seems more a choice than a failing.'[42]

The Israel Philharmonic represents the cultural heritage of a nation that is increasingly becoming polarized. Though the orchestra is regarded as the flagship of the whole country, in fact, it represents only the Ashkenazi (European) part of Israel. There are numerous divisions in Israel: left and right, religious and non-religious, white and black, Jews from Europe and those from the Arabic countries. The Israel Philharmonic Orchestra keeps turning for its identity to increasingly distant sources in cultural Europe and the Holocaust. As Dorman, a bassoonist with the orchestra for many years who chaired its executive committee for a decade, said, 'The way we play a Mahler symphony, we have a touch nobody else can achieve. In his music you can hear the suffering of the Jewish people. Other orchestras can't deliver that message.'

But many feel that despite all the attempts by the Israel Philharmonic Orchestra to include all sections of the population, it remains an elitist institution whose sounds are music to nobody's ears. In Israel, there are three Andalusian orchestras as well as an Arab one, but the choice of music of the Israel Philharmonic gives it a status which is immune to criticism as it is seen to be a part of the national Zionist enterprise. The support the ensemble receives is far more than what similar orchestras in Be'er Sheva, Haifa and Rishon Lezion get.

There is a direct correlation between the number of subscribers and the number of Ashkenazim in Israel and it is argued that the Israel Philharmonic Orchestra has little hope of flourishing if it directs its art to such a limited audience. The Heart at East coalition, which was established in 2009, has been agitating for a more equitable distribution of the culture budget. It has highlighted the huge disparity between what the arts that could be labelled as European get and what Arab, Mizrahi (Jews of the Middle East) and Ethiopian arts get by contrast. More importantly, Zubin's and Shoshani's stranglehold on the Israel Philharmonic Orchestra has attracted adverse comment. Many feel that young Israeli composers, conductors and singers have been unable to breach the walls of the music establishment monopolized by the Israel Philharmonic and the Israel Opera, both of which have been led by the same people for many decades. There now appears to be a mood for a change of regime. Zeev who had in 2006 urged Zubin to resign, reignited the issue in his article 'Should Israel Philharmonic Orchestra's Iconic Maestro Hand over the Baton' in the *Haaretz* in February 2015. While agreeing that Zubin was the best thing to have happened to the Israel Philharmonic Orchestra, he suggested that it was time for him to step aside and make way for a younger music director. His critics claim that Zubin has been on autopilot for years and is incapable of turning in anything other than a routine performance. It is also argued that with the members of the orchestra becoming younger, there is a need to work on style. When I asked him about this, he said, 'Not everyone likes whatever you do and even after fifty years, everyone in Israel does not like me.'[43]

In Zubin's defence, it is said that he earns much less than any other conductor of his stature and it is his love for the Israel Philharmonic Orchestra and Israel that keeps him there. He brings in top conductors and soloists to the orchestra—not an easy task, given the perpetual security problems the embattled nation faces. The real problem is the ultra-conservative taste of the Israeli people, coupled with the lack of public funds, which results in unimaginative programmes, a fact which Zubin himself laments. Young and new, it is argued, is not necessarily better, and they feel that those who seek to remove Zubin are being unappreciative of the treasure that is their maestro. What is really needed is the education of the conservative audiences and innovative means to rejuvenate the musical scene.

♫

In October 2007, the Mann Auditorium, the home of the Israel Philharmonic Orchestra, turned fifty. Zubin conducted the orchestra in a programme that was identical to the one played fifty years ago, a programme we have already noted in a preceding chapter. This time the players were French pianist Hélène Grimaud, Greek violinist Leonidas Kavakos and British cellist Steven Isserlis. Sheriff, for long a recognized name, was also present on the occasion. He was of the opinion that all the talk about the auditorium's bad acoustics was exaggerated and felt that it could be improved with minimum investment. He quoted conductor Celibidache who said that there are no bad acoustics, only bad orchestras and conductors, to prove his point.

But whatever Sheriff thought, the general feeling among many musicians and the audience was that the acoustics of the hall were far inferior to auditoriums the orchestra visited in other parts of the world. The orchestra musicians would 'return to their misery' at home, hoping that someday they would get a hall with better acoustics. In 2003, Zubin approached the Tel Aviv Municipality with his tale of woe. 'The acoustics are a mess,' he told the mayor.

It was the beginning of a long and difficult saga, since not all were convinced that the Mann Auditorium needed an overhaul. Plans for a $38-million renovation were set in motion in June 2005, when Zubin addressed a press conference on the subject. The renovation would focus on improving acoustics and changing the 'fan'-shaped seating arrangement to the more modern 'shoe box'. Capacity would come down to 2400 as the space for each chair was to be increased. Additional washrooms and improvements to the cafeterias were also planned. The exterior was to undergo only moderate increased. But these plans hit a roadblock when a petition filed by the Association for Tel Aviv's Cultural Heritage and the Association of Architects in Israel was upheld by the National Board for Planning and Building Appeals Committee. The petition held that the renovation involved material changes to a historic site in contravention of commitments made to UNESCO when it declared Tel Aviv's White City a World Heritage Site in July 2003.

There was a lengthy public debate on how the Mann Auditorium (known in Hebrew as Heichal Hatarbut, literally the 'temple of culture') was the preserver of the city's cultural code, a code not reflected in other public buildings built in Tel Aviv at the same time. It was argued that unlike others, it was not a mute building—it was the mouthpiece for an entire era and the values it embodied. Renovating the Mann Auditorium would be tantamount to disfiguring an urban monument that was one of the milestones that delineated the cultural landscape of the city.

Whatever the merits in the arguments of the naysayers, the $38-million project started in August 2011 and the new hall was ready in May 2013. Along the way, it got a new name, becoming the Charles Bronfman Auditorium, after the Jewish-Canadian billionaire and Seagram Co. beverage scion who had donated $10 million for its renovation. The Tel Aviv Municipality promised $18.9 million and the rest of the money was raised from various contributors. The Mann family agreed to the change after being assured that Fredric Mann would be memorialized within the renovated building. The building's façade—considered by the architects as one of the better examples of 1950s Tel Aviv architecture and one which was influenced by Le Corbusier—was retained.

The creation of the new hall has given the orchestra facilities it could only dream about before: adequate library space, soloist rooms, space for an archive, dressing rooms for orchestra members, a VIP room (named after Sara and Michael Sela) and a rehearsal room which converts into a chamber music facility. It was inaugurated on 25 May, with Zubin conducting Beethoven's Violin Concerto with Perlman as soloist. The conductor was suitably upbeat about the new acoustics. 'We have improved it in every way,' he said. At the dress rehearsal, he clapped his hands and told the press, 'Even this sounds different.'[44] The other two pieces were Mahler's Fifth and *Festival Prelude* by Sheriff, a piece which, as we have noted, was played under Bernstein's baton in the first-ever concert at the Mann Auditorium. On opening night, Mayor Ron

Huldai joked, 'A request made by a maestro is, as you know, stronger than a command.'[45] When I asked him about the new hall, he said it was a distinct improvement. 'There is much more air space, reverberation,' he said.[46]

# A Podium *on* Offer

ON NEW YEAR'S DAY 1976, Zubin received an important visitor at his Brentwood home. The visitor was Carlos Moseley, the president of the New York Philharmonic, and he was there to offer Zubin the music directorship of the orchestra. It was not something Zubin would have thought possible even a few years ago. Like most Parsis, Zubin speaks his mind frankly and forcefully, and what he has said has been seen as refreshingly honest by some and childishly indiscreet by others. He has a persistent tendency towards excessively frank public remarks and is known to both speak up and speak out, and sometimes even puts his foot in his mouth.[1] In December 1967, Zubin, who was rather more candid than he should have been, found himself at the centre of a controversy with the New York Philharmonic. In his most famous verbal gaffe till date, he made remarks which were uncomplimentary to the New York Philharmonic and the city of New York.

## 'FOOT IN MOUTH'

On Zubin's return from Bombay in 1967, speculation was rife that he was likely to succeed Bernstein at the New York Philharmonic. By 1967, Zubin was also beginning to become familiar to New York audiences. He had conducted the Philadelphia and the American Symphony orchestras in Carnegie Hall and had become one of the regulars at the Metropolitan Opera. But he had not conducted the New York Philharmonic since the Lewisohn Stadium concerts in 1960. To rectify this, the Philharmonic invited the rising star to conduct for two weeks during the 1968–69 season, Zubin's sabbatical year. Zubin accepted the invitation, with a proviso: he told Moseley that he wouldn't do it if it meant he was a candidate for permanent conductor.

Despite Zubin's protestations of non-candidacy, Schonberg's article in the *New York Times* headlined 'After Leonard Bernstein, Who?' on 10 December 1967 chose to discount his statements and proceeded to analyse his qualifications for the job. The next day, Los Angeles was abuzz with rumours about Zubin's move to New York. Zubin attempted to scotch the rumours at a reception in his honour that evening, which was attended by numerous members of the press. Zubin dismissed the New York job and the availability of the Boston and Chicago conductorships, saying they were of no interest to him. He said he delighted in the freedom he enjoyed in his Los Angeles post to pursue his other interests, most notably the conducting of opera. When asked about his chances of getting the job in New York, he bluntly said that he didn't want it and was happy in Los Angeles. For further emphasis, he added: 'My orchestra is better than the New York Philharmonic. We play better than they do. Artistically, it would not be a step up for me.'[2]

The *New York Times* correspondent filed his story, which appeared the next day with the headline: 'Mehta Prefers Los Angeles Job to Bernstein's at Philharmonic.' The same article quoted Joseph B. Koepfli, board chairman of the Los Angeles Philharmonic as saying, 'Zubin doesn't want his nose to the grindstone, and that's what he'd have in Boston or Philadelphia. We on the other hand are being as flexible as we can to suit him, because whatever this orchestra does, and is, is his.'[3] Koepfli and some prominent members of the symphony board's executive committee were speaking of Zubin in an interview after the reception, held at the studios of KCET, the local educational television station.

'I think all of this is wishful thinking,' said Behrendt, a member of the executive committee and later president of the Los Angeles board. 'The people in the East are thinking about how they're going to get him; it never crosses my mind that we'll lose him.'[4] Behrendt said she and the other board members did not consider the possibility of Zubin leaving for another orchestra because 'to him the challenge is right here'. 'He can do anything he wants; he has all kinds of recording possibilities. If he went to Philadelphia, he'd find that they had already recorded everything worth doing.'[5] (The Los Angeles orchestra had a four-records-a-year contract with London and was at the time the only American orchestra recorded by the British company.)

No harm had been done till the *New York Times* reporter left the party to file his story. But the *Newsweek* correspondent stayed longer and caught the remark that was to cause Zubin much heartache and also seriously impact his career. Zubin was reported as having said: 'An American should lead the Philharmonic. And he should be able to deal with both the orchestra—they step over conductors—and with New York.' Perhaps the most brutal utterance was, 'A lot of us think, why not send our worst enemy to the New York Philharmonic and finish him off once and for all.'[6] This tactless remark soon became the skeleton that rattled in Zubin's cupboard whenever the New York Philharmonic was discussed. Zubin had bad-mouthed the city of New York as well. 'I can't wait to get out of this town. It's claustrophobic. I absolutely loathe it.'[7] Zubin was also not too thrilled about the audience in New York even though he did not voice it publicly then. 'I never thought too much of the New York audience whose applause is only enough for a conductor to return twice to take a bow.'[8]

Zubin denied having spoken to *Newsweek*, saying that they hadn't got that remark from him. 'They didn't get it from me. I should have written them a note at the time. I can understand why the musicians would be upset.' He admitted, however, that he had made remarks similar to those quoted in the magazine to Moseley of the Philharmonic and to others. 'I told Mr Moseley, who the hell wants the job? It's never been offered to me anyway.' Zubin said he was most embarrassed about those words because in a *New York Times* interview from Los Angeles that same week, he had recommended the thirty-seven-year-old American conductor Maazel for the post. 'I just hope I don't get sued by Lorin,' he told the *New York Times*, laughing. 'He is one of my best friends.'[9] Zubin felt that the unfortunate inference that might be drawn was that Maazel was the 'worst enemy' he would like to send to the New York Philharmonic to be finished off. Even though Zubin denied giving the statement directly to *Newsweek*, Kermit Lansner, managing editor of the publication, said that the magazine stood by its report.[10] He said the statement was made to a *Newsweek* correspondent in Los Angeles and it appeared in the 18 December 1967 issue of the magazine. (Journalists later learned to distinguish between what Zubin wanted printed and what he didn't. When he preceded a statement with 'This is off-the-record,' he meant it. When he made a smart-alecky remark, followed by a scream of 'Don't print that!' one could be sure that 'he'd be crestfallen not to read a verbatim account of his felicitous way with words'.[11])

## THE APOLOGY

Zubin's statements snowballed into a controversy, which only ended with his meeting with the New York Philharmonic musicians. Zubin found himself at the headquarters of Local 802, the New York branch of the American Federation of Musicians, making a full-dress apology. Zubin was called by the executive board of the New York musicians' union to explain the statements he had made about them. 'They call him Zubi Baby,' remarked Max Arons, president of Local 802, American Federation of Musicians, 'but we will talk to him like an adult, no kid stuff.'[12] Arons said he wanted to check whether Zubin had indeed said what he was reported to have said in *Newsweek*, things like he wouldn't send his worst enemy to conduct the New York Philharmonic, and that the orchestra walks all over conductors.

In a ninety-minute session described by Arons as 'strict and stern, but friendly',[13] Zubin contended that he had been misquoted in the published remarks to which the union had objected the previous week. Zubin said he was 'happy to come in and clear up' the misunderstanding. He insisted that his views on the New York Philharmonic had been 'distorted out of all proportion'. Zubin disarmingly assured both the union and the committee of the Philharmonic musicians that he never meant to insult or degrade the players who, in any case, were his colleagues, and he promised to say as much in a letter for the Philharmonic bulletin board. He said that all he sought was respect for his own Los Angeles Philharmonic.

Zubin told the union board that he had 'the greatest respect for the great musicians of the Philharmonic', many of whom were his personal friends. He explained that the other remarks, cited in a *New York Times* interview in which he contended that 'my orchestra is better than the New York Philharmonic', were intended to express his pride in his own orchestra, not to disparage the New York Philharmonic. Zubin, who was scheduled to make his Philharmonic debut the next season in a two-week engagement, also agreed to meet with the players' committee of the orchestra, headed by Selig Posner, a violist, 'to clear the air'.[14] The union's invitation to Zubin for 'exploratory' discussions did not carry any threat of disciplinary action. Since Zubin was not an American citizen, he was not a member of the union. The union had to take the approval of the Immigration Department before inviting him to the meeting. Arons said that Zubin understood that the musicians' union could cause him trouble everywhere in the United States if it wanted to.[15]

After the meeting in the Local 802 offices, the union's executive board was satisfied that Zubin had not intended to slur the New York Philharmonic. Arons said the union—not the Philharmonic or its musicians—had initiated the complaint against the conductor because 'one thing the union wants is to have musicians respected'. Zubin even got some fatherly advice from the union president who told him to study what he said just like he studied a score, since an unkind word is like a bad note, which can't be taken back once it's played.[16] In his autobiography, Zubin says that his remark made in a private circle had been reported by the journalist and had caused him much embarrassment. Privately however, many agreed that Zubin was only repeating the standard opinion of the Philharmonic as a band of hard-boiled musicians who, if so inclined, could walk all over any conductor.

## A TOUGH BUNCH?

When the New York Philharmonic finally got a new music director, it was the Frenchman Boulez. Zubin could never have guessed at the time that this was the man he would succeed. Zubin had debuted with the orchestra in 1960 when he conducted at the Lewisohn Stadium. His regular season debut with the orchestra was to have come in 1968 but the rather tactless 'place-to-bury-one's-worst-enemy' remark came in the way. The orchestra dropped Zubin's name from its list of guest conductors for the 1968–69 season.

Moseley acknowledged that the two-week period originally reserved for Zubin had been vacated and no new engagement finalized. Zubin clarified to *Los Angeles Times* that he had been asked to withdraw but had refused to do so since he did not want it to look as if he had 'chickened out'.[17] He told the New York Philharmonic that it would have to make the move. It did, by removing him from its list of guest conductors for that season. Arons, however, said that the controversy was a forgotten issue and that the union had in no way made any suggestion to the New York management about cancelling Zubin's engagements as a guest conductor.

Zubin's remarks in 1967 kept him from the podium of the New York Philharmonic for the next six years. While this may seem like a long penance for a small transgression, in fact, resentment smouldered long at the Philharmonic because Zubin had touched a raw nerve. The players knew there was some truth to what he had said. While they discounted Zubin's claims about the superiority of the Los Angeles Philharmonic as the comment of a conductor loyal to his own orchestra, what rankled was the assertion that there was something amiss in the way the New York orchestra treated its conductors.

The New York Philharmonic comprised 106 of the most accomplished instrumentalists in the world. Fifty or sixty top players auditioned for every opening and, in many cases, a musician who played a principal position in his home orchestra was more than pleased to accept a last-desk chair in the Philharmonic. But precisely because the level of playing was so high, it became easy for the musicians to develop a feeling of superiority. This affected their willingness to accept the leadership of a conductor. The players insisted that their reputation as a 'tough bunch' was undeserved. And they resented, above all, the rumours that they sabotaged the efforts of conductors they didn't like by playing badly.

Still, all orchestral musicians know that 'stepping over conductors' does not necessarily involve purposeful false notes from players, but rather an unwillingness to subordinate their own musical personalities and ideas about music to the overall conception of the conductor. This subtler form of sabotage was not uncommon at the Philharmonic. Every musician thinks that he has something valid to say musically. So when a conductor wants them to conform to his idea of the piece, senior musicians resent it.

In addition, musicians are frequently jealous of conductors of the 'superstar' variety who soak in all the adulation and tend to deflect the spotlight from the orchestra's own virtuosity. In these cases an orchestra may develop a kind of Freudian 'baton envy' that can affect morale. However, even a superstar conductor can win over orchestral players if they respect him as a musician. A string player remarked: 'We don't like to see flamboyance just for the sake of personal aggrandizement, and to a certain extent we're put off by Mehta's "glamour boy" aura, but most of us think that Mehta is a very serious musician. Anyhow, a certain amount of that is necessary for the audience in this imperfect world of ours. And of course, we grew very used to that under Bernstein.'[18]

## MAKING UP

In spite of a lingering feeling of ill will towards Zubin among the Philharmonic players, by 1972, it began to seem short-sighted to continue to boycott him. At a meeting between Moseley and the musicians' advisory committee, an agreement was reached to engage Zubin for two weeks of concerts in 1974. Even then, however, the orchestra's animosity had not completely faded. It was only in May 1974 that he faced the orchestra in Philharmonic Hall as a guest conductor, breaking the seven-year-old ice with, 'Ladies and gentlemen, a few years ago I did something very immature and I am the one who paid for it.' At his first rehearsal, he addressed the musicians, 'I am coming to New York to make music. I can only do it with a hundred per cent involvement and I expect the same in return. If I cannot make that happen, I will pick up my hat, and let somebody else try.'

Former Philharmonic oboist Ronald Roseman recalled Zubin's first rehearsal that year: 'I was afraid of a very unpleasant scene; I thought the orchestra might chew him up. They were still quite hostile. But the first thing Mehta did when he stepped on the podium was to apologize, in a very dignified way, for what he had said about the orchestra. He didn't deny he had said it. He simply spoke in a very manly, straightforward way. I was very touched by it and so were most of the others. Then Mehta said briskly, "Now let's work together," and he began the rehearsal. I remember the orchestra played very well for him.'[19]

A few days later, they played their first concert together, one which had been chosen for dramatic effect by Zubin. He started with three overtures, all from rarely performed Weber operas. This was followed by Olivier Messiaen's enormous tone poem *Et Exspecto Resurrectionem Mortuorum* and by another big piece, the Organ Symphony of Saint-Saëns. If the aim was to grab the attention of the audience and the critics, Zubin certainly succeeded. Schonberg, while calling it an 'unusually noisy evening', praised Zubin as 'a conductor of temperament and of no mean technical skill'. He wrote, 'He is a man of virtuoso flair and makes the most of it.'[20]

Not long after this concert, Boulez announced that he was not going to renew his contract in New York since he had accepted the offer of taking over the new Institute of Musical Research in Paris. Speculation was rife once again but this time the critics, having been caught completely off guard by Boulez's appointment as Bernstein's successor, were less keen on hazarding an informed guess. Boulez, while he would not be drawn into any discussion with the press, said that he thought his successor should be from the younger generation with considerable experience and also proven leadership and ability—a choice which narrowed the field to two men, one of them Zubin.

## A CANDIDATE FOR MUSIC DIRECTOR

The Philharmonic board in New York was also thinking along the same lines but the big question was how to lure Zubin away from Los Angeles where, by all accounts, he was very happy. In an interview in November 1975, Zubin told Rockwell of the *New York Times*: 'I'm thirty-nine years old now, and I've developed three orchestras. Today I have a real Rolls-Royce in Los Angeles. Why should I go somewhere else and start the same rigmarole? I'm an old man now.'[21]

Los Angeles was at the centre of Zubin's personal life too. Nancy loved the city, and his parents, too, resided there. After fourteen years, a dozen international tours, more than forty recordings and nearly 1300 concerts in Los Angeles alone, Zubin's love affair with the Los Angeles Philharmonic seemed far from over. Why would he ever willingly leave an orchestra he had moulded into an international outfit and a city which he and his wife loved? Little did the Philharmonic board in New York realize that all they had to do was ask, for, in the same interview with Rockwell, Zubin had dropped a hint that the situation in Los Angeles was changing. 'I don't threaten to leave Los Angeles. I consider it all the time. It's human—one feels unappreciated. I would never leave for a better offer. I would only leave it if I thought my time was over.'[22]

Fleischmann thought that Zubin's cancellation of a month's engagement with the Berlin Opera in January 1976 was a crucial element in his decision to make the switch. Zubin denied the connection saying that Moseley's offer predated the cancellation. But the restlessness which Fleischmann had sensed was very real. Zubin had been quoted as saying that he was considering leaving since he thought it was better for both the orchestra and him to end their association. 'It was time,' he said, 'for us to move away from each other's influence.'[23]

Moseley, too, must have sensed something, since he changed his tactics from waiting and watching to active pursuit. In the end of December 1975, he called up old friends who owned a house on Malibu Beach and asked if he might stay with them for a few days. He ordered a round-trip ticket to Los Angeles and then placed a call to Brentwood, Zubin's home.[24] Moseley was a friend of Behrendt's, and he knew her devotion to Zubin. He remembered her words when the New York Philharmonic was scouting for a conductor to replace Bernstein. Behrendt had said, 'It never crosses my mind that we'll lose him.' But friendship counts for little when it comes to business. Boulez had just resigned and the Philharmonic needed a new music director. Moseley hoped Behrendt would forgive him.[25]

In 1975, Moseley was responsible for the day-to-day operation of the Philharmonic, and was thus a crucial figure in the orchestra's selection of a new music director. But he was weary of the complicated and delicate negotiations the task entailed. Back in 1967, finding a successor to Bernstein had been particularly difficult and the press had turned the situation into a horse race. Critics and journalists analysed the front-runners, even handicapping them in racing-form style. Those mentioned included Lorin Maazel, Zubin Mehta, Pierre Boulez and Colin Davis. It was a source of embarrassment for Moseley to have his business constantly in the public eye.[26]

Zubin enjoys visits from his friends, so when he got the call from Moseley, he asked him to visit. 'I love my friends to drop in, so when Carlos called from New York to say that he was coming to Los Angeles, I told him to come over for a visit. So he came, just like that. And he dropped this bomb in my lap. It just didn't occur to me that he had come out here especially to offer me the job. Really! He was staying with friends in Malibu, he told me, and so I assumed that's why he had come.'[27]

When Moseley sensed a change in attitude in Los Angeles, he realized that they had a chance of getting Zubin to New York. He came armed with the necessary permission to make a firm offer. He persuaded the members of the music-policy committee to empower him in case Zubin was really interested, and if he was willing to sign a three-year contract and give them a significant number of weeks of conducting. Moseley confessed that he was surprised to discover that Zubin had not made the connection between his call from New York and the forthcoming job offer. Zubin, too stunned to react, let Moseley do the talking.

Moseley told him of the orchestra's and the board's enthusiastic support of him as the choice for music director. He described the orchestra's need for a vibrant and energetic conductor, and stressed his own belief that Zubin was the best man for the job. This was not the way Moseley had talked to the other candidates on his list. When he had visited them, he had primarily sounded them out about their availability. As Moseley made his case, he was happy and relieved to see that Zubin was listening intently and with growing enthusiasm. And Moseley did not know it then, but Zubin had just refused the Berlin Opera a month earlier.

Zubin spent several hours in conversation with Moseley before leaving to conduct a New Year Night's concert of light music. Moseley took the flight back to New York the next day. That same evening, Zubin met Mehli and asked his opinion on the New York offer. Mehli told Zubin that he was old enough to decide for himself. When Zubin persisted, Mehli said that he should take it, since in his opinion it was the best thing that could have happened to him.

Mehli, it must be remembered, had wonderful memories of the New York Philharmonic which he had heard night after night at Carnegie Hall when he was learning the violin. It had a great sound in those days, being led by some of the most famous names in conducting history. Mehli felt that his son Zubin could make them play that way again. Zubin was well aware of the orchestra's tradition of greatness under Toscanini. He longed to meet the challenge of continuing that tradition and herein lay, at least in part, the attraction of Moseley's offer. Zubin told Mehli that he had already accepted the offer. 'I had a feeling you would say that. I already told Carlos Moseley I would take the job,' he said.[28]

Nothing, however, had been settled in that January meeting, though plans had been made for further discussions in New York. The devil is often in the fine print and a number of issues had to be resolved. The fee appears to have been the least of the problems and was settled 'in a conversation of five minutes'. No major conductor discloses his pay, but knowledgeable sources said that Zubin's salary was certainly 'in six figures'. (Zubin was rumoured to have been getting $1,75,000 in Los Angeles; his salary was surely higher in New York.)

Zubin's principal concern was to ensure that his position as musical adviser of the Israel Philharmonic was not affected. Moseley and the board realized that this was non-negotiable and quickly bowed before the inevitable, accepting his leadership of the Israeli orchestra.

Issues of authority were next on the list. Zubin was used to having a lot of authority in Los Angeles and he wanted to know how much of it he'd have in New York. One of the first things he saw was their orchestra contract. The orchestra contract, or 'trade agreement' between the New York Philharmonic Society and the musicians' union, spells out the details about hiring and firing, the number of rehearsals and concerts to be held each week, and various details of the orchestra's obligations and privileges.

Having final authority in hiring was of greater importance to Zubin than the rules of firing—he is, after all, he quips, not a 'firing conductor'. The orchestra contract contained provisions that made it tedious and time-consuming for a conductor to fire a player. But it also gave him the final authority in all hiring decisions, with the assistance of an advisory orchestra committee. Zubin believes that the music director must have the final say because he has a clear conception and vision of what he wants to bring into his orchestra. The players may sometimes be too concerned with virtuosity in an audition. 'It is the music director who knows exactly what kind of stone the orchestra needs to fill into a hole in the wall created by each vacancy.'[29]

Next the recording situation had to be settled before Zubin and the Philharmonic could reach an agreement. Intensive negotiations began between executives of London/Decca and CBS Records to see whether they could work out a plan to share the Philharmonic and Zubin. After complicated negotiations, both sides agreed to release each party from exclusivity in order to be able to record with the other.

In the end, there was only one issue that was not resolved to Zubin's complete satisfaction: the matter of the number of programmes the Philharmonic put on each year. Zubin preferred to have fewer programmes and to repeat them more often each season. He believes that the music gets digested better if you play a programme eight times instead of four. But because of the present set-up of Philharmonic programming, with twelve series running through the season, this was not possible.

A final meeting between Zubin and the Philharmonic officials sorted out the schedules of his concerts for the three seasons of the contract. Albert Webster, who became the Philharmonic's managing director upon Moseley's retirement in June 1978, said that they had asked Zubin for eighteen weeks each season and it was important to find out where those weeks would be on the calendar. After constructing a hypothetical schedule at some point in the discussion, they realized that a decision had been reached on what the actual schedule was going to be.

Zubin also asked Barenboim for his opinion once he made up his mind. Barenboim had guest conducted often in New York and was especially positive about the New York Philharmonic. Sometime later, Zubin conveyed his decision to the management at Los Angeles. On 19 January 1976, Fleischmann was sitting in his office chuckling over an article in the *New York Times* which discussed Zubin's candidacy for the music directorship of the New York Philharmonic. He told Zubin, 'Look, here they go again. They can't seriously think that you're still a candidate.' Zubin told a surprised Fleischmann, 'Well, I am. They're right. I'm going.'[30]

On 25 February, Behrendt, as president of the board of directors of the Los Angeles Philharmonic, announced that Zubin had decided not to renew his contract with the Los Angeles Philharmonic in order to accept the music directorship of the New York Philharmonic. Moseley made his announcement the same day. (On that very day a brief story had appeared in the *New York Times* headlined, 'Mehta May Get Boulez Place'. The story cited unconfirmed reports which neither the management in Los Angeles nor New York confirmed or denied.)

## SAYING GOODBYE

Behrendt, in her official statement to the press, lauded Zubin's role with the orchestra. She said that Zubin had contributed immeasurably towards making the Los Angeles Philharmonic one of the world's great orchestras. His superb artistry, wisdom and enthusiasm had given the people of Los Angeles an exciting and thriving musical culture of the highest international standards. She added that while New York was lucky to get him, Los Angeles had been immensely fortunate to have 'enjoyed his musical leadership for longer than most leading American orchestras can call on the services of a world-famous music director'.

The press release also included a brief statement from Zubin, which read: 'For some time I have been torn with the feeling that perhaps both Los Angeles and Zubin Mehta needed a change. At first I thought that devoting more time to opera would satisfy my urge to meet new challenges. It was, however, only when I was confronted with a firm offer from the president of the New York Philharmonic that everything came into focus.'[31]

After the meeting with the board, Zubin went to break the news to the orchestra. He did not beat about the bush and said: 'I might as well come to the point. I have decided to accept the musical directorship of the New York Philharmonic. Whether I'm doing the right thing or not, only time will tell.'[32] There was a hushed silence which was broken by an 'Oh Wow' from the violin section. Zubin—for all his feisty defence of the Los Angeles Philharmonic in 1967—was clearly stepping up. The next day Moseley met Chandler and Behrendt, and apologized for being a 'miserable robber'. He said they were awfully nice but greatly regretted losing Zubin.

On 5 May 1978, Zubin conducted his farewell concert in the Los Angeles Music Center. The audience rose and applauded him for almost a minute when he walked on to the stage. Things began poorly. First, the pianist, Barenboim, who had been scheduled to play Beethoven's Concerto No. 5, had to cancel because Du Pré had suffered a relapse. A programme consisting of Beethoven's *Egmont* Overture and his Concerto in C for Piano, Violin, Cello and Orchestra was then scheduled, plus the originally planned Mahler Symphony No. 1. There were two minor glitches which involved the starting time of the concert and the delay in the arrival of Zubin's formal clothing. Zubin had ordered that his formal clothing be delivered to the Music Center at 8.15 p.m. He borrowed a tuxedo for the overture, and the show went on, albeit about ten minutes late. He was properly garbed in tails for the Concerto and Symphony.[33]

At intermission, John Ferraro, president of the Los Angeles City Council, briefly thanked Zubin for his tenure, saying the city 'admired and loved the independence, self-discipline and dedication' he had brought to the orchestra. He added, 'We thank him for all the joy he has brought to this city.'[34] The farewell concert was a typically flashy conducting performance and the audience seemed to love every moment of it. After the programme, the audience gave Zubin a standing ovation for twelve minutes, recalling him seven times to shouts of 'Bravo!' The applause subsided only after Zubin shepherded the entire orchestra into the wings, leaving the stage empty.[35]

What prompted Zubin to switch? Zubin and the Los Angeles musicians had been inseparable for nearly sixteen years and the relationship may just have started to become a little stale. Zubin concedes in his autobiography that his players knew the pieces of the classical symphonic repertoire almost by heart and could have played these masterpieces just as well without him, though only in the way Zubin had interpreted them. Then there was the fact that in Los Angeles, his was the only show in town. He wanted more musical stimulation, the kind he had had in Vienna as a student. In New York he could work with his own orchestra during the day and go out and hear a visiting orchestra, an opera or a solo recital in the evening. New York was the centre of the musical world and that's where he wanted to be. The offer was an irresistible rite of passage for a conductor of the first rank whose ambition was matched by his courage. Zubin told *Time* magazine that his decision was a hard one 'but New York is the centre of the world now. And it is important to me that I be there.'[36]

He also said that he felt he should move there at his age rather than when he was fifty-five or so.

Zubin's appointment as music director of the New York Philharmonic from the 1978 season ended a year-long search at the Philharmonic. Sir Georg Solti, director of the Chicago Symphony Orchestra, had turned down the post the previous year, once again serving as Zubin's inadvertent benefactor. (According to Stephen E. Rubin who told the story in the *New York Times*, Moseley had flown secretly to Europe and offered Solti the job the previous spring. Solti declined the offer around December. Explaining the rejection, Solti took a subtle dig at Zubin. Calling it a difficult decision, he said, 'But as a close friend said to me, "If you have a Rolls-Royce, why change it."'[37] The allusion was to the remarks Zubin had made while protesting his disinterest in the New York Philharmonic.)

Maazel and Barenboim were also mentioned. Schonberg speculated in the *New York Times* that the shortlist may also have included Colin Davis, Ozawa and Haitink. Moseley was thrilled with his catch. Justifying the selection, he said Zubin was a fine conductor who had a dramatic personality, leadership qualities and audience appeal. His sixteen years at Los Angeles showed his *Sitzfleisch*: he could stick with an orchestra for an extended period of time. And he had built the Los Angeles Philharmonic from a second-rung orchestra to one of the dozen greats in the world. What would also have weighed decisively in Zubin's favour was that his contract called for a minimum of sixteen weeks with the orchestra, and a maximum of twenty-two weeks seemed a possibility—more time than the Philharmonic had enjoyed with a single conductor since Bernstein's early years.

## THE ZUBIN MEHTA LEGACY IN LOS ANGELES

While Zubin was credited with dramatically raising the artistic fortunes of the Los Angeles Philharmonic, he was criticized for a somewhat limited area of expertise. It was an acknowledged fact that he excelled in the grandiose German-Romantic repertory, but he was found wanting on occasion in dealing with earlier music, more delicate music, or adventurous music of the twentieth century. However, his glamorous image, energy and vitality—major assets in a position where public support is of crucial importance—remained beyond dispute.

*Los Angeles Times* music critic Bernheimer was Zubin's most trenchant critic throughout his tenure as music director. He accused Zubin of 'superficial performances which stressed bombast over subtlety and revealed impetuosity rather than maturity'.[38] He also took Zubin to task for programming which was frequently arbitrary in its combinations of dissimilarities. The components of a programme must suit each other in mood, style and content. They have to be complementary. Bernheimer said that at the Philharmonic one got the feeling that works were placed together only because the combination happened to fill the required time slot.

According to him, Zubin was also guilty of slighting the baroque and classical eras both in quality and quantity of performance. Bernheimer did credit him with expanding the repertory when it came to twentieth-century music, but felt that Zubin's service to contemporary composers was uneven. While he programmed numerous premieres, he seemed to undo some of the good work with performances that seemed 'dutiful if not disdainful' and made statements which bred a feeling of condescension in the audience. (He once laughingly declared that Krzysztof Penderecki's First Symphony would be played before the interval, because otherwise the entire audience might flee.)[39]

Zubin's absence from Los Angeles also attracted adverse comment ('busy hop scotching around the world and tending to his other orchestra'[40]). Zubin, Bernheimer said, had little time to pause, reflect, probe, digest and re-evaluate. 'He often seems to be coasting on his immense natural talent and on easy podium effects. It works well in the obvious Romantic showpieces, but in the long run it isn't enough to satisfy the most discerning listener.'[41] Unsurprisingly, the Los Angeles Philharmonic excelled in the grandiose Romantic indulgences which Zubin conducted best. Bernheimer also carped about the fact that the orchestra under Zubin hated to play softly. ('Bona fide, shimmering pianissimos are a luxury.'[42]) Although Zubin never had difficulty in pleasing the casual concertgoer, he did not always charm the musical cognoscenti.

Critics were of the view that, in general, refinement of expression and restraint of emotion were not what one normally associated with a Mehta performance. His interpretations often gave off sparks but seldom a mellow glow. Zubin's performance as an accompanist also came in for some stick accusing him of sometimes being disinterested, inflexible and even wilful in allowing the orchestra to overpower the soloist. This criticism, however, was strange given the fact that most soloists thought that Zubin was and is one of the best conductors to perform solos with.

That there was more than a grain of truth in Bernheimer's assertions became apparent in the tenure of his successor, Giulini. 'Under Mehta, the Philharmonic sounded brash, aggressive and a bit raw; under Giulini, it suddenly became a refined, subtle and responsive musical ensemble.'[43] There is a tendency of the local critic to become impatient if not bored with the local conductor, whose work can become too familiar and therefore dull. But there were other critics too, far removed from Los Angeles, who often echoed Bernheimer's views. Thomas Willis's *Chicago Tribune* review of a concert in which Zubin conducted Mahler called his interpretation 'basically middle-of-the-road, substituting energy for spirituality, and external drama for precise and careful analysis'. He wrote:

> For all the excitement, I still felt that I was floating on the surface instead of being submerged. With Mahler you should be able to drown and return to life.[44]

Several Los Angeles players, while recalling his days with the orchestra, praised Zubin's rehearsals as 'fun' and 'efficient' and lauded his rapid grasp of a complicated score. But they also recalled his indifference to detail, especially when the music did not deeply interest him.

The acoustics of the Dorothy Chandler Pavilion also came in for some adverse comment. From his customary location at the side of row F, Bernheimer said that the orchestra frequently overpowered the soloists and the climactic outburst tended to shatter. He held that in the centre of the orchestra section, if there was a piano concerto, you could not hear the piano because the sound just wasn't defined. He said that the hall, the conductor and his own location could be to blame. Zubin says that Bernheimer's opinion on acoustics should be taken with a pinch of salt because even though they tried to give him better seats, he insisted on sitting in the same place for every concert, the extreme left aisle, where he could be close to the exit and the first to leave.[45] The seeds of discord had been sown from the time of their first interview and it was often speculated that Bernheimer's constant criticism may have been the result of some personal animus. Given his independence of spirit, Zubin was (and still is) curiously sensitive on the subject of his relationship with his most acid-tongued detractor. 'It is hard to believe that in all these years, there is not one phrase of music he has found sensitive. He says all the bombastic passages were good. I won't accept that. I will not. I sincerely believe he doesn't listen.'[46]

Bernheimer deplored the 'aura of adulatory puffery' which engulfed Zubin in Los Angeles. The city had found a symbol to capture its cultural fancy and 'clasped the extroverted conductor to its collective breast'. Zubin, for his part, always claimed that he rejected the glamorous persona attributed to him but Bernheimer felt that the extravagantly feted conductor did little, if anything, to dismantle the cult figure image. He cited as examples the portrait of Zubin in the Pavilion, the ushers wearing Nehru-style coats, the huge billboard on Sunset Boulevard, remarks about women in orchestras and about New York City, among other things.

But what Bernheimer ignored was that in a bar located in a lower level of the Music Center, there were several exhibition cases, some containing models of operatic decor, including the costume worn by Merrill as Escamillo in *Carmen* and the Yves St Laurent gown Chandler donned on the opening night of the Pavilion. Zubin also pointed out that he has never at any point in his career employed a press agent; after Hearst passed away he never had a manager in the United States (though he had agents abroad) and so if there was a personality cult, it was a creation of the media.

Doryphore Bernheimer also gave credit where it was due. He observed that a Mehta reading of a piece of music could on occasion be unorthodox but never uninteresting, since Zubin knew how to 'enliven even the most standard standard'. 'Still he never craves nonconformity for its own sake. His brand of freshness seems to come from a new, unbiased examination of the score, coupled with a canny evaluation of—and perhaps, instinct for—the composer's intentions.'[47] Bernheimer said that Zubin was sufficiently talented to warrant the respect of the international music establishment, yet sufficiently flamboyant and romantic to capture the collective imagination of local supporters. He admitted that the specific matching of maestro and metropolis was 'fortuitous and mutually advantageous'. He called Zubin's tenure one which was marked by vitality and growth and on occasion by a halting spirit of adventure.[48]

When I asked Zubin about his most acerbic critic, he said that their first meeting lasting about half an hour had gone off very well. He was therefore surprised when a rather upset Chandler called and asked him why he had treated the music critic so badly. 'It was one of the very few times when she sounded really angry,' Zubin said. Apparently, Bernheimer had expected to be asked to stay for lunch and took what he considered a slight badly (and personally). 'I have never ever dined with a critic,' Zubin told me, 'so I don't know why he took it so amiss.' When I told Zubin that Bernheimer had also praised him on occasion, he said, 'Maybe, but it was mostly negative.'[49]

When Zubin left Los Angeles, even his worst detractors said that he had led a provincial orchestra to world-class status. During his sixteen years in Los Angeles, even Zubin's strongest critics admitted that the orchestra had improved. Part of that was due to what Zubin called a 'spirit of congeniality' he built among the players. He attributed his success to a fruitful relationship between him and his players' committees, and the presence of a strong administrator in Fleischmann. Zubin says that the worst thing for an orchestra is an uninvolved player. 'You don't make music by engaging the best people—the best people don't make the best music.' The involvement of the players and the orchestra's personality are important. 'Some of my first concerts in Montreal were fantastic, and I want to tell you that was not a great orchestra.'[50] (On 13 December 2012, Zubin conducted the same programme he had offered fifty years ago when he made his debut as music director of the Los Angeles Philharmonic. The day was declared Zubin Mehta Day in Los Angeles County and the city named him a Living Cultural Treasure, one of only five. It was after all Zubin who had put the Philharmonic 'on the map'. Taking the microphone at the end of the concert, Zubin remembered his 'friend and guru' Ravi Shankar who had passed away two days earlier.)

## AT THE HELM IN NEW YORK

Zubin succeeded the French composer-conductor Boulez, once the enfant terrible of the avant-garde. A supreme orchestral technician—his players called him the 'French Correction'—he was unable to charm the older subscribers or 'assert himself as an exciting interpreter of the bread-and-butter-repertory'.[51] Boulez had been a cool ascetic leader, more interested in the nuances of reticence than in the dynamics of expression. It was hoped that Zubin would be an antidote to his astringency and bring back some of the fire of the Bernstein days. On the other hand, there were some who were less than delighted. Zubin, they felt, had a reputation for more gloss than substance. There was also the question of his repertoire which stressed Tchaikovsky and Strauss to the detriment of the classics. And not all had forgiven his remarks about New York and its musicians.[52]

But Zubin was eager to begin afresh in New York. He was realistic about the job ahead of him and conciliatory towards the orchestra he would soon head. In September 1976, he had observed, 'You know the point comes—and I'm including myself because I made those terrible remarks once upon a time—that the New York Philharmonic gets too many blows below the belt. They play as many good and bad concerts as any other big orchestra. You don't improve a situation by knocking it.'[53]

On 14 September 1978, almost three years after Moseley came to

California to deliver his orchestra's proposal, Zubin conducted his first concert at Avery Fisher Hall as the new music director of the New York Philharmonic. 'Things went well right from the beginning—I could feel it in my stick,' Zubin said, looking back on his first months with the orchestra. 'I was a little nervous at the start. After all, I hadn't had a new job or a "first rehearsal" as a music director in sixteen years. But there was no trouble. We just made music together with goodwill on both sides. Now I just need a place to settle down. At this point, I'm allergic to hotel rooms.'[54]

The musicians in New York appeared to welcome the change. Concertmaster Rodney Friend said, 'There's a feeling in the orchestra of the beginning of a very exciting and productive period.' Violinist Oscar Ravina pointed out: 'Boulez was not trying to reach the audience with spontaneous feeling, or luscious phrasing. We'll be coming closer to that kind of thing with Mehta.'[55] The positive vibrations showed in Zubin's first rehearsals where he radiated pent-up emotion that electrified the orchestra. Zubin's first-season repertoire included lots of familiar fare. There were no plans for a major overhaul. 'Innovation,' he said, 'happens as you go along.'

Zubin and Nancy had relocated to Manhattan's East Side but retained their beloved villa in Brentwood. As for the Los Angeles Philharmonic, it inherited an unsurpassed replacement in the Italian Giulini. As one Los Angeles Philharmonic staffer put it: 'You could say that we've lost a Hercules, but we're getting a God.'[56] And almost all the credit for getting Giulini to Los Angeles went to Fleischmann. In what was probably his most brilliant managerial coup, he succeeded in persuading one of the great conductors of the day to accept the music directorship of the Los Angeles Philharmonic. Fleischmann promised Giulini that he would not have to conduct more than eight or ten subscription weeks a year, plus recordings and tours, all spread out in such a way that he could have weeks off between programmes and as much rehearsal time as he needed. He also promised to take on many administrative duties, something which the conductor greatly disliked. (In this Giulini was not alone, for many conductors are disinclined to take on managerial responsibilities and abhor daily administrative chores.)

Fleischmann was a gifted talent detector and was also responsible for hiring Finnish conductor Esa-Pekka Salonen who led the orchestra through an extraordinary period, beginning in 1992. The speed of his response to every situation was famously swift (he was nicknamed Flick-knife Fleischmann), especially when it came to spotting new talent. In 2009, the sensational young Dudamel from Venezuela, whom he had picked out in a German conducting competition six years ago, succeeded Salonen at the Los Angeles Philharmonic.[57]

Unlike the flamboyant Zubin, Giulini was shy and self-effacing and though his performances had been celebrated internationally for nearly three decades, most observers had regarded him as an unlikely choice for Los Angeles. Many felt that the critical factor was the reputation the orchestra had achieved under Zubin. Giulini himself acknowledged Zubin's role: 'Everything that has been done by Mr. Mehta in the past fifteen years to develop the orchestra has been perfect. All that is necessary now for me is to continue.'[58] As for Zubin's appointment, *Newsweek* magazine couldn't have put it any better: 'The world's most visible orchestra has chosen the world's most visible conductor.'[59]

# The New York Philharmonic

ZUBIN'S TENURE AS MUSIC director of the New York Philharmonic started with a free outdoor concert in Central Park's Sheep Meadow on 14 August 1978, before a crowd estimated at 1,40,000. It was in 1965 that the New York Philharmonic had given its first free concert in Central Park, ending the programme with Beethoven's Ninth Symphony under the baton of Steinberg. Zubin played Wagner's *Rienzi* Overture, Ravel's *La Valse* and Tchaikovsky's Fourth Symphony.

Before the start of the concert, the question on everyone's lips was whether the chemistry that fuses a conductor and an orchestra into a single music-making entity would be apparent. By the end of the concert, it was evident that the orchestra had begun to adjust to its new music director. The audience gave them a rousing ovation; the musicians too seemed delighted with the way things had gone—and the Philharmonic officials seemed enormously relieved. The day before the concert, Zubin had rehearsed at the Alice Tully Hall and there was palpable tension in the air. Zubin told the orchestra that he had been 'pretty shaky yesterday, but now I've calmed down and I really look forward to this rehearsal'.[1] They started with Ravel's *La Valse* and by the time the orchestra took a break at the end of the piece, most of the tension had vanished. When asked if the orchestra frightened him, Zubin replied in the negative and, with a smile, added that he hoped that he didn't frighten them either.

In one sense, Zubin had a lucky break in his first days with the Philharmonic since the New York papers were on strike and, though there was television and magazine coverage, the glare of publicity was less intense. The audience, too, had a chance to make up its own mind without being told what to think by the press. Zubin says that there were two responses when his New York tenure started: a section of the press harped on his comments about the Philharmonic a decade ago; the other drew attention to the coincidence of Zubin being born on the same day that the great Toscanini had conducted his last concert with the New York Philharmonic.

By mid-November, Zubin completed his first series of concerts and music critic Schonberg was full of praise:

> Mr. Mehta is a romantic through and through, and he has been getting the orchestra to play with an unusually rich sound. His beat is an orchestra player's delight. It is almost text-book in its motion, moving in fairly large arcs in an unfussy manner.[2]

But the last part of that review came with its words of warning, which in a sense were prescient:

> Whether the love affair will continue remains to be seen. The Philharmonic has been known to turn around and bite, and conductors have walked away bleeding. But right now all is harmony.

Zubin's first season with the orchestra was an unqualified success. He and the orchestra made four television appearances and five recordings, including the soundtrack of the Woody Allen film *Manhattan* which became one of the top-selling Philharmonic recordings of all time. He led the orchestra on tour in September 1978 to Argentina and, for the first time in the ensemble's history, the Dominican Republic. In April 1979, he led a tour to the East Coast, playing at Boston, Hartford,

Washington and Philadelphia. *Newsweek* referred to the 'honeymoon' between Zubin and the Philharmonic:

> The New Yorkers may have been expecting arrogance and erratic temperament; what they got was good humour—and musical authority.[3]

Schonberg called it 'The Year of Zubin Mehta'. The memory of Zubin's description of the orchestra musicians as a bunch of infamous malcontents was all but forgotten. His success in the first season was such that in May 1979, his contract was extended through 1986. He would conduct eighteen weeks of subscription concerts; in addition, there would be two to four or more weeks of touring and special events.

It was partly Zubin's accommodating and relaxed manner that helped him win over the hard-boiled Philharmonic. 'When Mehta conducts,' said flautist Julius Baker, one of the orchestra's best-known superstars, 'he invariably commands marvellous discipline. He has created a good atmosphere. And also, he has a way of relaxing the tension of a rehearsal by coming out with a Yiddish phrase suddenly. It warms the cockles of my Jewish heart.'[4]

More than anything else, it was his skill as a conductor that helped erase any lingering doubts among Philharmonic members. 'I've been concertmaster for some fifteen years on both sides of the Atlantic,' said Philharmonic concertmaster Friend, 'and I've never come across a conductor with a stronger stick technique. Technically, it's one of the most unbelievable experiences to play with Mehta.' Another orchestra musician explained, 'The greatest thing of all is that we sound better. Everybody's noticed it.' The critics too, commented on the new sound of the Philharmonic. 'The orchestra played well for its new conductor,' wrote Schonberg in the *New York Times*'s catch-up edition after the newspaper strike, '. . . The sound was exceptionally warm.'[5]

Andrew Porter of the *New Yorker* commented, 'In the Philharmonic's playing there was a more loving concern for expressive colors and for emotional phrasing than I've heard in a long time.' Not all the critics, however, found the new sound pleasing. Alan Rich of *New York Magazine* complained of 'horn glissandi incorrectly articulated, minor inner voices given undue prominence, a dynamic range so extreme that once again, all sense of line disappears'.[6] As for the orchestra's baton envy, percussionist Morris Langre remarked on Zubin's down-to-earth manner. 'He's not at all coming on like a superstar,' he said. 'We feel that he's extremely sincere. Actually, I haven't heard a negative word about Mehta. Even the most intense complainers seem pretty pleased with him.'[7]

For Zubin, the pace was hectic. On a typical high-gear day—and there were many of those—he was up at 8 a.m. Skipping breakfast, he spent the morning studying scores before crossing Central Park to get to the Lincoln Center. The morning rehearsal would last for two hours. By 5 p.m. he would be on his way home, returning for an evening concert at 7.30 p.m. On such days he was rarely in bed before 2 a.m.[8]

## THE MEHTA YEARS

The record of accomplishment, which the Philharmonic outlined in a privately published volume called *The Mehta Years*, was impressive. Whether the orchestra was better when Zubin left it than it was in 1978, as many believe, or merely different, it was undeniably Zubin's orchestra. He hired forty-four of the 106 players, most of whom remained with the orchestra, and were known for their fine musicianship and technical virtuosity.

While some questioned Zubin's commitment to contemporary music, his record of conducting premiere performances during his time with the Philharmonic left no doubt of his interest in the 'music of today'. He resented the fact that he was often accused of paying only lip service to contemporary music. Blunt and outspoken, he made no bones about the fact that he thought some contemporary music was complete garbage, something which none of his colleagues had the courage to say. When prodded for details, he said that he had no affinity with a whole period called neo-baroque or neo-modern, all the stuff written after the Second World War. 'It's European and American too, the whole school of pupils of Boulanger and Hindemith who write music that looks classical and sounds like it has got wrong notes in it. There's reams and reams of that stuff and I can't take it.' He added, 'A lot of it is wonderful. I love Luigi Nono and much of Krzysztof Penderecki.'[9]

Fifty-two works got their world premiere performances during his tenure, with thirty of them on programmes conducted by Zubin. These included Barber's Essay No. 3 for Orchestra which was part of the programme on Opening Night 1978. Other premieres over the years included Penderecki's Symphony No. 2 (May 1980), Bernstein's *A Musical Toast* (October 1980), *Raga Mala* by Ravi Shankar, William Schuman's *On Freedom's Ground* (October 1986), Ellen Taaffe Zwilich's *Symbolon* (June 1988) and David Del Tredici's *Steps* (March 1990).

Zubin took on composers-in-residence, first Druckman, and then Del Tredici who oversaw the Horizons series of festivals of contemporary music. Horizons '83: The New Romanticism featured performances of twenty-five different works, including four world premieres and seven New York premieres. The next year, Horizons '84: The New Romanticism—A Broader View featured forty-six works by forty-two composers, including seven world, eight US and five New York premieres. Horizons '86 had Music as Theatre as its theme and involved at least one semi-staged work or some form of visual display. Horizons '90, with Del Tredici as artistic adviser, was called New Music for Orchestra and was a smaller affair, featuring performances of works by six composers, including three world premieres. There were also other festivals: Music in May in 1979 where works for classic and baroque orchestra were played, a Beethoven Festival in 1980 and The Romantic Era in the year that followed. The Mozart–Stravinsky Festival was held in 1982 and in 1986 there was Boulez Is Back, which saw the former music director of the Philharmonic return for the first time in nine years.

In the autumn of 1989, *Strings* magazine referred to Zubin's 'penchant for discovering and fostering talented young players'. A total of 425 guest performers made their debut appearances with the Philharmonic during his tenure. One of them was the eleven-year-old Japanese violinist Midori whom Zubin discovered and featured as a surprise soloist on a New Year's Eve programme. Midori saw a poster in a record store of Zubin conducting and pestered her mother for a copy of it. The poster was soon up in her room. When she moved to New York, she heard Zubin conduct and finally got to meet the man in the poster. 'I heard many great musical works for the first time under his direction; works by Strauss, Mahler, Bruckner, Beethoven, Stravinsky. I was a young girl living inside the violin repertoire, and he introduced me to the world of symphonic repertoire,'[10] she said.

Other artistes who made their Philharmonic debut included sopranos Montserrat Caballé and Dame Kiri Te Kanawa, tenors Luciano Pavarotti and Domingo, violinists Shaham and Ughi, narrators Hans Hotter, Angela Lansbury and Kirk Douglas. From India, Ravi Shankar and L. Subramaniam made their debut with the Philharmonic in Zubin's time.

The Philharmonic's free Park Concerts held in summer were its largest public-service effort, reaching hundreds of thousands of people each year in the five boroughs of New York and the neighbouring counties. On 20 August 1990, Zubin conducted his final concert in Central Park, a salute to Carnegie Hall that initiated the celebration of its centennial season. It was a landmark occasion in which the Carlos Moseley Music Pavilion, a new permanent outdoor facility, was inaugurated. Stern, as guest soloist, offered his services pro bono for the event.

Zubin had often remarked on the excellence of individual talent in the orchestra and took great pains to put his players forward, both as soloists and in chamber settings. One of the most laudable aspects of Zubin's tenure with the Philharmonic was his habit of providing principal players and sometimes even musicians below the rank of principal with solo showcases. He encouraged regular solo appearances by artistes such as concertmaster Dicterow and principal clarinettist Stanley Drucker.

No fewer than thirty orchestra members made their Philharmonic debut in the thirteen years Zubin was music director. They included Baker (flute), Leonard Davis (viola), Friend (violin), Warren Deck (tuba), Renée Siebert (flute), Mindy Kaufman (piccolo) and Eugene Levinson (double bass). Zubin made it a practice to feature soloists both on tour as well as at home. In 1990, the Philharmonic's 'A Five Star Evening', broadcast on the award-winning PBS series *Live From Lincoln Center*, featured concertmaster Dicterow, principal clarinettist Drucker, principal trumpeter Philip Smith and principal cellist Lorne Munroe under Zubin's direction. 'We have such fine instrumentalists,' he told an interviewer in 1983, 'that they solo during the New York season also. And when we go on tour, I'm very proud to show them off.'[11]

It was also an effective method of varying the workload of the musicians and lifting them from their otherwise faceless routine. It saved money for the Philharmonic and, by all accounts, was also welcomed by the audiences who came to know these solo players by name and enjoyed seeing them showcased. Concertmasters traditionally get solo opportunities and it was no surprise that Dicterow played forty-one times with the orchestra in a solo capacity during a six-year period from 1980 onwards.[12] Bringing key players into the spotlight and encouraging them to suggest the repertory was also a good way for Zubin to reinforce their loyalty. It improved morale since many players have solo ambitions and have to adjust psychologically when they become cogs in an orchestral machine.

Another of Zubin's initiatives which became a cherished tradition was the New York Philharmonic Chamber Ensembles established in 1983, with its annual six-concert series. Spearheaded by an active orchestra committee which determined all aspects of programming, the Ensembles received wide exposure at home and on tour, and involved more than 90 per cent of the orchestra's membership.

The Philharmonic's Young People's Concerts entered their seventh decade during Zubin's tenure. His commitment to developing musicians was demonstrated early in the 'Young Performers' series, in which student musicians chosen in national auditions appeared as soloists with the Philharmonic. Soprano Beverly Sills narrates how once, during a Young People's Concert, they showed the children a page from a score by Penderecki. It was a circle with notes all over it. 'How do you conduct music from a circle?' one of the children asked. 'Simple,' quipped Zubin, whose sense of humour is well known. 'I just keep making cartwheels.'[13]

Zubin was equally supportive of educational activities, which took many forms during his years with the Philharmonic. The annual joint concerts with the All-City High School orchestra involved combined rehearsals and coaching support from members of the Philharmonic. In 1986, Zubin broke new ground in the orchestra's long-standing relationship with the Juilliard School. He conducted the Juilliard Orchestra in a series of rehearsals, with the support of coaches from within the Philharmonic, culminating in the first joint concert of the two ensembles. (In December 1988, he conducted the Juilliard Orchestra for a benefit concert on behalf of the American-Israel Cultural Foundation in Carnegie Hall.)

NBC's critically acclaimed cultural series *Live from Studio 8H* twice featured Zubin and the orchestra in the early 1980s. The inaugural programme on 9 January 1980, a tribute to Toscanini with guest stars Perlman and Price, won an Emmy Award for best classical performing arts programme. Zubin also regularly conducted the Philharmonic on *Live from Lincoln Center*, collecting a total of six Emmy nominations. Its 1982 programme *An Evening with Danny Kaye* reached an audience of 6 million and won a Peabody Award. His early biographer Bookspan who served as the radio and television 'Voice of the New York Philharmonic' all through Zubin's tenure narrates an anecdote which took place during a concert broadcast live from the United Nations. Zubin's sense of humanity was fostered early and he has always been known for his tenacious commitment to principles. After being recalled to the podium for five or six bows, he told the audience: 'My colleagues of the New York Philharmonic and I thank you for your warm reception. We have just joined here in mutual harmony . . . Why can't you do the same?'[14] He also refused to perform in South Africa because of the policy of apartheid. He asked them where he would stay as an Indian and they said that they would make an exception in his case. Zubin refused, saying that there would be no concert until it was open for all. They said they could not do that since there were no bathroom facilities for non-whites.

There were also some memorable opening nights for the Philharmonic under Zubin. The opening night at the Philharmonic is one of New York's most glamorous autumn galas and Zubin's tenure was studded with a succession of fabulous ones. In September 1980, Stern, Perlman and Zukerman played together as part of the Pension Fund Benefit Concert in honour of Stern's sixtieth birthday. Stern was to figure on the line-up again, eight years later, when he played in an opening night benefit concert. Other notable performers who appeared on opening night included sopranos Price and Norman and violinists Perlman and Zukerman. The concert on 12 September 1990, with Rostropovich on the cello was a special one because it was Zubin's 1000th concert with the Philharmonic. The programme consisted of Mozart, Bloch and Tchaikovsky. It was also a concert to benefit the Musicians' Pension Fund.

*Pension Fund Benefit Concerts*

The Pension Fund Benefit Concerts have been a rich source of artistic satisfaction for the Philharmonic's audiences. While they were all special evenings, possibly none was as memorable as the one with Kaye in September 1981, which was telecast on the *Live from Lincoln Center* series.

Kaye and Zubin were good friends. On 23 September 1981, Kaye conducted a New York Philharmonic Pension Fund concert. It was his third appearance with the Philharmonic, having made his first in 1958 when Mitropoulos was the music director. The orchestra had been trying to get him for several years and Zubin was instrumental in helping him make up his mind. Kaye came on stage with two bundles of batons—at least thirty-five of them—found his favourite one, gave a vigorous up beat and saw the baton fly about twenty feet behind him into the audience. He did imitations of conductors—the neurotic type, the narcissistic type, the aged type. He even managed to conduct a few pieces along the way. He played pieces by Rossini, Ravel, Beethoven and Verdi, some television commercials and a bit of Johann Strauss.

The orchestra members looked on in wonderment and laughter as Kaye kept them entertained with his many antics on stage. In fact, the musicians were laughing so hard that they could barely play and decided for the first time in many years—since 1965, in fact, which was Kaye's last Philharmonic appearance—not to look at the conductor.[15] Zubin participated in the programme, warming up the orchestra in Strauss's *Die Fledermaus* Overture, and then gave over the rest of the evening to his guest conductor. He, however, served as master of ceremonies for the intermission broadcast in which Kaye, Domingo, Stern and Kissinger participated. If Kaye's antics on stage drew laughter from both the musicians and the audience, his conducting skills were hardly that of a complete amateur.

As Zubin commented, 'Danny does the best he can, and his best is very good, it's real orchestral routine. He has a natural beat, he keeps a steady rhythm, he know exactly what he wants and knows exactly how to get it. The humour is superimposed. As far as the music itself, there is no distortion at all.'[16] Mitropoulos had the same opinion about Kaye's conducting abilities, even saying that Kaye elicited a better sound from the players than he himself did. As far as the actual music went, there was nothing at all funny about it. The guests at the concert included Grant, Peck, Sills and Rodman Rockefeller. There was a dinner for 800 under a huge tent in adjacent Damrosch Park. In the course of his career, Kaye raised over $5 million in support of musicians' pension funds.

In June 1982, the New York Philharmonic and the Israel Philharmonic combined forces in Berlioz's *Symphonie Fantastique* to entertain an audience which had contributed in excess of half a million dollars, with half of the amount going to each orchestra's endowment fund. Zubin is well experienced in conducting such dual-orchestra concerts and we have already noted in an earlier chapter how he played the same composition in a combined performance of the Montreal Symphony Orchestra and the Los

Angeles Philharmonic at Montreal's Expo 67. The Berlioz was the last piece on the programme. Before that, Zubin had led the white-jacketed New York Philharmonic in a performance of Tchaikovsky's *Romeo and Juliet* Overture-Fantasy, followed by the black-jacketed Israel Philharmonic playing Bartók's suite from the ballet *The Miraculous Mandarin*. The Berlioz was enthralling to watch, with the two orchestras and their 200-plus members marching and countermarching across the enlarged stage at Avery Fisher Hall where the first eight rows had been removed to permit the expansion.[17]

### *Taking the A1 Train*

Zubin had long championed the idea of special programming for minority audiences. During his years with the Los Angeles Philharmonic, he took his orchestra to such locations as the all-black Trinity Baptist Church and the Federal Prison on Terminal Island. In New York, he took his musicians to the Abyssinian Baptist Church, a social and cultural landmark of Harlem.

In April 1980, Zubin conducted the musicians of the New York Philharmonic in an expansive, brassy programme well suited to the occasion. On stage were ninety of the orchestra's 106 musicians (all that would fit on the church stage). The 125-voice chorus (sixty-five from the church's own choir, the rest from Harlem groups) sang several selections from George Frideric Handel's *Messiah*. Organist Leonard Raver played the Church's 4000-pipe organ in the finale of Saint-Saëns's Symphony No. 3.[18]

The highlight of the evening was a performance by Price who had got married in the same church in 1952. She got standing ovations before, between and after her performances of 'Pace' from Verdi's *La Forza del Destino* and *He's Got the Whole World in His Hands*. As an encore, she sang 'Vissi d'arte' from Puccini's *Tosca*. The audience of 2000 people laughed and waved, overflowing from the pews on to folding chairs, and into the street outside to enjoy this special evening. Zubin and the church had originally planned to make admission to the event free but since corporate contributions were not forthcoming, they were forced to charge from $5 to $25 for tickets. 'The orchestra had been to South Korea, the Soviet Union, every place in the world, and not to Harlem,' Zubin said. 'It was scandalous.'[19] The press also warmed to the orchestra and observed: 'The Philharmonic takes the A1 train.' (The A1 is a train to Harlem.)

It was a spectacular and happy fulfilment of Zubin's vision of a neighbourhood outreach concert in Harlem. On 22 April, the *New York Post* wrote:

> Last night the New York Philharmonic went to the Abyssinian Baptist Church in Harlem and gave one of the most stirring and appreciated concerts in its long history.[20]

Zubin said, 'We are going back to Harlem next year, that's for sure.' As one enthusiast shouted from the balcony of the church, 'A-men.'[21] Zubin was as good as his word. The success of this programme led to a succession of Harlem concerts and Zubin conducted five more, the last being in December 1986. As Samuel D. Proctor, former pastor of the church, put it: 'The world is not quite the way it was before Zubin Mehta took the initiative and brought Jews, Catholics, Protestants, Blacks, Whites, Asians and Hispanics for six moments in which time and space were touched by eternity.'[22] Zubin also conducted a concert in December 1988 at Harlem's famous Apollo Theatre, beloved of jazz and popular performers for many decades. Cellist Anthony Elliott made his Philharmonic debut in a concert which consisted of Schubert, Mendelssohn, Puccini, Bizet and Tchaikovsky.

A few months later, towards the end of July, Zubin led the orchestra at the White House on the occasion of Indian Prime Minister Indira Gandhi's visit to the United States. This concert with Dicterow as soloist marked the first appearance of the full orchestra at the White House. Nancy was a good friend of the Reagans and both Mehtas were frequent visitors to the White House. But high on Zubin's list of peeves was President Ronald Reagan's decision to cut art funding by half. Nancy had recently been selected for a presidential task force on the arts and humanities but Zubin remembered Reagan's attitude towards the Los Angeles Philharmonic with disdain, saying that in eight years as governor of California, Reagan had come to only one concert! When asked why there was no Indian piece, he said he had invited Ravi Shankar but the latter had told him that he would require half an hour for just one piece, when half an hour was the time allotted for the whole performance!

## BOMBAY MEETS BENARES

Never one to shy away from trying something new, Zubin also collaborated with sitar maestro Ravi Shankar in what can best be described as experiments in fusion. It has long been understood that Indian and Western classical music have little in common from a musical standpoint, since there is little opportunity for genuine interaction between an oral tradition, where improvisation is central, and a notated one. When Rudyard Kipling famously said 'East is East, and West is West, and never the twain shall meet,' he may well have been talking of Western and Indian classical music.

When Menuhin and Ravi Shankar won the Grammy for Best Chamber Music Performance for their 1967 recording *West Meets East*, they appeared to have proved Kipling wrong. Instances when a Western classical musician such as Menuhin has attempted to play Indian music with a measure of authenticity are rare, but there have been a few times when Indian musicians, notably Ravi Shankar, have composed music in a Western classical format. Ravi Shankar's *Concerto for Sitar and Orchestra* and *Raga Mala*, two of his most famous and popular works, both feature solo sitar alongside a Western orchestra. *Raga Mala* was dedicated to, and first conducted by, Zubin. Ravi Shankar remained a deeply traditional artiste on the sitar, but he was also forever trying to bridge the gap between Indian classical music and the music of the West, and *Raga Mala* was his most ambitious attempt.

Before Ravi Shankar began his studies with his guru, Ustad Allauddin Khan, he had already had extensive contacts with the West, thanks to his elder brother by twenty years, Uday Shankar, of whose dance group he was a member. In the 1930s, it was Uday Shankar's troupe that introduced the Indian performing culture to the West. From the age of ten, till he turned eighteen, Ravi Shankar spent considerable time in Paris, where he learned French and imbibed a great deal of Western classical music, though he never studied it formally. He met many famous Western musicians and artists, a list which included Enescu, Segovia, Toscanini and Ignacy Jan Paderewski. Ravi Shankar said that though they all liked Indian classical music, they found it monotonous after a while because it seemed to them to go on and on. That hurt him and he wanted them to understand and appreciate Indian music—which explains in part his need to compose for non-traditional ensembles despite his unquestioned success as a sitar player in the traditional idiom.[23] Ravi Shankar's popularity in the United States soared after the 1969 Woodstock Festival, when he and Beatle George Harrison shared the stage for a memorable set.

After his successful chamber music collaboration with Menuhin, Ravi Shankar began considering the possibility of bringing sitar into an orchestral context. He was afforded this opportunity in the late 1970s, when he was commissioned to compose a sitar concerto for the London Symphony Orchestra to be conducted by Previn. The *Concerto for Sitar and Orchestra* was dedicated to Ustad Allauddin Khan and the work was translated into western notation by Fred Teague, one of his American students. Ravi Shankar based the piece on a series of ragas, transposing them into different keys in order to give the illusion of harmony. The concerto presents only one raga for each of the four movements. In each movement, Ravi Shankar develops the given raga while the orchestra responds. The concerto was composed in two and a half months and debuted in January 1971 at the Royal Festival Hall in London.

This concerto was performed around the world by both Ravi Shankar and his daughter Anoushka, much more frequently than the complex and difficult *Raga Mala*. Ravi Shankar admitted that both concertos were challenging for Western musicians and that he himself had difficulties in synchronizing the improvised sitar passages with the orchestra. The work invited flak from critics who labelled it a bastardization of two distinct forms of music. The choice of Previn as conductor of the composition could not have been more appropriate, since he too was comfortable crossing musical boundaries in spite of criticism. Previn was not only a reputed classical music conductor but also an accomplished jazz musician. He was also musical director for the 1973 film adaptation of Andrew Lloyd Webber and Tim Rice's rock opera *Jesus Christ Superstar*. Though he received an Oscar nomination for his work, he was marginalized in the world of classical music for having participated in a rock musical. Both Previn and Ravi Shankar received scathing criticism for compromising their art for commercial appeal. And both ignored their critics and did exactly as they pleased.

Ten years after the 1971 London debut of *Concerto for Sitar and Orchestra*, Zubin would conduct Ravi Shankar's more difficult second concerto, *Raga Mala*, in New York. Ravi Shankar (whom Zubin called the Jascha Heifetz of India) first met Zubin in the early 1960s in Montreal, when he was conductor of the Montreal Symphony Orchestra. Ravi Shankar says in his autobiography, *Raga Mala*, that he was highly impressed by him but discovered that he had limited knowledge of Indian classical music. He met him again in the late 1960s in Los Angeles when Zubin was the music director of the Los Angeles Philharmonic.

Between 1967 and 1970, Ravi Shankar rented a succession of four houses in Los Angeles. Celebrities like Marlon Brando, Peter Sellers, Terence Stamp and the four Beatles attended his parties. It was during this period of glamorous Hollywood parties that Ravi Shankar came across Zubin again. He recalls that a young and handsome Zubin was much in demand at all the parties. Ravi Shankar called him charming and funny, and although he was years younger, they became good friends—a friendship which ended with the sitar maestro's death in 2012.

Ravi Shankar admired Zubin not only for his musical virtuosity but also for the fact that he was still very much an Indian at heart. In *Raga Mala*, he writes:

> It is wonderful to see an Indian attaining such a prestigious position in the Western classical field as one of its top conductors and, despite his involvement in music that is so completely Western,

still maintaining his innate Indianness: in his way of talking, his manner, and his love for his homeland and its people.

*Raga Mala*

Since making his acquaintance for the first time in Montreal, Ravi Shankar had met Zubin on and off, but it was only in 1980 that they formed a closer bond. By the late 1970s, Ravi Shankar was ready to experiment once again. Luckily for him, Zubin had taken over as the music director of the New York Philharmonic in 1978, when he himself was spending a lot of his time in New York. He lived near Gramercy Park with Sue Jones, and their daughter Geetali (better known as Norah, and now a famous singer) was a few months old. He discussed the idea with Zubin who seemed keenly interested in such a project.

Zubin obtained the commission from the orchestra and suggested that Ravi Shankar visit the Avery Fisher Hall at the Lincoln Center on the mornings that he rehearsed with his orchestra. That way he could get an idea about the musicians and their sound, their abilities and limitations, and the range of what he could do with them. In doing as Zubin advised, Ravi Shankar discovered some great musicians, including the flautist Baker. Zubin recalls that the composition practically grew in his home. Of this creative collaboration was born *Raga Mala*, Ravi Shankar's second sitar concerto. In fact, he wrote the piece with particular musicians in mind for the solo parts. There were four movements, which lasted an hour. Ravi Shankar worked with the soloists of the New York Philharmonic—the concertmaster, the first trumpet, the first clarinet—and they listened to what he wanted and advised him. He wrote extended solos for all of them. The tabla part was to be played on tom-toms. *Raga Mala* employed many instruments he had not used in the first concerto, which made it sound quite different. Ravi Shankar took about thirty different ragas one after the other, playing long pieces of each of the earlier ones followed by a progressively shorter elaboration of each of the succeeding ragas, so that in the end they were mere flashes of ragas, eight to sixteen bars each.

After the orchestral tutti that opened the concerto, Ravi Shankar entered with a solo in traditional alaap style. This sounded improvised at first but was, in fact, composed. Specific instruments responded to certain phrases, making it clear that there was nothing spontaneous about the entire solo. Zubin recalls that he would wait for Ravi Shankar to arrive at a certain note before he could continue.

Ravi Shankar and Zubin first performed this composition in April 1981 but it proved to be more difficult than the first concerto. Ravi Shankar said that the first movement with 'Lalit', a morning raga, was especially difficult. To Western ears, this raga seemed to have too unusual a pattern. Ravi Shankar recalled that before he composed the concerto, Zubin had suggested: 'Let it be something like hot chilli. Make it difficult.' He made it really complicated and the musicians had a difficult time playing the piece.

Ravi Shankar was hard on himself and said that he had not liked his own rendition. While he said that Zubin conducted it wonderfully, he felt that he had made a mess of his own playing. This was due in part, he says in his autobiography, to the 'discordant sounds or wrong rhythmic accents' he heard in the background which affected his concentration. Ravi Shankar admitted that playing with an orchestra is different and difficult. In a solo recital, he is his own master, leader, conductor and performer, and can improvise at will. But in an orchestral setting, he was completely shackled.

He said, 'In the first concerto I built my own prison and this one is going to be the same. With my sitar recitals, I'm free. Here, everything is fixed. Even in the portions in which I improvise, I have cues.' Zubin also realized that Ravi Shankar felt terribly handicapped during the rehearsals because he had to keep to the number of measures allotted to him. Zubin encouraged Ravi Shankar to play more, while the sitar maestro wanted to hear more of the orchestra. The music was well received. They played the concerto four or five times in New York and then in Europe to standing ovations.

In March 1982, Ravi Shankar and Zubin performed it with the London Philharmonic Orchestra at the Royal Festival Hall. The London musicians struggled to reproduce parts that had been written specifically for the New York players. Since the parts were player-specific, the players in London had to devote a lot of time to practise their parts. Zubin and Ravi Shankar also recorded the concerto which, despite many flaws, captured the excitement and emotional depth of the composition.

Speaking about their collaboration, Zubin says, 'It was really two friends getting together, wanting to be together on stage, that made our collaboration possible. Musicians appreciate one another. It is wonderful to have colleagues from different worlds speak and listen to each other. And my collaboration with Raviji during the second concerto was one that educated me more than anybody else.'

Regardless of its popular appeal, the reaction of the critics confirmed what has always been well known: Indian and Western classical music have almost nothing in common and therefore don't mix well. Rockwell, while calling the result 'never less than graceful and pleasant' wrote in the *New York Times*:

> But Mr. Shankar is not used to thinking in orchestral terms, and the concerto broke down into a strung together sequence of bits and pieces. This is very different from Indian music itself, which builds inexorably from spiritual meditations to the most exhilarating climaxes.[24]

In September 1985, Ravi Shankar's *Concerto for Sitar and Orchestra* premiered in New York under Zubin and the orchestra as part of the New York Philharmonic's 'Salute to the Festival of India', a gala concert that began the ensemble's new season. (Zubin conducted the first concerto again in 1997, at London's Barbican Hall, home of the London Symphony Orchestra.) Donal Henahan, music critic for the *New York Times*, wrote that while the concerto 'gave the orchestra some strikingly odd and beautiful sonorities to explore, the material was never transformed in any way that a Western listener could find interesting.' He added: 'It was, however, still easy to enjoy Mr. Shankar's fabled virtuosity and the crafty manner in which he let the orchestra support and highlight it.'[25]

Zubin's and Ravi Shankar's paths crossed once again in April 1989, when they toured together with the European Youth Orchestra, which consisted of talented musicians from all over Europe, roughly between the ages of eighteen and twenty-four. The itinerary included London and Madrid, and then Calcutta, Bombay and New Delhi. In Bombay, *Raga Mala* was first performed at Shanmukhananda Hall and later to a huge audience at Brabourne Stadium. Zubin turned out in a dagli and Shankar wore a silk kurta. During the performance, Ravi Shankar wove the tune of 'Happy birthday to you' into one of his improvisational solos: Zubin had turned fifty-three six days earlier.

*Raga Mala*, even if it had not completely won over the critics, had been popular with audiences abroad. But in India, it was a complete disaster. Zubin recalls that they played *Raga Mala* and Mahler's First for about 12,000 people in Calcutta. While Mahler received a standing ovation, *Raga Mala* was poorly received by the audience who considered it an 'amalgam of disparate elements'. It did not go down well with the Indian audiences since they wanted to hear the development of the raga—the improvisation that is hardly possible with fusion. Instead, all they heard was the orchestra trying to improvise, which again could hardly be given that label since all the improvisations were written out, and not the result of spontaneous creativity. Zubin says that in Indian classical music, the height of improvisation comes after three or four hours of just 'playing until you get hot', and they didn't appreciate that. 'Orchestra players cannot improvise, especially in the Indian vein, and Ravi Shankar, when he plays, is a free bird,' Zubin said.

### *Can East Really Meet West?*

There is little doubt that the two musical traditions are vastly different. There are fundamental differences between the two. Improvisation, which is the distinguishing feature of Indian classical music, hardly mixes with the complete organization which defines Western classical music, where a large group of individuals comes together to form a cohesive whole. Here individual brilliance is submerged in collective excellence. Numerous individual talents have to be organized into a harmonious group.

Then there is the music itself. In the Western stream, every piece of music is written down, with the composer defining the tempo of each movement and even the size of the orchestra. The conductor and the orchestra work within the confines of these fairly rigid parameters. The music demands not only the submersion of individual identity but also teamwork, with each musician being part of an ensemble. Most of all, both conductor and orchestra follow a written musical score which defines rigidly how a piece is to be played. Indian classical music by contrast has its emphasis on individuality, on improvisation, on mood and environment (morning and evening ragas), on a tradition with no written score and, finally, the complete absence of ensemble or team effort. While the Western score is characterized by structure, in the Indian classical tradition there is always improvisation, some addition being made to standard form or design in every performance.

On the face of it, it appeared that Zubin shared Ravi Shankar's inner drive to bridge the East and West. But he was well aware of the perils of mixing the two. Zubin told the *New York Times* that 'this isn't so much East meets West as Bombay meets Benares'. Zubin said, 'It's just two different parts of India getting together. His first sitar concert just confirmed my view that these two worlds of East and West can't mix. But Ravi and I have always been friends; I introduced him years ago to some jazz musicians I knew in Los Angeles. We've always kept in touch. He said he'd learned a lot from his first concerto and wanted to try another. This is just two friends getting together and trying to do something. Maybe it will be the start of something new, and maybe it won't. It's just an attempt.'[26]

Criticized as an iconoclast, Ravi Shankar in his defence said that this was because critics had mixed his identity as a performer and composer. As a composer, he said, he had tried everything, but as a performer he was getting more classical and orthodox and jealously protected the heritage that he had inherited. But Ravi Shankar still had one unfulfilled desire. If there was one fusion that he still dreamed of doing, it was performing with Zubin and the Israel Philharmonic Orchestra. Ravi Shankar said, 'It simply doesn't work out because of our schedules, but we are such great friends and I have performed with Mehta in India and all over the world, so yes, I would love very much to do it in Israel.' Unfortunately, that never happened and Ravi Shankar passed on in 2012. But Zubin did perform with his daughter Anoushka Shankar both in Florence and in Israel. (Anoushka and her film-maker husband, Joe Wright, named their son, born in February 2011, Zubin.)

## ANOTHER EXTENSION

The end of 1983 saw Zubin's contract with the New York Philharmonic being extended to 1990. The extension came two years before his contract was to expire. Despite the fact that Zubin had for several years been accused of inconsistency and that his effectiveness in dealing with the orchestra had been regularly debated, his extension was an acknowledgement that the management did not see him as the problem. The indisputable fact was that the New York Philharmonic's reputation for cynicism had survived or generations. As Henahan pointed out in the *New York Times*, this decision was not in itself surprising given the fact that a list of potentially available candidates would have been a short one indeed. He observed: 'Mr. Mehta actually is in the upper crust of a rather small loaf.'[27]

Cellist Naomi Graffman recalls playing with four leading orchestras in less than three months. She played with the Chicago Symphony, Cleveland Orchestra, the Orchestre de Paris and the New York Philharmonic. According to her, the last two were the *worst* orchestras in the world. She said, 'They contained the greatest instrumental elements you can imagine, but they are all such second grade, low-class kids that the moment any one comes to conduct them, they say, "get the teacher".'[28]

## A FORCED REST

In March 1984, Zubin underwent surgery for lateral epicondylitis, a severe chronic inflammation of the muscles attached to the elbow—an injury akin to tennis elbow, which was the result of vigorous arm and hand movements while conducting. Zubin was hospitalized for one week and housebound in New York for another. Frank Milburn, the music administrator of the New York Philharmonic, said that Zubin's elbow problems were not new. He remembered a performance in Berlin nine years earlier, when the intermission had to be extended while Zubin tried to recover from the discomfort in his elbow. Milburn said that he had known about his condition for a year and a half. Cortisone injections did not really work, though six months of rest might have done the job, but someone with Zubin's career and workload could hardly be expected to take that much time off.

Zubin had two years of non-surgical treatment for his condition but ultimately decided to opt for surgery. The operation was performed at the Hospital for Special Surgery in Manhattan by his friend Dr Leon Root, and was declared a success. Zubin's right arm was in a splint for three weeks. The operation meant that he would not be able to conduct his final six weeks of subscription programmes with the New York Philharmonic that season. He continued to stay in New York during his recuperation and attended to the administrative matters of the Philharmonic.

The 1983–84 season proved to be a trying time for Milburn and managing director Webster. Rafael Kubelík, suffering from a wrist fracture, had withdrawn from his two weeks of concerts, and Previn had cancelled a December engagement because of a broken toe. Eleven of the orchestra's thirty-five weeks of subscription concerts were affected by conductor replacements, an uncommonly high number given that the usual was about four weeks in a year.

In April 1984, Zubin found himself in an unaccustomed role at the Abraham Goodman House. Filling in for Tony Randall at the last minute, he had to play Robert Schumann opposite Nancy as Clara Schumann. Nancy had been cast all along in *The Schumanns: Romance in Music and Letters*, a Concerts Plus chamber music programme—a dramatic recitation about the Schumanns' love, drawn from their letters and diaries, accompanied with music by both of them. Zubin who was recovering from surgery appeared with his right hand in a sling (with a scruffy beard as he could not shave), and with reading glasses for his onstage stint. The artistic director of Concerts Plus was Simca Heled, a prodigy who had joined Zubin and the Israel Philharmonic as principal cellist while still in his teens. It was a new experience for Zubin since this was the first time he had ever been on *any* stage with his wife. Zubin's performance came in for praise, with critics calling it direct, intense and refreshingly natural. The text described the Schumanns' early love affair and then jumped to Robert's madness and death.[29] Zubin lauded his wife's performance and said that if his own was worthy of praise, much of the credit should go to Nancy who had coached him.

This was Zubin's second encounter with the dramatic arts: the first was in January 1983, when Zubin graduated from showing films at his concerts to acting in one himself. He acted as himself in Cyrus Bharucha's *On Wings of Fire*, a film about the Zoroastrian religion. In it, Zubin tries to discover his roots and understand them. He spent several days shooting sequences in Bombay, Navsari and Panchgani, which consisted of him engaging a Parsi priest in dialogue on the origins of Zoroastrianism. 'My part is only to ask a thousand questions,' he said.[30] The film, which premiered in September 1985 at the Ziegfeld Theater, New York City, also starred Nigel Terry, Paul Shelley, Saeed Jaffrey and Amrish Puri. Derek Jacobi (later Sir) was the narrator.

Bharucha relates how Zubin seemed a little nervous about remembering his lines.[31] Obviously a superb memory for music did not automatically translate into a memory for the dialogues of a docu-drama. Zubin took a lot of interest in the film and made numerous suggestions to its director as the shooting progressed. He even visited the Navsari home where his grandfather had once lived and was given a genealogy of the Mehta family, which included both him and Zarin.

In August 2004, Zubin was once again involved with cinema and his religion albeit in a different way. He complained against the use of the 'Farohar', a holy symbol of the Parsis, in promos of the movie *Alexander* to its director, Oliver Stone, with whom he was acquainted. Zubin told the audience at a meeting of the Zoroastrian Association of California in Irvine, where he was guest of honour, that he had called the director about the use of the 'Farohar' and registered his protest. The minuscule Zoroastrian diaspora was protesting against its use because, for Parsis, Alexander is far from being 'the Great'. In fact, he is the accursed: the man who murdered priests, destroyed fire temples and burned down Persepolis.

# The New York Philharmonic *on* Tour

ZUBIN HAD ONCE REMARKED, 'Touring is the lifeblood of an orchestra.' And, during his tenure, this was something the Philharmonic did a lot of. He and the Philharmonic travelled widely in thirteen years, 'bringing eclectic and innovative programmes to audiences worldwide with characteristic expertise and energy'. No one would deny that Zubin is an extraordinary musical ambassador, a role he not only revels in, but also endows with incredible energy, humanity, intensity and passion. Webster observed, 'His approach to touring with his orchestra is that of a missionary, a diplomat, an educator, and a *bon vivant* all rolled into one.'[1] He was also a tireless champion of his orchestra, of India and his adopted American home; and he exuded a sincerity which was seldom forgotten. Many noticed that Zubin seemed more relaxed, more himself, while on tour than at any other time with the Philharmonic.

The Philharmonic had a unique agreement with Citibank, in place since 1980, which gave the corporation the first option to underwrite any major foreign tour. The agreement which continued till Zubin demitted office in 1991 proved to be a 'joyful and rewarding adventure' in the words of Bill Koplowitz, former vice president at Citibank. Zubin is the consummate cosmopolite, at home in all parts of the world (the fact that he speaks half a dozen languages may have something to do with it).

An indefatigable traveller, Zubin's vast reserves of energy have elicited comment and much admiration. Indeed, many felt that Zubin had long liberated his body clock from the confines of the circadian rhythm. His touring day often started at the crack of dawn and continued into the wee hours. Begin with an early morning flight to the next city on the itinerary. Accept an airport greeting ceremony and handle a full press conference minutes after arrival at the hotel—something which was often followed by TV or newspaper interviews. Conduct a full rehearsal. Grab a catnap. Perform at the concert. Appear at a post-concert reception and address the audience with grace and humour. Not yet exhausted, gather a few friends for a small, late dinner, preferably in an Indian restaurant happy to keep its kitchen open for its famous compatriot. Often small openings in such a schedule would find Zubin and Nancy slipping away to a museum or art gallery or just a local market for a quick shopping stop. Nancy accompanies Zubin on all his tours.

## DOMESTIC AND OVERSEAS CONCERTS

Zubin's first overseas tour with the Philharmonic was to Argentina and the Dominican Republic in September 1978. It was the first-ever visit of the orchestra to the Dominican Republic which was preceded by concerts in Buenos Aires. The Philharmonic played in Santo Domingo, La Romana and Bonao. The repertoire consisted of Beethoven, Brahms, Kaye, Mahler, Sergei Prokofiev, Ravel, Tchaikovsky and Wagner. April 1979 saw a domestic tour (East Coast) with the Philharmonic performing at Boston, Hartford, Washington DC and Philadelphia. In August that year, the orchestra played in Tanglewood. In January and February 1980, there was a week-long tour of Florida and Washington DC, where they played Beethoven, Elgar, Haydn, Liszt and Strauss.

That was followed by an extensive ten-country tour of Europe in August and September the same year. It opened with a performance at Edinburgh where Penderecki's Symphony No. 2, written for and dedicated to Zubin, had its European premiere at the Edinburgh

International Festival. The other stops on the nearly month-long tour included Lucerne, Salzburg, Malmö, Stockholm, Oslo, Berlin, Hanover, Bonn, Vienna, Brussels, Paris and London. The famous German baritone Fischer-Dieskau performed with the orchestra in Mahler's 'Six Songs' from *Des Knaben Wunderhorn* in Berlin.

In May 1981, the Philharmonic undertook a tour of Mexico, playing in Guanajuato and Mexico City. Featured artistes included violinists Menuhin and Dicterow, and the repertoire included Bartók, Beethoven, Ravel, Strauss, Vivaldi, Wagner and Tchaikovsky. Mehli and Tehmina joined Zubin and Nancy during this trip. August and September 1982 saw a tour of South America with the Philharmonic playing in Caracas, Rio de Janeiro, São Paulo, Montevideo, Buenos Aires, Santiago and Quito. They played Bartók, Beethoven, Brahms, Bruch, Dvořák, Aaron Copland, Mozart, Schumann and Strauss.

### *The Asian Tour*

In September 1984, Zubin took the New York Philharmonic on a tour of India. It was part of a twenty-two-concert, thirteen-city Asian tour beginning in Tokyo on 15 August and culminating with five concerts in Delhi, Calcutta and Bombay in September. In 1978, he had had a heated disagreement with the Indian government about a tour with the Israel Philharmonic. Granting permission for the tour initially, the Morarji Desai-led Janata Party government later withdrew it for fear that the visit would offend the Arab countries with which India had close ties.[2] At that time, Zubin angrily said that he would never conduct in India until it recognized Israel.

Six years later, a calmer and less agitated Zubin told the *New York Times*: 'I can't hold the New York Philharmonic responsible for my statements, and when it came down to it, I could not conceive of an Asian tour without going to my own country.' He added, 'I love India, it is important for my spirit to go back. I feel I belong so much. When I land in Bombay it is like I never left. I never even changed my passport, though I could have become a Swiss citizen some years ago.'[3]

The tour began with concerts in Japan where the Philharmonic was well regarded but considered a notch lower than, say, the Vienna or Berlin philharmonics. Zubin himself ranked eighth in popularity behind such favourites as Karajan and local hero Ozawa, according to a poll conducted by a Japanese music magazine. There were concerts in Osaka, Nagoya, Yokohama and Tokyo. Enthusiasm was high, judging from the six bows Zubin took before agreeing to an encore in Kan-i Hoken Hall in Tokyo.

Concerts followed in Seoul, Taipei, Hong Kong and Bangkok. The Philharmonic had to deal with a number of difficulties. For one, because of the humidity in many of those places, a full-time violin maker had to be taken along to keep sensitive instruments in working order. In Zubin's words: 'Tours are very important for orchestras, because every night they have to play in different climatic and acoustic conditions, sometimes with no rehearsals and always in circumstances which demand that they put their best foot forward. The temperature in a hall affects the quality of sound, and so does humidity: as soon as it gets very hot, the strings tend to go down, while the woodwinds tend to go up, but the master contracts of American orchestras permit only one rehearsal a week while touring, so I have to find a place where we really need it, like the Philharmonic in Berlin, where no orchestra that doesn't know the Hall could possibly play without a rehearsal.'[4]

There was also the problem of having to reschedule part of the tour for Bangkok instead of Kuala Lumpur after the orchestra cancelled both its concerts in that city in response to the Malaysian government's resistance to the playing of Jewish compositions. The orchestra had not agreed to a request by the Malaysians to remove from its programme Bloch's *Schelomo: Hebrew Rhapsody for Cello and Orchestra*, because of the score's Jewish theme and origins. Malaysia is a predominantly Muslim country with Islam as the state religion, and authorities there claimed that discouragement of the portrayal of musical presentation of works of Jewish origin was part of government policy that had been spelled out clearly. Zubin said that they had no objection to the performance of works by Copland and Bernstein, probably because they did not realize that they too were Jewish.

There were widespread expressions of outrage from Jewish organizations and government officials, including New York Mayor Edward Koch, who denounced the Philharmonic's capitulation to the anti-Jewish policies of the Malaysian government. The Philharmonic announced that in the absence of a positive response by the Malaysian government to reinstate the Bloch piece, they could not proceed with the two concerts in Kuala Lumpur.

The Philharmonic also played in Indonesia, another Muslim country, but as luck would have it, did not put *Schelomo* on its programme. The principal underwriter of the Asian tour was Citibank which provided one-third of the tour's $2.5-million cost. In fact, it was through Citibank that the Malaysian government had requested the orchestra to cancel the Bloch piece.

Zubin and the orchestra played in a number of halls across Asia, of which only three met with his approval. Some he called 'lousy' but admitted that at such a time, acoustics were secondary, and it was the interaction between the orchestra and the people that was of prime importance. 'Jakarta had never heard a major symphony,' he recalled with a trace of wonder.[5] The last stop before India was Singapore. The Philharmonic played to 27,000 listeners in Singapore's National Stadium where it helped to celebrate the nation's twenty-fifth anniversary with Tchaikovsky's *1812 Overture*, complete with cannons and fireworks.

The tour of India was a grand success. It was the last leg of the Philharmonic's Asian tour spanning eight countries. Zubin, who was returning to conduct in India after seventeen years, was excited about making the trip back home. Zubin and the orchestra were given a traditional welcome with a vermilion tika and garlands. Two elephants whose services had been enlisted for a suitably exotic salute trumpeted their welcome. A senior member of the orchestra was quoted as saying, 'I have not seen him this excited ever. He is like a little boy bringing home a new toy.'[6]

The concert in New Delhi's Siri Fort Auditorium was attended, among others, by Prime Minister Indira Gandhi and was a huge success. Forgotten was what Zubin called 'a little social earthquake' when some forty orchestra members complained loudly about cockroaches and a mildewed smell in their rooms and walked out of the government-owned Ashoka Hotel into a more expensive privately owned one. Zubin explained to the Indian press, 'They are New Yorkers and New Yorkers tend to be both opinionated and vocal.'[7]

Alan Nazareth, secretary of the Indian Council for Cultural Relations, the main organizer of the event in India, described the visit as 'the biggest thing attempted by the Council'. 'It is the size, the renown of the orchestra and the fantastic public response and interest that is overwhelming, and a good part of that interest is because of Zubin,' he said.[8] In Calcutta, where the last internationally famous cultural group to appear was the Bolshoi Ballet, the audience stood on the seats to cheer, mobbed the stage door, and would not leave the concert hall for half an hour.

Understandably the greatest thrill for Zubin came in the city of his birth, Bombay. Despite an absence of thirty years, Zubin seemed to slip back into India easily and comfortably. When the lights were not just right, he called for the 'lightwalla', and spoke to his Parsi friends in Gujarati and to others in Hindi. Tehmina made the trip with Zubin but Mehli, still bitter and resentful, stayed away. A huge hoarding in front of the Air India building at Nariman Point had an appropriately affectionate message: *Arre Bawa, it's aapro Zubin* (Hey Parsis, it's our Zubin). In the words of Webster, 'In India, the prodigal son's return was greeted with the acclaim reserved for kings.'[9]

Zubin led the orchestra through the American melodic themes of Dvořák's *New World* Symphony and Wagner's *Ride of the Valkyries* to great applause. The delighted audience cheered, stood up, clapped and begged for more at the Shanmukhananda Hall. Zubin obliged with two encores, Dvořák's *Slavonic Dances* and Wagner's Prelude to the first act of *Lohengrin*. Adding to the charm of the evening were the floral tributes and garlands of roses given to Zubin. He later said he could feel on stage the love of the people. 'It's more than a musical effect. I feel the affection.'[10] In his last concert on 18 September, Zubin appeared for the final encore (John Philip Sousa's *The Stars and Stripes Forever*) wearing a Parsi dagli (wedding dress), making a powerful statement of identification with his community. Bombay's audience answered with a five-minute standing ovation which clearly moved the maestro. 'I've played all over the world, but through all the years I've kept my Indian identity,' he said. 'Standing there playing for my own people, I knew that I had been right in always being an Indian.'

Zubin also treated the orchestra to an authentic Parsi wedding feast, complete with banana leaves for plates. It was an evening to remember, 'exotic yet simple, sumptuous yet plain, and with a warm human glow throughout'.[11] During the major domestic and international tours that were such a prominent feature of the Philharmonic's schedule during Zubin's tenure, both he and Nancy were the perfect hosts. The entire orchestra was hosted on numerous occasions. Apart from the repast in Bombay, the most fondly remembered were parties at a wine cellar in Vienna and on an exotic island in Singapore Harbour; and a sumptuous barbecue and square dance at the Mehta home in Brentwood.

The Asian tour was followed by a five-week tour of nineteen different European cities from May to July 1985. The tour started in London at the end of May, and concerts in Frankfurt, Munich, Berlin, Dresden and Leipzig followed. Performances in Dresden and Leipzig were the Philharmonic's first in the erstwhile German Democratic Republic. At Leipzig, the audience's sustained ovation brought Zubin back for repeated bows even after the orchestra had left the stage. The repertory included Beethoven's Violin Concerto, Mahler's Fifth Symphony and Sousa's *The Stars and Stripes Forever*. Other cities on the tour included Amsterdam, Stuttgart, Budapest, Vienna, Paris, Bonn, Zurich, Florence, Milan, Vatican City, Madrid, Istanbul and Tel Aviv.

In July and August 1987, the Philharmonic embarked on a tour of Latin America. They played in Caracas, Brasilia, Belo Horizonte, São Paulo, Rio de Janeiro and Buenos Aires, and the programmes included pieces by Berlioz, Bruckner, Hindemith, Mozart, Ravel, Schubert and Tchaikovsky. On 9 August 1987, a special free noontime concert in a Buenos Aires public square was attended by 1,00,000 Argentinians. The Philharmonic's Ensemble concert in Iguazu Falls, Argentina, was nearly forfeit because the ground crew at the São Paulo airport had forgotten two instruments on the runway. Even as Citibank, the tour sponsor, dispatched planes to retrieve them, the ensemble members made a quick revision to the programme and the show went on.

## A SABBATICAL FOR THE MAESTRO

In 1987, Zubin took a year-long sabbatical from the New York Philharmonic. He said that he needed a break from his five-concerts-a-week-for-sixteen-weeks routine, not counting tours and extras. Scholars use their sabbaticals for many purposes—to undertake research, to teach, to vacation and generally to recharge their batteries. Zubin did a bit of all of those things. He said, 'I needed first of all a break from New York itself. Not so much from the Philharmonic, but from New York City; after ninety concerts a year each year, it really took its toll on me spiritually—every year five concerts a week for sixteen weeks plus tours and extras. Even though I worked very hard over these last twelve months, it really was a vacation.'[12]

In fact, he seemed to derive so much pleasure from his sabbatical that in typical Zubin style ('I say what I think'), he said that he was seriously considering calling it quits with the Philharmonic following the expiration of his contract at the end of the 1990–91 season. Never one to conform timidly to corporate rules, Zubin displayed his no-nonsense frankness once again. He, however, began to have second thoughts about such a definitive pronouncement, especially after nervous Philharmonic officials contacted him on the telephone and persuaded him to change his mind. Zubin hedged his bets, saying that his state of mind was inclined to retirement, but that he would only decide later.

It was during the sabbatical that Zubin led the Israel Philharmonic on its first tour of Poland and Hungary. It was the first visit of the orchestra to Eastern Europe. It was, as Zubin was quick to point out, an important political gesture for Israel, which was trying to establish closer relations with Eastern Europe. Neither he nor the soloists accepted fees. Zubin's forthrightness was once again on view when he reminded the Poles during press conferences of their complicity in Nazi atrocities. 'Sometimes I do really use my non-aligned Indian position to say things other people cannot,' he said. Zubin said that they came in friendship, but wanted the Poles to understand that they knew about what had gone on during the war and about Poles who had collaborated. 'We had members of the orchestra whose relatives had perished in the camps. The party officials sent back their tickets. But the public response was incredible, I would say almost an unnatural reaction. It was like a political demonstration.'[13]

The trip to Poland and Hungary was not the only time Zubin spent with the Israel Philharmonic that year. After he and the New York Philharmonic helped open the renovated Carnegie Hall in December, he presided over two Israel Philharmonic festivals, one marking the orchestra's fiftieth anniversary and the other honouring the late Arthur Rubinstein where they had fifteen of the finest pianists in the world playing everything he ever did with orchestra.

Zubin spent a large part of the next two and a half months on vacation, the highlight of which was a cruise to Antarctica. On the cruise, Zubin read a good deal—novels and his favourite genre, historical studies of Europe and India. But the most amusing result of that trip was a photo taken by Nancy, which showed a bearded Zubin, baton in hand and dressed in a tuxedo with a big smile on his face, standing in the midst of a colony of penguins. *Life* magazine ran a photograph of him in formal attire, standing among thousands of penguins, holding his baton aloft and saying: 'I finally found enough musicians to play Mahler's Eighth Symphony.' Rockwell, writing in the *New York Times*, said:

> The birds seemed to be looking every which way, but perhaps that's a plausible metaphor for the attention musicians pay conductors.[14]

The rest of his vacation was spent in his two Los Angeles homes, Brentwood and a beach house in Malibu, reading and studying scores. There was one interruption: a last-minute tour with the

Maggio Musicale Fiorentino orchestra to give two concerts for the Sultan of Oman and two in Bombay. The tour was paid for by an Israeli businessman, Bruce Rappaport, who wished to cultivate good relations in Oman; Zubin accepted on the condition that Bombay be included in the trip.[15]

By late spring, Zubin was in Vienna for a Mahler Third Symphony and a run of performances of *Otello* with Domingo at the State Opera. Every night he would go to the theatre or sit in the opera watching performances put on with no rehearsal at all. The most notable operatic venture by Zubin that year, apart from *Otello*, was a run of performances of *Tristan und Isolde* at the Los Angeles Music Center, with the Los Angeles Philharmonic in the pit. With stage direction by Jonathan Miller and decor by David Hockney, it attracted favourable attention and Zubin's conducting received much praise.

Other activities over the course of 1987 included his annual stint at the Maggio Musicale in Florence; several concerts in Paris; closing the Israel Philharmonic's season in July, touring with it for European summer festivals, opening its new season in October; and a special memorial concert in Philadelphia for his friend the philanthropist Frederic Mann. In fact Zubin lost three other friends in 1987: Kaye, Heifetz and Du Pré.[16] When Zubin heard of Du Pré's demise, he said: 'Jacqueline du Pré was the most phenomenal talent on any instrument I have had the privilege to be associated with. Her instinctive ability to communicate with musicians, with audiences and music on the whole was simply miraculous.'[17]

But Zubin hardly cut his ties with the New York Philharmonic during his sabbatical. He maintained contact with the Philharmonic officials, speaking on the phone twice or thrice a week, and also kept himself abreast of auditions and other administrative matters. He led a special concert at Avery Fisher Hall for the American Symphony Orchestra League, a Central Park free concert and, most importantly, a twenty-day, fourteen-concert tour of Latin America to which we have already alluded above.

## ON TOUR IN EUROPE AND ASIA

In May and June 1988, Zubin took the New York Philharmonic on a tour of the Soviet Union. In ten days, the orchestra gave three performances at Leningrad's Philharmonic Hall and three at Moscow's Tchaikovsky Hall, which included a concert led by the Soviet conductor Gennady Rozhdestvensky. As a grand finale, the Philharmonic and the State Symphony Orchestra of the Soviet ministry of culture gave a joint concert at the 11,000-seat Green Theatre in Gorky Park, a performance which was televised throughout the Soviet Union, and later broadcast on the Philharmonic's radio series the next year. Rozhdestvensky led the 200-player ensemble in the Dmitri Shostakovich Fifth Symphony and Zubin conducted Berlioz's *Symphonie Fantastique*. Undaunted by rain, thousands of Muscovites formed a sea of umbrellas as they enjoyed this rare musical event.

The Soviet tour was the result of a complex trail of negotiations that began as far back as 1986 and ended in April 1988. The sponsors were Coca-Cola, Combustion Engineering and RJR Nabisco. Webster, the orchestra's managing director, did most of the negotiating with Gosconcert, the Soviet arts organization, and had to explain to them the intricacies of corporate sponsorship. In fact, the contract was a model of detailed planning. It covered everything from the number of buses needed and when they would leave, to how the musicians would get their hotel room keys, and when and where they would eat their dinner. The Soviets took care of the internal expenses, paying roubles to the orchestra, which the musicians would use for their per diem expenses. Also included were master classes at the conservatories in Leningrad and Moscow.

This was the orchestra's third visit to the Soviet Union (the first was in 1959 and the second in 1976) and the musicians rated all three concerts at Leningrad as extraordinary. But a more virtuoso performance was in store in Moscow, when Zubin and the orchestra played Mahler's Ninth Symphony at Tchaikovsky Hall. Zubin who walked off the stage to roaring applause embraced a member of the orchestra who was standing in the wings. According to Zubin, it was the best performance the orchestra had ever given him. Webster said, 'I have never seen Zubin like that: so absolutely taken by the performance.'[18] What was even more remarkable was the fact that Zubin had conducted the Mahler work only once before—two weeks earlier in New York. The performance of the formidable piece left the audience silent for almost a full minute. But once the applause started, it lasted nearly fifteen minutes.

There were cries for an encore but Zubin declined. 'You simply cannot play anything after that. This was Mahler's farewell to the world. There is no way to follow up, to do an encore.'[19] Rozhdestvensky conducted the New York Philharmonic in works by Prokofiev and Gershwin, and the Moscow premiere of *Kein Sommernachtstraum*, a work by Alfred Schnittke who is widely considered to be the Soviet Union's most famous contemporary composer. Zubin also conducted a concert when they played works by Schubert and Stravinsky—and in an effort to share new trends in American music, *Symbolon* by Zwilich, a composition that was commissioned for the tour and which had its world premiere in Leningrad.

Always keen for musical diplomacy, Zubin said he could not disregard the political opportunity presented to him during this tour: the chance to appeal to the Soviet Union to change its stance on Israel. 'Soon I will be talking to a Soviet journalist from *Izvestia*,' he told the *New York Times*. 'I must talk to her about the refuseniks. I must. This cannot go on like this.'[20] Zubin referred to the case of Anna Rosnovsky in the Israel Philharmonic Orchestra whose sister, Lena, lived in Leningrad. The Soviets would not let her go because of some secret work she had done fourteen years ago. He said that he would write to the foreign minister. On the musical front, the New Yorkers donated a number of American orchestral scores and took back works by contemporary Soviet composers. As Zubin said, 'When musicians get together, there is an incredible camaraderie. We may have different accents, but we speak the same language.'

After the Soviet Union tour, the New York Philharmonic visited ten European countries and played sixteen concerts. The tour, scheduled from 17 August to 10 September 1988, was sponsored by

Citicorp. It opened on 20 August with a performance in the Herodes Atticus Theatre in Athens, at the foot of the Acropolis. As part of the Athens Festival, the orchestra played two performances there, the first dedicated to the memory of former Philharmonic music director Mitropoulos. Other cities on the itinerary were London, Frankfurt, Hamburg, Berlin, Stockholm, Helsinki, Amsterdam, Brussels, Lucerne, Madrid and Paris. The repertory consisted of works by Beethoven, Bruckner, Schoenberg, Schubert, Stravinsky, Wagner, Webern and the American composer Zwilich.

### *The Asian Tour*

The Asian tour of August and September 1989 was Zubin's last international tour with the orchestra. The stops were Singapore, Bangkok, Hong Kong, Taipei, Seoul, Osaka, Nagoya and Tokyo. More than 55,000 people heard the Philharmonic in a free outdoor concert at the Padang in Singapore, where Zubin's image was projected on to a large screen to the right of the stage. Several Philharmonic musicians were featured as soloists during the tour which featured works by Beethoven, Brahms, Dvořák, Haydn, Mozart, Puccini, Rachmaninoff, Nikolai Rimsky-Korsakov, Johann Strauss, Tchaikovsky and Richard Strauss.

## MUSIC AS SPECTACLE: THE THREE TENORS

Zubin has not been above, or indeed averse, to spectacular displays with his orchestras. Nor has he been hesitant to experiment, though sometimes with mixed results. However, for all his venturesomeness, he remains a serious artiste of the highest class. One of his most popular and best remembered exploits came in July 1990, a year before he left the New York Philharmonic. In what became one of the most memorable performances of all time, he led the three tenors Pavarotti, Domingo and José Carreras in a concert on the eve of the soccer World Cup final in Rome. Famous throughout the world as the Three Tenors concert, the performance, held on the outdoor stage of the third-century Roman baths of Caracalla in Rome before a crowd of 6500 people, led to the highest-selling classical music recording of all time.

On 7 July 1990, Pavarotti, Domingo and Carreras appeared together for the first time and treated the public to two and a half hours of operatic arias and popular tunes. The brainchild of Mario Dradi, a concert manager from Bologna, who dreamed of organizing an unusual, never-seen-before concert on the eve of the soccer World Cup final, it was primarily meant as a musical welcome for Carreras who was returning to the world of opera after a battle with leukaemia.

The concert intended to raise funds for his foundation for leukaemia research. Apart from the usual concert fees, all the gate profits went to Carreras's foundation. All three tenors agreed to give to charity their share of concert-related revenues, including the estimated $1 million in Caracalla box-office receipts. The event was criticized by some as being more of a spectacle and less of serious art. The programme comprised well-known selections from operas like *Tosca* and *Turandot*, and a medley of songs that included 'Maria', 'Cielito Lindo' and 'O Sole Mio'.[21]

The enthusiasm and spontaneity of the three tenors and Zubin were obvious as they ran through the regular programme and three encores, accompanied by the huge 198-member orchestra. Zubin had agreed to conduct the orchestra del Teatro dell'Opera di Roma, the orchestra of the opera in Rome, on condition that his ensemble from Florence, the Maggio Musicale Orchestra, be allowed to perform along with it. Since there is no trio for three tenor voices in operatic literature, Zubin suggested that each of the three choose their favourite pieces. He then asked Argentinian composer Lalo Schifrin to put together a medley to include their favourite selections.

It was the perfect combination for a great outdoor concert. Each tenor sang some of his popular arias; all were in top form and there was no rivalry on or off the stage. The jewel in the concert's crown was the final medley sung by the three in tandem. During the second encore, the audience could not resist joining in as the three tenors belted out a spirited rendition of 'Nessun Dorma' from Puccini's *Turandot*. In addition, the concert was broadcast live to a worldwide satellite audience estimated at 800 million, including ABC viewers in the United States. It was a huge financial success for the organizers and the record company Decca/London who had been given royalty-free recording rights.

No one had thought it would turn into such a success, least of all Zubin and the singers. In 1990, the tenors thought—as did everyone else involved—that their concert recording would at best be an interesting curiosity with average sales.

To almost everyone's amazement, the concert and the record emerged as a sensation, and Decca reaped the profits. It sold 10 million in records and more than 1 million on video. It was also by far the highest grossing fundraising programme in public-television history. A spokesperson for Channel 13 said the New York outlet of PBS had raised more than $1 million from its telecast of *The Three Tenors*. Pavarotti, who had an exclusive recording contract with Decca said he had no complaints but Domingo was furious and ostracized Decca. He suspected that they had paid Pavarotti a royalty.

While Zubin did not grudge Decca its unexpected windfall, he did comment on a certain lack of grace on the part of the record company: '... We are all sufficiently well-off so it did not hurt us not to get a share, but all the same we feel that Decca could at least have sent us a little Christmas card in appreciation of their enormous profits.'[22] The immense popularity of the 1990 concert was fuelled by repeatedly telecasting it on PBS television stations as it reached a wider viewing audience and brought classical opera to a more popular level. Zubin says that the concert was primarily a bright and happy event with a unique character. 'That the idea would later become a concept which is still valid almost to the present day, was something that none of us could have known back then,' he said.[23]

## STEPPING DOWN

On 2 November 1988, Zubin announced that he would be leaving the Philharmonic to pursue 'other artistic endeavours' when his contract expired in 1991. He said that he was turning down a contract extension in order to free himself of administrative responsibilities. Zubin, as we have seen, had given an indication of his intent during his sabbatical year but had also said that he could not entirely preclude the possibility that he might change his mind.

He told an interviewer in December 1991 that he wanted to continue to conduct the orchestra but didn't want to go back to New York. 'My rapport with the orchestra the last five seasons was such that I had only pleasure with them. In fact, New York wanted to extend the contract. I was the one who said no.'[24] Later in the interview, when asked about how it felt to leave New York behind, he threw both his arms in the air and said, 'I'm freeeeeee.'

As he stepped down, Zubin said in a statement: 'Having held the position of music director with various North American organizations since 1961, I must at this juncture pursue other artistic endeavours which have to do with less administrative activity than that with which a music director is usually involved.'[25] Stephen Stamas, the president of the Philharmonic, said that Zubin had provided outstanding musical leadership to the orchestra, and their musical life had been enriched by his contribution.

Zubin had received several offers but had declined them all. The London Philharmonic had actively sought his services and there were rumours that he might return to Los Angeles. But what was known for a fact was that Zubin had several operatic productions on his plate in Europe starting 1991, including at least one at the new Bastille Opera in Paris. His other opera engagements included programmes at London's Royal Opera in Covent Garden and the Maggio Musicale in Florence. Given his status as a conductor of the first rank, he was also considered a candidate for the Berlin Philharmonic once Karajan retired.

In the autumn of 1990, for Zubin's final season, Rostropovich and Barenboim performed as soloists with the orchestra. It was at the same time that the gifted Soviet pianist Kissin made his Philharmonic debut. In January 1991, Zubin conducted members of the Juilliard Orchestra in the opening concert of the Mozart Bicentennial at the Lincoln Center. In April, he travelled to Lucerne to inaugurate a new Easter Festival there, with concerts in Amsterdam and Brussels.

On 28 May 1991, Zubin conducted his last piece as music director of the New York Philharmonic. Fittingly, it was Schoenberg's *Gurrelieder*, a performance in which he had always dazzled. At six minutes to 11 p.m., covered with confetti, Zubin walked off the stage of Avery Fisher Hall with an arm around concertmaster Dicterow.

During the intermission, a number of speeches paid tribute to his achievements. One of them was from President George Bush Sr who said that the conductor had 'helped reinvigorate and broaden the appeal of classical music'. The Philharmonic had, in fact, been bidding farewell to its longest serving conductor in the modern era for the past two weeks. There were farewell dinners for Zubin at the Metropolitan Museum and Le Cirque. He also received two gifts which had a special connection to the Philharmonic's history: a page from the original score of Mahler's Ninth Symphony which was composed while he was music director of the orchestra, and a replica of the baton used at the first concert of the Philharmonic in 1842 along with a silver tray on which was inscribed a tribute to his 'immeasurable charm'. Members of the orchestra presented Zubin with a crystal orb with an eagle on it, manufactured by Steuben Glass Works. He was made an honorary member of the Philharmonic-Symphony Society of New York.[26] (The others who have received this honour include Bernstein, Stern, Copland, Serkin, Boulez, Drucker and Ax.)

Also at that farewell concert was Hutheesing and he recalls that Zubin tore off the cover page of the programme (which had his photo on it) and scribbled a note which read: 'Remembering 1960. I am glad that we haven't lost the thread that was woven in the 1940s—God Bless!' After the reception, Hutheesing was invited by the Mehtas to join them for dinner as part of the family. It proved to be a memorable evening, full of fond and funny recollections. He says the paper remains with him even today as a treasured memento of their friendship.[27]

Zubin's successor was the East German conductor Masur who was slated to take over in the 1992–93 season. The announcement in April 1990 that he would succeed Zubin surprised many, and ended a search that lasted nearly two years. Although he had led the orchestra regularly since 1981, he was not widely considered a leading contender for the post, with names like Colin Davis, Leonard Slatkin and Sinopoli frequently heard as prospects. In 1989, Abbado almost accepted but backed out when he was offered the Berlin Philharmonic after Karajan's departure.

# The Bittersweet Years *in* New York

WHEN ZUBIN BEGAN HIS thirteenth and final season as music director of the New York Philharmonic in 1990, it represented the longest incumbency of any chief conductor in the orchestra's history. Zubin had hardly received a uniformly favourable press during his tenure with the New York Philharmonic. The critical response to Zubin in New York was mixed: some admired him, others dismissed him and most pointed to the many concerts in which he gave a competent but uninspired performance. Zubin, according to the critics, had failed to realize his potential as a serious artiste. His leadership too, it was said, was less than inspiring. His perfunctory approach, they said, spread to his players, encouraging a pedestrian attitude among them.

While few questioned Zubin's technical mastery, there were complaints about the seeming indifference with which he approached most of his concerts. While his Bruckner and Messiaen were especially applauded, he seemed to dispatch the music in the standard repertory with more 'brusque efficiency than spiritual enlightenment'. It is of course possible that Zubin faced the problem of his critics being overfamiliar with not only his repertory but also his style and interpretive range. Apart from the tepid critical response, the unwillingness of major labels to record extensively with him and the orchestra was also an embarrassment.[1]

## MAESTRO AND METROPOLIS

Music does not happen in a vacuum. It is said cities get the conductors they deserve: there is a symbiotic relationship between a city and the music director of its orchestra. Any consideration of the Philharmonic during Zubin's time must begin with the realization that the personality of New York City also shaped that of its musicians. This applied to other cities and their orchestras as well. Thus Boston was viewed as aristocratic and elegant, Philadelphia seen as smooth and rich, and Chicago as big and brawny. But the New York Philharmonic was seen to be defined more by its corporate character than a definitive sound. 'That character is most commonly described as feisty, proud, intolerant, and sometimes, shockingly cruel to conductors it finds unsympathetic.'[2] Even the legendary Karajan was wary of New York where he had a shaky start on his first appearance there in 1955. Roger Vaughan, in his biography of Karajan, called it 'a rough abusive city with a tiresome plethora of superstars'.[3]

Stories of the musicians' rudeness to conductors were unsettling. Older players winced as they recounted the orchestra's ill-treatment of the kindly Mitropoulos in the 1950s. One of the most devastating and famous put-downs in Philharmonic history is diminutive Italian oboist Bruno Labate's single line to Klemperer: 'Klemp, you talka too much.'[4]

Foss had once slammed down his score and shouted, 'My four-year-old son would not have done that!'[5] when a musician mocked a soprano soloist with an imitation. During a performance under Boulez, a musician used his instrument to simulate bird calls. The reasons ascribed for such behaviour range from the soloist training at New York's Juilliard School to the surfeit of other musical institutions and freelance opportunities which ensure that a player would not starve, were he to resign. It is also possible that New York's long-standing union pride played a part. It is said that under Toscanini the orchestra had been 'whipped into shape'. The 'retroactive resentment' provoked by the Toscanini tenure may have led to a determination to resist the authority of lesser conductors as poor Barbirolli (not yet Sir), who succeeded Toscanini, found to his great chagrin.[6]

Given the orchestra's tough reputation, Zubin's job also had a lion-taming aspect to it. What Zubin gave to the orchestra as its director was perhaps exactly what the city had wanted him to. Tracing the history of orchestras, it is easy to find examples where city and conductor proved ideally paired. Stokowski and Koussevitzky in Philadelphia and Boston respectively, became inseparably linked with those cities in the public mind. The tenure of Szell in Cleveland and Reiner and Solti in Chicago were also good examples of what can happen when the right artiste and the right city get together. We have already noted the unhappy story of Barbirolli. Similarly, Rafael Kubelík and Martinon in Chicago proved to be the wrong men in the wrong place. In Bernstein's case, New York proved that it could recognize genuine artistic achievement provided it came clothed in charisma and a saleable personality.[7]

However, it is a well-known fact that few Philharmonic conductors in the last six or seven decades have received a favourable press in New York. Zubin's predecessor Boulez had a hard time. And before Boulez, Bernstein was the 'favourite whipping boy of the New York critics' who felt that his ego was getting in the way of his music. Mitropoulos had had a difficult time in the 1950s. While nobody questioned Zubin's professionalism, there was a feeling in many critical circles that he was more concerned with colour and effect than with substance. He was also accused of being inconsistent. 'That his strength lay mainly in the big Romantic showpieces, rather than Beethoven and his predecessors was also seen as a big minus. While the Philharmonic's musicians liked him well enough as a person, there were those who felt that he was not particularly inspiring musically even though they admired his clear beat and general technique.'[8]

Musicians of the best orchestras can be highly critical of their conductors and any major ensemble has a sizeable number of players who think they can do as well or better on the podium than any of the maestros who conduct them. In this regard the musicians of the New York Philharmonic had a track record which was much worse than their counterparts in other major orchestras. The New Yorkers, while gifted, were notorious for their supreme self-confidence and antagonism towards almost anybody who held the baton: a low regard for conductors seemed to be a symphonic tradition. Schonberg summed it up when he wrote:

> And the New York Philharmonic is, for better or worse, generally conceded to be an unparalleled bunch of prima donnas who individually are brilliant players but collectively are a pain in the baton.[9]

## UNHAPPY MUSICIANS

In June 1983, five or six members of the artistic committee—players elected by the orchestra to liaise with management—told the board members that the musicians were unhappy with the artistic and administrative skills of the music director and with the loss of the exclusive recording contract that the Philharmonic had with CBS Records for over forty years. The contract was a source of additional income for each member of the orchestra. The report to the board members was based on a questionnaire distributed to each member of the orchestra. The artistic committee reported that nearly half the players had returned questionnaires with all but six listing complaints about Zubin.[10]

The main reason appeared to be the loss of income from the cancellation of the CBS contract at the end of 1982. In the past, each player stood to make anywhere between $2000 and $3000 each year in recording fees. In addition, there was the $600 in royalty income. Though CBS cited the increasing cost of recording in New York as the reason for ending the contract, there were many who believed that it was Zubin's apparent inability to gain a large following among record buyers that had prompted the move. The orchestra had a specific problem in that Zubin did not sell many records at least with the Philharmonic and especially in Europe. Christine Reed of CBS Masterworks was quoted as saying that the label 'couldn't give away the orchestra and Zubin Mehta in Europe'.[11]

In response to the criticism about lack of recordings and poor sales, Zubin asked if he should send his royalty statements to the *New York Times*. He was part of as many as thirty-nine recordings with the orchestra. These included Brahms, Mahler, Beethoven, Wagner, Dvořák, Stravinsky, Strauss, Holst, John Knowles Paine, Verdi, Gershwin and Del Tredici. Among the record labels, CBS Masterworks predominated, with Colombia Records, New World Records and Deutsche Grammophon producing a few as well.

When Barbara Isenberg of *Los Angeles Times* asked him about this in December 1991, he said that the press never forgave him for the lack of recordings during a three-year period in the mid-1980s. 'They still say no record company wants to touch me. It's not true. I've been refusing recordings . . . Should I take out an ad?'[12]

Another cause for resentment among the musicians was the acoustics at Avery Fisher Hall. Even when it opened in 1962 as the Philharmonic Hall, its acoustics were unsatisfactory. It became the Avery Fisher Hall in 1976 after major remodelling. As Henahan wrote in the *New York Times*:

> Compared to Carnegie Hall, the Philharmonic's former home, Avery Fisher can seem cold and raw, kind to certain instruments such as brass and percussion but unflattering to the strings. Many Philharmonic musicians resent what they regard as unfair comparisons of their orchestra with international ensembles that annually stop at Carnegie to play a couple of intensively rehearsed concerts under optimum acoustical and psychological conditions.[13]

These became more glaringly obvious when Zubin's elbow injury forced him to turn over his orchestra to a series of conductors summoned at short notice.[14]

Critics also noted that there seemed to be a crisis of leadership at the Philharmonic. Zubin was a modern-day maestro who, apart from being music director of the Israel Philharmonic, also guest conducted. In Los Angeles, Zubin had the redoubtable Fleischmann, himself a strong personality bubbling with ideas and ambition, by his side. So, when Zubin was away, he knew that back home, Fleischmann was providing the concrete direction the orchestra needed. Webster, on the other hand, hardly had the same strong public image of Fleischmann and 'in the absence of any firm leadership the impression was of gentlemanly drift'.[15]

About halfway through Zubin's tenure, he thought that his relationship with the musicians had become more relaxed. Talking to Schonberg of the *New York Times* before the Asian tour in 1984, he said that he and the Philharmonic shared a more comfortable relationship. He indicated that pockets of resistance comprising the old-timers who had played under Toscanini, Reiner, Walter and Klemperer remained and they turned up their noses at any conductor. But with younger and more dedicated musicians entering the roster, the orchestra was playing with more enthusiasm. Zubin felt that the reputation of the orchestra as a conductor-killer was no longer true.[16]

The management felt that Zubin's efforts to enforce artistic discipline may have caused some discontent. He may also have alienated a few by his attempts to put his stamp on the membership of the orchestra. It was fortunate that from 1977 to 1982 an unusually large number of positions had fallen vacant and almost one-fifth of the orchestra had been chosen by the maestro. These included among others, the concertmaster, the associate concertmaster and three principals. New players were not the only change. At Zubin's behest, the orchestra began to acquire fine instruments in a bid to improve and polish the sound.

Regardless of what the critics and his own musicians thought of him, the musical administrators in New York had a great deal of respect for Zubin. They thought him a real professional who was genuinely interested in his orchestra and committed to its well-being. Zubin personally attended all auditions whenever there was a vacancy in the orchestra and worked well with the management. Bernstein—notwithstanding the criticism he faced when he was music director in the 1960s—was a huge audience hit. Boulez's regime was less successful in terms of audience appeal, with subscribers down to 27,000 by his last season in 1977–78. By 1987, they were up to 35,000 and, according to official statistics, the attendance at Avery

Fisher Hall sustained itself at more than 95 per cent during Zubin's tenure. It was argued that because Zubin did not force the issue of contemporary music, the number of subscriptions rose sharply from the time Boulez ended his tenure. In any case, the negative press seemed to happen to any conductor in New York. When a conductor first came in, he was a golden boy; then ennui set in on the part of the press.

While many were highly critical of Zubin's music-making during his tenure in New York, especially in the later years, the more level-headed critics also gave him his due. For one, he gave the orchestra a lot of his time, an average of twenty weeks a season. A strong personality with a decisive stick technique, he was not the kind to be bullied or musically overpowered by the players in New York. He showed rectitude in his programmes and made an effort to balance concert hall familiarities with new or difficult music. Writing in the *New York Times* in August 1983, Holland observed:

> Conducting is an impossible job requiring the brutality of a corporate executive, and the soul of a poet, and perhaps we expect too much of those who fill the job. Mr. Mehta has used his skills and personality admirably, and he can make this difficult orchestra's assemblage of skill and temperament pay him heed. Expecting him to be a profound musician as well may be a little greedy.[17]

## MEHTA DISAPPOINTS?

Henahan, the *New York Times* music critic who was known for his curmudgeonly reviews, continued to be relentless in his criticism of Zubin. He said:

> Mr. Mehta disappoints more often than not . . . And yet in spite of his abilities as a leader and a musician, he somehow does not regularly produce concerts that are exciting to experience or, failing that, stimulating to think about.

As far as the state of the orchestra was concerned, Henahan was a little more charitable:

> The notoriously erratic and capricious Philharmonic has its bad nights but it has been kept in trim under Mr. Mehta's guidance and throughout this season has played with reasonable enthusiasm and alertness.

He went on to add that solid professional routine had its place but what was required 'on any given evening was inspired conducting and playing of the uncommon sort'. Henahan was also critical of Zubin's programming saying that whatever his other merits as music director were, Zubin had not demonstrated remarkable talent as a programme builder.

When Zubin replaced Boulez, the Philharmonic trustees thought it was another Bernstein coup. But in reality, Zubin did not fit any such stereotype. He did not engage the public imagination the way Bernstein, or even Toscanini, did. Zubin's technical prowess was recognized—as was his penchant for quick and 'economical' rehearsals. Though the easy relationship he shared with his musicians who respected his 'willingness to treat them as colleagues' was well known, he gave the impression that he was all too willing to be satisfied with routine.

Critics pointed out that 'time after time the listener had to leave a perfectly responsible, carefully prepared Mehta performance wondering why it made so little impact'.[18] While he struck a chord with the Philharmonic's conservative audience, he could not manage to rally much support beyond that. However, critics concede that Zubin was a responsible leader, spending considerable time each season at the head of his technically sound orchestra. Henahan wrote:

> Unhappily, his regime has fallen between stools, neither a model of serious artistry nor a genuine public relations coup.[19]

Inevitably, living conductors are constantly compared with the older masters who have since passed on. As Henahan put it, 'Like it or not, contemporary musicians are in nightly competition with ghosts and you know who usually wins these bouts.'[20]

When Zubin replaced Boulez as music director of the New York Philharmonic, it was universally expected that he would quickly impress his own personality on the orchestra, its repertory and on New York's musical life. But after three years in charge, the critics said that change had been slow in coming. While they agreed that there was a level below which Zubin and the orchestra never slipped, and several sections, particularly those of the wind and brass instruments, showed a clear improvement under Zubin's direction, his three seasons had given no indication that he meant to change the Philharmonic's jaded image seriously.

Henahan wrote in April 1981:

> By now you might think that a Mehta plan for revitalizing the Philharmonic's reputation and broadening its audiences would be discernible, even if far from realization. But an examination of next season's programs, which are now at hand, simply confirms that in spite of a few new ruffles and flourishes the Philharmonic will go on playing pretty much the same old tune. Details of programming change, but the status quo prevails.[21]

Henahan did give Zubin some compliments, even if they were backhanded:

> Unlike Mr. Boulez, Mr. Mehta rarely gives a thoroughly and unrelievedly boring performance, even if the work at hand is something as tiresome as *Ein Heldenleben*. In fact, it sometimes seems that he plays the worst music best, perhaps because it tests him most. He can be counted on to play any work well enough so that it can be recognized, at very least.[22]

Zubin took all the criticism philosophically. He insisted that honest criticism never bothered him. What he does not like is snobbishness in criticism. He thinks that too many critics today are overly anxious to parade their knowledge and he has little respect for them. He narrates how he conducted a contemporary piece of music that he thought was sheer junk, and could not understand one critic who went to three performances of the work, wrote reams about it, and never mentioned the other pieces on the programme. This, he says, is just bad journalism.[23] He was critical of music critics who pretended to know more than they actually did. 'Critics try to show you how much they know, asking you these multiple choice questions. They ask you a question and answer it three ways, only to show you what they know. It gets tiring.'[24] He told Ralph Blumenthal of the *New York Times*, 'What was never understood in the United States is that my whole musical background is Viennese. Nobody really realized where I was coming from. I didn't make a point of broadcasting it.' He also believed that a lot of critics didn't know the scores.

In his memoirs, he gives the example of how he beat the time for the blank bar at the end of Schubert's Fourth Symphony as a joke. The musicians laughed and this was reported by a critic as the 'conductor's unbelievable ignorance at which the players too had laughed'.[25] He was known to have remarked that the better the orchestra got, the worse the reviews became: 'So what was sad about this whole newspaper business was that the better the orchestra got, after the first four or five seasons, the worse the reviews. This is what nobody could understand—didn't they listen those first years? Now when it's going so well, why are they picking on us?'[26] Zukerman had observed, 'I'm getting sick of it. I don't read the papers any more.' He said that Zubin's personality was so magnetic that it actually interfered with the listening process to some extent. But that, he said, was only superficial.[27]

Zubin noted with a mixture of irritation and amusement that many regarded him as a glamour-boy conductor and could not quite figure out why. He considered himself a serious musician who had mastered his scores and had very few platform mannerisms. A picture of him semi-nude and standing on his head against the wall in a yogic position (*oordhwapadmasana*) appeared in a large number of newspapers and magazines. When I asked him about that famous photo, he smiled and said, 'I can always do that, but I gave up doing yoga when I went to Vienna.'[28] Zubin also refuted reports about the orchestra calling him 'Zubi Baby'. He clarified to Schonberg, 'Nobody ever called me "Zubi baby" and the writer who first used the expression later admitted to me that he had made it up. I don't have the time to be a glamour boy.'[29]

Loved by his musicians in Los Angeles and projecting a glamorous image, he seemed just the right person to revive the heady days of Bernstein. But that glamorous image quickly became suspect in New York. Zubin's first years at the Philharmonic were 'pronounced a honeymoon on all sides'. He told the press in January 1980 that there is 'a certain joy in the music-making now' and he hoped the public realized that. 'It is about time the Philharmonic lost its reputation of being monsters.' He said that it was possible to have frank conversations with players and it was never ugly or taken personally. 'For instance, they didn't like Bruckner. I told them, "I cannot order you to play with your hearts but I love this music." It worked for a few of them ... And the performance took spirit. In the concert they really played with love, and I hope things like that are noticed.'[30] He stressed his openness with the musicians, and even the friendships with some of the players—friendships that he insisted didn't interfere with his professional relationship with the orchestra. There was the occasional tiff but he said that he had great musical fun with the players. In interviews in later years, he praised their musical virtuosity.

But as time passed, the criticism grew. Either the conductor's performances were becoming shallower, some thought, or his true colours were showing through. As Holland wrote in the *New York Times*:

> Zubin Mehta inspired the expansive and the self-indulgent. . . . Mr. Mehta, gifted as he was, alternated between fits of boredom and an almost childlike fascination with noise. Armed with an extraordinary collection of orchestra virtuosos, he cultivated the large, the loud, the explosive, the colorful, and the shiny.

It appears that Zubin's problems in New York had less to do with the players and more to do with the critics. When I asked him about the criticism in New York, he said, 'I got along well with the musicians in New York. In every assembly, there is always someone who doesn't like you. Even in Israel, everyone doesn't like me. After the first few years, the reviews started getting worse. I am an honest musician who tries to interpret the composer's intention the best I know. If somebody doesn't like the interpretation, there is nothing I can do.'[31]

The musicians, at least in the later years, were more than pleased with Zubin's music-making, but his glamour, candour and love of the good life made him an attractive target for critics. At a rehearsal in Los Angeles in the early 1990s somebody had tacked an Italian magazine opened to a photo of the maestro with a scantily clad Brazilian dancer during a South American tour. Walking past it, Zubin laughed and said he had better ones, including one of himself, the dancer *and* Nancy.[32] He also pointed out that New York had a sort of self-destructive attitude towards its institutions: 'It's a constant fight against people trying to put you down, whether you're an artistic organization or a university or a sports team. I've never read such drastic newspaper articles about any sports team as they write about their own. In Chicago, they die for their teams. In New York, (if) they lose two games, they are the worst in the world.'[33]

Reflecting on his assignment in New York, he said, 'My time in New York with the musicians, I would say 80 per cent of it was only good times.' When asked about the bad times he said that those came when he had to replace players and make other changes. 'When I first came, the orchestra was at a certain level. I don't want to comment on that.'[34]

Despite these troubles, Zubin did stay in New York for thirteen years, the 'longest tenure of any Philharmonic music director in this century'. He also took on considerable administrative burdens, making it quite natural that he would finally want to be free of it all. He achieved a great deal during his tenure in rebuilding the subscription base of the audience and restructuring the orchestra itself. But the unrelenting criticism rankled. Werner Klemperer, one of Zubin's closest friends and son of the conductor Otto Klemperer, described Zubin's reaction to the harping criticism as 'surprised sadness'. If there was one area in which Zubin's New York experience fell short of his hopes it was in the relationship between critic and music director. 'I feel that the critic and music director should have such a good relationship, they can pick up the phone and call each other any time,' Zubin said in 1976. 'We should not be adversaries.'[35]

Towards the end of his tenure repeated requests by the *New York Times* for an interview with Zubin drew no response for almost a month. Then it was denied. 'They haven't asked me for thirteen years,' Zubin told Carl Schiebler, the Philharmonic's personnel manager, who acted as an intermediary. 'Why should I do it now?'[36] (Zubin had, in fact, been interviewed by *The Times* critics and reporters periodically throughout his tenure.) Zubin, Schiebler reported, felt that he and his players had been treated unfairly, and that every time he tried to do something good, he had been stung in the press.

Zubin was far from alone in thinking that he had been abused by the press. James Oestreich writing in the *New York Times* said that what always struck him was the great respect and affection accorded to Zubin by many of his fellow artistes and by music professionals, speaking not only for publication but also in private. 'Through conversations with his colleagues runs a corrective litany: undervalued, unappreciated, underestimated, unrecognized, underrated, and misunderstood.'[37]

Fleischmann blamed New York itself for whatever problems Zubin encountered at the Philharmonic, remarking that he (Zubin) had not received enough support within the organization to allow him to use his enormous gifts to full potential. But Joseph H. Kluger who collaborated closely with Zubin as orchestra manager of the New York Philharmonic said that there was nothing that Zubin wanted to do that he could not do, and felt that he attempted much, and achieved much, and that his record as music director needed no apologies.[38] Zubin told me that he didn't always get the best advice from his senior musicians. He also said that the management was very supportive and accommodating.

Kluger also expressed puzzlement at the intensity of the criticism. 'It was almost hatred,' he said, 'which I really don't understand. The only perspective that makes sense is to look at it in the context of the history of the Philharmonic and its music directors. What was written about Bernstein in the early 60s? Scathing criticism. Only after he left the Philharmonic did he attain critical acclaim. Was it because he became a much better conductor? Maybe. Maybe not.'[39]

Zubin led the orchestra on successful tours of the United States, Mexico, Central and South America, Europe, the Soviet Union and Asia. It was on these trips that he really came into his own. And notwithstanding all his travels, and his being music director of the Israel Philharmonic simultaneously, Zubin spent more time with the New York ensemble than most other music directors did with their orchestras. His final five-year contract stipulated twenty weeks per season in New York, and Zubin sometimes offered more.

Many believe that there was no Zubin Mehta problem and, with hindsight, this may just be true. In their view, it was merely a figment of the press's fevered imagination. Zubin showed signs of being a more assiduous orchestra builder than many of his generation, and indeed than most of his predecessors at the Philharmonic. Unlike many conductors who flitted restlessly from one podium to another, he has stayed rooted with the orchestras for which he has felt responsible. But in Zubin's case, critics felt that it appeared as though the Philharmonic musicians thought they did not deserve him. 'Their detached, pedestrian playing of some of the world's greatest music reveals a deep-rooted cynicism that will not be easy for a new music director to displace.'[40]

Still, Zubin's problems with critics had not been confined to New York. We have already noted his famously adversarial relationship with Bernheimer, the chief music critic of *Los Angeles Times*. He did not get particularly favourable reviews in London either, though he was generally well received in Europe. John Willan, a former managing director of the London Philharmonic, suggested that conductors like Zubin who are adored by the public would come to England more often, were they not given discouraging reviews. He cited the example of a performance of *The Rite of Spring* in 2005 which was called 'humdrum'—odd given that it was Zubin's flashiness that irritated critics.[41] Willan had tried to hire Zubin as the music director of the

London Philharmonic in 1987 but gave up after trying for two years. Understandably, Zubin wanted a break and the freedom to do what he wanted, without having to attend to the administrative duties which most conductors dislike.

## A GENTLEMAN CONDUCTOR

Even Zubin's admirers acknowledged that the performances left something to be desired. Some blamed the Philharmonic. Others argued that Zubin's virtues did not always work to his advantage. He was often described as gentle, kind, fair, generous—traits not associated with conductors who had terrorized orchestras from the podium. Werner Klemperer said, 'Most of the time, orchestras—and I don't mean the New York Philharmonic specifically—need a benevolent dictator. But dictator is a big word there. Zubin is benevolent, but he's not a dictator. He's very kind, and with an orchestra maybe sometimes less than kindness is necessary.'[42]

Charles Rex, the Philharmonic's associate concertmaster at the time, called Zubin a complete gentleman who always treated the musicians with fairness, respect and generosity. 'If he has a fault in rehearsal,' Rex said, 'it's that he might be a little too gentle. New York is not a gentle city.'[43] Zubin's assistant conductor, Wong, said he used to think the same but discovered that Zubin could effectively stop the fooling around when he wanted to. Philharmonic flautist Siebert put things in proper perspective when she said, 'He hasn't gotten where he is by being weak.'[44]

'Orchestras and their music directors constitute a marriage of sorts; and in whatever configuration, matrimonial success is best measured by endurance,' wrote Holland in the *New York Times*. By that yardstick, Zubin's was a very successful tenure but critics pointed out that his 'worst qualities precisely matched the worst qualities of the New York Philharmonic and insured a long period of mediocrity for both'.[45] What nobody can deny is that Zubin left behind a group that was loaded with talent, largely because of his many superb hires. Of the 107 orchestra members, forty-two were hired during his thirteen-year-tenure, and many thought that this was his finest and most lasting achievement in New York. What Zubin was less successful in doing in the later years of his directorship was to efficiently use the resources he had mustered to full artistic advantage. His musicians seemed bereft of morale and it was left to Masur, his successor, to instil the needed spirit, pride and sense of discipline among the players.

'The interesting thing about Mehta,' Deck said, 'is that he let individuals be a little creative. Too much so. But he let individuals be creative in how they were going to turn a phrase, and he was always willing to listen to a new idea even in a concert. It can have horrible results, but there's a certain spontaneity and a certain excitement.'[46] There was no denying Zubin's genius as a conductor. But, as Holland put it—a view echoed by several critics—'A confident command of detail and minutiae in the midst of size and complexity went hand in hand, unfortunately, with a lot of questionable taste. What truly seemed to engage Mr. Mehta's attention was a love, almost childlike, for the loud and the large.'

However the Philharmonic experience is evaluated, it hardly hampered Zubin's career. Orchestra managers in other cities appeared united in thinking that New York's loss would be their gain. Zubin was booked ahead for several years. Zarin, who had just become the executive director of the Ravinia Festival in Illinois, was reluctant to speak about Zubin's plans, but confirmed that the schedule was packed enough for him to be unavailable to come to Ravinia. It was expected that Chicago would see a lot more of Zubin. Not only had Zarin taken over at Ravinia, Barenboim was now the music director of the Chicago Symphony. Zubin was also set to embark on a four-year *Ring* project at the Lyric Opera in the 1992–93 season. He was in talks with the Met as well, but no firm commitments had been made. Zubin was set to return for the Philharmonic's 150th anniversary celebrations in 1992–93 and, when asked about other appearances, acting director of the New York Philharmonic, Allison Vulgamore, said, 'We are constantly at his door.'[47] (Zubin returned to conduct the New York Philharmonic in 1992, 1996, 1997, 2000, 2003, 2007, 2009 and 2012.)

# Florence

IN 1985, MIDWAY THROUGH his tenure at New York, Zubin was appointed chief conductor of the Maggio Musicale Fiorentino orchestra in Florence. His association with that orchestra was almost as old as his connection with Israel. He visited Florence for the first time in 1956–57 when he went to Siena. His debut in Florence came in February 1962, at the Teatro Comunale. The first opera he conducted in Europe, *La Traviata*, was also performed there in July 1964. This was followed by repertoire performances of *Tosca* in July 1965.

If Vienna introduced Zubin to orchestral sound, and Israel encouraged his innate belief that music could be used to foster peace, Florence won him over with its beauty and helped him grow musically. Zubin says that Florence warmly welcomed him when he was a young, unknown and inexperienced conductor. Florence and the Maggio Musicale Fiorentino orchestra represent a second home for Zubin.

Florence, the cradle of the Italian Renaissance, is the place where almost every great Italian writer and artist, including Dante, Petrarch, Giotto, Brunelleschi, Da Vinci and Michelangelo made their mark. It is famous the world over for its priceless art treasures and attracts millions of tourists every year. Some say the whole city is a museum. And in this glorious setting of art and culture, music has played a crucial role. The capital of Tuscany is also the birthplace of opera. A group of aesthetes called the Camerata Fiorentina created a new art form in 1597 called *opera lirica* or lyric work. Their aim was to produce something new by combining poetry, music, dance, costumes and stagecraft.

Like many new art forms which take a while to develop, *opera lirica* was, in the beginning, rudimentary and awkward and the very first operas such as *Euridice* by composer Jacopo Peri and librettist Ottavio Rinuccini were stiff and formal. It took the arrival of Claudio Monteverdi from Cremona to breathe life into the form. Using a libretto by Alessandro Striggio, Monteverdi composed the first opera that is still staged with any frequency, *La Favola di Orfeo* (1607). His music evoked both the sound and the meaning of the words. The music in both the vocal and the instrumental parts communicated emotion relating to the story, something that Peri and the others had failed to do. In so doing, Monteverdi laid the foundations for opera as we know it today.

The Maggio Musicale Fiorentino orchestra was founded on 9 December 1928 by conductor Vittorio Gui as the Stabile Orchestrale Fiorentina. In 1933, the orchestra created what would become one of the oldest and most prestigious music festivals in Europe: the Festival del Maggio Musicale Fiorentino. It is from this festival that the orchestra took its name. Created as a triennial event, the festival was founded by Gui and aimed to present contemporary as well as forgotten operas in dramatic productions.

It stood in contrast to the grand spectacles such as *Aida* that had been staged in Verona since 1913. The forward-looking Maggio Musicale exemplified Florence's tradition of innovation. It was Italy's first such event for music and soon joined Salzburg and Bayreuth as one of Europe's most acclaimed music festivals. It attracted outstanding conductors, stage directors and singers whose work was admired by Florentines, Italians and Europeans who wanted something challenging and compelling. It was a May (*maggio*) festival that gradually expanded to begin in mid-April and conclude in mid-June. The first opera presented was Verdi's *Nabucco*.

The festival that now begins in late April and runs into June, typically presents four operas. Its success led to the organizers turning it into a biennial event in 1937. After 1937, it became an annual

Photograph by Nancy Mehta

34. Zubin conducts a vast ensemble of penguins during a visit to Antarctica, 1987.

35. Mario Miranda's Zubin.

36. With film director Cyrus Bharucha.

Photograph by Jacob Aviram

37. With a young Midori.

38. A bearded Zubin.

39. With Ravi Shankar.

Photograph by Gianluca Moggi

40. In Russia with the Maggio Musicale Fiorentino orchestra.

Photograph by Bert Bial

41. Zubin with Mindy Kaufman of the New York Philharmonic playing the piccolo in Mexico, 1981.

42. With Itzhak Perlman.

43. (Left to right) Plácido Domingo, Barbara Frittoli and Zubin.

44. Zubin at a function in Mumbai when he brought the Maggio Musicale Fiorentino orchestra to India. To his left is Mstislav Rostropovich and to his right is Mehroo Jeejeebhoy.

45. Maureen Wadia, Itzhak Perlman, Zubin, Nancy and Michael Ecker.

46. Zubin and Nancy with Nusli and Maureen Wadia and their two sons.

47. Yusuf and Farida Hamied with Zubin and Nancy.

48. Zubin and Nancy outside the
Mehli Mehta Music Foundation, Mumbai.

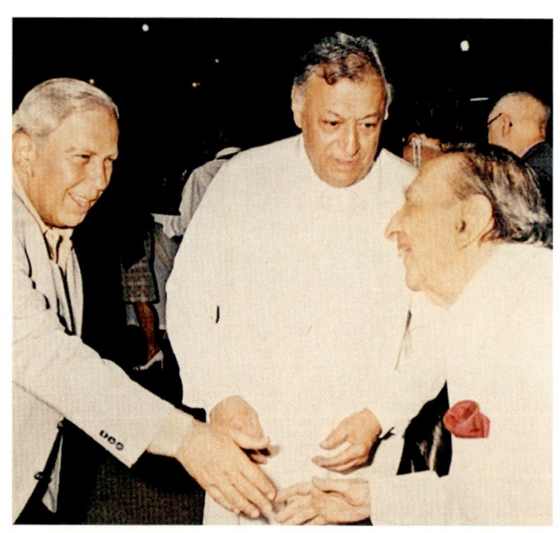

49. With Yusuf Hamied and Jamshed Bhabha
(extreme right).

50. With the trustees of the Mehli Mehta Music Foundation.

Photograph by Jacob Aviram

51. Sixtieth anniversary concert of the Israel Philharmonic Orchestra.

52. Seventieth anniversary of the Israel Philharmonic Orchestra.

53. With Natalia Ritzkowsky.

54. Four generations of the Mehta family.

55. The extended Mehta family.

56. Zubin hosting a traditional Parsi dinner in Mumbai.

57. Zubin and Nancy lighting a ceremonial lamp at the Mehli Mehta Music Foundation, with Mehroo Jeejeebhoy looking on.

58. Zubin and Daniel Barenboim at Zubin's seventieth birthday celebration.

59. With Shimon Peres and Sophia Loren, 2006.

60. Zubin at the Jamshed Bhabha Theatre, Mumbai.

61. With Sachin Tendulkar.

Photograph by Gianluca Moggi

62. With Pope Benedict XVI at the Vatican.

63. Zubin rehearsing at Brabourne Stadium, Mumbai.

64. Shimon Peres awarding Zubin the Presidential Medal of Distinction, 2012.

65. German ambassador to India Michael Steiner honours Zubin with the Commander's Cross of the Order of Merit of the Federal Republic of Germany, New Delhi, 2012.

Photograph by Yossi Seliger

66. With Shimon Peres.

67. Zubin and Nancy with Queen Sofía of Spain.

festival (except during the Second World War) and has since become an indispensable appointment for music lovers the world over.

The festival attracted the attention of the musical world from the start, thanks to its original ideas. One of these was the importance given to the visual aspect of opera: some of the finest theatre and film directors have collaborated alongside a large number of painters and sculptors for the design of the sets and costumes. It also had a decisive impact on the development of modern operatic and dramatic art.

The home of the orchestra is the Teatro Comunale, though performances take place in the smaller arena of the Teatro Piccolo as well as the historic Teatro della Pergola. The musicians perform opera and ballets in autumn and symphony concerts from January to April. The Teatro Comunale was partially destroyed twice, first by an air raid in 1944 and then by flood waters in 1966, but each time it has been restored immediately. A new opera house opened in 2011.

The quality of the orchestra soon attracted the best talent and it was not long before some of the world's greatest conductors led it: Walter, Furtwängler, Mitropoulos, Klemperer, Karajan, Solti, Bernstein, Böhm, Wolfgang Sawallisch, Rodziński, Carlos Kleiber, Giulini and, what was then the best of the younger generation, Abbado, Ozawa, Maazel and of course Zubin Mehta. After Gui left the post of permanent conductor, he was succeeded by Mario Rossi, Markevitch, Piero Bellugi and Bruno Bartoletti. Illustrious composers such as Richard Strauss, Hindemith, Stravinsky, Penderecki and Luciano Berio have conducted their own music with the orchestra, often as premieres. The celebrated soprano Maria Callas also sang here.

The life of this Florentine orchestra has been marked by two distinct periods, the first under Muti and the other under Zubin. Muti was its permanent conductor from 1969 to 1981 and it was in Florence that he made a name for himself. Zubin has been its principal conductor since 1985. The orchestra has also had a close association with Myung-Whun Chung and Semyon Bychkov, principal guest conductors since 1987 and 1992 respectively.

## 'MY ITALIAN FAMILY'

Zubin's association with the orchestra started on 11 February 1962. It must have been an auspicious day, for it was the start of a relationship which lasts to this day. (Zubin has said that he will not renew his contract which ends in 2017.) He made his debut at the Teatro Comunale, with a programme which consisted of Giovanni Giorgi, Schumann's Concerto for Piano and Orchestra and Mahler's First Symphony. His accompanist on the piano was Gulda whom Zubin had known in Vienna and they collaborated in perfect harmony on Schumann's concerto. Mahler's music was a rarity in Florence in those days. But for Zubin, with his musical origins firmly rooted in Viennese soil, it was only natural for him to play Mahler.

The concert in Florence was, however, not his Italian debut. That had been with Milan's Angelicum Orchestra in 1961, with Webern and Beethoven. After his debut in Florence, he made his debut at La Scala in Milan in 1962. Impressed with his performance with the Angelicum Orchestra, Francesco Siciliani invited him to conduct his first concert at La Scala. Siciliani was a musical prodigy, composer and conductor, but was best known for managing La Scala in Milan and the San Carlo in Naples. He helped promote the early careers of such artistes as Callas and Renata Tebaldi, apart from working with many leading conductors.

It appears that Siciliani had stuck his neck out to get Zubin to La Scala. He had to prevail upon the superintendent Antonio Ghiringhelli to invite Zubin to conduct. Ozawa had conducted there the previous year and Ghiringhelli, alarmed by the exotic conductors Siciliani was inviting, admonished him saying, 'Last year you called a Japanese conductor, and now you want an Indian with a turban conducting from Toscanini's and Victor de Sabata's podium.'[1] It didn't turn out to be as bad as that though, since Zubin did not conduct with a turban, but his debut was a success. Webern's *Six Pieces for Orchestra* and Richard Strauss's *Don Quixote* were on the programme. Webern proved to be a wrong choice and did not go down well with the audience. A couple of times he heard the doors being slammed.

There is an amusing anecdote concerning Zubin's visit to Milan to conduct at La Scala. Siciliani had bought Voltaire's opera *Omnia* in Vienna but had balked at the idea of carrying the numerous volumes back with him to Milan. He had delegated the task to an agent to ensure that they reached him in Milan. The agent distributed them among people travelling to Milan, with a request to deliver them to Siciliani. Zubin's services were also enlisted as a courier. When Zubin was changing trains at Innsbruck, he forgot the books in the train. He quickly ran back across the tracks to retrieve his precious cargo just as the train started to move. Zubin says that had he failed to deliver the books, his debut in La Scala may just have 'vanished' since it would have ruined Siciliani's set of the opera.

Zubin returned to Florence for concerts of Mozart, Webern and Brahms in October 1962; and Brahms, Stravinsky and Dvořák in February 1964. The concerts were well received and Renato Mariani, the then general secretary of the Teatro Comunale, offered him a chance to do an opera. They chose Verdi's *La Traviata* and Zubin recalls that he memorized the entire opera, of which there were four performances in July 1964, directed by Riccardo Moresco. Virginia Zeani was Violetta and the famous Met baritone Mario Sereni played Giorgio Germont. This was a turning point in Zubin's career, though he maintains that real success came a year later, in July 1965, when he conducted six performances of Puccini's *Tosca*, directed by Lorenzo Frusca.

In February 1967, Zubin returned to conduct a concert of Mozart, Beethoven and Bruckner. The year before, Florence had been ravaged by floods and Zubin had been greatly pained as he watched those images on television. He wanted to return as quickly as possible to Florence. Since the Teatro Comunale was under renovation, the concert was held at the grand Salone dei Cinquecento (on the first floor of the Palazzo Vecchio) which was used for the assemblies of the General Council of the People after the reforms brought about by Girolamo Savonarola. The walls of the hall, originally decorated by Michelangelo and Da Vinci, were worked on by Vasari and his pupils, and date back to the second half of the sixteenth century. The hall also exhibits the *Genius of Victory* by Michelangelo.

In that beautiful setting, Zubin conducted Beethoven's Concerto No. 3 for Piano, with Barenboim as the accompanist. His connection with Florence was now strong and he returned in October 1967 with his Los Angeles Philharmonic orchestra in a programme of Weber, Liszt and Bruckner. The soloist for Liszt's Piano Concerto No. 1 was Watts.

The year 1969 was hectic but also a highly satisfying one, artistically speaking. Zubin received an invitation to be the music director of the Maggio Musicale Festival that year. Even though he was music director at Los Angeles and had engagements with the Israel Philharmonic, he found that he could take up this assignment quite easily. There was a new production of *Aida* staged by Carlo Maestrini, and Zubin's favourite, *The Abduction from the Seraglio*, a remake of the Salzburg Festival (1965) production, directed by Strehler, who also directed the *Fidelio* which followed. The same year, Zubin conducted the Israel Philharmonic Orchestra in a concert with Rubinstein, and Abbado came with the London Symphony Orchestra, while Barenboim and Du Pré performed with the English Chamber Orchestra. Florence saw so much of Zubin that season that 'Mehta Maggio' was coined to humorously describe the young conductor's exploits that year.

*Aida* premiered on 6 May 1969, but not without its share of controversy. The opening had to be postponed because Carlo Bergonzi who was to play Radamès was forced to retire with a bad throat. With no substitute available, the opening of the festival was delayed and this led to some controversy. Finally, there were six performances of Aida and they went off smoothly. Zubin says that Verrett made a wonderful Amneris and Zeani a great Aida. In the last performance, a recovered Bergonzi made a perfect Radamès. Zubin remembers this *Aida* fondly. The scenes and costumes had been done by his friend Enrico d'Assia with whom he collaborated closely. 'Do what you want, but I want to feel the desert . . . the heat, the breath that emanates from the desert,' Zubin told him and he succeeded in transmitting this feeling in almost every scene.[2]

*The Abduction* was staged at the Teatro della Pergola at the end of May and the four performances of this opera were directed by Strehler, who had attained legendary status in the world of theatre and opera by the time he died in 1997. Zubin called him a man of great culture and musical sense. He and Strehler shared a cordial relationship despite the fact that the latter was a difficult man to get on with. Strehler was upset that *Aida* was directed by Maestrini, though if Zubin is to be believed, he had no grounds for feeling this way. They had offered him that opera, or any other for the opening of the festival, but he had refused saying that he intended to direct only the remake of *The Abduction* he had done at the Salzburg Festival with Zubin in 1965, and *Fidelio*. Zubin says that his feelings were suitably assuaged by the superintendent of the festival, Remigio Paone.[3]

*The Abduction* was a great success both for Zubin and for Strehler. Zubin was all praise for Strehler's general conception and staging where everything fell into place like clockwork. His chiaroscuro of light and shadow for the speeches and songs was, according to Zubin, a stroke of genius. It had a superb cast, with most of the original singers of the Salzburg debut also appearing in Florence. (The Salzburg production was extremely popular and was performed continuously for eight years.) Rothenberger played Konstanze; Werner Hollweg, Belmonte; Gerhard Unger, Pedrillo; Grist, Blonde; and Spiro Mallas, Osmia.

*Fidelio* was staged in early June and Zubin and Strehler clashed once again. The opera depicts how Leonore, disguised as a prison guard named Fidelio, rescues her husband, Florestan, from death as a political prisoner. Some notable moments in the opera include the Prisoners Chorus, an ode to freedom sung by political prisoners. A story of personal sacrifice, heroism and eventual triumph, its underlying struggle for justice and liberty mirrored the political movements in Europe at the time when Beethoven wrote it. In the end, to celebrate the defeat of tyranny, Strehler, who had socialist leanings, asked the chorus to wave red flags. When Zubin asked him the reason for the red flags, he was told, 'It is homage to my socialist faith.' Zubin politely demurred saying that was not the place for political propaganda. The red flags ended up having yellow stripes and Strehler sulked for five days. But the performance was superb and Zubin says that he does not remember another staging of *Fidelio* as good as this one.[4]

In between the *Fidelio* performances in early July 1969, Zubin conducted a concert at the Teatro Comunale with the Israel Philharmonic Orchestra. An added attraction was Rubinstein who played Beethoven's Concerto No. 3. The rest of the performance consisted of Schoenberg and Brahms. After the Maggio Festival of 1969, Zubin did not conduct in Florence for the next eight years. The controversy over the delayed *Aida* and petty politics in the Teatro Comunale hurt him and he preferred to stay away from Florence. But when Massimo Bogianckino took charge in Florence, everything changed. Zubin brought the Los Angeles Philharmonic to Florence in May 1977 and they played Mozart, Richard Strauss and Mussorgsky. The concert was a great success and Zubin told an interviewer many years later that he still remembered the warmth of that applause. In June of the same year, there were three performances of Richard Strauss's opera *Salome* directed by Boleslaw Barlog, with Zubin conducting the Vienna State Opera. He recalls that Gwyneth Jones made a convincing Salome.

Even though he had not conducted in Florence for some years, a connection remained. Zubin has had a close relationship with the orchestra for many years now. When he is in Florence, they rehearse every day and he has a deep personal bond with the musicians. He knows every player, including each member of the chorus which he feels is excellent and can sing in any language.

### *The* Ring *in Florence*

In 1978, after Zubin had been appointed music director in New York, he received an offer from Florence to conduct Wagner's *The Ring of the Nibelung.* Luca Ronconi would be the director, while the staging would be done by Pier Luigi Pizzi. It was a first for Zubin and he was happy that he was finally getting a chance to engage with Wagner in a manner he had never done before. Since he would be doing one opera of the four-part *Ring* each season, he could approach

Wagner's tetralogy in a leisurely but thorough manner. From 1979 to 1981, the highlight of Zubin's association with the Maggio orchestra was his involvement with the performance of the *Ring* cycle.

The *Ring* is one of the greatest and most challenging enterprises an opera company can undertake. It is probably the grandest, most complicated and controversial work in the music theatre repertory. Wagner selected ninety melodic fragments or leitmotifs to represent characters, places, emotions and actions. All the elements in the symphonic dramas of Wagner—the orchestration, the singing, the words, the setting—are woven into a definite pattern. The unit which binds the various parts into a compact whole is what Wagner called the leitmotif. These leitmotifs, little strands of melody, run throughout his operas like repeated figures in a tapestry. They identify the characters in the operas and endow the music with a recognizable personality. Wagner did not invent the leitmotif but he gave it life. It was only in the *Ring* that he turned this symbol into a concrete form of musical portraiture. With its perfection, Wagner introduced a new instrument into orchestral music. His genius, it must be remembered, was primarily orchestral. The voice in a Wagnerian opera is but a part of the orchestra.

Opera is a composite art form. It makes use of vocal and instrumental music; the poetry of the libretto; dance; and sets and costumes to appeal to the audience on musical, dramatic, visual, emotional and intellectual levels. Staging even one opera, much less a whole season, is a staggering task. Given Wagner's complex orchestral scores and staging, and the almost impossible vocal demands made on the singers, assembling the necessary financial and artistic forces for staging one of his operas is indeed a daunting task. Few singers across the world are able to cope with the score, especially the roles of Siegfried and Brünnhilde, who dominate the last two operas. Thus a *Ring* has come to symbolize accomplishment, seriousness and range for any self-respecting opera company.

Sawallisch and director Ronconi had planned a full *Ring* in La Scala but could put together only *Die Walküre* and *Siegfried*. Bogianckino agreed to resume the *Ring* in Florence. While *Das Rheingold* and

*Götterdämmerung* were new productions, *Die Walküre* and *Siegfried* were modified versions of the La Scala performances.

*Das Rheingold* was staged in May–June 1979 under the direction of Ronconi, with sets and costumes by Pizzi. This was followed by *Die Walküre* in February–March 1980. A new *Das Rheingold* was interspersed with it and *Siegfried* was staged in January–February 1981, and *Götterdämmerung* in June 1981. The same month, there was also a concert of Beethoven and Mahler, with Barenboim playing the piano in Beethoven's Concerto No. 5 on 12 June. Two days later, Zubin conducted Tchaikovsky's Concerto for Violin and Orchestra, with Perlman as violinist. Mahler's First Symphony was common to both programmes.

Performing the *Ring* always takes a monumental effort and Zubin recalls that the Italians took to Wagner exceedingly well. *Das Rheingold* was a success, especially from the production point of view. Pizzi's simple but effective staging was much appreciated. While *Die Walküre* and *Götterdämmerung* were of a high standard, *Siegfried* was not up to the mark. The singing was not particularly good, though Jones was a splendid Brünnhilde. Learning from this, Zubin made sure that he got singers of the highest quality for his performances. At times, the singers protested against Ronconi's unconventional direction and complained to Zubin that they did not like the director's interpretation. Zubin somehow managed to placate them. As Brünnhilde, Jones, who in *Die Walküre* had to fall asleep for eighteen years, was asked to do so with her head on a table. This radically anti-hero interpretation did not appeal to Jones initially, but she toed the line. The end result, however, was most satisfying. Zubin says they had demonstrated that an Italian theatre, orchestra and chorus could perform Wagner's tetralogy as well as any opera house in Germany or Austria, and perhaps with greater inventiveness.[5]

In May 1983, there were three Brahms concerts at the Teatro Comunale with the Los Angeles Philharmonic. Zubin was standing in for an indisposed Giulini in response to frantic entreaties from Los Angeles to save the tour. The soloists were of the highest class: Gidon Kremer (violin) and Yo-Yo Ma (violoncello).

## CHIEF CONDUCTOR

In 1980, Muti, the music director who was responsible for greatly improving the level of the orchestra, left Florence rather suddenly. Stranded without a music director, the committee of the orchestra came to Israel and requested Zubin to help them tide over their artistic crisis. Zubin agreed and stepped in as guest conductor. However, he did this free of charge, making it clear that this was only a temporary arrangement; he was only 'helping out'.

In 1985, however, that temporary arrangement became permanent when he was named chief conductor of the orchestra. In 1986, they invited him to become artistic director for the Maggio Festival that year. One of the reasons Zubin accepted was because he really loves working in Florence. This has something to do with the system there. From the very first rehearsal and through all the performances, Zubin says, he can count on the same cast. He adds that while this is not possible in bigger opera houses with a higher number of performances, like in some German cities, it is nice to always work with the same musicians.

The artistic directorship of the forty-ninth Maggio Festival was a great honour as well as a great responsibility for Zubin. He opened the festival on 19 May 1986, conducting the Israel Philharmonic Orchestra in Bruckner's Eighth Symphony. In June, there were four performances of Wagner's *The Mastersingers of Nuremberg* directed by Michael Hampe, with stage and costumes by John Gunter. Four performances of *Tosca* followed at the end of the month, with Jonathan Miller (later Sir) directing Puccini's opera in an acclaimed 'non-realist' interpretation. Miller, a British theatre and opera director who trained as a medical doctor is an author, television presenter and a familiar public intellectual in both Britain and the United States.

Zubin also conducted the orchestra in a performance of Schoenberg's *Gurrelieder* with Klaus Maria Brandauer as the narrating voice at the Palazzetto dello Sport, where the acoustics turned out to be surprisingly good. Zubin had conducted Beethoven's Ninth Symphony there the previous year. The festival closed with 'Music in the City', a joyful festivity involving many orchestras and ensembles that covered the entire city of Florence. The last performance of Verdi's *Requiem* at the Piazza della Signoria in the presence of the leaders of the European Economic Community marked the opening of the year of Florence as the Capital of European Culture.

In February–March 1987, Zubin took the orchestra on a tour of Oman and India. They played in Muscat and Bombay and the soloist was the violinist Ughi. The programme consisted of Wagner, Beethoven, Brahms, Mozart, Tchaikovsky and Ravel. A year later, there was a tour of Turkey where they played Wagner, Beethoven and Tchaikovsky in Ankara and Istanbul. Once again Ughi was the soloist.

The Frenchman Messiaen, considered one of the major composers of the last century, was good friends with Zubin who appreciated his music and performed it many times. Messiaen's last work, *Éclairs sur l'au-delà*, which he composed in 1991, was commissioned by Zubin and the New York Philharmonic and the maestro conducted this orchestral piece in Florence in June 1993. In 1988, he played *Turangalîla* in the presence of Messiaen—who had just entered his eightieth year—in a concert in Florence held in his honour. Playing the piano was Messiaen's wife, Yvonne Loriod, an accomplished pianist, and on the ondes Martenot (an electronic instrument for which Messiaen often wrote parts) was her sister, Jeanne. (Yvonne was his muse and accredited interpreter of his piano pieces and, for three decades, also his devoted wife. She was his muse not only for his piano works but for his orchestral ones as well. When the German musicologist Heinrich Strobel commissioned what would become *Chronochromie*, he felt obliged to specify, 'This time, no ondes Martenot and no piano.' Messiaen's students included big names like Boulez and Karlheinz Stockhausen.) Two days later, there was a repeat performance of *Turangalîla* in Paris, and again the next day at the Salerno Festival. Zubin said that contemporary composers were performed in Florence and it was his duty as music director to make sure that new works made it to the programme even if the response of the audience was initially one of irritation.[6]

The year 1989 was marked by two meaningful performances: an intense Mahler's Ninth in March and a concert to express solidarity with the people in China after the Tiananmen Square tragedy in early June. The concert developed as a spontaneous response to the event and they played Beethoven's *Eroica* and 'Free Me' from Verdi's *Requiem*. The soprano was Cecilia Gasdia. At the end of the concert, hundreds of Florentines crowded into the Piazza della Santissima Annunziata to show their support.

The fifty-third Maggio Festival the next year was memorable for two operas: *Il Trovatore* and *Don Giovanni*. *Il Trovatore*, a favourite of Zubin's, was staged in June, a performance made more special by the return of Pavarotti to Florence after many years, as Manrico. The rest of the singers were no less distinguished: Giorgio Zancanaro, Dolora Zajick and Barbara Frittoli.

The same month also saw the first of Mozart's Da Ponte operas, *Don Giovanni*. The other two of the trilogy, *Cosi fan tutte* and *The Marriage of Figaro*, were completed in the next two years. Lorenzo da Ponte wrote the librettos for three of Mozart's operas which are considered his most famous and the collaboration between the two must be counted among the most successful in the history of opera. Da Ponte had led a bohemian life as a teacher and priest. A friend of Giacomo Casanova's, he had been expelled from Venice for sexual depravity. He had an extraordinary gift for languages and understood that creating an opera was all about collaboration between the composer and librettist, both of whom had to know when to give way: sometimes words had to yield to notes and vice versa.

This was the first time Zubin was conducting these operas and they were produced by Miller, whom he considered a good friend. He had a high regard for Miller's skills as a director and counted himself as a fan. Miller displayed an uncommon ability to guide singers who were not natural actors, with comic timing or urgency, depending on what the situation demanded. Most of the real action in these operas takes place during the recitative passages and Miller was exceptional in guiding the singers in these.[7]

The year 1991 was marked by two tours—the first in June to

Siena and Ravenna, and the second, an international tour to South America and Spain. They visited Venezuela, Argentina and Brazil and ended the tour in Madrid. The orchestra played in Caracas, where the tour started, Buenos Aires, Santos, São Paulo and Manaus. In Manaus, they inaugurated the newly renovated Teatro Amazonas, playing Verdi, Beethoven and Berlioz. At the end of the concert, Zubin shared his concern for the destruction of the Amazon rainforests, something which did not go down too well with the governor of Brazil's biggest state. Amazonas is the largest tract of tropical rainforest in the Americas and is home to more than a third of all the species in the world. Zubin also recalls sailing to the confluence of the rivers Negro and Amazon, comparing it to the power and beauty of a great symphony.

The highlights of 1993 were Bizet's *Carmen* and Mozart's *The Magic Flute*. The latter was directed by a relative newcomer to Italy, Julie Taymor, who subsequently went on to become the first woman to win a Tony Award for directing the stage musical *The Lion King*. Zubin called her production sensational: full of poetry, mystery and authentic fantasy. The frequent scene changes were a difficult test for everyone but in the end it was worth it. Over a decade later, Taymor premiered *The Magic Flute* at the Metropolitan in 2004, and it quickly entered the repertoire there.

The year was also noteworthy for the debut of sixteen-year-old Sarah Chang in Florence. A child prodigy, Chang had, at age eight, auditioned for Zubin and Muti, who were music directors of the New York Philharmonic and Philadelphia orchestras respectively. Both granted her immediate engagements. Chang played Tchaikovsky's Violin Concerto in D Major and, according to Zubin, performed the formidable piece with great aplomb.

The bomb attack in May on the Accademia dei Georgofili, in which the Uffizi gallery was damaged, also took place in 1993. Zubin conducted a concert at the Piazza della Signoria on 27 June as a tribute to the victims, playing the Overture from *The Magic Flute*, Verdi's *Requiem* and the fourth movement from Beethoven's Fifth Symphony. This concert was to start the tradition of concluding the Maggio Musicale every year with an impressive open-air concert in the Piazza della Signoria, the civic heart of Florence, with an audience of 30,000 in attendance. Zubin says that it turned into a celebration, a way to conclude the festival in grand style—an embrace of the city, its musicians and its theatre.

The highlights in 1994 included Schoenberg's *Moses und Aron* and *Il castello del principe Barbablù* by Bartók in concert form, and Richard Strauss's *Salome*. Zubin was awarded the Abbiati Prize for the Best Conductor of the Year for his performance in conducting Schoenberg's masterpiece. The Abbiati Prizes, established in memory of Italian musicologist Franco Abbiati (1898–1981), are Italy's most distinguished music awards, and are given annually by the Italian National Association of Music Critics, comprising more than 150 Italian critics and journalists. Under Zubin's baton, it was the first time that the Italian chorus sang in German, and they faced formidable difficulties initially. Zubin called it an eloquent demonstration of the chorus's high level of professionalism and virtuosity. The orchestra then undertook a tour of France and Spain in August, where they performed at the ancient Roman theatre in Orange and in Santander.

In 1995, Zubin conducted the Berlin Philharmonic in three concerts in April and May. Every year, the Berlin Philharmonic plays in a city known for its artistic and cultural heritage, and in 1995 the orchestra chose Florence. The concerts were held in the grand Salone dei Cinquecento. Zubin, who has had a fifty-year association with that orchestra, conducted a programme of Beethoven, Boris Blacher, Paganini and Stravinsky. Young Sarah Chang was the soloist. There was also a concert at the Teatro Comunale in which they played Stravinsky and Brahms. These concerts were telecast worldwide. Later in the month, Zubin substituted for an indisposed Celibidache, conducting the Munich Philharmonic in Bruckner's Fourth.

The year 1996 saw stage performances of Gaetano Donizetti's *Lucia di Lammermoor* and Luigi Dallapiccola's *Il Prigioniero* in concert form. There was also a concert at the Boboli Gardens on 21 June. But the highlight of the year was the tour of Austria and Denmark. They played at the Salzburg Festival, where the venue for the concert was the Salzburg Cathedral, the seventeenth-century Baroque cathedral which still contains the font in which Mozart was baptized. Zubin says that the success of the orchestra in Salzburg marked the coming of age of both the orchestra and the chorus at the highest international level. The programme consisted of *Il Prigioniero* in concert form and Verdi's *Four Sacred Pieces* and the *Requiem*. The first two were performed at the festival. The four choral works written separately by Verdi in the last decades of his life with different origins and purposes, but published together, are often performed as a cycle.

They played the *Requiem* again in Copenhagen. That year was also special because they staged *Aida* twice, first at the Teatro Comunale and then at Yokohama and Tokyo on their tour of Japan in September. It was directed by Raffaele Del Savio who had hand-painted the sets and, drawing inspiration from the *Aida* staged in 1969 by D'Assia, didn't need Zubin's suggestions. Zubin told me that unlike the constant criticism he faced in New York, none of his performances in Florence received negative press.

## *TURANDOT* IN THE FORBIDDEN CITY

One of the most spectacular performances with which Zubin has been associated (and there have been many) was the staging of Puccini's *Turandot* in Beijing's Forbidden City in September 1998. This dramatic and musical extravaganza staged under the direction of Chinese film director Zhang Yimou was performed by a cast of 1000 in the Forbidden City, the vast imperial compound in the heart of Beijing. The seed for the idea was sown in 1994, when Zubin was on a tour of China with the Israel Philharmonic Orchestra. In 1996, he took the Vienna Philharmonic to China. It was during this trip that he took a walk through the Forbidden City with Austrian promoter Michael Ecker. The latter broached the idea of staging Puccini's last opera in its original setting. Ecker, the chairman of Opera On Original Site, Inc., was a specialist at staging opera performances at original locations. He had put up a lavish production of Verdi's *Aida* at the Temple of Luxor in Egypt in 1987.

*Turandot* was not only Puccini's swansong but also his masterpiece.

It is one of the twenty most performed operas and the aria 'Nessun Dorma' sung by Pavarotti in the role of the unknown prince Calaf (described as two and a half minutes of melodic perfection) is among the most famous recordings in classical music. Turandot is a princess who doesn't want to get married. Her extreme hatred towards men is reflected in the fact that she gets her father, the emperor, to decapitate any man who aspires to possess her. To ward off suitors, she asks them three riddles and if they fail to answer, their heads are chopped off instantly. In the end, Calaf, an unknown prince, solves the riddles but promises to sacrifice himself if she can learn his name. Liu, a slave girl commits suicide to avoid betraying his name. Finally, the princess succumbs to Calaf's passionate embrace and kiss, and announces that she has learned his name: Love.

Puccini died in 1924, before he could finish the opera, having completed the score up to the death of the slave girl in the final act. He did, however, leave behind enough material to indicate how the opera was to close. It was finished by Franco Alfano, a minor composer of operas. The premiere was conducted by Toscanini at Milan's La Scala in April 1926 and the temperamental maestro gave the unfortunate Alfano a hard time, first rejecting his work and then cutting it drastically. At the premiere, he did not perform Alfano's conclusion, but stopped with the suicide of the slave girl, Liu. Turning to the audience, he said: 'Here Death triumphed over Art.'[8] The audience left in silence. (There is an interesting anecdote about a performance of *Turandot* in Verona with Nilsson and Domingo as Turandot and Calaf respectively. Nilsson describes how Domingo's kiss in the final act was so long that the audience began to shout, *'Basta, Basta, adesso'* ['Hey, that'll do, thank you']. In the process, he ended up infecting her with tonsillitis which almost jeopardized her subsequent performances.) Different and unique, *Turandot* was the consummation of Puccini's creative career.[9]

Ever since *Aida* was commissioned for the opening of the Suez Canal, opera entrepreneurs have been thinking of ways to draw audiences to exotic locations outside conventional opera houses. While many of these productions were mediocre, with poor sound, two of the more exciting and authentic operatic performances were initiated by Zubin. The maestro, who loves the lavish nature of opera, was involved with the staging of Saint-Saëns's *Samson et Dalila* and *Fidelio* with the Israel Philharmonic in Caesarea's Roman amphitheatre in the 1970s. He has also conducted a virtual reality production of *Tosca* in Rome. Primarily made for television and video, each of the three acts was set in Rome, where the story of *Tosca* actually unfolds. Zubin conducted the orchestra in a studio and the sound was transmitted via monitors to the locales where the singers performed. The result was a traditional and spectacular production that was both extravagant and exuberant. This was conceived and produced by Andrea Andermann.

Ecker's idea greatly interested Zubin since it had long been his dream to stage *Turandot* in its original setting. But he realized that they would face many bureaucratic hurdles. He also knew that Karajan and Franco Zeffirelli had been turned down in the 1970s. The Chinese had been a little wary of allowing filming, or any other cultural events, in the Forbidden City since the minor damage caused by the shooting of Bernardo Bertolucci's *The Last Emperor*. But Zubin was interested enough to try his luck with the Chinese minister of culture. During a break in the concert with the Vienna Philharmonic, Zubin tried to convince him that a grand performance of the kind he had in mind would not only be a magnificent spectacle but would also enhance China's image internationally.

In June 1997, Zubin did a new production of *Turandot* in Florence with Chinese director Yimou. It was around this time that Ecker approached Zubin with a serious offer to take the opera to Beijing. Zubin says that he persisted with the minister and finally, at one meeting, he said, 'Yes. We trust you and you are Asiatic. Do it.' Zubin quips that he even took a box of the choicest Alphonso mangos to soften him up!

Zubin was no stranger to Puccini or to *Turandot*. He is considered one of the finest Puccini conductors of this generation, if not the best, and his 1962 recording with Joan Sutherland and Pavarotti was one of the best on the market. The idea of involving Yimou in the project was Zubin's. When they were planning a new *Turandot* in Florence, he thought of approaching the Chinese director whose Oscar-nominated film *Raise the Red Lantern* had made a deep impression on him. Yimou was known internationally for films such as *Ju Dou* and *Raise the Red Lantern*, and used the colour red to tell his stories to great effect. He said that he knew nothing about Western opera until he was asked to direct it. 'At first it was confusing—another heavy-set person on stage and I didn't know who's who,' he told an interviewer. 'But then they sang and it hit me how beautiful the human voice is. Exquisite. It was very moving.'[10]

Yimou has not always been on the right side of the authorities in China—some of his films were even banned. His films portrayed a China never seen before: his characters struggle with stifling tradition, repression and fear. (Given his humble beginnings, this is not surprising. His first job was as a farmhand and then as a labourer in a cotton mill. It is said that he sold his blood over a period of many months to earn enough to purchase his first camera.) Unsurprisingly, when Zubin first tried to contact Yimou, the Chinese created problems for him. Finally, they managed to start negotiations with him and, after some thought, Yimou agreed to come on board for *Turandot* to be staged in Florence, with Zubin and the Maggio Musicale Fiorentino orchestra.

*Turandot* premiered in Florence on 5 June 1997, opening the sixtieth Maggio Musicale Festival. There were eight performances in June followed by two more in July. The cast included Sharon Sweet, Jane Eaglen and Audrey Stottler (as Turandot); Lando Bartolini, Giuseppe Giacomini and Keith Olsen (as Calaf); and Cristina Gallardo-Domâs, Lucia Mazzaria and Chiara Angella (as Liu).

Yimou and his team of costume and set designers and choreographers—all in their late twenties—put up a sumptuous production. In the course of the production, Yimou learned about opera, something which was altogether new for him. Although he was familiar with Chinese theatrical traditions, he knew nothing about fitting chorus movements with music and he was very eager to learn. Zubin says that Yimou's understanding of music grew as he worked on *Turandot*. And if he knew nothing about opera, he had a great sense of theatre. That Yimou knew nothing of opera did not worry Zubin; he understood that with opera, it is flexibility that counts. Within a few days of their collaboration, he knew all would be well. 'He knows the musical cues. He knows exactly when a piece of music needs another fifty people brought in,'[11] he had said. The magnificent costumes were all handmade. The production was a great success.

It was this success that made Zubin call on Yimou again when they decided to take the opera to Beijing. What also weighed in Yimou's favour was that he was Chinese: he would ensure an authentic production. Zubin's first few meetings with Yimou in Beijing were worthy of an espionage thriller. He picked him up from an undisclosed location and their visit to the Forbidden City was a closely guarded secret. When the Chinese authorities came to know about it, they were less than thrilled. But Zubin persisted with his demand for Yimou as director and they finally relented. Staging *Turandot* in the Forbidden City was also a coup of sorts. It was the biggest event to have taken place there since the wedding of the then non-sovereign monarch of China, Pu Yi, in 1924.

That year, *Turandot* became the must-attend performance for the rich and famous. Aircraft were chartered across the world to bring socialites and their billionaire husbands to Beijing for this one of a kind concert. The first of the eight performances scheduled on consecutive nights was on 5 September 1998, in the 580-year-old Ming Dynasty temple where emperors once made sacrifices to their ancestors. A sprawling courtyard in one corner of the Forbidden City was converted into an open-air amphitheatre for the most extravagant Western cultural event ever to take place in China. Two specially constructed pagodas and two artificial pavilions enhanced the magnificent stage setting at the top of twenty-one stone steps that led to the imposing doors of the majestic, disused palace. Drums heralded the opening of each show and red hand-painted panels covered in gold-leaf took the place of a stage curtain. Two performances—one, a grand rehearsal, and the other, an official performance—were reserved for Beijing residents at reduced prices.

Since the roles are so demanding, the singers alternated in the main parts. Giovanna Casolla, Stottler and Sweet played Turandot; Angela Maria Blasi, Frittoli and Barbara Hendricks played Liu; and Bartolini, Kristján Jóhannsson and Sergei Larin, Calaf.

Ecker, whose Opera On Original Site along with the China Performing Arts Agency was responsible for this coup after years of haggling with Chinese officials, called it 'the last great cultural event before the millennial festivities begin'. The extravaganza which cost $14 million was a huge success artistically but less so financially. Expenses for the site, disappointing ticket sales in recession-hit Asia, lower-than-expected sponsorship and some unsold tickets made it a disappointing project financially. The Chinese government charged a high rent for the venue, with the producers also having to pay for electricity and cables.

The Italian culture ministry put in $1.5 million for costumes and flying the orchestra and chorus of the Maggio Musicale Fiorentino to Beijing. The orchestra knew the opera by heart thanks to the Florence staging. Special *Turandot* tours were organized to draw opera lovers from Europe and North America.

More than 1000 people were involved, including local Chinese singers and extras and 300 Chinese soldiers who played warriors; 100 dancers replaced the twelve who had performed in Florence. Yimou demanded that the costumes be remade in Ming rather than Tang dynasty–style, adding another $3,30,000 to the cost. The costumes were hand-stitched by 600 members of the same village where the imperial family had their clothes tailored 500 years ago.

On stage, Yimou had added two smaller pavilions on rails and he used them deftly. He employed the chorus like a Greek one because the architecture of the pavilion restricted movement. 'What he did with the space available to him was miraculous,' Zubin said. The singers were nearly twice as far from Zubin as they would have been in a regular opera house. The Chinese were obsessed with the fact that no harm should come to any architectural detail in the Forbidden City, so the opera team had no choice but to stay within its confines. They did six rehearsals—two with each of the cast members—to get used to the distances involved. Another problem was miking up the stage for the audience, as the performances were outdoors and open-air sound is quite dry.

Business guests comprised roughly half the 4200-member audience each night and more than 200 companies paid large sums for tickets, dinner with the cast and advertising recognition. The Chinese authorities requested and got a large number of free tickets and one journalist who covered the event said that he found it difficult to find a Chinese who had paid to witness the opera.

At the end of it all, there was an air of self-congratulation even if it had not been a financial success. 'Although it is a Western opera, I am Chinese, everything I think is Chinese and it will be a Chinese production,' Yimou had said. And so it was. It made the Chinese very proud that they were part of such a high-level production. There was a line of thought which held that the reluctance of Chinese officials to let Yimou do the project initially stemmed from doubts about his ability to handle such a high-profile project as he lacked experience in this genre. But they need not have worried. In the end, critics and performers enthused about the innovations—more symbolic, animated movement; bright and elaborate costumes; and Chinese ballet dancers. For Zubin, it was a dream come true and he called it the experience of a lifetime. (Alan Miller's documentary *The Turandot Project* takes the viewer behind the scenes of this history-making production.)

The staging of *Turandot* was a turning point in China's willingness to embrace the West. Suddenly, after decades of suspicion, censorship and rejection of Western culture, Beijing had opened its doors. It is said that this gave China the confidence to host the Olympics a decade later. In fact, it may have played a role in helping Beijing win the bid to host the Olympics. It was this liberal exchange, coupled with the excitement of artistic freedom that marked China's entry on the world cultural stage.

One-time enfant terrible Yimou went on to choreograph the opening and closing ceremonies of the Beijing Olympics in 2008 to great acclaim. He became a national icon and was voted *Time* magazine's Person of the Year in 2008. While describing the opening ceremony, Hollywood director Steven Spielberg said: 'In one evening of visual and emotional splendor, he educated, enlightened and entertained us all.'[12]

Yimou revisited *Turandot* in October 2009 for the sixtieth anniversary celebrations of the founding of the People's Republic of China, in which he offered a high-tech, near-total reinvention of his lavish 1998 production in the Forbidden City. It was an amazing turnaround, given that *Turandot* had been banned by the Kuomintang Chinese government when it first appeared. Perhaps the ultimate irony is that *Turandot* has, for all practical purposes, ended up as China's national opera.

♫

In the years that followed, Zubin led *Tristan und Isolde* (1999), *La Traviata* (2000) and *Il Trovatore* (2001). *Tristan* was, according to Zubin, a bit of a 'graduation exam' for the orchestra which, he says, they passed with full marks. In *Tristan*, he explains, every instrumentalist is a soloist and once an orchestra masters that, it is ready to face any musical challenge. There was another tour of Japan in 2001 and *La Traviata* and *Turandot* were staged, the latter again under the direction of Yimou. There was also a tour of Monte Carlo where they played Beethoven and Brahms at the Grimaldi Forum, Salles de Princes, in November.

Asked about how the Maggio orchestra had changed in the forty years that he had known it, Zubin, in an interview with Franco Manfriani in 2002, said it had improved in every way. As an example, he pointed out how the horn players now played with their hand inside the instrument in order to control the emission and intonation better, just like in other international orchestras. In the 1960s, this method was unknown in Italy. Zubin says that the repertory of a great symphonic orchestra rests on the classic–Romantic tradition with its centre in Vienna. He proudly said that the orchestra now had this 'Viennese sound' which unfortunately the music lovers of Florence could not fully appreciate because of the acoustics of the Teatro Comunale. He cited a recent visit to Turin where the acoustics were much better: he said that it did not seem right that the Florentine should travel to Turin to appreciate the music of his own orchestra. There was a crying need, he stressed, to build a new auditorium because the orchestra, the chorus and the city all deserved it.[13]

His dream finally came true when a new hall opened in December 2011. With all the talk in Italy of austerity measures, lay-offs, additional property taxes, pension reductions and salary freezes, the inauguration of a modern concert hall came as a breath of fresh air. The local administration had bet big on culture and, instead of halting construction on this massive project, ended up executing the plans on time.

The inaugural celebrations of the Nuovo Teatro dell'Opera were marked by a series of concerts and ballets, including the fourth act of *Otello* and the first act of *Tosca*, from 21 December 2011 to 1 January 2012. The new theatre has an auditorium entirely devoted to opera which can seat 1800 people. A symphonic hall with a capacity of 1100 and rehearsal rooms for musicians and dancers has yet to be built. There is also an outdoor amphitheatre that can hold upwards of 2200 people and a terraced garden for public use. This is the new home for the historic Maggio Musicale Fiorentino. 'The Maggio' of course consists of not only the Maggio Orchestra, but also the Maggio Chorus. (The ballet troupe, Maggio Danza, was closed in May 2013 as a cost-cutting measure.) However, the new facility was far from complete at the time of its inauguration and it was only in May 2014 that it was finally ready.

In 2011, Zubin took the orchestra to twelve countries (France, Luxemburg, Spain, Germany, Japan, Taiwan, China, India, Hungary, Russia, Austria and Switzerland) to celebrate the 150th anniversary of the Italian Unification under the expert guidance of director general Francesca Colombo. It was named the 'World Ambassador of Italian Culture'. (In 2008, on the eightieth anniversary of its founding, it received the Gold Florin of the city of Florence.) Zubin and Nancy have a home in Florence (a second 'home' apart from Brentwood) and Zubin is an honorary citizen of that city, apart from being awarded an honorary doctorate by the University of Florence. He says this makes him 'doubly Florentine'.

To mark fifty years of Zubin's debut in Florence, the Maggio Musicale Fiorentino dedicated a special Mehta Festival in his honour from 9 November to 5 December 2012 at the Teatro dell'Opera. It consisted of three concerts, six other performances and the opportunity to go backstage after the show. The programme included music by Mahler, Hindemith, Bartók, Dvořák and Puccini, all conducted by Zubin. Mahler's *Resurrection* opened the festival which ended with *Turandot*. On 30 November, there was *Mathis der Maler* by Hindemith, Bartók's Concerto for Two Pianos, Percussion and Orchestra featuring the Pekinel sisters, and Dvořák's Seventh Symphony.

The year 2012 also marked the seventy-fifth edition of the Maggio Musicale Festival. The *fil rouge* of the festival, 'The travel from Middle Europe to South America', was dedicated to Italian explorer Amerigo Vespucci on his 500th death anniversary. The Florentine explorer, navigator and cartographer was the first to demonstrate that Brazil constituted an entirely separate, hitherto unknown land mass. Colloquially called the 'New World', this continent came to be called 'America' deriving its name from Americus, the Latin version of Vespucci's first name. The highlight of the festival was a line-up of four performances of Richard Strauss's opera *Der Rosenkavalier* which was being presented in Florence after twenty-three years. It was directed by Eike Gramss, with sets by Hans Schavernoch.

A contemporary opera commissioned by the Teatro Comunale, *La Metamorfosi*, based on Franz Kafka's story and composed by Silvia Colasanti, premiered at the festival. Other performances included the ballet *The Miraculous Mandarin* and the opera *Bluebeard's Castle*. Hindemith's ballet *The Four Temperaments* and Schoenberg's *Verklärte Nacht* were also performed. A Bartók evening was to be conducted by Ozawa but he cancelled owing to ill health, and was replaced by Hungarian conductor Zsolt Hamar. In August, Zubin and the orchestra toured South America, visiting Chile, Uruguay, Argentina and Brazil, dedicating their tour to the memory of Vespucci.

A noteworthy event in February 2013 was when the orchestra

led by Zubin played for Pope Benedict XVI in the Paul VI Hall of the Vatican. It was a concert from the Italian Embassy to the Holy See on the occasion of the eighty-fourth anniversary of the Lateran Accords. The repertoire included Verdi's *La Forza del Destino* and Beethoven's *Eroica*. Addressing the audience briefly after the performance, the Pope said that the choice of *La Forza* was a fitting tribute to the great composer on the 200th anniversary of his birth. Less than a week after the concert, the Pope abdicated.

♫

The majority of Italy's fourteen lyric and symphonic foundations, including the Maggio, had been losing money for years. From 2004 to 2008, they lost €100 million with approximately 70 per cent of the funds received going towards salaries. In May 2013, Maggio Danza, the ballet company formed in 1967, was shut down citing serious financial constraints and mounting debt which had to be repaid. The banks blocked further credit and the situation was precarious enough to endanger the future of the entire Maggio Festival.

In 1999, the Maggio became one of the first theatres to try to supplement its funds with private sponsors. But most Italians were not accustomed to that method and tax laws did not make such donations particularly advantageous. Zubin has spoken out strongly against the fact that Italy does not allow tax-deductible donations, a system widely prevalent in the United States which benefits both the donor and the receiver. He even spoke to the authorities about introducing such a system in Italy but nothing happened. Artistes and stage directors were not paid on time and some preferred not to come to Florence at all or demanded guarantees in their contracts specifying payment by a certain date, which the theatre could not meet. Zubin himself did not receive payment for over one and a half years.

Since the 1960s, it had been assumed that the Maggio name and the Florence mystique would suffice to keep things solvent but those hopes were belied. The mayor of Florence traditionally heads the opera board, but many of them had political agendas, as did the general managers, and there was an uncontrolled increase in expenditure and employees. Things got progressively bloated and expensive even as ticket income and funding declined. The fact that opera was invented and perfected on Italian soil should have been reason enough for government support. But Berlusconi's government showed startling indifference towards opera and other traditional genres when it announced that the Unified Fund for the Performing Arts which covers opera, theatre, dance and film would be cut by more than a third.

Zubin said that they needed to get a strong fundraising arm because Florence was not an industrial city like Milan or Turin and it was more difficult to raise money there. Banks helped out but they were affected by the cash crunch too. The government paid lip service to tax deductibility but there were no concrete steps and no incentive to give money. He compared the situation with Munich where there were always packed houses and a €50-million subsidy kept them in the black.

The theatre had accumulated a deficit of €34 million in 2009 and the cutbacks had affected Zubin and the orchestra as well. That year they were forced to cancel the operas *Macbeth* and *Billy Budd* because of financial constraints, though *Die Walküre* survived. In 2013, Verdi's *Don Carlos* was reduced to a concert version. The commissioner, Francesco Bianchi, had a mandate to save €6 million by the end of 2013 and there were cuts all around. The singers had not been paid their wages and the Performing Arts Endowment slashed funding further.

Zubin bemoaned the fact that the budget for culture which was already at .04 per cent of the GDP in Italy was brought down to .02 per cent, with chances of it being reduced even further. There appears to be no let-up in the financial woes of the Maggio. When I asked him about the current state of finances, Zubin said, 'They're still in great need of finances.'[14] In 2015–16, he led Verdi's *Falstaff* and *Rigoletto* and Beethoven's *Fidelio* with the Maggio orchestra. From 2017, Zubin will be conductor emeritus. His successor, Italian conductor Fabio Luisi, is currently principal conductor of the Metropolitan Opera and general music director of the Zurich Opera.

# The Podium *and the* Pit

WHEN ZUBIN WAS WINDING down his thirteen-year stint as music director in New York, he received an offer from Chicago's Lyric Opera to perform Wagner's *The Ring of the Nibelung*. Starting in 1993, when the first of the four *Ring* operas was to be staged, Zubin would conduct an opera a year until all four were presented as a cycle during the Lyric's 1996 season. They were to be produced by the influential opera director August Everding. Ardis Krainik, the general manager of the opera, had assured Zubin that he could engage singers of his choice. Zubin accepted the offer as one of his reasons for not taking up the conductorship of another orchestra was to make time for opera. As we have seen, he had conducted the entire *Ring* cycle in Florence from 1979 to 1981. This would be the first time since the Second World War that the entire *Ring* would be performed in Chicago.

Though Zubin's experience with the *Ring* in Florence would prove useful, it had been many years since that production. He had approached Wagner with some trepidation as a student in Vienna. The first Wagner opera he had conducted was *Lohengrin* in Vienna in 1974. It had not been particularly successful, with the atmosphere at rehearsals being vitiated by the overbearing attitude of the East German stage director who seemed at odds with the choir and the singers. But that experience did have the merit of giving him his first important insights into Wagner's style.

This was followed by a 'half' *Ring* in Vienna but Zubin believes that *Das Rheingold* and *Die Walküre* were failures from a production point of view. In fact, the premiere of *Das Rheingold* was memorable for another reason: it was the first time that Zubin was publicly booed. Maazel, who was the music director of the Vienna Opera, comforted him by calling it an occupational hazard but it appears that the heckling had been orchestrated by a famous conductor who felt slighted at not having been asked to conduct that opera. This was corroborated by an old usher who knew Zubin from his student days. He told him that the hecklers had entered the opera house only at the end of the performance.[1] The ill-fated *Ring* was abandoned on Maazel's advice, both agreeing that it had no real future.

Zubin was booed one more time in Vienna when he conducted *Il Trovatore* under the direction of Hungarian film director István Szabó. The audience did not like the staging and booed Szabó when he came on stage to take his bows. When Zubin embraced him as a gesture of conciliation, he was booed as well. The fact that Mehli, Tehmina and Nancy were in the audience that day only added to Zubin's discomfiture.

## THE LYRIC OPERA'S *RING*

The Lyric Opera's four-year survey of Wagner's four-opera masterpiece opened in January 1993 with eight performances of *Das Rheingold*, the Prologue of the *Ring*, with performances running through 12 February at the Civic Opera House.

*Das Rheingold* was well received by audiences in Chicago with Zubin's conducting coming in for praise. The production by Everding, with designs by John Conklin, evoked a mixed response. A postmodern interpretation, partly influenced by puppetry and Japanese drama, the production was puzzling for many. But the music was considered admirable. Edward Rothstein of the *New York Times* wrote:

> Mr. Mehta, who often seems seduced by opportunities to proclaim rather than suggest, submitted himself to the demands of the

score, attending to its line and colour, deferring to singers, casting a long line.[2]

*Die Walküre* followed in the next season, *Siegfried* in 1994–95 and *Götterdämmerung* in 1995–96. The *Ring* cycle culminated in the spring of 1996, with all four operas presented over a week, the way Wagner had intended it. The Lyric's stars included such world-class Wagnerians as James Morris (Wotan), Éva Marton (Brünnhilde), Siegfried Jerusalem (Siegfried) and Matti Salminen who did all four bass roles.

After presenting *Götterdämmerung* in three special performances in March 1996, Zubin embarked on three week-long cycles of the complete *Ring*, starting March 11. If Everding's and Conklin's vision came out second, the critics reserved their most fulsome praise for Zubin's conducting. They said that he had coaxed playing from the orchestra that was little short of spectacular. Tim Page, writing in the *Washington Post*, said that 'at times one might have thought this was the Chicago Symphony Orchestra itself rather than "just" a pit ensemble.' Zubin had moved to Chicago two months before the programme to prepare for the *Ring* and it had paid off. Page observed:

> Mehta conducted with greater insight, sensitivity, authority and seriousness of purpose . . . He fully deserved the bravos that thundered over his head when he took his bows.[3]

Unlike Italian operas, Zubin does not conduct Wagner from memory because he cannot learn the text by heart. He says that the conductor often recites the text along with the singers, like a kind of prompter. He must accompany the singers not only musically but also with words. According to Zukerman, 'Zubin is more extraordinary in some ways in the pit than on the stage. Because he is theatrical, it seemingly lends itself better to his style.'[4] Zubin feels that an opera orchestra is not just a background for what's going on onstage. 'The movement flows from the pit to the stage to the pit. Apart from playing the notes, you have to let the audience partake of a complete theatrical experience,' Zubin said.[5]

When a singer has mastered his part in terms of both the music and the acting, Zubin gives him a lot of freedom of expression, but he believes that it is still the responsibility of the conductor to lead the performance. He also believes that for non-Germans, a conductor must give his singers more time to get used to the alliterations if he wants each word in the text to be intelligible. Old-timers reminisce about the days when conductors like Walter and Toscanini spent months coaching singers individually. Today opera is part of the jet age and the time that singers and conductors have together is limited. Zubin says that his friend Barenboim practises very thoroughly with his singers and it is a pleasure to work with them afterwards. Singers are always on the move and if they are unintelligible, it is because there is just no time to work on their diction.[6] Zubin observes that not many performers have mastered the art of simultaneous singing and acting, though some formidable talents like Callas and Jon Vickers had done so beautifully. Some roles, however, are more demanding and Zubin is happy if the performers just stand and sing their roles correctly.[7] Today the new generation combines both with greater frequency than in the past and he observes this favourable development from the orchestra pit with much pleasure.

♫

When Zubin was doing the *Ring* in Chicago, he received an invitation from the opera in Munich to conduct a production of Wagner's *Tannhäuser* in 1994. It was to be produced under David Alden's direction. Sir Peter Jonas who had been assistant manager of the Chicago Symphony Orchestra and later the general manager of the English National Opera in London had become the general manager at Munich, succeeding the redoubtable Sawallisch who had been both music director and general manager there. Zubin had been offered the post of music director when Everding was general manager, but had declined as he felt that he did not have the experience for it.

His only experience with the Bavarian State Orchestra until then had been in February 1975 during Sawallisch's time, when he had conducted a concert of Haydn, Penderecki and Strauss. Zubin had never conducted *Tannhäuser* before, nor for that matter, an opera in Munich. He says that the orchestra had a sound which closely resembled the Vienna Philharmonic. The musicians, no strangers to Wagner, were an experienced lot and the rehearsals began at a very high level. Alden's concept of the staging created problems at times but Zubin says that he understood his contemporary view of musical theatre. It was during this time that Zubin took leave, once to lead a concert at Sarajevo's National Library, and again to conduct the second Three Tenors concert in Los Angeles. He made a deal with Sir Peter, promising to conduct a *Tannhäuser* in the autumn free of charge if he released him from one of the summer performances. Zubin narrates in his memoirs that he would not have been surprised if, after all that, Sir Peter thought him to be a rather 'dubious partner'.

## *REQUIEM* IN SARAJEVO

Zubin has for long used the power of music to essay his role as an ambassador of culture and peace. Music for him is not only a means of fundraising for worthy causes but also a way to communicate solidarity and forgiveness. He has a passionate belief (some believe a bit naively) in the capacity of music to make peace and break down ethnic, religious and cultural barriers, if only momentarily.

The concert in Sarajevo on 20 June 1994 in which he conducted the Sarajevo Symphony Orchestra and Chorus was just one of many such occasions in his long career. He conducted a televised benefit performance of Mozart's *Requiem* in the charred shell of the National Library which had been destroyed by Serbian bombardment. Some 10,000 people had died or disappeared during the Serbian nationalists' shelling of the city since the Bosnian war had begun two years ago and the *Requiem* was chosen as homage to those killed. Zubin flew in with Nancy in a military aircraft from Ancona in Italy. The orchestra, understandably, was in poor shape. The string musicians were without strings and the clarinet players had no reeds, and they were happy to use the supply Zubin brought with him. The hotel they stayed in had windows which were blacked out because of the strife.

The ruin of the library was certainly one of the eeriest venues chosen for a performance of the *Requiem*. Workers erected a tiered stage over the piles of bricks and cinder, and the ash of tons of paper on the floor. Joining Zubin for the performance was tenor Carreras, soprano Gasdia, mezzo-soprano Ildikó Komlósi and the bass Ruggero Raimondi. The objective of the 35-minute concert was to raise money for refugee aid and reconstruction of the city from donations called in during the live telecast in Italy, Japan and the Middle East, and taped broadcasts to other countries. The man who had brought them all together was Dradi, the Italian promoter who, as we have noted before, was instrumental in putting together the hugely successful the Three Tenors concert in Rome in 1990. It was also later distributed as a DVD.

While the rehearsals at the city's ornate National Theatre were open to the public, the actual concert was closed to all except some fifty invited guests, including the United Nations commander in Bosnia, Lt Gen. Michael Rose. Zubin said, 'We just hope . . . Something to convince somebody to stop this madness. Maybe we'll come someday and play the Second Symphony of Mahler's *The Resurrection*.' In a rehearsal earlier in the day, Zubin had tears in his eyes when the chorus sang 'Amen'. 'We have come for you to bless us more than we bless you,' he said.[8]

## THE THREE TENORS ENCORE

Less than a month after he conducted the concert in Sarajevo, Zubin was in Los Angeles for an encore of the Three Tenors concert which had succeeded beyond all expectations in 1990. The spectacular success of that concert led to a repeat performance four years later, in July 1994, in Los Angeles, once again on the eve of the soccer World Cup final. Zubin and the three tenors reprised the popular concert in Encore! The Three Tenors, a performance which joined the ranks of Hollywood Oscar night as a global event, being telecast live in 100 countries and reaching an audience of over 1 billion people. Organized by Tibor Rudas Production at the Dodger Stadium in association with World Cup USA, the staging of Encore had all the glamour of a Hollywood extravaganza. Home of the Los Angeles baseball team, the Dodger Stadium has been the site of some illustrious events, including the original Beatles tour and Pope John Paul II's visit in 1987. But Encore was a special occasion—it filled the entire infield and outfield for the first time—and the scale of this grandiose concert outdid all previous events.

Bidding for the recording and video rights to Encore involved some of the most mind-boggling sums of money ever offered for a one-time classical music event. After negotiations that involved all the major labels, the Warner Music Group ended up with the rights by committing $10 million to the project, including everything from performing fees to marketing. This time the tenors and Zubin were reportedly paid $1 million each simply to perform at the event, apart from earning royalties on the recording and video sales from Warner. Zubin said, 'By the time we reached the second Three Tenors concert, we made sure that we would have our share in the profits as well.'[9]

This time, Pavarotti's Hungarian-born promoter, Tibor Rudas, was the presenter. Born in Budapest in 1926, Rudas studied voice and toured Europe singing in variety shows before establishing a dance studio in Australia. He took his 'French style revues' to Las Vegas in 1963 and expanded into casino entertainment, including classical performances, in Atlantic City. In 1982, he teamed up with Pavarotti, presenting him first in a tent in Atlantic City, then in recitals and arenas around the world.

Rudas, the producer and organizer of the event, said the income from tickets for the new show was a record take for a musical event: $13.5 million for 56,000 tickets priced from $15 to $1000. Rudas dismissed the whining of music and social critics. 'We didn't realize in Rome that we created the Beatles for the senior citizens,' he said. 'It's something the people have been waiting for for a long time. Only nobody knew they were waiting for it.' Rudas said that initially the three tenors were not interested in coming together again. They thought it was a great one-time event, and wanted to keep it that way.

But he kept pushing. In the meantime, he got the rights to promote the final concert of the 1994 World Cup and thought that the tenors would agree if he told them it would be an official part of the World Cup. He was right.

In an attempt to evoke the ambience of the first concert, designers from three continents collaborated with Hollywood craftsmen to transform the ballpark into a neo-classical amphitheatre. An enormous painted backdrop of a landscape dotted with live palm trees stretched across the stage set in the centre of the field, flanked by waterfalls and classical columns. All this had been put together in less than a week by 600 artists and craftsmen working around the clock. The four principal artistes were supported by a team of nearly 1000 people comprising musicians, performers, technicians, engineers and administrative staff. The Meyer Sound system developed by Rudas and Pavarotti carried the voices with pristine clarity all around the stadium.

At a full-dress rehearsal two days before the show, an audience of 3000 people got a first look at the concert as the three tenors sang and horsed around with Zubin and members of the audience. In June, a similar dress rehearsal-cum-charity concert had been staged in Monte Carlo for Prince Rainier and Princess Caroline, and 1000 guests. On 16 July 1994, the voices of Pavarotti, Carreras and Domingo dazzled an audience of 56,000 people as Zubin led the 104-member Los Angeles Philharmonic along with the 60-member Los Angeles Music Center opera chorus. Performing a new repertoire that included arias by Verdi and Puccini, they also presented traditional tunes, like 'The Impossible Dream' and 'Ave Maria'. As a tribute to Hollywood, the tenors saluted the best of showbiz music, singing a medley of nostalgic tunes from Gene Kelly's 'Singin' in the Rain' to Frank Sinatra's 'My Way'. In the audience, both Sinatra and Kelly took a bow as cameras zeroed in on them. It was obvious from the synergies generated between the four that the camaraderie was perfect.

Zubin, who arrived two days before the concert from a European tour, remarked, 'I'm flying on a magic carpet with them. As an accompanist, as a man who makes music with them, I have such confidence. Sometimes when you work with a soloist, either instrumental or a singer, you feel you have to be careful in case something goes wrong. With them it just doesn't happen, and it's a great satisfaction. They don't know what a fan I am.'[10] With the tenors singing arias and popular songs of many nations, it was good entertainment apart from being a major media event. It also had its moments of high art. Absentee hostess Elizabeth Taylor honoured the four performers at a post-concert dinner. Benefiting the Elizabeth Taylor AIDS Foundation, the star-studded party, held under a tent on the stadium grounds, was attended by Hollywood heavyweights such as Tom Cruise and Nicole Kidman, Arnold and Maria Schwarzenegger, Dustin Hoffman, Gregory and Veronique Peck, Kirk Douglas, Frank and Barbara Sinatra and Walter Matthau.

Zubin recalls that while the original concert was great fun, the second was more controlled and less spontaneous. The tickets were more expensive and the concert was sold out. The end result was certainly entertaining but less spectacular. 'It was still great fun but it was very different from what we established four years earlier.'[11] The disc too sold well but not as well as the 1990 recording.

Though the effort was applauded by some for introducing opera to a wider public, some purists scorned it as not so much 'music for the millions' as 'music for millions'—a disparaging reference to the large payments that the four received. As Joseph McLellan wrote in the *Washington Post*:

> On the downside, this concert embodied trends building for years that threaten the long-range health of classical music. These trends include celebrity worship, in which the performer and his personality are more important than the material performed; least-common-denominator programming, which avoids material that audiences might find unfamiliar or challenging; fixation on profits and spinoffs; and the substitution of electronic contact for direct experience.[12]

It was also felt that the concert helped to undermine traditional musical enterprises: music was bound to suffer if a substantial part of the billion-member audience succumbed to the delusion that what they had heard was the best of classical music. The financial angle too was important. The benefits to music were questionable in a project that, as McLellan put it, 'may skim off more than $50 million for the classical equivalent of a rock concert' when that money could have been used for more substantial projects such as commissioning new works and training young artistes.

Four years later in 1998, the three tenors got together again for another concert in Paris with the majestic Eiffel Tower in the background. Zubin was unavailable and his place was taken by James Levine, the conductor of the Metropolitan Opera. Unfortunately, it was a dull, forgettable concert which captured none of the magic of the earlier two.

## LEADING AN OPERA HOUSE

Zubin's contact with Munich had been sporadic in earlier years. In the 1980s, he had conducted *Gurrelieder* and Bruckner's Ninth with the Bavarian Radio Symphony Orchestra. Celibidache who was the music director of the Munich Philharmonic Orchestra from 1979 till his death in 1996 had invited Zubin to conduct on numerous occasions. Often Zubin would substitute for him when he fell ill. One particular occasion stands out in his memory: a performance of Bruckner's Fourth in Florence and Vienna. He was so moved by the way the orchestra played in Vienna that he donated his fee to set up a fund to support young musicians. Zubin developed a good rapport with the Munich Philharmonic and they played Schubert, Brahms, Bruckner and Mahler together.

In February 1996, after Zubin had conducted eight performances of *Siegfried* in Chicago, he received a visitor from Munich. The visitor was Sir Peter and he was there to offer Zubin the music directorship of the Bavarian State Opera starting 1998. Zubin, as we have noted before, had been offered the Berlin Opera in 1976 and he wasn't ready then, but by the time the offer came from Munich in 1996, he had done *Fidelio*, *The Magic Flute*, the three Mozart Da Ponte operas, lots of Puccini and Verdi, and two cycles of the *Ring* and felt confident enough to accept. In the 1980s, offers from the London Philharmonic and the Royal Opera at Covent Garden had also been turned down.

Zubin had made his debut at Covent Garden in 1977 as a result of the coaxing of Helga Schmidt who was in charge at that time. (She would also lure him to Valencia nearly three decades later.) He conducted *Otello* with Vickers as the tenor. In the same year, he conducted *La Fanciulla del West,* a rarely performed opera by Puccini. Carol Neblett sang the part of Minnie and Domingo played Dick Johnson alias the bandit Ramirez. It was a huge success. But on the whole Zubin rates his experience at Covent Garden as not particularly good, though the New Year's Eve performance of Johann Strauss Jr's light-hearted, romantic and wickedly funny operetta *Die Fledermaus* was a success. In it, Hermann Prey played Eisenstein and Te Kanawa, Rosalinde. The next year Zubin conducted it again with Nilsson as a surprise guest. Zubin continued to conduct in London till the 1990s. Sir John Tooley, general director of Covent Garden, visited Zubin in Los Angeles in the 1980s to offer him the music directorship, but Zubin, already at the helm in Israel and New York, simply did not have the time.[13]

The contract in Munich was for one of five years and Zubin was expected to conduct forty performances a year. In addition, he had to give two Academy Concerts with the opera orchestra. Zubin had conducted many more concerts than operas before his appointment as general music director of the Bavarian State Opera. But that was to change soon. Conditions were propitious. Zubin had a good orchestra which he soon grew fond of, an excellent choir and unmatched acoustics. In Sir Peter, Zubin had an experienced music administrator who was an excellent mediator between art, politics and business. According to Zubin, their shared love of cricket turned it into a match made in heaven.[14]

The Bavarian State Opera is by far one of the most productive opera house in the world. It stages 380 performances of more than fifty operas and twenty ballets, including ten new productions in a year. The festival that sees the end of the season mounts more than thirty operas in six weeks, as many as Covent Garden does in a year. This is possible because of the 860-strong permanent staff who, as employees of the government, work more flexibly than in many houses. Also, there is total identification with the opera house, a house, which for them is also a home.[15]

The appointment was Zubin's first permanent engagement in Germany; it was also the first time that he was expected to conduct an opera after just one rehearsal. He says the repertoire performances gave him quite a few strands of grey hair. It was a challenging task at best, forcing him to learn something new in his early sixties. Zubin made his debut as music director in Munich with a festival performance of Wagner's *Tristan und Isolde*, an opera he knew very well, having conducted it more frequently than any other. It was also the flagship production of the Munich Opera Festival that year, which was to continue through the rest of July. Munich, unlike Salzburg or Edinburgh, is never caught up in a festival fever nor is opera an obsession the way it is in Bayreuth or Verona, but there is more opera every July in Munich than in any other city in the world. While Salzburg gets the glitterati and Bayreuth the Wagner adherents, for people in Munich, attending opera in the National Theatre on Max-Joseph-Platz is a way of life. Zubin had first conducted *Tristan* in Rome in a concert performance with Nilsson. Later he also conducted it in Montreal, Berlin, Vienna, Florence and Los Angeles. While there was praise for the orchestra, the singers and for Zubin's conducting, Peter Konwitschny's production was controversial. Still Zubin was pleased that he had started off on a positive note.

As far as the repertoire performances were concerned, Zubin began with Verdi's *La Traviata* on 9 July 1998 and it was well received. *Aida*, which was produced by David Pountney, followed in October. Next was a successful new production of Weber's *Der Freischütz* on 31 October 1998, with Thomas Langhoff and Jürgen Rose. Puccini's *Tosca* followed on 1 November. Zubin faced some problems when he undertook Mozart's *The Marriage of Figaro* in three performances, starting on 13 November. The performances were nothing to write home about. Zubin says that with Mozart, one always needs more rehearsals. Though the singers had not changed since the *Tristan* premiere, Zubin's way of doing things was different. Also, Zubin and the singers lacked experience in working together.

He said that it is much more difficult to suddenly step into a repertoire set than to start a new production where one is involved from the beginning and grows with each performance.[16] But the musicians in Munich were nothing if not professional and were able to understand the travails of a conductor who was assuming the music directorship of an opera for the first time. It takes time for a relationship to develop between musicians and a conductor so that even the smallest gesture is interpreted and articulated in the performance. By the end of his tenure, Zubin says that they had developed such wonderful understanding that they could even perform Wagner's *Die Meistersinger von Nürnberg* without any rehearsal, with excellent results. The year 1998 closed with a performance of *Die Fledermaus*.

In April 1999, Zubin conducted the *Ring* produced by Nikolaus Lehnhoff and designed by Erich Wonder. This was the legacy *Ring* which he had inherited. However, in 2002–03 there was a new production under Herbert Wernicke who not only directed it but also designed the sets and costumes. *Das Rheingold* premiered on 24 February 2002 and *Die Walküre* on 30 June, but unfortunately, the production lost its director in April when Wernicke died unexpectedly of a lung haemorrhage in Basel. A comparatively rare phenomenon in the operatic world—a designer who was also his own director—he created the costumes, sets and sometimes even the lighting of his own productions. Much loved by singers, managers and conductors, nobody had a bad word to say about him.

The unfinished *Die Walküre* was brought to completion by Hans-Peter Lehmann who remained faithful to Wernicke's original concept. *Siegfried* and *Götterdämmerung* were produced under the direction of Alden, with Gideon Davey doing the design and costumes. They premiered on 3 November 2002 and 28 February 2003 respectively. In May 2003, there was a premiere of *Die Walküre,* this time under the direction of Alden.

Zubin says that he learned a lot in Munich, adding significantly to his repertoire. Apart from *Tannhäuser* which had been a personal premiere, he was able to add three more Verdi operas to his repertoire: *Don Carlo, Falstaff* and *Rigoletto*. *Don Carlo* which was produced under Rose's direction is a complex and difficult opera, and Zubin who held the work in awe, waited quite a few years before attempting it in Munich. It premiered on 1 July 2000, and Zubin was happy that he could perform it in the five-act version (including the Fontainebleau Act). It was a success. *Falstaff* had its premiere on 17 January 2001 under the direction of Gramss, and *Rigoletto* four years later on 21 February 2005 under Doris Dörrie. Zubin was, however, no stranger to the music of Verdi. Of Verdi's early operas, he had conducted only *Jérusalem,* the French adaptation of *I Lombardi alla Prima Crociata* in Vienna, and in 2001, the death centenary of Verdi, he gave a guest performance of this production with the Vienna Philharmonic at La Scala in Milan. And of course Zubin has been conducting his *Requiem* for the past fifty years.

One of the high points of Zubin's tenure at Munich was the premiere of Aribert Reimann's opera *Bernarda Albas Haus* based on Spanish dramatist Federico Garcia Lorca's *The House of Bernarda Alba*. Reimann, known especially for his literary operas, also wrote the opera *Lear*, based on Shakespeare's *King Lear*, at the suggestion of lyric baritone Fischer-Dieskau who sang the title role. Zubin had seen Lorca's play in London and had always wanted to conduct this opera. The premiere was scheduled for 30 October 2000 and Zubin received the score six months earlier. Studying a score takes time—it needs to be absorbed slowly so that the music can sink in.

Reimann was on hand to guide and advise the conductor and the musicians, and impressed Zubin with his knowledge of music. The fact that he was an excellent pianist himself also helped. The orchestra drawn up by Reimann was an unusual one. There were four pianos of which two were specially adjusted to produce unconventional sounds. There were twelve cellos, a woodwind section, brass instruments and percussion—but no violins, violas or bass. Apart from the unusual orchestra, even the singing parts were extremely difficult. Despite the novelty of it all, the performance which was produced by Harry Kupfer received a positive response from the audience.

Booing, according to Zubin, is a thing of the past. Gone are the times when poor Stravinsky had to face the ignominy of being pelted with tomatoes after a performance of *Le Sacre du Printemps*.

Another opera Zubin had always wanted to conduct was Berlioz's *Les Troyens*. It premiered on 30 June 2001. Zubin says that he required a bit of pushing from Sir Peter before he took it up. Barenboim gave him the opportunity to get some practice with the piece when he invited him to conduct the concert version of this opera in Chicago where he was music director. It proved to be a wise move.

The last premiere Zubin conducted in Munich as music director was Schoenberg's *Moses und Aron*. It was staged by Pountney and opened on 28 June 2006. Thanks to Swarowsky, Zubin had discovered Schoenberg early and this was to him the perfect way to end his tenure in Munich. The piece is so challenging that Zubin doubled the usual number of orchestral rehearsals. It paid off. The result was high-level precision coupled with intense musicality: every phrase lived and breathed.

It was also a farewell premiere for Sir Peter who was leaving with Zubin after thirteen years as general manager of the opera. The 'rangy Englishman with clipped grey hair' who has battled cancer many times in his life told *Opera* magazine in 2006 how Zubin's appointment came about. He said that Zubin and he were playing cricket at the Munich Cricket Club, when the maestro sat down on the lawn with him and talked about his jet-setting lifestyle. He told him he needed something serious and suggested the Munich Opera. Sir Peter pestered him ever since and Zubin finally joined in 1998.

He was all praise for Zubin both as a person and as an opera-house music director:

> For a start, he's got this Indian thing about gossip and is interested in everything. He doesn't just come in and conduct a performance and go back to the hotel ... He loves conducting. When he's here, he conducts twice a day, every day, a rehearsal and a performance. He does fourteen productions a season, which makes for wonderful stability.[17]

Sir Peter also praised Zubin's down-to-earth attitude and behaviour. '... he has no airs or graces ... just another member of the company.'[18] He called Zubin one of the nicest people who was also very clever except that he did not wear his intellect on his sleeve and this was often misunderstood by critics who thought it wasn't there. Zubin is legendary among musicians as an accompanist of near psychic responsiveness. Sir Peter echoed something similar when he said, 'Above all, he's totally humble before music, and his way of following singers makes him a real opera conductor.'[19] Sills was known to have remarked that you've never sung with an exciting conductor until you've sung with Zubin Mehta.

Sir Peter too was leaving on a high note. He had taken many positive steps in his years in Munich: he had expanded the repertory, introducing the conservative Munich audience to the virtually unknown Baroque masterpieces of Monteverdi, Francesco Cavalli, Henry Purcell and Handel. He had commissioned new operas and solidified the company's financial base by working to increase private donations. Sir Peter had given a new direction to the opera in terms of artistry and aesthetics, and in Zubin he found a congenial partner.

*Moses und Aron* was, however, not the last performance of Zubin's tenure. That came on 31 July 2006, when he conducted Wagner's *Die Meistersinger von Nürnberg* as his farewell concert. Adding to that evening's sense of occasion was the fact that the performance marked the end of an era. The great German bass Kurt Moll also delivered his swansong that night. It was his last opera performance on any stage and the audience cheered him for a full ten minutes.

After the performance there was a party backstage for about 1000 celebrants who had gathered to say goodbye to Zubin and Sir Peter. Ushers and electricians mingled with musicians and divas as a huge amount of Bavarian beer and pasta were consumed. Nobody was in a hurry to go home because, for many, this was home.

Zubin had also toured with the orchestra, making successful visits to Europe (1999 and 2004) and Japan (2001 and 2005). The first European tour in September 1999 saw the orchestra play in

Birmingham, London, Turin, Cologne, Zurich, Vienna and Frankfurt. Five years later, in September 2004, the stops included Gstaad, Rimini, Leipzig, Madrid, Vienna, Budapest, Brussels, Dortmund and Barcelona.

His last overseas tour with the Bavarian State Orchestra was when he brought the ensemble to India in December 2005 for a whirlwind trip of three days, discussed in a later chapter. Though the short trip was a strain on all of them, it forged a deep human bond among the musicians and between the musicians, and Zubin. He and Nancy were also happy that they could give the musicians a glimpse of India.[20]

Zubin's successor was Kent Nagano while Sir Peter's originally appointed successor was Christoph Albrecht, who withdrew in 2005. The next intendant, Nikolaus Klaus Bachler, could not take up the post till 2008 on account of his contractual commitments as chief of the Burgtheater in Vienna, leaving incoming music director Nagano as interim opera director sharing responsibility with two other senior figures, Ronald Adler and Roland Felber.

It was also during Zubin's tenure at the Bavarian State Opera that he met Natalia Ritzkowsky who subsequently became his assistant (which she remains). Natalia, who was working in Sir Peter's office, became Zubin's assistant when he started his tenure there in 1998. She says that from the beginning a warm and friendly atmosphere prevailed, though the job certainly had its challenging moments. Her job responsibilities, she says, were never clearly specified. 'I just try to ease his life so he can concentrate on what is to me the main aspect of his work, conducting. So I try to organize everything around the music. A big part of my responsibility is certainly to be the contact person [as this author knows only too well] for everyone who wants to contact him and sometimes to be the dragon in front of his door.' Natalia who works from Greifenberg in Germany told me that she considered it an honour to work for the maestro. She describes him as 'a great musician and a truly wonderful "Mensch"'.[21]

## VALENCIA

One of the reasons Zubin gave for not taking up the music directorship of another orchestra after his tenure in New York ended was his desire to free up more time to do opera. In 2005, Zubin got another chance to further engage with opera when he became the director of the Festival of the Mediterranean at the Palau de les Arts Reina Sofia, the opera house and cultural centre in Valencia, Spain. The opera house designed by leading architect and native son of the city, Santiago Calatrava, is the final piece of the City of Arts and Sciences, a complex of beautifully integrated white buildings that include a planetarium, a science museum, a botanical garden and Europe's biggest marine park.

The egg-shaped dome of the opera house which has been compared to an ocean liner's hull, a spaceship and a helmet is, as *Time* magazine put it, 'part of a gleaming composition: curved walls, rolling stairways; turquoise reflecting pools topped by a detached feather-like roof'. The spectacular buildings along 86 acres of abandoned riverbed are a futuristic vision shaped with steel, concrete, glass and white ceramic tiles. A city within a city, it is designed to combine education with entertainment and leisure. Calatrava wanted his creation to represent the sea and the sky of the Mediterranean, and the brilliant white structures and mirror-like pools produce intense reflections.

The jewel in the crown, however, is the Palau, Europe's biggest opera house, with its three halls seating 4000 people, including about 1700 in the Sala Principal, the main hall. It represents, according to the architect, 'a correlation between spectator, musician and artist'.[22] With its ample rehearsal and performance spaces, and fine acoustics (Calatrava brought in his own team to ensure quality), the Palau's appeal for both artiste and spectator is undeniable. Zubin told me that he collaborated with Calatrava in designing the orchestra pit. He also advised him to design a hall which would at most seat 1700 spectators. A €120-million symbol of civic braggadocio, it takes pride of place at the City of Arts and Sciences along the serpentine garden that was once the River Turia. It is the centrepiece of what local politicians hope will be a cultural renaissance for a resort better known for its beaches than its love of opera. It was hoped that it would come to symbolize the city like the opera house of Sydney.

In a world where opera is still seen as the highest of high culture, a new grand theatre immediately heralded a new-found status. Whatever its arriviste pretensions, Valencia's biggest draw for the music aficionado was the talent that it attracted. The late Maazel was appointed music director for the first three years and Zubin was put at the helm of the annual Festival del Mediterraneo (Festival of the Mediterranean). Maazel, as the Palau's inaugural music director, hand-picked its new orchestra. The Palau's intendant, Schmidt, formerly artistic director at Covent Garden, London, strove to assemble world-class operatic offerings. When Zubin heard that Schmidt was heading Palau, he was convinced that the artistic quality would be extremely high.[23]

It was her vision not just to attract stars from opera's firmament but also to seek out lesser-known artistes and to create a world-class opera house that also provided opportunities for young performers to develop. Maazel personally conducted all auditions for the opera's musicians, first in Spain, and then around the world, hearing some 5000 performers play to find the ninety-plus musicians from twenty-five countries that made up what Zubin called his 'virgin' orchestra: the Orquestra de la Comunitat Valenciana. Most were in their early thirties and some had no prior experience of playing in an orchestra.

### *A New Opera House Is Born*

The Palau opened on 8 October 2005, and Zubin conducted the first-ever concert at the new hall on 24 October, leading the Israel Philharmonic Orchestra in a programme of Beethoven's *Leonore* Overture, Mozart's *Jupiter* Symphony and Brahms's First Symphony.

*Fidelio*, the first production of the new opera house was staged in October–November 2006 and inaugurated its first full season. Pierluigi Pier'Alli's traditional production was firmly set in the period of the opera with soldiers wearing tall cylindrical hats and crossed belts over their chests. The singers included Peter Seiffert, Waltraud Meier, Ildikó Raimondi and Rainer Trost. The production included the interpolation of the *Leonore* Overture No. 3 between the two scenes of Act 2. Increasingly, productions of *Fidelio* are doing away with this but including it here gave the new orchestra ample opportunity to showcase its skills. Zubin's conducting also attracted praise. 'Mehta's reading had a traditional spaciousness but also a strong dramatic element.'[24]

The first two parts of the *Ring*, *Das Rheingold* and *Die Walküre* were staged in April and May 2007. They were co-produced by the Palau de les Arts Reina Sofia and the Maggio Musicale Fiorentino and directed by Carlus Padrissa of the innovative Catalan theatre group La Fura dels Baus. Nancy had seen their production of *Damnation de Faust* in Salzburg and been impressed with their work. It struck Zubin that it would be exciting to work with them, but he put the thought out of his mind till Schmidt came to him with the idea of doing something at Valencia (before the opera house had even been built). When the discussion turned to Wagner, Zubin told her that he had done enough *Rings* and didn't want to come to Valencia for another unless it was something radically different. Zubin then remembered the La Fura dels Baus and told Schmidt that he would be interested only if she could get the Catalan group on board. She talked to them and they loved the idea. Zubin then met their director Padrissa. He was doing a new *Ring* in Munich at the time and came to all the performances. It was his first *Ring* and that way he could work out what he liked and what he didn't. They discussed it afterwards and then Padrissa went away to work on his own conception.[25]

For almost thirty-six years, La Fura dels Baus has mixed theatre and film to create shows of surprising originality and visual splendour. What the group did in *Das Rheingold* could perhaps be described as a twenty-first-century attempt to achieve what Wieland Wagner did at Bayreuth in the 1950s—the creation of an abstract collection of images to complement Wagner's music. Just as in the theatre spectacles which made La Fura famous in Europe and East Asia, their staging of *Das Rheingold* was full of images moving slowly on a giant screen; athletes hanging from ropes (usually upside down); and an assortment of ladders and cranes moving around the stage to depict power. It was vastly different from the string of productions that had been inspired by the highly influential centenary 1976 *Ring* produced by Patrice Chéreau and conducted by Boulez.

The young Finnish bass baritone Juha Uusitalo was a virile, emotionally charged Wotan and Anna Larsson used her even mezzo to great effect as Fricka. As in Chicago, Salminen played all the bass roles. The other players also came in for praise from the critics. Zubin and the orchestra got a mixed response. 'In the famous *Rheingold* opening . . . the brass seemed disconnected and disengaged, the strings rushed through their opening bars and the sense of a musical flower slowly opening was lost. Later on, Mehta managed to guide his forces to a more coherent reading, and in the end, the public could sit back and enjoy the intersecting lines expressed with eloquence, clarity and verve.'[26]

*Siegfried* and *Götterdämmerung* were performed in June 2008 and May–June 2009 respectively. Before that there had been a staging of *Turandot* in May–June 2008 under the direction of Chen Kaige. The first staging of the *Ring* tetralogy as a compact cycle came in June 2009 when all four parts were performed in a sequence. It was Spain's first indigenous staging of the *Ring*. For an opera house that had got its performance hall just under four years ago, and which was now at the end of only its third season as an opera-producing entity, the Valencia *Ring* was nothing short of astonishing. The achievement was made even more remarkable by the fact that Schmidt had created a company from scratch.

Padrissa, in collaboration with Franc Aleu (video projection), Roland Olbeter (scenes), Chu Uroz (multimedia costumes) and Peter van Praet (lighting) as well as a small army of nimble extras and performing stagehands who played Nibelungs in *Das Rheingold*, slain heroes in *Die Walküre* and the dragon Fafner's tentacles in *Siegfried*, put together a production that was a triumph of technology and acrobatics.

The cast included seasoned veterans such as Domingo, an eternally heroic Siegmund; Salminen as Fasolt, Hunding, Hagen and the dragon; Larsson; Gerhard Siegel and Franz-Josef Kapellmann. Lance Ryan made a convincing Siegfried; Uusitalo played Wotan and Jennifer

Wilson, Brünnhilde. Critics called it 'one of the most consistently well sung *Rings* of recent times'.[27] From the musical point of view it was declared an unqualified success 'thanks to the experienced hand of Zubin Mehta in the pit and the marvellous young Orquestra de la Comunitat Valenciana, already a *Ring* ensemble to be reckoned with, offering a sonorous depth of Wagnerian sound and transparent accompanying textures, so the singers' words cross from the footlights effortlessly.'[28] Acoustically the theatre turned out well by treating voices favourably. And the large orchestra pit which stresses instrumental clarity over blended richness, proved to be an asset in accommodating the Wagner-sized orchestra of the *Ring*.

Zubin rates this collaboration with La Fura as one of the more memorable productions of the *Ring*. He told *GBOpera* magazine that it was a unique partnership because they were both flexible in their approach. While the staging was modern, they remained faithful to Wagner's instructions, and the use of cutting-edge technology did not prevent the audience from getting everything it expected from a Wagner opera.[29]

♫

Richard Strauss's *Salome* and Bizet's *Carmen* were staged in June 2010, and *Tosca* and *Fidelio* followed in May–June 2011. Mahler's Third Symphony was next, including a performance at the Festival of Music and Dance at Granada. After that was a trip to the Ravenna Festival where Richard Strauss's *Don Quixote* and *Ein Heldenleben* were on the programme. *Don Giovanni* was staged in early 2012 and *Il Trovatore* and Luigi Cherubini's *Medea* followed in May and June of the same year. Next, *Tristan und Isolde* were performed in concert form.

There was a new production of *Otello* directed by Davide Livermore in June 2013. The Cor de la Generalitat Valenciana, the main local-government-funded chorus, was celebrating its twenty-fifth anniversary that year and the programme was designed to be a homage to Verdi and Wagner. *La Traviata* under the direction of Willy Decker was staged in October–November and a La Fura dels Baus production of *Die Walküre* followed. There was a tour of China in December–January where they visited eight cities, including Beijing, Shanghai and Wuhan.

In June 2014, Verdi and Puccini again took centre stage with a new production of *La Forza del Destino* directed by Livermore and old favourite *Turandot* under the direction of Kaige. There was also a concert to celebrate the 150th birth anniversary of Richard Strauss; the programme consisted of *Also Sprach Zarathustra* and *Der Rosenkavalier* (suite) before the performances of *La Forza del Destino* and *Turandot*.

*Turandot* was Zubin's last opera in Valencia and the applause after the final performance on 15 June lasted an astounding eighteen minutes. At the end of the month, Zubin announced his decision to part ways with Valencia. Zubin told a press conference on 27 June 2014 that he could not put up with the government cuts at the Palau de les Arts. Subsidy had fallen drastically and the number of musicians in the orchestra dropped from ninety-six to fifty-seven. Zubin was also miffed that Barcelona's Liceu Opera received considerably more than the Palau. He warned that at the rate things were going, it would soon become a provincial theatre. He did, however, say that he was saving room in his 2016 schedule in case things at Les Arts improved.

♫

Scandal hit the opera house in January 2015 when Schmidt was arrested on charges of financial irregularities. It was alleged that the house contracts awarded by the organization did not follow the appropriate processes and that funds had been misappropriated. There were also accusations of conflict of interest. She was simultaneously earning two salaries—one as a representative of the Palau de les Arts and another as a representative of the Patrocinio de les Arts, the company created to attract private sponsorship for the Palau, which reportedly awarded her commissions amounting to €5,08,000. Likewise, Schmidt's personal business expenses which were said to be considerable also came under scrutiny. She was released on bail almost immediately though questions were raised about the manner of her arrest and the unnecessarily high-handed treatment of the veteran opera administrator. The case is still in court and the authorities have impounded her passport. Zubin told me that it had also been put about falsely that she had taken a percentage from him, Domingo and Maazel. 'It was of course a complete fabrication,' he said.[30]

# Music *in the* Family

MUSIC PERMEATED MEHLI'S LIFE and he, in turn, as founder of the Bombay Symphony Orchestra and the American Youth Symphony, filled many other lives with music. He moved to England in 1955 where, as we have already seen, he worked as concertmaster with the Hallé Orchestra. Until 1959, he worked as leader of the Hallé Orchestra under the extremely supportive Barbirolli whom he described as 'one of the greatest influences of my conducting life'.

The next five years were spent as second violin in the Curtis String Quartet in Philadelphia, with which Mehli toured extensively all around the United States. In later years he was to state, 'the string quartet has been the prime, basic factor of my entire musical philosophy'.

## MENTOR AND CONDUCTOR

Mehli finally ended his peripatetic existence when he settled in Los Angeles in 1964. His official position—which he held until 1976—was director of the orchestra department at University of California, Los Angeles (UCLA), where he succeeded Foss. At that time the music department at UCLA was primarily focused on music history and ethnomusicology. The orchestra consisted of an uneven group of instrumentalists who played more for their love of music than to become professional musicians. Performances were also a rarity. However, if the students at UCLA could not achieve full symphonic status, Mehli soon found a group of musicians who could. Within two months of arriving in Los Angeles, he took over the leadership of the American Youth Symphony, comprising university students from Southern California. Zubin, who by then was music director of the Los Angeles Philharmonic, had recommended his father for the post. Zubin recalls, 'The mandatory auditions and tests came off perfectly and my father was entrusted with this wonderful assignment.'[1]

The American Youth Symphony—the members of which are between sixteen and twenty-five years old—was his pride and joy. He conducted thirty-three seasons, only retiring at the age of ninety. Under his guidance, the orchestra grew to 110 in size and began a series of international tours. He was particularly pleased that fifteen of his 'graduates' were playing in the Los Angeles Philharmonic and about 100 others were members of professional orchestras in the United States, Canada, Europe, Israel and South America.

Acknowledged as one of the outstanding youth orchestras in America, the American Youth Symphony has over the years provided important performance opportunities for talented young instrumentalists. The orchestra presents six free concerts a year from May to October as part of the UCLA Performing Arts programme. In his biography of Barbirolli, Michael Kennedy quotes the great conductor as saying, 'I . . . attended Mehli's concert with the American Youth Symphony. I am glad I did, for dear Mehli was magnificent. Made those children play really quite splendidly. I was really thrilled and impressed.'

The American Youth Symphony was a group made up of the most talented university and college students from Southern California. Most of them came from institutions that did not have the resources to play the big orchestral repertory of the nineteenth and twentieth centuries. It was Mehli's aim to introduce the young players to this kind of music. 'The students know nothing and they must begin somewhere to dedicate their lives to learning this repertory. When they leave here they will have performed all the symphonies of Beethoven, Brahms, Tchaikovsky and Dvořák, plus the last six symphonies of Mozart, five of Mahler, two of Bruckner and all the Strauss tone poems,' he said.[2]

Mehli also conducted the Philadelphia Orchestra in 1978, 1980, 1982 and 1984 to high acclaim. In addition, he conducted the RIAS Berlin, Israel, Tokyo, Yokohama, Jerusalem, Venezuela and Brazil Symphonies; the Israel Sinfonietta; and the symphony orchestras of San Antonio, Grand Rapids, Milwaukee, Miami, Puerto Rico, Rhode Island, Jacksonville, Memphis, Ashland and Eugene. In March 1983, he made his New York debut at Carnegie Hall to undisputed appreciation with another youth orchestra, the National Orchestra Association Symphony.

'Any time I go to Chicago or New York, I meet people who played with him in his orchestra,' said Zubin. 'They were all very, very fond of him. Of course, they always had stories about how strict he was.' Mehli was passionate and cared deeply for what he did. Lawrence Sonderling, a former concertmaster of the American Youth Symphony, recalled that he was a man of great intensity and his profound love for music was obvious in everything he did. 'In rehearsal with the orchestra, he would badger us, he would yell and scream; sometimes he would tell stories of things he had heard and seen in his musical youth. Always the intensity was there. And the passion.'[3] Mehli was indefatigable—he was bursting with energy even in his eighties, energy which had as its source his unquenchable passion for music.

Mehli made no bones about the level of commitment he expected from his players. 'I make the effort . . . you make the effort or don't play in my orchestra.'[4] And there never was any doubt that Mehli made the effort, and then some. He was known as a tough leader and a persuasive communicator. He yelled, cajoled, browbeat and did whatever it took to impart his love and passion for music to his young students. He was passionate about music and demanded perfection from his orchestra and from his students. He was strict. He could spend hours on one measure, one bar, until he got it exactly right. He also got carried away at times. He considered his students part of his extended family. Mehli no doubt followed the dictum of the man he admired most as a violinist: Jascha Heifetz. Heifetz was amused when people expressed surprise that he still needed to practise after fifty years. 'I agree with Liszt,' he said. 'If I don't practise for one day, I know it; two days, the critics know it; three days, the public knows it.'[5]

As a teacher Mehli was an inspiring taskmaster. Prospective American Youth Symphony members had to answer three questions: their age, their teacher (Mehli was particular about the pedigree of the student) and if they were willing to spend three and a half hours rehearsing every Saturday. The aim, according to Mehli, was to train them in great orchestra playing. He seemed to have unlimited energy. 'There is probably no greater dynamo of a person in the whole musical world,' observed Fleischmann when he was executive director with the Los Angeles Philharmonic in the late 1980s. The roster of the Los Angeles Philharmonic then boasted eight American Youth Symphony alumni. Others had also remarked that Mehli could never sit still for a minute and, even in repose, his gestures and facial expressions were always animated. Two heart attacks in four months in 1969 did not slow him down. The doctors had told him that he shouldn't conduct another concert, but Mehli ignored them. He conducted for nearly thirty years more, proving his doctors monumentally wrong. Zubin told me that Kaye had once said about Mehli: 'Your father is the very definition of terror.'

Mehli built each season around a theme, such as notable fifth symphonies, or the music of one composer. This way the students could cover many more masterpieces. His interpretations were based on copious research because he believed that a conductor must really understand the composer's idiom, language and philosophy. When asked why so much of his career encompassed working with young musicians, he said, 'One develops a special knack for it, and also patience. God sends us on missions. I've dealt with young people all my life. That's my destiny.'[6] Bharucha who directed the film *On Wings of Fire* in the mid-1980s recalls going to Mehli for violin lessons as a young boy, and remembers being chided for not practising enough.[7] While Mehli was a fine violin player and a competent conductor, there is no doubt that it is as an inspiring teacher that he will always be remembered.

Mehli's students echo Zubin's description of him as a lovable dictator. 'My seat in the orchestra was directly in front of him, literally under his nose,' said Abhijit Sengupta, the former artistic director of the Michigan-based Fontana Chamber Arts, who trained with Mehli in the American Youth Symphony in the mid-1990s. Mehli had the habit, much to the disapproval of his doctors, of getting excited and agitated while conducting. Sengupta recalls Tehmina telling him, 'Abhijit, if he falls off the podium, please promise me you will catch him.' If anyone made careless mistakes, he became so angry, he practically frothed at the mouth! But no one took it personally because his young wards knew he had a great deal of affection for them and that his histrionics were partly an act.

Ponti Jr, Sophia Loren's son, and the conductor of the San Bernardino Symphony Orchestra, who privately studied with Mehli, calls him his greatest influence. Mehli would make him sing all the significant orchestral parts in a score, so much so that to this day 'singing' the score is one of the most integral and important elements in the way he learns and assimilates a score. Aside from that, Mehli would almost invariably chide him for singing out of tune!

Mehli was renowned for his amazing ability to conduct flawlessly from memory. De Mello, former Bombay String Quartet second violinist recalled Mehli's phenomenal memory. 'If there was a phone call, he would say, "Excuse me, please carry on." When he would return, we didn't have to tell him where we were. He knew the music so well.' While De Mello went on to perform with more experienced conductors, he retained a soft corner for Mehli whom he admires the most. 'I'm so proud that I was not only a member of his string quartet but also a sincere friend of his,' he said. 'He was my great guide and my inspiration.' But even more than his incredible skill and his impeccable memory, the one thing that people remember the most about Mehli is his warm and loving personality.

Zubin says that his father had two loves—his family and his music. 'This was his entire life.'[8] Mehli took enormous pride in the achievement of his sons. Zubin began working with the Los Angeles Philharmonic two years before Mehli moved to the city and had the satisfaction of the presence of his father during his tenure with the orchestra: 'Any concert of mine that he attended, there was no doubt to whom my message was going. That is what I will miss in Los Angeles, because he will not be there.'[9] In later years, Zubin told interviewers that he picked up everything he knew about classical music from Mehli. He said his father was the source of his musical education until the age of eighteen when he went to Vienna for further studies.

Mehli attributed his continuing vigour to hard work: 'Conducting is one of the most physically tiring things in the world. We not only concentrate, and think of the music and remember the music and all that. But we have to impart it to a hundred boys and girls or men and women who are in the orchestra. A good conductor uses this arm, the right arm, for the tempo and for the rhythms and all that, and the left arm for the expression. You see, so both arms are working together. The chest is working, lungs are working, brain is working, everything is working together except the legs. And even the legs.'[10]

Mehli disdained the score and conducted from memory, a practice which Zubin also adopted. His logic was simple: 'Just as we keep our body in good shape by exercising, you have to exercise your memory also. And therefore every concert throughout the season, a whole season, I [conduct] from memory ... I come from what I call the golden age of music, when no one used a score. Today's great conductors—let's even leave my darling son Zubin out of it—but Abbado, Maazel, Ozawa, all conduct from memory.'[11]

Mehli was a highly competent conductor in his own right. But for many, he was placed in the curious position of potential paternal also-ran. In April 1968, he filled in for Munch who had cancelled his concerts with the Montreal Symphony. The brutal question on everyone's mind before the performance was, who is Mehli Mehta, other than Zubin's father? True, he played the violin and had conducted some minor orchestras, but would he have qualified as the head of the orchestra department at UCLA had Zubin not been his son? Bernheimer of *Los Angeles Times*, who was often unkind to the son, gave the father an unqualified testimonial. He wrote: 'Now that we have heard the performance, the doubts are resolved and rude questions seem academic. Mehli Mehta is a fully qualified conductor with a thorough knowledge of his craft.'[12]

The praise was again fulsome when he conducted the National Orchestra of New York in his debut in the city at Carnegie Hall in March 1983. The critics said Mehli had proved that his son Zubin had actually followed his own talented baton. 'He led the group with expert attention to detail; nothing was overdone. Each musical phrase was warm, direct and to the point.'[13]

In March 1994, Mehli and the American Youth Symphony presented the orchestra's twenty-ninth Annual Gala Benefit Concert at the Dorothy Chandler Pavilion. It featured the nineteen-year-old Russian violin virtuoso Vengerov as soloist. Mehli, who was recovering from a bout of pneumonia, conducted the performance seated on a chair. He opened with Bernstein's *Candide* Overture and Vengerov displayed his virtuosity in Jean Sibelius's Concerto for Violin and Orchestra. The evening concluded with Mussorgsky's *Pictures at an Exhibition*.

Such was Mehli's popularity that Los Angeles Mayor Richard Riordan proclaimed 6 March 1994 as Mehli Mehta Day. In his greetings, Riordan said, 'The American Youth Symphony is a credit to our community, serving as the launching pad for outstanding musicians. We are proud of its many graduates now filling chairs with many of the world's great orchestras.' Earlier, California Governor Pete Wilson had congratulated Mehli on his Governor's Art Award, modelled on the lines of the Kennedy Center Awards (which Zubin received in 2006). In a letter to Mehli, he lauded his contribution over three decades to providing invaluable musical training to young musicians.[14]

In September 1988, Mehli turned eighty and in his honour the American Youth Symphony board, affiliates and friends gave him a birthday banquet at the Beverly Hills Hotel—a small token of appreciation for his inspirational leadership of young musicians. Eventually, age and failing health forced Mehli to slow down. He suffered heart attacks in 1995 and 1996 and in March 1997, he announced that he was finally retiring the next year. Returning to the podium on 3 March 1997 after an absence of ten months for the annual benefit gala at the Dorothy Chandler Pavilion, he conducted Beethoven's Third Piano Concerto with guest pianist Ax, followed by a rendition of Prokofiev's Fifth Symphony in the second half. 'The doctors say no, Tehmi and Zubin say no, but God willing, I will conduct a few concerts in the next season.'[15]

The verve with which Mehli conducted is fresh in the minds of his colleagues and students even today. His final performance with the American Youth Symphony in May 1998 at the age of ninety is the stuff of legend. Even though he suffered a seizure during the farewell concert, he refused to leave the stage. 'We tried to convince him not to go on, but he wouldn't listen,' said Zubin. 'After thirty-three years of being music director of the American Youth Orchestra, he wasn't going to let that go. He conducted the symphony brilliantly.'

Mehli left the stage after his farewell concert with the American Youth Symphony at UCLA's Royce Hall in obvious discomfort: 'The doctor said that were it not for the defibrillator regulating my heartbeat, I would have been dead on the spot.'[16] But he took his advancing age philosophically: 'Maybe I was quicker and I was sharper when I was younger, but I'm much more mature just now. I understand music better, I feel it better, I understand the meaning of the composer and his language better. And so I consider myself a much better musician as I get older.'[17]

Alexander Treger, a long-time member and assistant concertmaster of the Los Angeles Philharmonic, who succeeded Mehli in the fall of 1998, spoke of Mehli's great love of music and his total dedication to it. 'Music was totally his love. His knowledge of music, of certain phrasings, bowings, just name it, it's amazing. I call it the Mehta genius . . . The generations of musicians he trained, it's absolutely marvellous.'[18]

'He was always talking about music,' said countertenor Bejun, Dady's son. 'Music was never far from his conversation. He was an incredibly passionate man.' Though Mehli was often unwell during the last years of his life, he managed repeatedly to will himself back to health. 'In the last five years he was very close to death many times. He'd battle back each time and he would be fine, not diminished in any way but absolutely fine.'

## LAYING DOWN THE BATON OF LIFE

Mehli's last days were not happy. In July 2002, Zubin flew from Israel to Los Angeles when he was told that his father was sinking fast. As soon as Zubin heard that his condition had worsened, he flew to him immediately, cancelling his appearances with the Israel Philharmonic. Mehli spent the last three months of his life in hospital. After Zubin arrived in Los Angeles, Mehli found out that his son was supposed to go on an Australian tour with the Israel Philharmonic soon. He insisted that Zubin go on tour as planned. Faced with no choice, Zubin agreed.

When Zubin returned from Australia, Mehli was still alive but his lungs were barely functioning and he was being fed through tubes. The doctors forbade him to drink water because he would choke. He did not feel any hunger, but only begged that they put some ice on his tongue. He simply wanted to feel a drop of water. The doctor allowed this once in a while, but Mehli always asked for more and Zubin was forced to refuse because he knew that it could kill him. He was very angry with me and said: 'You are a traitor. You prefer to listen to the doctors and are not looking after me.'[19] Mehli's last days were full of suffering. On 19 October 2002, Mehli finally laid down the baton of life at the Santa Monica UCLA Medical Center, survived by his wife, two sons, four grandchildren, and two great-grandchildren. Zubin had flown in from Munich to visit his ailing father only to learn that he had passed away.

Zubin says that since his demise, his father has always been in his thoughts. 'I loved him attending my concerts. I felt that I was conducting for him personally.' Mehli had last watched Zubin on stage in December 2001 when he had guest conducted the Los Angeles Philharmonic at the Dorothy Chandler Pavilion. By divine coincidence that last concert was the *Requiem* by Verdi. And all his life Mehli was nothing if not proud of his son's achievements. 'Once

Zubin was known as the son of Mehli: Now I am known as the father of Zubin. And I am very happy about that,' he said.[20]

## THE MATRIARCH

If Mehli, Zubin and Zarin were the famous ones in the family, it was Tehmina, known to the international music community as 'Tehmi' (and 'Bhulki' to her friends and family in Mumbai), who was the quiet strength of the family. As a loyal helpmate, Tehmina copied Mehli's orchestral scores, typed his correspondence, saw to it that his clothes were in order, and prepared his meals to fit his concert schedule. A passable piano player herself (she could accompany Mehli in certain easy sonatas), she remained traditional enough to be dressed in saris all her life but, as a small concession to fashion, wore Chanel shoes. 'I think the family should come first,' she told *Los Angeles Times*. 'If you put yourself first, then don't have children.'[21] Mehli summed up her contribution when he said, 'Though her body is frail, her mind is stronger than all of us put together. She's the centre of our family and the one person who holds it all together.'[22]

She received the Mother of the Year award from the Helping Hand of Cedars-Sinai Medical Center in 1984. Behrendt, then vice chairperson of the Los Angeles Philharmonic board, acknowledged the contribution of this selfless homemaker. 'She's always giving credit to others, but it's Tehmi who makes things possible . . . She is the definitive mother.'[23]

Tehmina passed away on 22 April 2005 after a brief illness. Zubin, who was in Los Angeles in January and was not scheduled to return until August, had a presentiment that she would not live long. He cancelled his concerts with the Israel Philharmonic in March so that he could be with his mother for two weeks. Zubin then had to fly to Mumbai to conduct three concerts in April with the Maggio Musicale Fiorentino orchestra under the auspices of the Mehli Mehta Music Foundation. It was in Mumbai that he learned that his mother had a tumour in the brain. It came as a shock to him as she had never displayed any symptoms. Zubin returned to Los Angeles just as she was about to undergo surgery. She recognized him but could not speak. She passed away a few days later.

## MEHLI MEHTA MUSIC FOUNDATION

While Mehli left Bombay many years ago, disillusioned with the lack of support for Western classical music, there still remained a small group of people enthusiastic about the genre. In 1996, the smouldering embers of the fire that he had lit so long ago, were reignited by the formation of the Mehli Mehta Music Foundation. Today, the foundation's premises at Banoo Mansions, in Kemps Corner, Mumbai, resonate with the strains of piano, string and wind instruments and singing voices. The moving spirit and leading light behind the foundation is its managing trustee, Mehroo Jeejeebhoy, who continues to render yeoman service to the cause of Western classical music in Mumbai.

One of the main objectives of the foundation is to foster in children an active awareness and interest in music. The Discover Music Series now has an enrolment of 150 children with many waiting to join. The Singing Tree Choir has given public concerts and presented children's musicals. To encourage the learning of instruments, the foundation has an ongoing programme of visiting music teachers who reside at the foundation for a fixed period of time. The Sangat Chamber Music Festival was initiated in the same year that the foundation was set up. Every December, musicians, Indian and foreign, who participate without a fee, come here for two weeks. Ten days prior to the concerts, the Sangat musicians rehearse together, give classes and interact with local students and teachers. The positive audience response to the Sangat concerts endorses the conviction that there is a need, and a place, for Western classical music in Mumbai's cultural life.

The foundation also plays host to guest speakers who give video presentations and lead discussions on different aspects and types of classical music. These intimate evenings are structured for smaller audiences and give an opportunity to interested amateurs and professionals to explore new areas and genres in the world of music. Both Zubin and Zarin are advisers to the foundation. Zubin's visits to India have involved him personally in all aspects of the foundation and enabled it to invite some of the great orchestras of the world to Mumbai.

As a result of performances by these orchestras, the foundation has been financially secure and in a position to implement new programmes. Its trustees include director Shyam Benegal, Hamied, lawyer Iqbal Chagla and industrialist Nusli Wadia. The trustees are responsible for all policy decisions and meet four times a year. A volunteer executive committee, which meets weekly, supervises the daily operations of the foundation. It includes Jeejeebhoy, Pheroza Godrej, Roshan Chagla and Smita Crishna.

Mehli, initially at least, was less than thrilled when he heard in 1995 that a foundation was being set up in his name to promote Western classical music in Mumbai. Eighty-seven-year-old Mehli had never returned to the city of his birth since he left it and was concerned about the quality of music being performed there. 'He didn't want to lend his name to something that didn't have a certain standard,' says Jeejeebhoy. But Mehli began to warm up to the idea the next year, when the foundation got off the ground with its festival of chamber music, Sangat. 'We made recordings of the concerts and sent them to him,' Jeejeebhoy said. 'He got very excited and said, "How wonderful that they can play music like this." He wrote back, giving me a critical appreciation of the playing.'[24]

Mehli's initial reluctance is not surprising when one considers the fact that he was always known for his exacting standards—whether it was while teaching his son Zubin, leading the Bombay Symphony Orchestra or the Bombay String Quartet (which he founded in 1935 and 1940 respectively) or training students in the American Youth Symphony. 'My father used to terrorize me,' said Zubin. 'He was very strict but it helped me in the long run, believe me.'

Mehli was soon convinced of the good work being done in Mumbai. In a message to the foundation in 1998, he wrote:

> My dear friends, you all have no idea how joyful and elated I feel deep in my heart, that at last my dear home town is achieving, in full bloom, my dreams, hopes and longings of making beautiful, great music . . . And now at 90, I realize that you all my dear, dear musical friends have remembered and rekindled the flame I lit in 1935, and that too in my name and honour.[25]

It was vindication for the man who was so bitter at being unappreciated that he never returned to Mumbai once he left it in the 1950s. When I asked Zubin about it, he said, 'He was very happy. And I am very happy too. My dream is to have a real school in Bombay. We are working out of a few apartments just now. I hope one day we have enough money and encouragement to have a real school.'[26]

Another development of relatively recent origin that would have pleased Mehli no end, and another belated vindication of all he stood for, is the formation of the Symphony Orchestra of India under the auspices of the NCPA, Mumbai. The brainchild of Suntook, the Symphony Orchestra of India was set up in 2004 and is keeping the flame of Western classical music burning bright in Mumbai. (Suntook narrated an amusing anecdote to me. In the mid-1980s Suntook, Zubin and some other friends had been to a concert of Verdi's *Requiem* conducted by Sinopoli at London's Festival Hall. During the performance, Zubin fell asleep. This was noticed by a lady in the audience and she took the celebrated conductor to task for showing disrespect to a colleague. Caught on the wrong foot, Zubin was charm itself. He was conducting *Aida* in London the next day and, as if by magic, produced a few tickets from his coat pocket and invited the lady to attend the performance. Suntook did not say if the star-struck admonisher had by then become apologetic.[27])

Zubin was the only show in town when he visited India. The Symphony Orchestra of India is going from strength to strength and slowly Western classical music, which till recently had only a niche clientele, is finding a bigger audience. 'They are doing good work. I congratulate them,' Zubin said.[28]

## ZARIN MEHTA: CELEBRITY MUSIC ADMINISTRATOR

If Zubin is a celebrity conductor, then Zarin, who was born in 1938, was a big star in the small world of classical-music management. In the 1970s the Montreal Symphony Orchestra's administration fell into disarray because a suitable executive could not be found (fluency in French being the major hurdle). Zarin took on the management of the ensemble in 1976 when it appeared that there would be no end to the futile search for an executive. Zarin, who had achieved professional distinction as a chartered accountant before turning to music management, turned around the ailing finances of the Montreal Symphony Orchestra. He was a partner at Coopers and Lybrand before joining the board of the orchestra in 1981, and then became its vice president and managing director. In his years as managing director, the operating budget of the orchestra had tripled to $15 million annually and fundraising had increased fivefold. Zarin's stewardship of the orchestra guided it into an era of international acclaim that lasts to this day.[29]

In December 1989, Zarin was named the executive director of the Ravinia Festival, the open-air music festival in Highland Park, near Chicago, the summer home of the Chicago Symphony, starting 1 June 1990. As William J. McDonough, festival chairman and head of the search committee, saw it, 'Ravinia was dedicated to great music-making, but it was also a business which had to have a balanced budget.' Zarin was seen as a man with the artistic commitment and financial skills to deal with both areas on the highest level.

Zarin ran the festival successfully for ten years from 1990 to 2000 and, besides his advocacy for young artistes and his extraordinary ear for identifying emerging talent, he was remembered most for his interest in music of all kinds. In addition to its long-standing commitment to classical music and its summertime hosting of the Chicago Symphony Orchestra, Ravinia under Zarin became a home for serious jazz and a reliable presenter of contemporary music.[30] In 1995, the festival unveiled a $12-million plan for renovation of its facilities. Zarin formed the Ravinia Festival Orchestra and instituted programmes in jazz and contemporary music as well as forums for young performers.

Though he developed a broad familiarity with music early on, Zarin, unlike his brother, never aspired to be a performer. Zarin told the *New York Times* in September 2000 that though there was always music and musicians in the home, none of his children have the same interest in classical music that Zubin and he had from listening to music on 78s in India. The business of music, however, is something quite different. 'That comes kind of naturally. My father ran his own concerts and chamber music concerts, so it became a kind of business and it was talked about at the dinner table. Zubin and I both went into normal directions for a time. At that stage there was never any thought of our going into the profession, because in Bombay there really wasn't a profession.'[31]

In the autumn of 1999, Zarin signed another five-year contract with the Ravinia Festival. But when the New York Philharmonic Chairman Paul B. Guenther came calling, he found the offer difficult to refuse. Zarin was one of forty candidates offered by a recruiting firm to the New York Philharmonic as possible executive directors, but it quickly became clear that he was the star the ensemble really wanted. In fact, each of the other candidates interviewed for the position suggested that Zarin was the best man for the job. The disappointed management at Ravinia tried to talk Zarin out of it, realizing at the same time that this was just the opportunity he needed. According to Guenther, Zarin was 'the best executive director in the country'.

For Zarin, the offer was irresistibly appealing, as was the prospect of change. He said, 'Without ever planning it, it has just worked out that every ten years, I have a natural change of direction. I certainly didn't plan this.'[32] Zarin, who took charge on 2 September 2000, replaced Deborah Borda who left for a similar position with the Los Angeles Philharmonic. Zarin, at sixty-one, was considered a star in the small world of classical-music management. He told *India Abroad*: 'I am pleased and honoured to have the opportunity to work with the New York Philharmonic and with my old friend maestro Kurt Masur. I look forward to continuing the grand tradition of this great orchestra and exploring and developing new visions of its future with the board, the orchestra and the staff.'[33]

In June 2004, Zarin was named the president of the New York Philharmonic. He kept the title of executive director and his day-to-day responsibilities remained the same. Among his accomplishments in four seasons was the hiring of Maazel as music director in September 2002. Guenther said: 'This title of distinction is given to Zarin Mehta by the Board in recognition of his four seasons of exemplary leadership and dedication to the New York Philharmonic . . . With each season, he is steadily transforming this orchestra and this organization to meet the demands of the twenty-first century. He has won the total trust and admiration of the organization, and I believe, has set a standard in the industry.'[34]

In September 2010, Zarin announced his retirement saying he would leave at the end of the 2011–12 season. His accomplishments included cordial labour relations, a record of exotic touring, including a visit to North Korea, and bringing Credit Suisse aboard as global sponsor. He also negotiated new agreements with the players on recordings and other uses of performances in the media, making them more cost-effective through revenue sharing with the musicians rather than high fixed payments up front. But he failed to merge the orchestra with Carnegie Hall, and attempts to tour Cuba and Georgia proved abortive. He is now retired in Chicago where he lives with his wife, Carmen.

## 'SON' RISE

The career of Mervon, Zubin's son, has seen him on both sides of the curtain. He did take piano and violin lessons but had limited musical talent. He loved sports, playing ice hockey, soccer and tennis. He went to Colgate University in upstate New York where he discovered that drama was his first love though he had enrolled to study Russian and political science. He did everything related to theatre—acting, directing, writing and producing—and it was his professor there who advised him to go to theatre school.

Mervon went to New York, to Sanford 'Sandy' Meisner and the Neighbourhood Playhouse School of the Theatre, a full-time professional conservatory for actors and the home of what is called the Meisner technique. He spent two years there, and then the next six years doing TV shows and Off-Broadway productions in New York, also working as a singing waiter to help pay his way. He came to Toronto in 1985 where he had friends. With the help of an agent, he joined the Stratford Festival where he spent two happy years. The Stratford Festival is an internationally recognized annual celebration of theatre, running from April to October in Stratford, Ontario. It is famous for its production of Shakespearean plays which is its primary mandate.

He returned to Toronto but couldn't get work because of the commonly held belief that once someone did Stratford, one couldn't do TV or stage. He went back to Chicago where there were many acting projects but very little money. When Zarin took over in Ravinia, he asked Mervon in 1994 to babysit the pop concerts. One thing led to another and, in 1998, Mervon became director of programming, going on to become director of production three years later. He soon earned valuable experience programming classical jazz, world music, country, pop and music theatre artistes. He then made the move to the Kimmel Center for the Performing Arts in Philadelphia in February 2002, where he became vice president of programming and education. Over eight seasons, he instituted music education programmes for thousands of children and presented the who's who of classical, jazz, pop and world music, including the Berlin and the Vienna philharmonics, Ravi Shankar and Oscar Peterson.

In April 2009, he returned to Toronto to become executive director of performing arts for the Royal Conservatory of Music and to open its stunning new facility, Koerner Hall, which has quickly become one of the finest halls in North America, known for its acoustics and diverse programming of jazz, world, classical and pop music. He is responsible for directing all aspects of the Royal Conservatory's performing arts business, including programming and management of Koerner Hall.

He has acted in over 100 theatrical performances, including residencies at the Williamstown Theatre Festival and the Citadel

Theatre in Edmonton, apart from several seasons at the Stratford Festival. He has also performed for the Court, Steppenwolf and Apple Tree theatres in Chicago. He has made several appearances on television and in films, and taken the stage frequently as a narrator of orchestral works with orchestras in Ottawa, Los Angeles, Chicago, Budapest and Lisbon. In Florence and Munich, he appeared in Bernstein's *Kaddish* with his father conducting.

He is married to Carey Suleiman who was in the marketing division at Ravinia and they have a son, Zed. They were looking for a name which began with 'Z'—like Zubin and Zarin—and settled on Zed.

# The Maestro *on* Tour

ZUBIN HAS BEEN TOURING the world with his orchestras for many decades now and his visits to India, especially Mumbai, have always fostered nostalgia. We have already noted his first visit to India when he brought the Los Angeles Philharmonic in 1967. He toured with the New York Philharmonic in 1984 and his first visit with the Maggio Musicale Fiorentino orchestra was in 1987. In 1991, he brought the European Community Youth Orchestra and, since the mid-1990s, he has been a frequent visitor to India, especially after the Mehli Mehta Music Foundation was set up in 1995. In this chapter, we look at his tours to India which, as Western classical music attracts the younger generation and takes firmer root in Mumbai, are eagerly looked forward to by an increasing number of music enthusiasts in the city. We also look at some of his more recent tours with the Israel Philharmonic Orchestra and his world tour with the Vienna Philharmonic in 2009.

## TOURS TO INDIA

In April 1997, Zubin brought the Munich Philharmonic Orchestra to Mumbai for three concerts, one in New Delhi and two in Mumbai. The Munich Philharmonic was founded near Stuttgart by Franz Kaim, the son of a piano manufacturer. Under Weingartner, the orchestra went on numerous tours abroad and gained an international reputation. Mahler himself conducted the orchestra for the premiere performances of his Fourth and Eighth symphonies. Ferdinand Löwe (1908–14), who was a pupil of Bruckner, organized the first large-scale Bruckner Festival and thus founded the Bruckner tradition which the orchestra maintains to this day. In more modern times, the name of Celibidache, who was music director from 1979 until his death in 1996, has been associated with the orchestra.

Zubin's concert in New Delhi was held at the Indira Gandhi Stadium under the auspices of the Time and Talents Club, the Mehli Mehta Music Foundation and the Confederation of Indian Industry. The programme consisted of Beethoven's *Leonore* Overture No. 3 and Bruch's Violin Concerto, with David Garrett as soloist. A prodigy, Garrett had made his American debut with the Los Angeles Philharmonic under Zubin's baton. Tchaikovsky's Fifth Symphony comprised the second half of the programme. At the concert at the Homi Bhabha Auditorium two days later, Tchaikovsky's Fifth was replaced by Schubert's Ninth Symphony. In the second concert in Mumbai, Beethoven's Fifth and Tchaikovsky's Fifth were on the programme.

A tour with the Israel Philharmonic Orchestra in October 2001 saw them perform for the first time at Mumbai's Jamshed Bhabha Theatre under the auspices of the NCPA, the Mehli Mehta Music Foundation and the Taj Group of Hotels, in association with the Times of India Group. The first concert on 13 October comprised the Scheherazade Symphonic Suite by Rimsky-Korsakov and Tchaikovsky's Fourth Symphony. The next concert had Schubert's *Rosamunde* and Tchaikovsky's Concerto in D Major for Violin and Orchestra, with Chang as soloist. Brahms's Second Symphony followed after the interval.

Zubin brought the Vienna Philharmonic to Mumbai for two concerts in March 2003, under the auspices of the Mehli Mehta Music Foundation. The tour was supported by the Austrian Embassy and they played Schubert's Fifth, Haydn's Trumpet Concerto and Beethoven's Third (*Eroica*) in the first concert on 28 March. The next morning, the orchestra players interacted with and played for children, allowing them to explore Western classical music in an informal setting. The evening's concert comprised the Overture to the comic opera *Merry Wives of Windsor* by Nicolai, the Philharmonic's founder; *Sinfonia Concertante* in B-flat Major by Haydn and, after the interval, Mahler's Symphony No. 1 (*Titan*).

A visit with the Maggio Musicale Fiorentino orchestra supported by the Italian government was the highlight of 2005. The April tour was made more special by the fact that Mstislav 'Slava' Rostropovich accompanied Zubin and the orchestra. Addressing a press conference, Zubin said that it was Rostropovich who had come up with the idea of the concerts when they met in Munich the year before. 'Mstislav said to me that once in my life, I want to go to your country and play two concerts to raise funds to start a music school in memory of your father,' Zubin said. (Mehli and 'Slava' were good friends.) The Maggio Musicale also agreed to perform for a much lower fee. The idea was that the funds raised from the concerts would eventually help the Mehli Mehta Music Foundation become a more structured music school. While the proceeds from the first two concerts in Mumbai were used by the foundation for the benefit of music in the city, the funds raised by the third went into relief efforts for the devastating tsunami of December 2004.

The concert on 8 April opened with the Overture to Verdi's *La Forza del Destino*. Joining Zubin and the orchestra in Dvořák's Concerto for Violoncello and Orchestra in B Minor was Rostropovich. The programme after the interval was given over to a perennial favourite, Beethoven's Fifth, where out of three short notes and a long one, the composer created one of the world's most famous symphonies. The next day, they played the Overture to *I Vespri Siciliani* by Verdi and Dvořák's Concerto for Violoncello and Orchestra in B Minor. The programme after the interval comprised Brahms's First Symphony.

The idea of holding the third concert on 10 April in aid of tsunami relief and rehabilitation was Zubin's. He was supported by violinist Rachlin who played Beethoven's Violin Concerto along with the orchestra. The concert opened with the *Egmont* Overture and the audience was treated to Beethoven's Seventh after the interval.

At the end of the year, in December, Zubin brought the Bavarian State Opera Orchestra to India, his last tour with it as music director. More than ninety musicians and two tonnes of musical equipment were flown in from Germany to present Verdi's Overture from *La Forza del Destino*, Schubert's *Unfinished* Symphony No. 8 in B Minor and Beethoven's Fifth in concerts in Chennai and New Delhi. On 26 December 2005, the first anniversary of the Indian Ocean tsunami, Zubin and the Bavarian State Orchestra performed for the first time in Chennai at the Madras Music Academy.

This special Tsunami Memorial Concert was organized by the Chennai German consulate along with the Max-Mueller Bhavan/Goethe Institute. The team performed to a packed hall of select invitees, which included Nobel laureate Amartya Sen. On 28 December, Zubin performed in Delhi at the Indira Gandhi Stadium in a concert that included sitar maestro Ravi Shankar in the audience. Zubin made a special mention of him at the show: 'I pay my tributes to my dearest friend and the greatest musician of India, Ravi Shankar. It has been a long time since we made music together. I will never forget the last time we worked together.' Ravi Shankar stood up and acknowledged the tribute.[1]

Zubin tours India once in two years. In October 2008, it was the turn of the Israel Philharmonic Orchestra to tour Mumbai with its music director for life. Accompanying Zubin and the orchestra was a host of superstars: Barenboim, Zukerman, Domingo, Frittoli, Amanda Forsyth and Tatiana Goncharova. There were four concerts, including one at Brabourne Stadium. The first, on 7 October, featured the Overture from Verdi's *La Forza del Destino* and Beethoven's Piano Concerto No. 3 in C Minor, with Barenboim as soloist. After the interval, they played Dvořák's Symphony No. 9 in E Minor (*From the New World*) which was commissioned by the New York Philharmonic and premiered in 1893 at Carnegie Hall. Two days later, the programme consisted of Paul Ben-Haim's 'Psalm', Brahms's Violin Concerto in D Major and Schubert's Symphony No. 9 ('The Great').

The concert on 10 October featured Zukerman (violin), Forsyth (cello) and Goncharova (piano). Schubert's Sonata in D Major for

Violin and Piano and César Franck's Sonata in A Minor for Violin and Piano were played before the interval. Gabriel Fauré's *Après un Rêve* for Cello and Piano and *Berceuse* for Violin and Piano featured in the second half, along with Kodály's Duo for Violin and Cello and Kreisler's Liebesfreud for Violin and Piano.

Perhaps the most exciting concert was at Brabourne Stadium of the Cricket Club of India on 11 October where superstars of the opera Domingo and Frittoli sang solo pieces as well as duets. The programme opened with Prelude to Act I of Bizet's opera *Carmen*. Among the solo pieces by Domingo were 'Prière' from *Le Cid* and 'Granada' which ended the concert. Frittoli's solos included 'Vissi d'arte' from *Tosca* and Micaela's Aria from *Carmen*. The duets included 'Tonight' from *West Side Story*, 'Brindisi' from *La Traviata* and 'Gia Nella Note Densa' from *Otello*. The Israel Philharmonic also played some polkas, including the favourite 'Tritsch Tratsch'. A final concert on 12 October consisted of Richard Strauss's *Till Eulenspiegel* and *Four Last Songs*, and Mussorgsky's *Pictures at an Exhibition*.

It is rare for the people of Mumbai to be treated to Zubin's concerts in quick succession, but that is just what happened when he returned after five months, in March 2009, with the Vienna Philharmonic. The year also marked the birth anniversary of the founder of modern science in India, Homi J. Bhabha, and it was fitting that the concerts were held at the Homi Bhabha Hall located at the southernmost tip of Mumbai.

Apart from being an outstanding scientist and institution builder, Bhabha was also a man of culture (and the elder brother of Jamshed Bhabha who was the equivalent of Chandler in Mumbai). We have already noted his association with Mehli in organizing the Yehudi Menuhin Concerts in 1952 and his playing the violin with Mehli at a party he hosted. An accomplished artist, his sketches and paintings were comparable to those of a professional. At Cambridge, he designed the sets for Mozart's opera *Idomeneo*. He was an important patron of the Bombay-based Progressive Arts Group which included M.F. Husain, K.H. Ara, S.H. Raza and F.N. Souza, and acquired many of their early works for the Tata Institute of Fundamental Research,

Mumbai, which he founded. Bhabha died tragically on 24 January 1966, when his plane crashed on Mont Blanc in the Alps. He was on his way to Vienna to attend a meeting of the International Atomic Energy Agency's Scientific Advisory Committee.

This was Zubin's second appearance with the Vienna Philharmonic in the city of his birth, having first played there in 2003. Mumbai (then Bombay) had also been a stopover on the 1959 world tour with Karajan. Playing in Mumbai has always been an intensely emotional experience for Zubin and this occasion was no different. The programme of the first concert on 11 March consisted of the Overture from Mozart's *The Marriage of Figaro*, Piano Concerto No. 2 in F Minor by Chopin and Beethoven's Seventh Symphony. Two works of Johann Strauss served as encores: Strauss's perennial favourite the 'Emperor Waltz', and the polka 'Tritsch Tratsch'. The next day, there was Schubert's Piano Sonata No. 20 in A Major and Bartók's Piano Sonata BB 88 Sz. 80, Debussy's *Preludes* and Chopin's Polonaise in A-flat Major ('Heroic').

Mumbai got to hear and see the virtuosity of the Chinese phenomenon Lang Lang for the first time. A superstar in the world of pianists, Lang Lang, a former child prodigy, was the first Chinese to play with the Berlin Philharmonic, the Vienna Philharmonic and top American orchestras. In August 2008, over 5 billion people heard him play at the opening ceremony of the Beijing Olympic Games. He also played with the Vienna Philharmonic under Zubin's baton during the closing of the Euro Cup final the same year, in front of the majestic Schönbrunn Palace in Vienna. In a unique first for piano manufacturer Steinway, five versions of pianos designed for the early musical education of children were named Lang Lang™ Steinway in his honour. He was also the first ambassador of the YouTube Symphony Orchestra.

Zubin's next visit to Mumbai in March 2011 with the Maggio Musicale Fiorentino orchestra was preceded by much tension. Zubin and the orchestra had been touring Japan when an earthquake and a devastating tsunami hit the island country on 11 March. A day after the calamity, they performed a concert in Tokyo. It was only after the nuclear emergency was declared in Japan that panic set in; they cancelled the shows and tried to leave the country as soon as possible. It was difficult for them to get flights and they finally managed to fly to Taipei and then to Shanghai.

The concerts in Mumbai on 30 and 31 March presented the violinist Arabella Steinbacher and tenor Fabio Sartori. The programme on 30 March included the Overture from *I Vespri Siciliani* by Verdi, Concerto for Violin and Orchestra in D Major by Tchaikovsky and Mahler's *Titan*. Mozart's *Jupiter* Symphony and arias from *Rigoletto*, *Macbeth* and *Tosca* were the highlights of the next day's programme. Present at both the concerts was Matteo Renzi, then mayor of Florence, and now the prime minister of Italy.

## BEETHOVEN'S FIFTH IN KASHMIR

Zubin has long dreamed of taking the Israel Philharmonic Orchestra to Cairo. While that has yet to be realized, another dream—of playing in Kashmir—came true when he brought the Bavarian State Orchestra to India in September 2013. Zubin had last visited Kashmir on a family trip in 1974 before violence enveloped the valley. While he has travelled far and risen high, he retains a sentimental attachment to the country of his birth. He had always wanted to play for an audience of 'Hindus and Muslims sitting together' enjoying the music, and he had in mind a symbolic gesture similar to leading the Israel Philharmonic before an all-Arab audience in Nazareth or the performance in Sarajevo's bombed library.

It was the German ambassador to India, Michael Steiner, who turned Zubin's dream into reality. When Zubin told him about it in 2012, Steiner said he would see what he could do. He was as good as his word. The Shalimar Gardens in Srinagar constructed by Emperor Jehangir were restored and on 7 September 2013, elegantly dressed people started filing past the pink pavilion and whispering fountains under four-century-old chinar trees to hear the Bavarian State Orchestra play Beethoven and Haydn. The 2700-strong audience did have government officials and the elite, but also comprised the public, with students being allowed free entry.

It attracted widespread criticism in Kashmir where much of the population chafes at the heavy police presence in the state. There were calls for a *bandh* (general strike) to protest the event. Zubin said, 'By coming here with this great orchestra and these wonderful soloists who will perform for you this evening, there are those we have hurt inadvertently. But we only want to do good. And I promise, next time, let's do this concert free for all Kashmiris in a stadium. We don't want only a select few.' Zubin told me that 70 per cent of Kashmir had watched the concert on TV. As the capacity of the venue was limited, he wanted to perform in a stadium the next time.

'*Hum bahut khush hoon,*' said Zubin in his pidgin Hindi (he readily agrees that it is not his strong suit) as he kicked off the historic concert. Opening the concert was Abhay Rustum Sopori's folk ensemble which played with the orchestra in a 'Tribute to Kashmir'. (Sopori is a third-generation santoor player, composer and conductor.) Later, the muezzin's cry mingled with the chirping of birds and with Beethoven's Fifth Symphony and *Leonore* Overture No. 3, Haydn's Concerto for Trumpet and Orchestra (soloist Andreas Öttl) and Tchaikovsky's Violin Concerto in D Major (soloist Rachlin). Actress Gul Panag was the presenter for the evening and in the audience were Zubin's friends Hamied, and Nusli and Maureen Wadia. Hamied and Wadia are old friends of Zubin's. He says that he is beholden to them for all the financial support they have extended for his concerts in India over the years. The one in Kashmir was no exception, he says. Wadia had even provided the services of aeroplanes free of cost. Ratan Tata, who was Zarin's classmate in St Mary's, is another benefactor who has supported Zubin's concerts on numerous occasions. 'I am very grateful to them all for all their help,' he told me. Zubin ended the concert with a short encore by Sopori's group, announcing in Hindi that they had started the concert with a Kashmiri piece and they would go home after hearing another.

The programme in Srinagar was repeated at Mumbai's Jamshed

Bhabha Theatre on 9 September. The next day's line-up had the Overture from *The Marriage of Figaro*, Beethoven's Violin Concerto in D Major with Midori as soloist and, after the interval, Brahms's Fourth Symphony.

## WORLD TOUR WITH THE VIENNA PHILHARMONIC ORCHESTRA

In February 2009, the Vienna Philharmonic and Zubin embarked on one of the longest tours in the history of the orchestra in terms of the distance travelled. Some fifty years after Karajan's world tour in 1959, the orchestra gave fourteen concerts in nine cities, in six countries, across three continents.

The tour began with a concert in London in the newly renovated Royal Festival Hall on 19 February. The next day's venue was the Théâtre des Champs-Élysées in Paris, after which the ensemble flew to Philadelphia for the next concert on 24 February at Verizon Hall.

In February–March 1989, the first 'Vienna Philharmonic Week in New York' took place under the direction of Karajan. Its success made it a permanent fixture in the calendar of both the Vienna Philharmonic and Carnegie Hall. In honour of the twentieth anniversary of this event, four concerts, instead of the obligatory three, were given in 2009. The concerts included pieces by Schoenberg, Bruckner, Wolf, Marx, Schubert, Mozart, Haydn and Richard Strauss.

After the last concert, the orchestra flew to Los Angeles, Zubin's 'home' for many years, where he conducted the Vienna Philharmonic for the first time in the city. At the end of the opening concert which included Wolf, Marx and Bruckner, he turned to the audience at Walt Disney Hall and said, 'Since 1962, I have dreamed of being able to perform with this orchestra for you.' The concert was an unqualified success, with *Los Angeles Times* enthusing about the way they had made Bruckner 'glow with a special radiance'.

Much tension had preceded the event. With five hours to go for the concert, the instruments of the Philharmonic had not yet arrived and, for an orchestra whose sound is so distinct, this could have been disastrous. Zubin was a worried man. Although the Los Angeles Philharmonic had offered to lend them instruments, he knew that it simply wouldn't be the same. The musicians had arrived two days ago, but the instruments which had been placed on a later flight were delayed because of a snowstorm. In the end all was well, much to Zubin's relief. With barely an hour to spare, the plane landed in Los Angeles and the instruments were rushed to the concert hall.

As always, the Mehtas hosted a lunch for the entire orchestra at their Brentwood home on the eve of the first concert. 'There were 130 people in the garden, the whole orchestra and their wives and guests,' Zubin told an interviewer. The fare consisted of barbecue and cheesecake. Zubin said that Nancy had organized the lunch with great attention to detail. Every musician was given a Stetson cowboy hat as a gift.

The second concert consisted of Wagner's *Rienzi* Overture, the 2nd Piano Concerto of Chopin with Lang Lang as soloist, as well as Schubert's *Great* Symphony. Polkas followed as encores.

Next on the orchestra's itinerary was Beijing. It would be their fourth appearance in China following performances in 1973 (with conductors Abbado and Boskovsky), 1996 (with Zubin) and 2004 (with Ozawa). They played Schoenberg, Strauss, Mozart, Haydn and Schubert in two concerts at the spectacular National Centre for Performing Arts on 8 and 9 March 2009.

The next stopover was Mumbai, which we have discussed in detail in the previous section. The world tour concluded with another first-time event—a guest appearance of the Vienna Philharmonic in the United Arab Emirates. On 13 and 14 March, Zubin and the orchestra performed in an open-air concert at the Al Jahili Fort in Al Ain.

Zubin had been designated as conductor-in-residence at the Abu Dhabi Classics, a season of concerts aiming to bring Western classical music to new audiences in that part of the world. In April, Zubin returned to Abu Dhabi with the Maggio Musicale Fiorentino orchestra for a performance of Mahler, followed by a programme of 'Russian Landscapes' featuring the music of Mussorgsky and Tchaikovsky.

## TOURING WITH THE ISRAEL PHILHARMONIC ORCHESTRA

Zubin has been touring the world with his orchestras for decades now, and the passion and intensity he brings to his music is incredible. Most of his tours have been with the Israel Philharmonic Orchestra and, over the years, the maestro and his musicians have travelled to all corners of the globe. Few orchestras tour as much as the Israel Philharmonic, which also happens to be Israel's foremost cultural institution and ambassador of peace and goodwill. Zubin once observed, 'Anywhere the Israel Philharmonic Orchestra plays, a whole new dimension permeates the audience at each and every concert, spreading the word about the face of Israel that very few know.' He has harnessed the power of music to spread peace and has never been afraid to speak up even at the risk of being impolitic. In this, he has followed Israel Philharmonic founder Huberman who once remarked, 'The artist does not create art as an end in itself, he creates art for human beings. Humanity is the goal.'

### *South America and Spain*

In August 2009, Zubin and the Israel Philharmonic Orchestra toured South America, performing in Argentina, Uruguay and Chile. The tour started in Buenos Aires on 19 August, with a concert at the Teatro Gran Rex. The programme of Strauss and Beethoven was followed by encores of Mozart and Strauss. In a concert the next day, they played Mahler's Ninth Symphony; a piece that stands alone with no overture or concerto preceding it.

A high-speed ferry across the Plata River took the orchestra to Montevideo next. They played at the magnificent Teatro Solis which is a gem of architecture with excellent acoustics. The concert, consisting of Strauss and Beethoven, received a standing ovation. Returning to Buenos Aires, they played at the Luna Park Auditorium; it was an electrifying performance where a crowd of 6000 cheered the orchestra.

In a concert at Rosario, Argentina's third largest city, they played for an audience of 3000 people at the Metropolitano Centro de Eventos. Rosario also got a new citizen that evening with the mayor granting Zubin honorary citizenship. After a concert at Córdoba, the Israel Philharmonic Orchestra flew to Santiago in Chile. But this visit was not without its share of excitement. Bringing fruit into Chile is strictly forbidden and attracts a stiff fine. Some of the musicians, through oversight or ignorance, were guilty of doing just that and were detained at customs. Enrique Maltz, the orchestra's Spanish-speaking cellist, pleaded with the authorities that the musicians spoke only Hebrew or Russian and could not read the warnings at the airport. They had to face a trial judge but were let off—without a fine and with a stern reprimand.

The concert consisted of Mahler's Ninth, the last time they played that piece on that tour, at the beautiful Teatro Municipal. The very last concert of the tour took place in an indoor arena with an audience of 12,000, enough to fill Tel Aviv's Charles Bronfman Hall about five times. The arena is enormous and a youth orchestra was brought in a day before to rehearse and try out the sound system. It was a festive programme featuring Beethoven and old favourites by the Strauss family. The Israel Philharmonic's programmes opened Chile's celebration of 200 years of independence.

In October 2009, the orchestra performed at Madrid and Barcelona. The tour was a tribute to impresario Alfonso Aijon who had for three decades hosted the Israel Philharmonic Orchestra on their visits to Spain, organizing concerts at Madrid, Barcelona, the festivals of San Sebastian and Santander, Bilbao, Valencia and Zaragoza. In Madrid, after the ensemble played Brahms's First and Second Symphonies, Queen Sofia honoured the musicians with a visit backstage. The next evening, the orchestra performed the Third and Fourth Symphonies by Brahms. Also accompanying the orchestra was an enthusiastic group from the AFIPO. The next stop was Barcelona with a performance at the Palau de la Música. There, Aijon invited the eighteen musicians who had participated in the first Israel Philharmonic Orchestra tour thirty years ago to a festive dinner.[2]

### *Far East Tour*

A trip to Japan and South Korea followed in November of that year, with the orchestra playing in Tokyo, Nagoya and Fukuoka. They also played for the first time in a place called Tsu, a ninety-minute bus ride from Nagoya, where the 'amazing' concert hall left Zubin highly impressed. 'You can't even find it on the map, and look at what a great hall they have,' he said. The last concerts in Tokyo consisted of Beethoven's Sixth and Seventh Symphonies and were telecast live as part of a Beethoven Cycle by visiting orchestras. The Israel Philharmonic Orchestra and Zubin had been guests of Japan nine times in the past thirty years and the last evening of each visit had always been reserved for a reception for the entire ensemble at the home of Tadatsugu Sasaki, the organizer of all their tours. Zubin expressed the wish to return to Japan at least once more to make it a round figure! As we shall see, this was realized when the orchestra returned in 2014. In South Korea, they performed at the Selong Music Center in Seoul with a programme of Rachmaninoff and Mahler. The last programme was at the Arts Center.[3]

### *Azerbaijan*

The year 2010 marked the first visit by the Israel Philharmonic Orchestra to a Muslim country. In December, the orchestra visited Baku, the capital of Azerbaijan. While the Israel Philharmonic in its earlier avatar as the Palestine Orchestra had been a frequent visitor to Cairo and had even played in Beirut, this was the first time in its modern history that they performed in a Muslim country. There were two concerts which took place at the Heydar Aliyev Cultural Palace as part of the Rostropovich Festival. (Rostropovich was born in Baku.)

### *United States Tour*

The Israel Philharmonic Orchestra began its seventy-fifth anniversary tour of the United States in February 2011 with a concert in Naples, Florida. Zubin chose a programme of Haydn's Symphony No. 96,

Liszt's *Les Préludes* and Schubert's *The Great*. After the Schubert he was recalled to the stage six times, something unprecedented for Naples. The next concert was in West Palm Beach where they played Haydn's Symphony No. 96 again and Mahler's Fifth. Both came in for much praise from the critics. The *Miami Herald* wrote:

> Mehta . . . showed the orchestra's flexibility and its players' glorious ability to vary their sound from a whisper to substantial forte . . . Mehta coaxed divine sounds from his players.

The next stop was New York's Carnegie Hall where Bronfman joined the Israel Philharmonic Orchestra for Liszt's Second Piano Concerto. Then Zubin performed Mahler's Fifth which again attracted very good press. A *New York Times* review said that the orchestra made 'Mahler's borrowings from Jewish folk and liturgical traditions sound authentic and soulful . . . Mr. Mehta too is a seasoned Mahlerian.' After performances in Seattle, came concerts in San Francisco.

In San Francisco, the Israel Philharmonic Orchestra met up with the Vienna Philharmonic (led by Bychkov) and reviewers had a special opportunity to compare two world-class orchestras performing two great symphonies on the same day: Mahler's Fifth and Sixth Symphonies. Both orchestras could claim a special connection with him since Mahler had Jewish roots and was also music director of the Vienna State Opera. The *San Francisco Chronicle* observed that 'the imposing Viennese forces . . . gave the most potent performance of their stay' and the Israelis led by Zubin 'played with enormous subtlety and tact, giving the most nuanced and elegant performance' that the reviewer could remember in many years.

The US tour celebrating the seventy-fifth anniversary of the orchestra and Zubin's fifty-year association with it ended in Los Angeles at Disney Hall. An important personal milestone for Zubin was his being honoured with a star on the Hollywood Walk of Fame in a special ceremony. In a fine gesture, Nancy secretly arranged for brass players from the Israel, Los Angeles and Vienna philharmonics, who were touring Los Angeles at the time, to play at the ceremony.[4] Though the tour was marked by sporadic demonstrations against Israel's policies in the West Bank, the praise for the music was unanimous. Mark Swed, writing in *Los Angeles Times*, observed:

> And this was a very distinguished Mehta . . . demonstrating that he has aged far better than many of us who once dismissed him as brash and slapdash could ever have imagined.

### *European Tour*

At the end of August 2011, the orchestra embarked on a month-long concert tour of European festivals: twenty-one concerts in eighteen cities. They flew to Milan and then drove to Stresa on the shores of Lake Maggiore. At the Stresa Festival, which was celebrating its fiftieth anniversary, Zubin conducting the Israel Philharmonic Orchestra was a central event. The concert featuring Webern, Liszt and Tchaikovsky was greatly appreciated.

From there, they flew to Vienna for the Grafenegg Festival—held annually in a seventeenth-century castle 60 km from downtown Vienna—directed by pianist Rudolf Buchbinder. That year, events included performances by the Philadelphia Orchestra and the Vienna Philharmonic, among others.

On 1 September, an event occurred that was unique in the history of the orchestra. On that day the Israel Philharmonic Orchestra's BBC Proms Concert at London's Royal Albert Hall was disrupted, the very first time that any programme of the ensemble had suffered such a fate. The Palestine Solidarity Campaign had earlier called on the public to boycott the concert and urged the BBC to cancel it. Several demonstrators shouted as Zubin conducted Webern's *Passacaglia*. Zubin says they remained dignified and silent on stage, and continued to play the piece which typically lasts for about ten to twelve minutes.

The programme consisted of Webern, Bruch, Rimsky-Korsakov and Isaac Albéniz, with Shaham as the soloist. The performance which had been divided into four parts was targeted by protestors seated around the hall in groups. When the first group was thrown out, other groups took over and disrupted the concert four times. The rest of the audience yelled back. BBC Radio 3 had to interrupt its live telecast twice. The pro-Palestine group claimed the Israel Philharmonic Orchestra showed 'complicity in whitewashing Israel's persistent violation of international law and human rights'. Zubin who has made no bones about the fact that he considers settlements to be counterproductive to the future of both Israel and Palestine, observed, 'Even if I personally feel a Palestine should exist, that's not the way to demand it. It's self-defeating and counterproductive.'[5]

On 11 September, the Israel Philharmonic Orchestra dedicated its 9/11 concert at the Beethovenfest in Bonn to the memory of Herman Sandler, former chairman of the AFIPO board, whose life had been cut short tragically in the attack on the twin towers of the World Trade Center in New York. The orchestra was welcomed by the Beethovenfest director who reminded them that it was also the fortieth anniversary of the Israel Philharmonic's first visit to Germany. That year, the festival commemorated the 200th birth anniversary of Liszt who, like Beethoven, was a pioneer of the modern concert tradition.

During the intermission, Zubin was presented with the Furtwängler Prize for his life's work in music by his friend Sir Peter, the former general director of the Bavarian State Opera. With this, Zubin joined the ranks of conductors Masur and Nagano. While the award was a great honour for Zubin, he said, 'I don't think it's necessary to give me a special award, however. I am a musician, I make music with my favourite orchestra, and that's enough for me. Each concert is an award and a gift to me. That's enough.'[6]

The next concert was in Milan at the Teatro degli Arcimboldi which was built as a substitute while La Scala was being renovated. The concert of Liszt and Mahler was broadcast live on Italian radio. A concert followed at the Agnelli Building, the old Fiat factory in Turin. With the Israel Philharmonic Orchestra in the third week of its tour, Zubin was known to have remarked, 'At this point, I don't know what city I'm in when I wake up.' Marck, the Israel Philharmonic Orchestra bass for the last three decades, offered a quick solution: Keep the tour book open to the right page, preferably under the pillow.

A concert in Rotterdam at the Gergiev Festival where they played Mahler's Fifth brought a spontaneous standing ovation from the audience. After a concert in Luxembourg the Israel Philharmonic Orchestra played in Paris where the audience again applauded the Mahler Fifth with a standing ovation.

The next stop was Bucharest for the first concert at the Enescu Festival. The Sala Mare a Palatului which can accommodate 2500 people, was packed beyond capacity as hundreds of music lovers thronged the aisles to hear the Israel Philharmonic perform an all-Tchaikovsky concert. The second concert at the festival—where Bronfman joined Zubin and the orchestra—was even more crowded than the first and understandably so. A great soloist and a great programme were the draw.

The Israel Philharmonic's next concert, in Madrid, had Queen Sofia of Spain—a committed patron of the arts—as an honoured guest. (Madrid's museum of modern art bears her name.) During the intermission, she received Zubin, with whom she has a personal friendship, for a private audience. Queen Sofia and her late husband, King Juan Carlos, attended one of Zubin's concerts in Granada in 1968 and the royal couple and the flamboyant conductor hit it off perfectly. The programme had a Spanish flavour: Albéniz's *Iberia*, Manuel de Falla's 'Evenings in the Gardens of Spain', Debussy's *Iberia* and Rimsky-Korsakov's *Capriccio Espagnol*.

The concerts continued in Rimini where they played Mahler's Fifth for the last time on the tour. The Mahler symphony had been a staple of the seventy-fifth-anniversary year, having been played in Tel Aviv and the United States, with seven more performances on the European tour. Zubin's parting remarks as he left the stage reflected that overdose: 'That's it! Now do it with someone else!' The month-long marathon ended with a concert in Verona where the 'Spanish' programme of Albéniz, Debussy, Ravel and Rimsky-Korsakov was a huge success.

*Summer Tour of 2012*

In July 2012, Zubin and the Israel Philharmonic Orchestra had the honour of opening the prestigious Salzburg Festival. The theme of the festival was 'Ouverture Spirituelle' and Judaism was the first religion selected. Sheriff's *Revival of the Dead*, commissioned thirty years earlier for the opening of the Holocaust Museum in Amsterdam, made for a sensational start to the visit and received a fifteen-minute standing ovation. The story of the Holocaust is central to the piece which is replete with traditional Jewish music, recognizable quotations and prayers. The Collegiate Choir, baritone Thomas Hampson and cantor Carl Heiger were part of the performance which received front-page coverage in the *New York Times.*

The Israel Philharmonic played three programmes shaped by Zubin and the festival director, Alexander Pereira, each with Jewish and Israeli content: Schoenberg's *Kol Nidre*, Mahler's *Kindertotenlieder*, Sheriff's *Revival of the Dead* and Bloch's 'Sacred Service'.

They also had some fun at the festival. Since 2011 marked Zubin's fifty years of concerts, the 'benefizkonzert' which was open to the public at reduced rates had hundreds of extra seats. On the stage for a programme of Verdi, Puccini and Franz Lehár were Zubin and Domingo, both icons of the music world, and they got a standing ovation even before they started. Zubin relinquished his baton to his friend Domingo for a performance of Verdi's Overture to *La Forza del Destino.* Domingo conducted with great confidence as Zubin peeked from the wings.[7]

The penultimate concerts of the ensemble's short tour of European cities were in northern Germany where they played in Kiel and Lübeck. The programme included Beethoven, Rimsky-Korsakov and Dvořák. The tour ended in early August with concerts in Santander and Girona in Spain.

*Fall Tour, 2012*

The Israel Philharmonic began its Fall Tour in October at Vienna's

Musikverein, a concert hall celebrated both for its rich acoustics and beautiful interiors. The programme included Hindemith, Mozart and Richard Strauss. The second concert had Mendelssohn's First Piano Concerto—Chinese pianist Yuja Wang's debut in Vienna—and Mahler's Fifth. The excitement of performing Mahler in his home town and on his own stage was not lost on the players who received a standing ovation at the end of the show. Later that month, Zubin and the orchestra were part of a fundraiser in Monte Carlo to benefit the Institut Pasteur in Paris and the Weizmann Institute of Science in Rehovot.

The success of Sheriff's oratorio *Revival of the Dead* at the Salzburg Festival earlier in the year resulted in that piece being played at a New York gala sponsored by the AFIPO at Carnegie Hall. Zubin's conducting was not only technically perfect but also emotional, moving and expressive. Sheriff sat in on the rehearsals and was in the first box seat at the performance. The response from the New York audience was overwhelming. The programme also featured Schoenberg's *Kol Nidre*, and Wang joined the orchestra in Mendelssohn's First Piano Concerto, later playing two encores. A small anti-Israel demonstration did nothing to dampen the spirits of the orchestra or the audience.

The orchestra performed at a brand new concert hall in Las Vegas at the end of October. They were lucky to have escaped the battering of the deadly Hurricane Sandy that struck the East Coast; it would also have meant cancelling the concerts in New York. The orchestra, which arrived by a chartered plane, had its own security check on the runway. The programme consisted of Schubert and Brahms, with Wang as the soloist, and was received with a standing ovation. The Israel Philharmonic wound up its short tour of the US with a triumphant concert at the Disney Hall in Los Angeles. The standing-room-only crowd applauded Zubin and the orchestra both at the beginning and the end of the concert.

*Far East Tour*

In 2013, the ensemble embarked on a tour of the Far East to

celebrate the New Year in China, playing at the Great Hall of the People in Beijing, which had been decorated to look like Vienna's Musikverein. The orchestra regaled the audience with Strauss waltzes and polkas, with China's ballet stars performing the waltzes. The orchestra also played in Guangzhou and Shenzhen.

In Taipei, the highlight of the concert came when the audience—performing as if it had studied the score beforehand—joined the orchestra in the *Radetzky March*, with Zubin helping them with some conducting. The tour continued in Seoul with two concerts at the Seoul Arts Center. A reception was held in honour of the conductor and the orchestra, which was attended by the heads of two of South Korea's most powerful chaebols, Kia and Hyundai.

The Far East tour ended in Bangkok where they played an outdoor concert in front of the palace. It was organized by Kuku Uberoi, an Indian publisher of books and magazines living in Bangkok. The entire stage was filled with orchids. The concert, held in honour of the Queen's eightieth birthday, was televised live to the entire country. The programme included Beethoven, Mozart, Brahms and Rimsky-Korsakov. The soloists for the Mozart Concertante were concertmasters Ilya Konovalov and Roman Spitzer.

### *South America*

The orchestra toured South America in August of that year, performing in Bogota and Lima for the very first time. At Lima, a special visitor—Israel Philharmonic benefactor Charles Bronfman—joined the orchestra and the AFIPO for a reception. In Brazil, there were concerts in Rio de Janeiro, Campinas and São Paulo. In the outdoor concert at Campinas, the orchestra had to brave the cold, wind and rain. The entire first violin section had to crowd left into the orchestra to escape the rain. 'You were all heroes. No other orchestra would have stayed on stage under those conditions,' was Zubin's pat on the back to his musicians.

At one of the concerts in Santiago de Chile—the last stop of the tour—there was neither a programme nor presenter; as a result the audience did not realize that the concert had come to an end. When the orchestra left the stage, the audience remained in their seats, thinking the music would continue. Within minutes, the musicians rallied for a quick return and Zubin spoke to the audience to clear up the confusion before going on to play three encores. This time, there was tremendous applause for both the maestro and his ensemble.

*East Europe and Far East, 2014*

In the summer of 2014, the Israel Philharmonic Orchestra toured Russia, Finland, Lithuania, Estonia and the Czech Republic. In Prague, the orchestra played in the final concert of the Dvořákova Music Festival where, during the interval, Zubin was congratulated by none other than Dvořák's grandson. The programme featured Beethoven, Mozart and Strauss, with the last receiving a standing ovation and eliciting an encore.

Three weeks after its tour of East Europe, in October 2014, the orchestra left for the Far East. The first stop was Bangkok, a return visit to the Bangkok Festival of Dance and Drama. A tour to Ulsan in South Korea followed. It is a city which boasts of the largest car-manufacturing facility in the world and also the largest shipyard (both owned by Hyundai). Rami Ungar, an Israeli businessman whose ships transport cars, was the sponsor. (His ships carry a large number of Hyundai and Kia cars.)

In Tokyo, the Israel Philharmonic joined the Tsunami Violin Project, performing on a unique quartet of string instruments made out of wood torn from homes affected by the 2011 tsunami. They also played in Osaka, Mie, Nagoya and Fukuoka. The highlight of the visit was the orchestra's first performance in Singapore. The tour ended after concerts in Beijing, Xiamen and Zhuhai in China. In Zhuhai, they made a print of Zubin's hand for the concert hall.

# 'Conducting *Is* Communication'

A CONDUCTOR'S TASK IS Herculean. He must not only direct in the sense intended by the composer, correct the faults of the players, many of whom may themselves have formed a conception of that work, but above all, he must be a focal point—an evocative and inspirational unifying force for 100 or so musicians who look up to him for guidance. A composer depends on a host of intermediaries to bring his work before the public—intermediaries who may be intelligent or stupid, active or inert, who have the power to illuminate or destroy the work. According to the French composer Berlioz, a bad musician ruins only his part; the incompetent conductor ruins everything.

Being a conductor is not just an onerous responsibility but a mysterious undertaking as well, because it must be accompanied only by gestures, something which cannot be taught beyond a rudimentary point. Conductor Leinsdorf has written that the 'gesture is of crucial importance in conducting as long as it carries a message'. Walter Legge, an influential figure in the recording of classical music in years gone by, who was the founder of the Philharmonia Orchestra of London, said that 'sound comes from gesture' and a conductor's gesture is the prolongation of his musical will. It is his means of communication. Conducting is the power of communicating a musical idea by the use of the hands.[1]

Power seems to go with the profession. Consider this: One person enters a hall and it becomes quiet automatically. He raises a small white stick and there is silence followed by music. Such a response to one's presence is more than what most mortals can be expected to bear without effect. The ego which must be immense for even entering the profession is further enlarged. Price once said, 'The great conductors have egos that are indescribable. They have no business being on the podium if that is not the case.'[2]

Zubin does not see his position as conductor as one of all-encompassing power or omniscience. While he agrees that the conductor is in a privileged position to know all the parts, he believes that his primary job is as a communicator. 'First of all, he is a communicator. He must communicate his knowledge, his perception, and his vision of the composer's message. As conductors we analyse the score and since we conduct music that spans 400 years, we have to know all the styles in order to interpret it to an orchestra.'[3] In an interview to *The Hindu* in December 2005, Zubin said, 'What is conducting? Conducting is communication. And what I communicate at the moment is what I feel and what my musicians need. Because I am there for them. They also appear in the music. One should never forget that.'

♫

In the 1930s there were two poles of conducting. At one end was Toscanini, the literalist who refused to read anything into music but music itself. His polar opposite was Furtwängler who seldom conducted the same piece of music the same way twice. He once said, 'The conductor has one arch-enemy—routine.'[4] History bears testimony to the fact that he never gave a routine performance. Mystical and metaphysical in his approach, he represented fluctuation of tempo spontaneity, a German tradition that stemmed from Wagner's ideas about conducting. Music is more than black and white notes on a printed score. The important thing is what lies between the notes.[5]

Music critic Cardus wrote in the Manchester *Guardian* in 1954 of Furtwängler's conducting style:

> He did not regard the printed notes of the score as a final statement, but rather as so many symbols of an imaginative conception, ever changing and always to be felt and realised subjectively . . . Not since Nikisch, of whom he was a disciple, has a greater personal interpreter of orchestral and opera music than Furtwängler been heard.[6]

An admirer of Furtwängler, Zubin notes how he spoke of the 'message between the music sheets'. Listening to Furtwängler, he said, one felt that he had inspired his players to give something over and above the score and their normal abilities. Furtwängler made every concert an intense, emotional experience for himself and his audience. He remembers Krips telling him that with Furtwängler, the orchestra played more colourfully than with other conductors.[7] Schonberg says that Furtwängler divided the responsibility of interpretation between himself and the orchestra and, given his unconventional baton technique, this was also inevitable: the orchestra would have had to have a great deal of initiative since his beat lacked the decisiveness that helps enforce precision in an ensemble. Nor was he very articulate. Cellist Piatigorsky told a charming story of Furtwängler pleading with the orchestra. 'Gentleman, this phrase must be—it must—it must—you know what I mean—please try it again—please.'[8]

The two conductors who influenced Zubin the most are Toscanini and Furtwängler—the former for his fidelity to the score and the latter for being 'emotionally staggering'. Toscanini did inject emotion into his conducting and there was great fervour and strength in it but on the whole he presented the work as he felt the composer put it down on paper. When I asked Zubin about this he said, 'My generation was fortunate that it inherited both these philosophies. Both are completely valid. We want to know what is between the notes, what the composer really intended, but in keeping with Toscanini, we do not depart from the written score for even a one-eighth note.'[9] Some of the musicians who played under Toscanini, however, took literalism to its extreme. They followed the score blindly and, in the process, became mechanical musicians. Zubin says that one is likely to discover something new in a piece one is familiar with, just as one is likely to discover something new in a painting while scrutinizing it carefully.

♫

Some conductors do not give the players the feeling that they are being led. When Wagner conducted, each player believed himself to be freely following his own feeling; in reality, it was Wagner's mighty will that had prevailed, so that all the musicians were doing was following the leader. The kind of effect the personality of a conductor has on the orchestra is narrated by Vaughan in his biography of Karajan. He examined a video of Kaye doing his comedy routine with the New York Philharmonic, something we have already touched upon in a previous chapter. After the fun had ended, he spent five or ten minutes conducting in a straightforward manner. Vaughan says that Kaye was 'a funny, sort of goofy, erratic fellow'[10] and that is exactly how the orchestra was sounding: slightly goofy and erratic. The conclusion is inescapable that the conductor brings to the podium not only his musical knowledge and talent, but also his personality. 'His is a form of naked leadership, the results of which are immediately apparent. All else being equal, the conductor plays what *he* is.'[11] As Schonberg put it, 'Conducting, like any other means of expression, is the man.'[12]

An incident will explain what this means. Karajan was rehearsing Wagner's *Tannhäuser* at La Scala and, when he came to a slow choral section, he told the orchestra to go on because he wanted to hear it from further back. The conductor Sabata who happened to be present at that rehearsal, stood in for Karajan. The moment he took over, there was a change in the music just by the personality he brought to the orchestra. Because he had conducted the orchestra for twenty-five years, there was a way of conducting that was *his* way. The moment he took over, the players automatically slipped into *his* way of conducting. Thus when we entrust someone with the playing of a piece, we must realize that it is *his* playing of it. Zubin agrees that personality does seep in but it is the message of the composer that should be of primary importance.[13]

Music, according to Walter, has a 'curious propensity': in 'acoustic representation music becomes a transmitter of personality' in much the same way that metal transmits heat. It transmits the ego of the performer more directly to the listener than any other medium of direct communication from one human being to another. In Zubin's case, his innate showmanship displayed what Munch called the 'magic emanation' and what his fans see as sensual magnetism. 'The image of both man and his music remains at best flaming, romantic, daunting, majestic, muscular, hot-eyed, ego-based and swinging.'[14] Zubin has never been known for the choreographic movements that characterized Bernstein; his beat is clear and podium mannerism restrained and economical. 'Nevertheless an unusual degree of personality and sex appeal does get transmitted from his podium to the audience.'[15]

Every orchestra has a distinctive character but because of a conductor's influence, ensembles can start sounding similar. Zubin says that the orchestras he has been associated with have started becoming similar, perhaps because 80 per cent of his repertoire revolves around the old and new Vienna sound, although they don't play Wagner in Israel. 'It all depends on the repertoire. Today's orchestras are so deft and flexible that it is simpler to absorb different styles within a single concert. I remember a concert with the Berlin Philharmonic when we played French pieces in the first half and German pieces in the second half. So one can hear different colours in the same evening, if the conductor is capable. It all depends on his knowledge and way of conducting the orchestra,' he said.[16]

Conducting is a mystical experience and the ability to transmit one's musical convictions is something that is inherent. But it can be polished and refined. For Karajan, conducting without a score was just such a refinement. He said that the score came between him and the music. 'When I have learned scores,' he said, 'I try to forget at the end what I have seen, because seeing and hearing are two different things.' During a concert he didn't hear the music any more—he just lived it. 'Every concert is a mystical experience, an ecstasy. You step out of yourself, or what you think is yourself. You no longer command it. It is a form of grace.'[17]

Zubin too believes that conducting is a mystical profession. He feels that it is a suggestive craft and after one knows the score, the style and the composer, there is a mystical element in the performance of a work that transcends practicality. 'Something that you cannot describe happens between the conductor and the orchestra.' Explaining the process behind the magic, Zubin says that in rehearsals, the conductor concentrates first on the practical aspects: is the orchestra playing together; is it playing in tune? With a great orchestra like the Israel Philharmonic, he takes 90 per cent for granted but they still have to work on the remaining 10 per cent. He says, 'That part is not so mystical, it is hard work getting that pack of cards to stand on its own. Then you laminate it, you shine lights on it, you paint it . . .'

He believes that people should first see a work the way the composer intended it. While he does not underestimate the concern for *Werktreue* (being faithful to the score) which he thinks is very important, he also believes that a concern for *Werktreue* which becomes a slavish faithfulness to the score, makes for a mechanical rendering of the music. An artiste has everything to do with how the music sounds. All the composer can do is to suggest. Notation is an inexact science. A composer writes 'allegro' but his ideas of the pace of that 'allegro' have to be interpreted by an artiste born 200 years later and no two artistes have exactly the same idea about the original marking. Composers have been willing to give interpreters a great deal of liberty as long as the intent and feeling of the piece are observed. 'That's why we call it interpretation. You have to know the composer's style, his other works where similar allegros were written, to correlate them. A lot of study and thinking goes into the analysing of any score.'[18]

There is a vast difference in the way different artistes play, for example, a Chopin piece. According to Schonberg the notes and note values are all faithfully observed, the tempi are more or less similar, and the 'work is recognizably the same, but it still sounds different'. He writes:

> Most musicians today insist that their primary aim is 'to express the wishes of the composer'. But every age sees a composer differently. . . . Too many things have changed, not the least of which are the instruments themselves, not to mention pitch or problems of ornamentation . . . The closer we try to 'express the message of the composer' by playing exactly what he wrote and no more, the farther we may be getting away from his message. [19]

The German physicist Werner Heisenberg believed that just the act of studying something would transform it. Similarly Karajan believed that with music, just taking a composition and giving it to an orchestra transforms it. 'Unless one agrees with this, one shouldn't make music.'[20] Sometimes just the printing of music alters the way it is played. On one occasion, the Vienna Philharmonic was given new music sheets because the old score had faded. The orchestra got lost because it was different visually and the breaks came at different times.

The reading of a piece changes over time. Zubin says that he never gets bored with a classical piece like *Eroica* and can play it every day but the same could not be said of a composition like Strauss's *Ein Heldenleben*. 'When we play something like that again and again on tour, it's hard to stay fresh. So sometimes, I invent things in the middle of the performance to keep the players on their toes.' In Vienna, Zubin says, he learned the importance of clear communication with his musicians and to that end he has mostly avoided the podium acrobatics used by some of his colleagues. He calls his relationship with his orchestra 'a benevolent dictatorship'. But there is a limit to being democratic, he cautions.

While Zubin is open to discussion, he insists that a certain basic discipline be maintained without which there would be chaos. Someone has to take the final musical decisions and that person is the conductor. For example, pick up and tempo can only be decided by the conductor since it would be nothing short of catastrophic to let each of the sixteen violinists decide which tempo a symphony should have. Similarly, if a soloist has a particular idea about how a piece should be played, Zubin gives him that liberty, provided he plays it within his general conception of the music. 'If he is completely opposite then, of course, we have a discussion. It happens rarely though.'[21]

The best way to make musicians follow the conductor is by coaxing and cajoling, with a lot of give and take. Often musicians rehearse with a conductor who is different from the one who is finally going to conduct the performance, and this requires the musicians to be flexible in their approach to music-making. His approach can be likened to that of Mendelssohn who strove for a community of equals, united by a love of music. But he does not let anybody take advantage of him.

He feels that the musicians should be able to depend on him and his 'fundamental musical perception'. Zubin sees himself as more of a coordinator and facilitator. The art of conducting, according to him, lies in inspiring, but with discipline—the musicians must have a sure feeling that they can trust the conductor and his musical conceptions. A conductor must be the conscience of the orchestra and is not only obliged to be true to the discipline (of conducting) but also to the intent of the composer.

Zubin also believes in giving respect to his musicians. They have played with different conductors, gathering vital experience from those performances. He also believes in a free exchange of ideas with his musicians and encourages them to express doubts if they think a certain piece has not been interpreted correctly. But a line has to be drawn somewhere. Every conductor, by virtue of his position, must have something of the dictator in him. Zubin regrets it if he has hurt musicians under him unintentionally or otherwise and sees himself as a father figure, confessor and musical adviser to his players. He is known to have reprimanded society ladies for treating orchestra players as social inferiors and, on one occasion, he even refused to attend a party unless they were invited.

Zubin admits it is difficult dealing with different orchestras and different musicians. The New York Philharmonic 'was not an easy orchestra to deal with' and, he says indulgently, the members of the Israel Philharmonic argue with him often. 'Musicians like to discuss,' he says. 'I am the kind of conductor who invites that. There are conductors who stand aloof; they have more peace of mind than some of us. But we invite discussions and criticism.'

Nothing upsets him more than an uninvolved musician. The work of a conductor is to create zest and not boredom, and this is why Zubin is distressed by players who merely do their 'job'. Zubin believes in giving and asking for 100 per cent. The love Zubin feels for a piece of music always shines through. Zubin also has the ability to present music which is not in the top league in the best possible light. Also, he can make a familiar piece sound different because, according to him, 'music is more than black notes on a white page. The important thing is what lies between the notes.'

♫

An orchestral player once told the great Hans Richter of the Vienna State Opera about his first experience of conducting. 'How did it go?' asked Richter. 'Very well indeed,' replied the player and then added, 'this business of conducting is really quite simple.' From behind a shielding hand, Richter said, 'I beg you, don't give us away.'[22] That conducting is not only easy but also a mechanical activity is what some naively believe. They think that the essential function of a conductor is beating time and his foremost task is to keep the players together. No doubt this is an error fostered by appearances: one sees a single person in front of many musicians and his task appears to be to bring order and unity among the players.

What the spectator does not see is the transmission of spiritual impulses from the conductor to the players; nor does he realize the musical and emotional understanding that has been established in the preceding rehearsals. Contrary to appearances, it is in fact, as Walter wrote, a 'single person who is making music, playing on the orchestra as on a living instrument', transforming its many components into a unity. Both the conductor's conception of the music and his personality resonate in the way the orchestra plays: it is a conductor's recreative inspiration which reveals through the musicians the inner meaning of a piece of music as he understands and interprets it.

A conductor has to make music by exerting his influence on others both as a man and as a musician; his task is as much a personal one as it is an artistic one. He who cannot deal with people or exert his influence on them is not fully qualified for this profession. It is the conductor's will, and it is the musicians' obligation; and since such obligation which has an element of depersonalization in it cannot yield artistic results, the conductor must persuade his musicians to become willing participants.

A player's task is a partial one; a conductor, on the other hand, bears the entire responsibility for the performance. In this task, empathy is most important. It is this empathy which will enable him to play on the orchestra, his instrument, with the freedom of a soloist. But the means by which a conductor can find audible expression of his conception are obscure. A conductor, by virtue of his inner musical intensity and the sheer power of his personality which he exerts on his musicians, must create an atmosphere of spiritual communion. 'Every keen observer will have perceived in this collaboration the workings of deep instinctive forces of the soul; at the very least he will have received an intimation of an irrational element in the influence of the one on the many.'[23] It is this instinctive faculty for immediately transmitting one's own musical impulses to the orchestra that is the sign of true talent for conducting. Musicians can immediately sense innate talent and flair. As Barenboim puts it, 'An orchestra tolerates inexperience but not lack of talent.'[24]

A conductor must not only have the talent, he must also know his music inside out. Zubin says that if a conductor mounts the podium without knowing exactly what he wants, the orchestra senses that immediately and he loses his authority. He firmly believes that music comes from within and the conductor has to further it through his capacity for communication with his musicians. Can conducting be taught? Many of the greats learned on the job, but Zubin feels that being taught the art helps because communicating with the body does not come naturally to everybody. Knowledge, psychology and human relations have a lot to do with it.

The concertmaster is like the prime minister of the orchestra and it is essential that he shares the conductor's musical conception. When differences arise, Zubin listens and, if convinced, gladly accepts the other point of view. In either case, he says, 'A logical end must result.' Commenting on the soloists, he says, 'The soloists have individual lines written for them by the composer. They are great musicians, the best in their profession. They have an opinion about how to play their solos. When it matches my concept of the piece, I, as a conductor, give them the freedom to follow that interpretation.' On another occasion, he said, 'My position is to make the orchestra feel comfortable in interpreting my vision of the piece. The overall picture is mine. The details I leave very often to the individual musicians playing their little solos.'

One of the greatest pitfalls a conductor must avoid is routine. Habit and complacency are dangerous, and older musicians especially show a resistance to change. The 'I have always played it this way' syndrome, whether it expresses itself verbally or through a hostile silence, can threaten a performance if the conductor is not careful. The more frequently a work has been performed and the better the technique has become, the more careful a conductor must be to avoid a habitual performance. When interpretation and rendering have become stale, and when the heartfelt content has vanished, then only the empty shell remains.

Zubin feels that routine which doesn't touch the soul, even if it is of a very high standard, is not appealing. He gave the example of a tour to South America with the Maggio Musicale Fiorentino orchestra. The response they received was better than anything the New York Philharmonic or even the Israel Philharmonic Orchestra had ever got. The quality of the Florence orchestra was not as good as the other two but Zubin said most members of the public don't really understand the finer nuances and they don't care! What made the concert a success was the involvement of the orchestra and love for what they were doing. They were playing with their heart and that made all the difference.

In this connection it is pertinent to point out that the masterpieces become greater and more beautiful with every encounter. A classic endures over time by revealing new and unexpected aspects of itself in interpretation and performance. As Walter said of Mozart's Symphony No. 40 in G Minor: 'Today I think I know it, but tomorrow it may be new to me; for I have often thought before that I have known it, only to find later that it was new to me.'[25]

Some degree of external discipline is indispensable in the process of making music but when that impedes the free flow of ideas, it becomes a barrier to the artistic communication between the conductor and the players. In any case, the harsh orchestral discipline of the podium tyrants has long since given way to a socially dignified form of orderly cooperation. The concept of discipline—in its general connotation of dutiful obedience—is of a negative nature: the more it is stressed, the more detrimental it becomes to the spiritual rapport between the conductor and his orchestra. In general, methods such as psychological empathy, persuasion and moral intermediation will have a more productive effect than a violent manner which will breed resistance and result in the intimidation of the orchestral players.

If a musician doesn't like the conductor and doesn't feel inspired, he cannot open up to him. Zubin recalled an incident in Los Angeles when there was a bit of tension between him and his orchestra. They played correctly but there was no love in it. Sometimes the boot can be on the other foot as well. He talks about how, on one occasion, he was mad at the orchestra and stopped cooperating while they were playing Brahms's First Symphony. He just let them play and they didn't know what to do. They were furious with him afterwards but he says he was upset with them first.[26]

Zubin is acclaimed by players, soloists and critics for his 'baton technique', the technical facility that allows a conductor to present a beat that is clear and easy to follow, to cue in entrances dependably, and to unify the playing into a crisp, precise sound. But a distinguished performance is not just a matter of clear conducting and good baton technique. The orchestra must be willing to follow the conductor's lead. A conductor must, as we have noted before, possess the inbred talent to lead, something Zubin possesses in abundant measure. But his leadership manifests itself in a deceptively collaborative manner, often couching his orders in the form of a question, 'Can we do that again just one more time?' He may be a 'nice guy' but his strength of will leaves no doubt and demonstrates unequivocally that he is the boss. Timpanist Kraft of the New York Philharmonic said that Zubin was never rude. He would draw out discipline with just a look or a shrug. 'He was always concerned about hurting others' feelings. He corrected many mistakes privately.'[27]

♫

Zubin does not keep track of how frequently he has played a particular musical piece but there are some he has played at least a hundred times. Brahms's Second Symphony or *Eroica* he can play with little rehearsal, but if it is a Schumann symphony, he always has to rehearse well and, when the performance is a success, it gives him a sense of fulfilment. Bruckner's Eighth is a personal favourite that he looks forward to conducting each time. Mahler's music, he says, is always a challenge to conduct, requiring all his energy and concentration. He considers Mahler's Seventh Symphony—which he has led several times—one of the most difficult pieces to conduct in the entire corpus of musical literature, but in his opinion, it has not been adequately recognized by the public. He is also rather proud of his recording of Mahler's Fifth with the New York Philharmonic.

At home, Zubin listens to chamber music, especially late quartets of Haydn and Beethoven. He admits he doesn't particularly care for British composers, with the exception of Elgar. An interesting fact about the master conductor's career is that he has never conducted at Bayreuth (the annual festival in Bavaria devoted to Wagner's operas) despite invitations from Wieland Wagner, the opera director and Richard Wagner's grandson, in the early years because his commitments with the Israel Philharmonic did not afford him the opportunity to get away for three months.[28]

He is particularly fond of Brahms, as was his father. Since his first exposure to the German composer's music, Zubin says, he has felt a kind of spiritual connection with it. In an interview, he once said that the four Brahms symphonies comprised one of the reasons he wanted to be a conductor. 'I knew all four Brahms symphonies, I wouldn't say intimately or even analytically, in Bombay, but I knew them.' He also heard the great conductors in Vienna lead all four Brahms symphonies. It was Brahms's First conducted by Böhm that introduced Zubin to the magic of orchestral sound. Again, he auditioned the first movement of the Brahms First for Solti when he wanted to be his assistant in Los Angeles, and Solti loved it. Sony Records asked him to record all four symphonies. He did so, first with the New York Philharmonic, and later with the Israel Philharmonic.

Like many others, Zubin conducts from memory. His method of committing scores to memory involves a detailed study of the structure of the music. He has a definite system and there is no mental photography involved—he does not attempt to see the printed page in his mind's eye. 'I always study with the form of the music in mind. I dissect a score completely when I study it. Memorization occurs when I put it back together again. I make no attempt to memorize everything I conduct—only the music I want to keep permanently in my repertoire.'[29]

Critics have commented on Zubin's 'visually arresting style' which they feel is designed to conduct the audience. Zubin, who considers showmanship to be an asset in his profession, defends his style, saying, 'Intellectual snobs forget that showmanship is a great asset to the profession. We have to be able to bring certain things over to the public magnetically, and that requires acting.'[30] Also, there is rare electricity that flows between him and the instrumental soloist or singer. 'Sometimes I purposely exaggerate my actions for the sake of drawing out the players, or to make the music sound more powerful. But on the whole, I think I am a very economical conductor.'[31] When questioned about his flamboyant style by *Frontline* magazine, the maestro replied, 'It all comes from the music . . . I do whatever the music demands.'

For Zubin, every movement he makes has a purpose. 'The conductor must think ahead and build an arc or a point of great intimacy. The musician is too busy. It's like jumping with a horse over a fence. It's the horse that is jumping but you are holding the reins. Otherwise, you are going to fall on your head.'[32] Commenting on the stage mannerisms of classical musicians, Zukerman observes that since conductors are not actors, they do not practise in front of the mirror. But the public exhibition factor cannot be ignored. The audience is a critical mass for any performer and he or she will, to a greater or lesser degree, make some extramusical effort to engage them.[33]

Zubin is also acutely aware that his eyes are as communicative as his baton and his hands. The fact that he conducts from memory enables him to use his face and eyes to good effect. He maintains eye contact with the musicians at all times. He also has a lively repertory of facial expressions: nods, smiles, frowns, quizzical looks. His face and gestures serve as an instant reinforcement for the players. He said, 'Half of our trade is in the eyes. There is a certain split second when the conductor gives with his eyes the indication of what and how the orchestra should play. It is a highly personal relationship. There is an implicit trust and understanding between conductor and musicians that cannot be imparted with the hands alone. And you cannot have a conversation on stage.'[34]

Like Zubin, Abbado believed that much of what he sought from his musicians was communicated through his eyes and called them his most important tool. For Ozawa, too, eye contact with players is critical. On the other hand, Karajan used to conduct with his eyes closed. He conducted from memory and hence needed to look at nothing. This was partly to avoid visual distraction but, as he later explained, 'After I learn a score, at the end I try and forget what I have seen, because seeing and hearing are two such different things.'

Walter tells us of the time when deteriorating eyesight forced him to abandon the score while conducting. Once that happened, he felt as though nothing stood between his internal image of the music and his communication with the orchestra. He agreed with conductor Bülow who decisively drew the line between those conductors 'who have the score in their heads and those who have their head in the score'. Independence from the score adds to the intensity and spontaneity of music-making, and fosters a close spiritual contact with the orchestra. Thus, in conducting, there are no rules, only guidelines. If the end result is successful, then even the most eccentric approach can be tolerated.

♫

Even the most complicated task that a conductor has to carry out in the concert hall is, in a sense, straightforward compared to the responsibilities he has in opera. The problems symphonic works pose to the conductor can be solved by purely musical endeavours. In opera, however, things are very different. Here his vision has to make itself felt in conjunction with the singers, always keeping the dramatic process in mind. He must allow the singer an adequate position in the interpretation as a whole. The singer too must not merely view his task as a musician but also be an active participant in the action on the stage. It is not enough for the conductor to take an interest in the music alone: his impulses should travel from the proscenium to the stage. Many good conductors fail in opera, and many opera conductors are unable to make a tangible difference to symphonic music. And, once in a while, there are conductors like Zubin who can acquire a technique without operatic training.

The conductor must be able to identify with the characters of an opera if he is to be a convincing interpreter of the music of these scenes. From such participation will grow his understanding of the individual tasks of the singers. It will enable him to be their adviser and to lend them that feeling of freedom which they need in order to give an individual stamp to their roles; and yet limit them sufficiently for their stage presence to be musically and emotionally compatible with one another and with the conductor's general interpretation. Thus a conductor's vision must manifest in an opera by encompassing all individual impersonations on the stage and by integrating all dramatic elements of the action in his unified interpretation of the work. 'It's possible that conducting a Mozart symphony could sometimes prove more challenging but opera has many more facets to it,' Zubin told me. 'You are conducting singers, following singers, the orchestra is following singers, singers are following the orchestra—it is all very complex.'[35]

The combination of the visible and the audible, of word and music, action and scenery and lighting—though related, are yet heterogeneous and do not easily become a perfect organic unity. A conductor's heart 'must beat with the orchestra and at the same time pulsate in the stage action; he must proffer his own ego, but also that of every dramatic personage on the stage; he must dictate, and at the same time adapt himself.'[36] The conductor has to be a complete musician but his music-making must complement those dramatic impulses that find their expression in the stage action. It takes many years to gain sufficient experience with opera, even with the symphonic repertoire. In opera, he must conduct it once just to know what is going on.

Zubin feels that opera and the symphonic repertoire present completely different challenges. With opera one has to be in control of both the stage and the orchestra at the same time. And this dialogue between the stage and the orchestra is based on the conductor's knowledge of when it is time to accompany, rather than conduct, a singer. Similarly, he must know when to conduct a scene. For instance, in the second act of *Tosca*, if the conductor makes the mistake of accompanying the singers, all the suspense is lost. It is fundamental to conduct the drama. Zubin gives the example of a performance of *Tosca* in Valencia in 2011 where there was a real partnership between him and Bryn Terfel who played Scarpia. Many singers do not feel this relationship but he says that his friend Domingo is an expert in maintaining this contact with the conductor.[37]

Zubin is not averse to giving singers flexibility—an opportunity to express themselves. In Wagner, where the words are more important, he gives the singers more liberty. *Das Rheingold* and *Siegfried* are a conversation from beginning to end and therefore he feels that the text should be highlighted and the music perceived as part of the background. This, he believes, is the most important goal to be achieved in Wagner's operas. The conductor and the director have to help the singers develop the drama on stage.[38]

# Epilogue

IN 2016 AS THIS volume goes to press, Zubin is a few months shy of his eightieth birthday. Not many will dispute the fact that he has spent at least the last three decades of his life at the summit of his profession. His devotion to his art borders on obsession and his place in its hierarchy is unassailable. As Judy Pasternak put it in *Los Angeles Times*, Zubin Mehta has 'adroitly manoeuvred through a long career from wunderkind to *éminence grise*, attracting criticism for his flamboyance while inspiring affection for the way he wields both his baton and the political power of his fame'. Today, there are several Indian musicians in world-class orchestras abroad. For them, the impossible became possible because Zubin Mehta blazed a trail. They could do it because he did it first. This also explains the buzz which accompanies Zubin's visits to India. He has risen to the very top in a profession which is in a sense alien, and one in which an Indian was hardly expected to shine, let alone bestride the podium like a colossus.

The labyrinthine depth of Zubin's musical knowledge is staggering. He is best known as a leader of the late-Romantic and early-modern repertoire, and his sharp insights into the Second Viennese School can be explained partly by his teacher Swarowsky's training at the feet of the flagbearers of that school, Schoenberg and Webern. His treatment of the old masters Mozart and Beethoven was initially described as 'more uneven' but over the years his interpretation of their work has also attracted praise. Zubin is a big fan of the music of Mozart. Ever since he started doing Mozart operas with some regularity, he says, the composer's music has enriched his life.[1]

An astrologer had foretold greatness when he was about to leave for Vienna in 1954, and his professors and colleagues, and older conductors saw great potential in him. Zubin himself has always been aware of the presence of unseen powers in his life. As he told his early biographers Bookspan and Yockey, 'Always at the right time, the idea comes or the opportunity presents itself. Something guides me. I feel that very strongly, that protecting force over me.'[2]

Unsurprisingly, it has also been a life rich with honours, awards and appreciation. In 1976, the Italian government awarded him the honorary title of 'Commendatore'. France awarded him the Medaille d'Or Vermeil and Commandeur des Arts et des Lettres. He has been bestowed the Hans von Bülow Medal by the Berlin Philharmonic and the Defender of Jerusalem Award by Israel, the only non-Israeli to receive it. Zubin received honorary doctorate degrees from Brown University, the Hebrew University of Jerusalem, Tel Aviv University and the Weizmann Institute of Science, Florence University, Westminster Choir College, Jewish Theological Seminary, Brooklyn College and Colgate University.

Böhm willed him the Nikisch ring, testimony that Zubin is regarded by many to be the true torchbearer of the Wagnerian tradition. In 1979, two years before he died, Böhm told Zubin in New York that he planned to leave the Nikisch ring to him. Böhm died in August 1981 and in November of that year, his son Karlheinz presented Zubin with the ring at a brief event in Vienna's Musikverein. Böhm wore the ring—a rare, dark-brown pearl set within a circle of diamonds—for many years. Zubin, less trusting of his ability not to lose it, kept it safely locked away. As a fitting end to the day on which the ring was given to Zubin, he conducted the first of five scheduled performances of *Die Walküre* at the Vienna State Opera. Zubin told me that he has given the ring to Barenboim who, he is sure, will pass it on to another conductor in keeping with Böhm's original vision.[3]

Zubin was one of eight distinguished recipients of the first Global Youth Peace and Tolerance Award presented by the DaCapo Foundation in association with Children Uniting Nations and Friends of the United Nations. Other awards include the Israel-based Wolf Foundation Prize for music, the Vienna Philharmonic Ring of Honor and the Gabriela Mistral Prize.

In 1999, Leah Rabin presented Zubin the United Nations' Lifetime Achievement Peace and Tolerance Award. In 2001, he was made an honorary member of the Vienna Philharmonic. He is an honorary citizen of both Florence and Tel Aviv, and was made an honorary member of the Vienna State Opera in 1997. In 2001, the government of India honoured Zubin with the Padma Vibhushan, India's second highest civilian award (he had received the Padma Bhushan as far back as 1965). In April of the same year, the then President of France, Jacques Chirac, named him Chevalier de la Légion d'Honneur. In January 2004, the Munich Philharmonic Orchestra bestowed the title of Honorary Conductor on Zubin and, in 2005, he was awarded the Bayerische Verdienstorden, the Bavarian Distinguished Service Cross. Recently, he added the Deutsche Verdienstkreuz, the German cross of merit, and the Cavalieri di Gran Croce of Italy to his collection.

In December 2006, Zubin was among the five stalwarts who were honoured by the John F. Kennedy Center for the Performing Arts for their lifetime contribution to arts and entertainment. The other four recipients were Dolly Parton, Smokey Robinson, Steven Spielberg and Sir Andrew Lloyd Webber. The award meant a lot to Zubin who said that anyone who has worked and dedicated himself for over thirty years to the arts in the US as he has done, knows the immense honour that the Kennedy awards signify. Kennedy Center chairman Stephen A. Schwarzman declared that Zubin's profound artistry and devotion to music made him a 'world treasure'. In 2007, Zubin shared the Dan David Prize with French composer Pascal Dusapin (for the present time dimension) for his contribution to music and won the Praemium Imperiale from Japan in October 2008. A rare honour for a classical music conductor came his way when he received a star (No. 2434) on Hollywood's Walk of Fame in 2011. It coincided with his fiftieth anniversary as a conductor. Actor and friend, ninety-four-year-old Kirk Douglas, joined Zubin at the ceremony near the north-east corner of Hollywood Boulevard and Vine Street. Zubin said that he didn't know how many classical musicians had stars to their name, but accepted the honour on behalf of them and for all the other classical musicians who had yet to be honoured. Later that day, he conducted the Israel Philharmonic Orchestra in a concert at the Walt Disney Concert Hall.

He is the only classical musician with a Kennedy Center Award, a star on the Hollywood Walk of Fame and even a Muppet named after him, making him the only living conductor to enjoy a career that spills over into pop culture. This and the Three Tenors concert have helped establish him as a name beyond the traditional classical music community. Google his name and there are 5,60,000-plus results—and this, when Zubin has no online presence on Twitter or Facebook. He does have a homepage, though he cannot remember having seen it. For such matters, he relies on his assistant.

Zubin, now one of the grand old men of the baton, is valued by orchestral players wherever he goes. Talent is not the only prerequisite for becoming a superstar. It is a unique and fortuitous combination of other elements that complement the talent to produce the superstar. Zubin retains the immense musical virtuosity and magnetism coupled with theatrical flair which brought him to international notice five decades ago. He still cuts a dashing figure and, no doubt, like Karajan, believes that his 'musical mission puts him beyond reproach'.

What Rockwell wrote in the *New York Times* couldn't be truer of Zubin:

> Star conductors and patient orchestra builders can be combined within one man, as Stokowski and Koussevitzky proved. But more commonly they are separate. Charismatic conducting demands flair, drama, flamboyance and . . . interpretive genius. Orchestra building requires stern but gentle attributes: a willingness to enhance the orchestra's discipline and sense of self through clear, efficient direction and a firm yet kindly ability to prod underachievers and

root out incompetents. Orchestra building is an administrative skill as much as anything else . . .

Notwithstanding the tepid and sometimes hostile reviews of Zubin's style of conducting in New York, his track record in Montreal, Los Angeles, Israel, New York, Florence and finally Valencia clearly shows that he is that rare conductor who is both a superstar on the podium and a remarkable institution builder. (He has also been known to encourage and nurture a large number of musicians and conductors. In recent times, Zubin spotted the talent in Carlo Montanaro, formerly a violinist at the Maggio orchestra, and encouraged him to take up conducting, even writing a letter of recommendation to the academy in Vienna. Israeli conductor Nir Kabaretti, formerly an assistant to Zubin in Florence, was another who received much encouragement.)

The trademark Central European tone of the Israel Philharmonic Orchestra is always in evidence—another testament to Zubin's strength as a conductor. He says that because of his influence, over the years his other orchestras have developed a similar sound. The renowned mezzo-soprano Christa Ludwig said that the only places where she heard the sound Karajan evoked from the Vienna Philharmonic were in Philadelphia and Tel Aviv.

♫

In 2014, Zubin lost two old friends: in January, Abbado succumbed to cancer and passed away at his home in Bologna, Italy, while in July, Maazel died in Virginia, United States. A few days after Abbado's demise, Zubin conducted the Berlin Philharmonic in a concert in his honour. After a speech by Martin Hoffman, the director of the Berlin Philharmonic, the audience honoured the memory of the departed maestro by observing a minute's silence. They then played the Adagietto from Mahler's Fifth Symphony. During his tenure with the Berlin Philharmonic from 1990 to 2002, Abbado devoted much attention to Mahler and the Adagietto was followed by silence rather than applause as a mark of respect. The concert continued with works by Webern, Beethoven and Richard Strauss. After the sad passing of Maazel, Zubin led the Munich Philharmonic in his place in October 2014 and also conducted the new production of *Aida* at La Scala, and two other concerts in February and March 2015.

♫

In October 2015, Zubin led a unique ensemble, the Australian World Orchestra, in performances in Mumbai, Chennai and New Delhi. The ensemble which unites the global diaspora of Australian classical musicians with virtuoso performers at home was born in 2011 from a dream of peripatetic Australian conductor Alexander Briger. He approached fellow Australian Nick Deutsch, an oboist in the Israel Philharmonic Orchestra, and, with his help, cobbled together the ensemble. The orchestra debuted in Sydney in August 2011 and, in a coup of sorts, netted Zubin for its 2013 season.

The concept is unique—the only professional orchestra representing one nationality coming together from all over the world. It consists of more than 100 musicians drawn from orchestras which include the Berlin Philharmonic, the Vienna Philharmonic, the Chicago Symphony Orchestra and the London Symphony Orchestra. Zubin conducted the 2013 season and Briger considers his association not only a great gift for Australian music lovers but also a boon for the ensemble's prospects on the international music calendar, given how rare it is for a conductor of Zubin's calibre to lead an Australian orchestra first at home and then on tour.

Briger narrates how the India tour came about. Deutsch, Zubin and he were having lunch together, when the maestro said that the orchestra should become Australia's cultural ambassador. When the two friends brought up India, Zubin invited them to tour the country of his birth. The strengthening of cultural ties between India and Australia consequent to Prime Minister Narendra Modi's visit in 2014 meant that the orchestra did not have any problem finding sponsors: the Australian government backed it with $2,50,000.

♫

Other than the rare actor, only conductors perform into their eighties with such regularity, which is a phenomenon in itself. An amalgam of various cultures, Zubin is the finest product of the cosmopolitan spirit of Mumbai, a spirit that still lurks under the surface despite the onslaught of modern philistinism and primitive parochialism. He is a brilliant example of how music has a universal language. As he closes in on Willem Mengelberg's record of five decades as music director of one orchestra (Concertgebouw Orchestra), his desire to make music burns as strongly as ever, as does his wish to share great music with others. This and the sheer joy he feels in conducting means that retirement is still far away. His only regret is that he has not been able to spend enough time with his family.

It is no longer fame or money but simply his unquenchable passion for music that propels him. Zubin has now reached what music critic Henahan described as 'elderhood'—a time when the talent, the accomplishments and the influence become entangled in myth. The resultant mystique is unlike that associated with any other profession. For almost sixty years now, Zubin Mehta has been at the core of the fairy tale, the centre from which the drama unfolds.

# Acknowledgements

A BOOK IS MADE possible by many people and institutions. Writing is a solitary activity but the publication of a book is almost always a collaborative effort. Inevitably, in a venture such as this, one is indebted to those who have gone before. My first debt is to three books: *Zubin: The Zubin Mehta Story*, his early biography written by Martin Bookspan and Ross Yockey; Zubin's own memoirs, *The Score of My Life* and Harold Schonberg's *Great Conductors*. My debt to the first, especially, has been immense. Much of the account of Zubin's early career as well as his time in Montreal and Los Angeles draws substantially from this biography. Zubin's own autobiography was useful too, coming as it did from the horse's mouth (or the conductor's baton if you will), but was often short on detail. Schonberg's magisterial *Great Conductors* has been a constant companion over the years and I have drawn liberally from it. Apart from providing an authoritative knowledge base for a neophyte, it has served as the basis for the Prologue.

My debt to people starts with Nandu and Shaila Sirdeshmukh who gave this book its first major boost in mid-2010 by getting me a copy of *The Mehta Years*, a slim book published by the New York Philharmonic on Zubin's tenure, which has proved valuable (a fact acknowledged by the maestro himself when I got him to autograph it). My thanks to Barbara Haws, archivist and historian, and Richard Wandel, of the New York Philharmonic archives, who made this possible. My gratitude also to Gabryel Smith for advising me on which photos I could use from this commemorative volume.

I have been in touch with Natalia Ritzkowsky, Zubin's assistant, on email for many years and she has always responded with admirable promptness and courtesy. She has described her role as 'sometimes to be the dragon at the maestro's door' but in my case she was the angel who let me in. Most of my communication with Zubin has been through her and I am grateful for her professionalism. She also fixed my appointment with him on his last visit to Mumbai, leading me to the maestro with the words: 'Make the most of your time. I don't know how much of it he will give you.' In the event, Zubin was kind enough to indulge me for an hour (and that too after six hours of rehearsal) though he did tell me in Gujarati that he was feeling sleepy and that the orchestra was waiting to have dinner with him. Thank you, Natalia, for all your help.

Zubin's longest association as music director has been with the Israel Philharmonic Orchestra and I gratefully acknowledge the assistance of its secretary general, Avi Shoshani, who responded promptly to my questions via email and also couriered material and books on the orchestra to me. My thanks also to Avivit Hochstadter and the Murray S. Katz Photo Archives of the Israel Philharmonic Orchestra who promptly provided photographs, with a promise of more, in case they were needed. Perhaps my greatest debt in this whole enterprise is to Peter Marck, the lead bassist of the Israel Philharmonic, Zubin's associate for nearly four decades, and the writer of the orchestra's blog. Peter generously gave me permission to refer to his blog on the recent tours of the orchestra and it is this material which forms the basis for much of the chapter 'The Maestro on Tour'. I have pillaged, paraphrased and precised shamelessly and it is only appropriate that I acknowledge his help with a special mention. Peter also offered photographs from his collection, apart from providing information on Zubin's early days with the orchestra. His inputs have been invaluable and I cannot thank him enough for being so forthcoming and helpful to a complete stranger.

I also owe an immense debt of gratitude to Francesca Zardini, formerly with the Maggio Musicale in Florence, and now in Naples, for her help in providing me with material on Zubin's concerts at the Bavarian State Opera and also his time in Florence. Francesca herself is in the process of compiling a book which enumerates every single concert conducted by Zubin, which she plans to bring out at about the time this biography will be published. Similar thanks go to Ester Francia Arenas who supplied me with details of the maestro's concerts in Valencia.

Cyrus Bharucha spoke to me at length about his association with Zubin and shared details about his experiences during the filming of *On Wings of Fire*. He was also instrumental in putting me in touch via email with a childhood friend of Zubin's, Ajit Hutheesing. Ajit supplied the answers to my questions and also volunteered other information about Zubin. NCPA Chairman Khushroo Suntook, another childhood friend, filled me in on details about their lifelong bond and some of the anecdotes he narrated find mention in the book.

Mehroo Jeejeebhoy, managing trustee of the Mehli Mehta Music Foundation in Mumbai, has been a pillar of support from the start. Apart from talking to me at length about her association with the maestro and the activities of the foundation, she generously provided photographs, some of which are reproduced in the book. She also allowed me unrestricted access to the excellent collection of books on music which the foundation possesses. My grateful thanks also to Bakhtavar Pestonji, Mehroo's assistant, for her help.

I am grateful to Silloo Billimoria, now well into her nineties, for her perfect recall of events which occurred many decades ago. Silloo corresponded with Tehmina who kept her informed about her son's prodigies in the United States and elsewhere. Thanks also to her daughters, Roda Billimoria Desai and Dina Dastur, for their recollections of Zubin and his family. When I told the maestro about Silloo, he remembered her with obvious affection. 'I wish I could meet her. A very dear lady,' he said.

T. Vijayalakshmi, my former secretary, organized and bound the enormous number of newspaper and magazine articles which provided the basis for a large part of the book. She uncomplainingly rendered assistance, never voicing the doubt which I am sure must have assailed her on occasion about whether the book would ever be published. My assistant, Jagat Singh, performed a similar role, photocopying mounds of material and spiral-binding successive drafts of the book, playing the role of odd-job man to perfection. He has, I suspect, over the years become a fan of Maestro Mehta.

Milee Ashwarya who commissioned this book was enthusiastic about it from the start and brought her usual energy to the venture. She and I are old friends and this is our third book together. An editor is often an author's best friend and Arpita Basu was an inspired choice. Her diligent and conscientious editing has added polish, grace and clarity to many rough edges, and greatly improved the book. In addition, I have also benefited from her fine sense of language and punctuation. All mistakes, of course are mine, apart from those of punctuation which are now mostly Arpita's. While all efforts have been made to ensure that the facts are accurate and that no citation has been inadvertently missed out, I will be happy if errors, which I hope are not too numerous, are brought to my notice.

This book has been in the making for eight years now and has undergone long periods of dormancy. The person responsible for bringing it back into focus was Kekoo Nicholson, president of the Cricket Club of India, Mumbai, whose passing remark in December 2014 was the spark for me to finish what I had started. He said that Zubin would be conducting a concert at Brabourne Stadium for his eightieth birthday, which for me was the conversational equivalent of a serendipitous find.

I would like to thank my sister, Tushna, and brother-in-law, Phiroze, who not only shared me with Zubin all these years, but also provided great moral support in a venture where I was often beset by self-doubt. Above all, I would like to thank my mother, Rati, whose faith in me never wavered when sceptics warned that my idée fixe was a classic case of overreach. It is to her that this book is dedicated.

I would also like to thank Anuradha Naik for her moral support and for being such a good friend. Thanks also to Dr Yusuf Hamied for his kind words of appreciation and to my friend Devendra Singh for the excellent photograph which appears on the cover.

And now for the biggest thank you of them all. Maestro Zubin Mehta, the subject of this biography, was generous and kind enough to entertain an unmusical stranger who wanted to write about his life. He cooperated fully once he realized that his uninvited biographer had done his homework reasonably well. When I first approached him for his approval, he was candid enough to say, 'I don't doubt your goodwill but I don't want to end up correcting everything you've written,' or words to that effect.

When the manuscript was sent to him, he made some preliminary observations and then set about reading it in right earnest. I cannot thank him enough for sparing the time to peruse the lengthy manuscript, given his extremely busy schedule. I know enough about his life to safely say that time is the maestro's worst enemy: he simply doesn't have enough of it. He pointed out a number of factual inaccuracies, for which I am most grateful. Zubin is probably the only person alive who could have made those corrections, given the fact that many of them pertain to his early life and career, and his father Mehli's early career.

Readers will have realized that this book is not a hagiography. Not once did Zubin tell me to delete anything which was uncomplimentary. In fact, when I drew his attention to the criticism during one of our long telephone conversations, he said, 'But you cannot have a book which only has compliments. That would be no good.' During the latter part of our collaboration (if I can take the liberty of calling it that), he even played the role of editor and proofreader. He wanted me to chop and change to avoid repetition, pointed to missing umlauts on some of the German names, and much else. Only when I told him that the editorial team was on the job and these little corrections would be taken care of, did he concentrate exclusively on the content. He was also kind enough to send me photographs from his private collection, telling Natalia that it would be a good idea to have new photos in this book. I would also like to thank Nancy Mehta who read parts of the manuscript and provided important information.

At the end of it all, Zubin sent his approval, making this an authorized biography. Thank you, maestro, for this happy ending.

# Notes

## PROLOGUE

1. Harold C. Schonberg, *Great Conductors* (New York: Simon & Schuster), 1967, p. 25.
2. Schonberg, 'Everybody Kissed and Made Up', *The New York Times*, 21 January 1968.
3. Stephen E. Rubin, 'What Is a Maestro', *The New York Times*, 26 September 1974.
4. Schonberg, 'Everybody Kissed and Made Up', *The New York Times.*
5. Schonberg, *Great Conductors*, p. 21.
6. Ibid., p. 22.
7. Ibid., p. 19.
8. Ibid., p. 167.
9. Ibid., p. 74.
10. Ibid., p.138.
11. Ibid., p. 254.
12. Ibid., p. 255.
13. Karajan played an important role in the development of the original compact disc digital audio format. He championed this new technology, lent his prestige to it, and also appeared at the first press conference announcing the format. The maximum playing time of the early compact disc prototypes was sixty minutes, but the final specification enlarged the disc size, extending it to seventy-four minutes. It is believed that it was due to Karajan's insistence that the format was given sufficient capacity to contain Beethoven's Ninth Symphony on a single disc.
14. Roger Vaughan, *Herbert von Karajan* (New York: W.W. Norton & Company, 1986), p. 146.

15. Schonberg, *Great Conductors*, p. 22.
16. Ibid., p. 23.
17. Sir Adrian C. Boult, *Thoughts on Conducting* (London: Phoenix House Ltd, 1963), p. xiii.

## INTRODUCTION

1. *Time*, 'Gypsy Boy', 19 January 1968.
2. Donal Henahan, 'Mehta Has a Mandate Now to Change the Philharmonic', *The New York Times*, 13 November 1983.
3. Mehli Mehta Music Foundation, *Applause: A Tribute to Zubin Mehta*, 2011, p. 8.
4. Ibid.

## A CHILD OF MUSIC

1. Naresh Fernandes, *Taj Mahal Foxtrot: The Story of Bombay's Jazz Age* (New Delhi: Roli Books, 2012), pp. 61–62.
2. Bomi S. Billimoria, 'Western Classical Music: Performers and Nurturers', Nawaz B. Mody ed., *Enduring Legacy*, vol. II (Mumbai: Published by the author, 2005), p. 716.
3. Zubin Mehta, interview by the author.
4. Martin Bookspan and Ross Yockey, *Zubin: The Zubin Mehta Story* (New York: Harper & Row, 1978), p. 5.
5. Zubin Mehta, *The Score of My Life* (New Delhi: Roli Books, 2008), p. 72.
6. Peter Lavezzoli, *Bhairavi: The Global Impact of Music* (Noida: HarperCollins Publishers, 2009), p. 216.
7. Mehli Mehta Music Foundation, *Applause: A Tribute to Zubin Mehta*, 2011, p. 10.
8. Bookspan and Yockey, *Zubin*, p. 4.
9. The Craens reigned over the Western classical music scene in Bombay in the 1940s and 1950s. Olga who played under Jules married the conductor who, at fifty-one, was twice her age. They remained married till Jules's tragic death in 1959. The last years were not happy. Jules pleaded single responsibility in a case of financial malfeasance to save his wife from jail. Olga who suffered from carpal tunnel syndrome stopped her public

performances in 1958. She supported herself with piano lessons till she succumbed to cancer in 1986. A film *Olga and Jules Craen: A Tribute* was put together by students of the husband-wife duo and screened in Mumbai in February 2013. The Olga and Jules Craen Foundation was established by Olga's students in 2012 and promotes a Young Musician of the Year to nurture outstanding ability in any instrument or voice. (*Parsiana*, 7 April 2013).

10. Dorit Gabai, 'The Conductor Dares', *Maariv*, 29 July 2005.
11. Mehli Mehta Music Foundation, *Applause*, p. 37.
12. *Musical Opinion*, 'Homi Kanga's 80th Birthday Concert on the South Bank', 1 July 2002.
13. *Little India*, 'Zubin Mehta: The Maestro from Mumbai', 2 February 2007.
14. Bookspan and Yockey, *Zubin*, p. 6.
15. *Little India*, 'Zubin Mehta'.
16. Zubin Mehta, interview by Noopur Tiwari in Zurich, NDTV, 28 September 2008.
17. Silloo Billimoria, interview by the author in Mumbai, 7 February 2015.
18. Mehta, *The Score of My Life*, p. 3.
19. Bookspan and Yockey, *Zubin*, p. 7.
20. Mehli Mehta Music Foundation, *Applause*, p. 32.
21. Homi Dastoor, *Musical Journeys* (Mumbai: 49/50 Books, 2014), p. 10.
22. Bookspan and Yockey, *Zubin*, p. 7.
23. Chris Pasles, 'Obituaries; Mehli Mehta, 94; Youth Symphony Conductor', *Los Angeles Times*, 20 October 2002.
24. Mehli Mehta Music Foundation, *Applause*, p. 20.
25. Zubin Mehta, 'Star Conductor Zubin Mehta Receives Furtwängler Prize', interview by Anastassia Boutsko, 11 September 2011.
26. Ajit Hutheesing, email to author.
27. Bookspan and Yockey, *Zubin*, p. 10.
28. Ibid., p. 11.
29. *India Abroad*, 'The Yoga Romance', 23 July 2004.
30. Yehudi Menuhin, *Unfinished Journey* (London: Macdonald and Jane's Publishers, 1977), p. 246.
31. Zubin Mehta, interviewed by the author.
32. Zubin Mehta, interview by Noopur Tiwari in Zurich, NDTV, 28 September 2008.

33. Zarin Mehta, 'Mad about Music', interview by Gilbert Kaplan, 6 November 2005.
34. Zubin Mehta, 'Mad about Music', interview by Gilbert Kaplan, 4 February 2007.
35. Bookspan and Yockey, *Zubin*, p. 12.

## CUFFE PARADE TO VIENNA WOODS

1. Zubin Mehta, *The Score of My Life* (New Delhi: Roli Books, 2008), p. 12.
2. Ibid.
3. Martin Bookspan and Ross Yockey, *Zubin: The Zubin Mehta Story* (New York: Harper & Row, 1978), p. 18.
4. Roger Kamien, *Music: An Appreciation,* 7th ed. (New York: McGraw-Hill, 2000), p. 223.
5. Vienna inherited a body of instrument types which at the end of the eighteenth century reflected the intellectual spirit and value system of central Europe. The emergence of national schools of composition in various countries at the beginning of the nineteenth century led to variations in the way instruments were constructed. However, such developments bypassed Vienna, where nothing much changed. Viennese music remained essentially faithful to concepts of sound originating from the classics of the country. Viennese instruments are richer in overtones (the sound tone is brighter), have a wider dynamic range thus making possible greater differences between 'piano' and 'forte', and enable greater modulation of sound. The Viennese sound is created by significant differences between Viennese woodwind and brass instruments and those used by other orchestras. The fingering on the clarinet is different and the mouthpiece has a variant form which in turn requires a special kind of reed. The bassoon too has special fingering and reeds. The trumpet has a rotary valve system and, in places, a narrower bore. There are differences in the trombone, tuba and oboe as well. Vibrato is used sparingly. The greatest difference is to be found in the Viennese (F-) horn, which has a narrow bore, an extended lead pipe and a system of piston valves. Viennese percussion instruments are all made from genuine goat parchment which gives a richer range of overtones than artificial skin.

However, Viennese string instruments are not of prime importance in producing the unique Viennese sound.

6. Bookspan and Yockey, *Zubin*, p. 15.
7. Ibid., p. 16.
8. Khushroo Suntook, interviewed by the author.
9. Mehta, *The Score of My Life,* p. 18.
10. Zubin Mehta, interviewed by the author.

## *DER INDER*

1. Zubin Mehta, *The Score of My Life* (New Delhi: Roli Books, 2008), p. 15.
2. Albert Goldberg, 'Conductor Zubin Mehta—at 26, a Long Way from Bombay', *Los Angeles Times*, 19 August 1962.
3. John Allison, 'Zubin Mehta', *Opera*, May 2009.
4. Zubin Mehta, interviewed by the author.
5. Zubin Mehta, 'Turning Point: Buoyed by Brahms', as told to Barbara Isenberg, *Time*, 17 February 2003.
6. Zubin Mehta, 'Mad about Music', interview by Gilbert Kaplan, 4 February 2007.
7. Martin Bookspan and Ross Yockey, *Zubin: The Zubin Mehta Story* (New York: Harper & Row, 1978), p. 19.
8. Ibid., p. 20.
9. Mehta, *The Score of My Life*, p. 15.
10. Ibid.
11. Ibid., p. 16.
12. Ibid., p. 17.
13. Bookspan and Yockey, *Zubin*, p. 22.
14. Mehta, *The Score of My Life*, p. 17.
15. Ibid., p. 22–23.
16. Ibid.
17. Bookspan and Yockey, *Zubin*, p. 21.
18. Mary Ann Callan, 'Wife's View of Zubin Mehta', *Los Angeles Times*, 19 January 1962.
19. Ibid.
20. Mehta, *The Score of My Life*, p. 20.
21. Many years later, Zubin befriended the Schoenberg family in Los Angeles.

They lived in the same neighbourhood. Once, after a barbecue party at his Brentwood residence, Zubin went to the Schoenberg home with the members of the Vienna Philharmonic, where the two sons Ronnie and Larry took them on a lecture tour. Gertrud, Schoenberg's wife, was kind to Zubin but was known to be snobbish in her choice of music. She was very upset when Zubin invited her to a concert where he conducted the 'Dance of Vengeance' from Samuel Barber's ballet *Medea*. 'How dare you invite me to such a programme?' she said.

22. Mehta, *The Score of My Life*, p. 20.
23. *Time*, 'The Art of the Little Movement', 1 March 1968.
24. Ibid.
25. Albert Goldberg, 'Good Conductor's Style Is Not His Own', *Los Angeles Times*, 7 March 1965.
26. Philharmonic-Symphony Society of New York, Inc., *New York Philharmonic: The Mehta Years*, New York, 1990, p. 60.
27. Bookspan and Yockey, *Zubin*, p. 29.
28. *Time*, 'The Art of the Little Movement'.
29. Zubin Mehta, interviewed by the author.
30. Goldberg, 'Good Conductor's Style Is Not his Own', *Los Angeles Times*.
31. Ibid.
32. Bookspan and Yockey, *Zubin*, p. 30.
33. *Time*, 'The Art of the Little Movement'.
34. Ibid.
35. Mehta, *The Score of My Life*, p. 23.
36. Ibid., p. 21.
37. Bookspan and Yockey, *Zubin*, p. 27.
38. Ibid., p. 29.
39. Goldberg, 'Good Conductor's Style Is Not His Own', *Los Angeles Times*.
40. Mehta, *The Score of My Life*, p. 25.

## SIENA AND AFTER

1. Zubin Mehta, interviewed by the author.
2. Daniel Barenboim, *A Life in Music* (New York: Arcade Publishing, 2002), p. 34.
3. Ibid.
4. Ibid.

5. Ibid.
6. Martin Bookspan and Ross Yockey, *Zubin: The Zubin Mehta Story* (New York: Harper & Row, 1978), p. 35.
7. Ibid., p. 36.
8. Zubin Mehta, *The Score of My Life* (New Delhi: Roli Books, 2008), p. 28.
9. Bookspan and Yockey, *Zubin*, p. 37.
10. Ibid.
11. Ibid., p. 39.
12. Ibid., p. 40.
13. Ibid.
14. Ibid., p. 38.
15. Mehta, *The Score of My Life*, p. 120.
16. Bookspan and Yockey, *Zubin*, p. 41.

## A RISING STAR

1. Martin Bookspan and Ross Yockey, *Zubin: The Zubin Mehta Story* (New York: Harper & Row, 1978), p. 45.
2. Zubin Mehta, *The Score of My Life* (New Delhi: Roli Books, 2008), p. 25.
3. Bookspan and Yockey, *Zubin*, p. 47.
4. Zubin Mehta, interviewed by the author.
5. Bookspan and Yockey, *Zubin,* p. 48.
6. Ibid., p. 49.
7. *Time*, 'Are You a Windmill?', 2 June 1958.
8. Bookspan and Yockey, *Zubin*, p. 53.
9. Ibid., p. 57.
10. Ibid.
11. Zubin Mehta, interviewed by the author.

## LIVERPOOL LET-DOWN

1. Zubin Mehta, *The Score of My Life* (New Delhi: Roli Books, 2008), p. 32.
2. Martin Bookspan and Ross Yockey, *Zubin: The Zubin Mehta Story* (New York: Harper & Row, 1978), p. 62.

3. John Allison, 'Zubin Mehta', *Opera*, June 2009.
4. Mehta, *The Score of My Life*, p. 33.
5. Bookspan and Yockey, *Zubin*, p. 63.
6. Ibid., pp. 63–64.
7. *Time*, 'Gypsy Boy', 19 January 1968.
8. Zubin Mehta, interviewed by the author.
9. Bookspan and Yockey, *Zubin*, p. 65.
10. Ibid., p. 66.
11. Ibid., p. 69.
12. Ibid., p. 71.

## DESTINY'S CHILD

1. Harold Schonberg, *The Great Conductors* (New York: Simon & Schuster, 1967), p. 196.
2. Philip Hart, *Conductors: A New Generation* (London: Robson Books, 1980), p. 130.
3. Tim Page, 'Fredric R. Mann', *The New York Times*, 8 September 2008.
4. Ibid.
5. Zubin Mehta, *The Score of My Life* (New Delhi: Roli Books, 2008), p. 36.
6. Martin Bookspan and Ross Yockey, *Zubin: The Zubin Mehta Story* (New York: Harper and Row, 1978), p. 74.
7. John Rockwell, 'Zubin's Father—and More', *Los Angeles Times*, 22 March 1972.
8. Allen Hughes, 'Music: Indian Conductor', *The New York Times*, 27 July 1960.
9. Albert Goldberg, 'Zubin Mehta's Plans and Dreams for L.A.', *Los Angeles Times*, 15 December 1963.

## MONTREAL

1. Martin Bookspan and Ross Yockey, *Zubin: The Zubin Mehta Story* (New York: Harper and Row, 1978), p. 88.
2. Zubin Mehta, interviewed by the author.
3. Helena Matheopoulos, *Maestro: Encounters with Conductors of Today* (New York: Harper & Row, 1982), p. 234.

4. Zubin Mehta, interviewed by the author.
5. Ajit Hutheesing, email to author.
6. Zubin Mehta, *The Score of My Life* (New Delhi: Roli Books, 2008), p. 39.
7. Zubin Mehta, interviewed by the author.
8. Bookspan and Yockey, *Zubin*, p. 92.
9. Mehta, *The Score of My Life*, p. 40.

## ANNUS MIRABILIS

1. John Barnes, 'Young Man with a Baton', *Los Angeles Times*, 23 January 1961.
2. Philip Hart, *Conductors: A New Generation* (London: Robson Books, 1980), p. 131.
3. Ibid., p. xvii.
4. Abe Cohen, interview by Peter Marck (Transcript given to the author by Marck).
5. *Time*, 'Solti and Chicago', 7 May 1973.
6. *Time*, 'Buffie & the Baton', 14 April 1961.
7. Ibid.
8. Murray Schumach, 'Feuds and Confusion Preceded Appointment of Coast Conductor', *The New York Times*, 11 November 1961.
9. *The New York Times*, 'The Mail Pouch: Hassles in Los Angeles', 26 November 1961.
10. Ibid.
11. Ibid.
12. *Time*, 'Brightness in the Air', 18 December 1964.
13. Schumach, 'Feuds and Confusion Preceded Appointment of Coast Conductor', *The New York Times*.
14. C. Robert Jennings, 'Zubin Mehta: Allegro Con Brio', *Los Angeles Times*, 5 April 1970.
15. Zubin Mehta, interviewed by the author.
16. Jennings, 'Zubin Mehta: Allegro Con Brio', *Los Angeles Times*.
17. Zubin Mehta, *The Score of My Life* (New Delhi: Roli Books, 2008), p. 50.
18. Marie Winn, 'Zubin Comes to Town', *The New York Times*, 19 November 1978.

19. Ibid.
20. Zubin Mehta, interviewed by the author.

## THE NEXT TOSCANINI?

1. Zubin Mehta, *The Score of My Life* (New Delhi: Roli Books, 2008), p. 127.
2. Martin Bookspan and Ross Yockey, *Zubin: The Zubin Mehta Story* (New York: Harper & Row, 1978), p. 132.
3. Ibid.
4. John Allison, 'Zubin Mehta', *Opera*, June 2009.
5. *Time*, 'Gypsy Boy', 19 January 1968.
6. He used his European contacts to draw some of the biggest stars to the Met and broke the company's racial barrier by hiring Leontyne Price in 1953 and Marian Anderson in 1955. In 1968 he 'fired' Maria Callas but later made attempts to win her back. He revolutionized the Met's productions by inviting the world's greatest directors and designers. He also possessed a quick wit. When told that the conductor George Szell, with whom he had crossed swords several times, was his own worst enemy, he responded, 'Not while I'm alive.' He suffered from Alzheimer's disease in later life and died in 1997 aged ninety-five.
7. Mehta, *The Score of My Life*, pp. 84–85.
8. Zubin Mehta, interviewed by the author.
9. (Quoted in) Walter Arlen, 'Mehta on Podiums of Europe Concert Halls', *Los Angeles Times*, 7 August 1965.

## ALLEGRO CON BRIO

1. *Time*, 'Gypsy Boy', 19 January 1968.
2. Ibid.
3. Albert Goldberg, 'Conductor Zubin Mehta—at 26, a Long Way from Bombay', *Los Angeles Times*, 19 August 1962.
4. Albert Goldberg, 'Mehta Conducts First of Season Concerts', *Los Angeles Times*, 16 November 1962.
5. *Time*, 'Gypsy Boy'.
6. (Quoted in) Philip Hart, *Conductors: A New Generation* (London: Robson Books, 1980), p. 134.

7. Zubin Mehta, interviewed by the author.
8. *International Musician*, 'With 600 Concerts to Go, New York Philharmonic Concertmaster Glenn Dicterow Will Make Each One Count', 1 August 2012.
9. Martin Bookspan and Ross Yockey, *Zubin: The Zubin Mehta Story* (New York: Harper & Row, 1978), pp. 200–01.
10. Thomas Thompson, 'The Importance of Being Ernest Fleischmann', *The New York Times*, 11 April 1976.
11. Ibid.
12. Ibid.
13. Ibid.
14. Hart, *Conductors,* p. 136.
15. Zubin Mehta, interviewed by the author.
16. Thompson, 'The Importance of Being Ernest Fleischmann', *The New York Times*.
17. Judy Klemesrud, 'Is Women's Lib Coming to the Philharmonic?', *The New York Times*, 11 April 1971.
18. Philharmonic-Symphony Society of New York, Inc., *New York Philharmonic: The Mehta Years*, New York, 1990, p. 22.
19. Zubin Mehta, interviewed by the author.
20. Albert Goldberg, 'Rare Strings for the Philharmonic', *Los Angeles Times*, 9 November 1965.
21. Mark Swed, 'Zubin Mehta's Heady Days as Los Angeles Philharmonic Music Director', *Los Angeles Times*, 8 December 2012.
22. Ibid.
23. Ibid.
24. Emily Coleman, 'Mehta: I Have Never Been Told What Programs to Do', *The New York Times*, 2 April 1967.
25. Zubin Mehta, interviewed by the author.
26. *Time,* 'Brightness in the Air', 18 December 1964.
27. Ibid.
28. *Los Angeles Times*, 'Seat at Music Center Endowed by Maestro', 12 August 1962.
29. Zubin Mehta, interviewed by the author.
30. *Time,* 'Brightness in the Air'.
31. Ibid.

32. Ibid.
33. Zubin Mehta, *The Score of My Life* (New Delhi: Roli Books, 2008), p. 125.
34. Albert Goldberg, 'Heifetz Adds Brilliance to Gala Event', *Los Angeles Times*, 7 December 1964.
35. Harold Schonberg, 'Jascha Heifetz Is Dead at 86; A Virtuoso since Childhood', *The New York Times*, 12 December 1987.
36. Diane Haithman, 'On and Off the Podium', *Los Angeles Times*, 5 December 1998.
37. Harold Schonberg, 'Music: Heifetz Inaugurates Los Angeles Music Hall', *The New York Times*, 8 December 1964.
38. Ibid.
39. Yehudi Menuhin, *Unfinished Journey* (London: Macdonald and Jane's Publishers, 1977), p. 321.
40. *Los Angeles Times,* 'Music Center Tour Thrills Zubin Mehta', 20 January 1963.
41. Zubin Mehta, interviewed by the author.
42. Haithman, 'On and Off the Podium', *Los Angeles Times*.
43. J.J. Bhabha, 'The Problem of Establishing an Innovative Institution', Kumud Mehta ed., *The NCPA 1966–1988* (Bombay: Bombay NCPA, 1988), p. 13.
44. Maki S. Masani, 'Dr Jamshed J. Bhabha: Innovating an Institution', Nawaz B. Mody ed., *Enduring Legacy: Parsis of the 20th Century,* vol. III, (Mumbai: Published by the author, 2005), p. 947.
45. *Tata Review*, vol. XXXIV (4), December 1999, p. 17.
46. William Bender, 'Audience, Critics Applaud Mehta's Metropolitan Debut', *Los Angeles Times*, 31 December 1965.
47. Hart, *Conductors*, p. 149.
48. Bender, 'Audience, Critics Applaud Mehta's Metropolitan Debut', *Los Angeles Times*.
49. Ibid.
50. Plácido Domingo, *My First Forty Years* (New York: Alfred A. Knopf, 1983), p. 45.
51. Hart, *Conductors*, p. 147.
52. Ibid.
53. Zubin Mehta, interviewed by the author.

54. Mehta, *The Score of My Life*, p. 86.
55. Swed, 'Zubin Mehta's Heady Days as Los Angeles Philharmonic Music Director', *Los Angeles Times*.
56. Ibid.
57. The orchestras of Boston, Philadelphia, Chicago, Cleveland and New York.
58. Howard Klein, 'Mehta Leads L.A. into the Big Time', *The New York Times*, 28 January 1968.
59. Judy Klemesrud, 'Mehta's Mystique: Baton In Hand, Foot in Mouth?', *The New York Times*, 18 October 1970.
60. *The New York Times*, 'Imperious on Podium: Zubin Mehta', 26 February 1976.
61. *Time*, 'Gypsy Boy'.
62. Coleman, 'Mehta: I Have Never Been Told What Programs to Do', *The New York Times*.
63. *Chicago Sun-Times*, 'Zubin Mehta Hot for Chilis', 16 May 1991.
64. Ibid.
65. T.P. Sreenivasan, 'India in His Marrow', Rediff.com, 1 March 2005.
66. Paul Hume, 'Order of the Lotus Bestowed on Mehta', *Los Angeles Times*, 9 May 1967.

## THE LOVE OF ZION

1. *Los Angeles Times*, 'Mehta Helped into Israel by Premier', 13 June 1967.
2. Zubin Mehta, *The Score of My Life* (New Delhi: Roli Books, 2008), p. 89.
3. *Time*, 'Gypsy Boy', 19 January 1968.
4. *Time*, 'Waiting for Mr. Right', 17 June 1966.
5. Zeev Steinberg, interview by Peter Marck (Transcript given to the author by Marck).
6. *Time*, 'Waiting for Mr. Right'.
7. Ibid.
8. *Time*, 'Home for Wanderers', 14 October 1957.
9. Yaacov Mishori, *Smiles, Pranks and Coughs at the Israel Philharmonic Orchestra* (Tel Aviv: Graphisoft Systems, 2002), p. 73.
10. Mehta, *The Score of My Life*, p. 115.

11. Ibid., pp. 116–17.
12. Judy Pasternak, 'The Pit and the Podium', *Los Angeles Times*, 28 April 1996.
13. Adolph Green, 'The Day They Made Music on Mt. Scopus', *The New York Times*, 6 August 1967.
14. Ibid.
15. *Time*, 'Inside the Outside Family', 7 December 1970.
16. Maureen Cleave, 'Triangle: Daniel and Jacqueline Barenboim and the Cello', *The New York Times*, 16 March 1969.
17. Daniel Barenboim, *A Life in Music* (New York: Arcade Publishing, 2002), p. 75.
18. Ibid.
19. *Time*, 'Gypsy Boy'.
20. *Time*, 'Inside the Outside Family'.
21. Cleave, 'Triangle: Daniel and Jacqueline Barenboim and the Cello', *The New York Times*.
22. *The New York Times*, 'Israel Philharmonic Flies in for Benefit Tour', 28 July 1967.
23. Ibid.
24. *Time*, 'Gypsy Boy'.
25. Ibid.
26. Barenboim, *A Life in Music*, p. 35.

## A BUSY CONDUCTOR

1. Martin Bookspan and Ross Yockey, *Zubin: The Zubin Mehta Story* (New York: Harper & Row, 1978), p. 159.
2. *Time*, 'Bucharest Battle', 29 September 1967.
3. John Rockwell, 'Mehli Mehta: Zubin's Father—and More', *Los Angeles Times*, 22 March 1972.
4. Zubin Mehta, 'Turning Point: Buoyed by Brahms', as told to Barbara Isenberg, *Time*, 17 February 2003.
5. Arthur J. Dommen, 'Bombay Homecoming for Zubin Mehta', *Los Angeles Times*, 7 November 1967.
6. Silloo Billimoria, interviewed by the author in Mumbai, 7 February 2015.
7. *The New York Times*, 'TV: Profile of Zubin Mehta, a Study of Dynamics', 16 December 1967.

8. Albert Goldman, 'Symphony and Rock? Forget It', *The New York Times*, 15 March 1970.
9. John Rockwell, 'Four "Contempo '70" Concerts Slated by L.A. Philharmonic', *Los Angeles Times*, 24 March 1970.
10. *Time*, 'Hit It Zubin', 1 June 1970.
11. Ibid.
12. Ibid.
13. Philip Hart, *Conductors: A New Generation* (London: Robson Books, 1980), p. 134.
14. Zubin Mehta, interviewed by the author.
15. Stephen E. Rubin, 'From Mehta—With Chutzpah and Love', *The New York Times*, 5 September 1976.
16. Mark Swed, 'Zubin Mehta's Heady Days as Los Angeles Philharmonic Music Director', *Los Angeles Times*, 8 December 2012.
17. Zubin Mehta, *The Score of My Life* (New Delhi: Roli Books, 2008), p. 160.

**'I DO'**

1. Mary Ann Callan, 'Wife's View of Zubin Mehta', *Los Angeles Times*, 19 January 1962.
2. She was born Anastasia Stratakis to a struggling Greek family in Toronto. She won a scholarship to the Toronto Conservatory and got her big opportunity when Rudolf Bing gave her a contract with the Met. Her lucky break came when she replaced an ailing soprano as Liu in *Turandot*. She never looked back after that performance.
3. *Los Angeles Times*, 'Zubin Mehta Confirms Engagement to Singer', 11 February 1965.
4. Ibid.
5. Joseph Roddy, 'Teresa Stratas Is a Lulu, a Soprano Siren Who Wowed the Met and Mehta (Among Many Men)', *People*, 21 January 1980, vol. 13 (3).
6. Zubin Mehta, interviewed by the author.
7. Judy Klemesrud, 'Mehta's Mystique: Baton in Hand, Foot in Mouth?', *The New York Times*, 18 October 1970.
8. Ibid.

9. This was told to the author by Silloo Billimoria, now ninety-four, at the same Cuffe Parade home where the Mehtas had once lived, 7 February 2015.
10. Sharon E. Fay, 'Mehta and Kovack Vows Read Twice', *Los Angeles Times*, 21 July 1969.
11. Zubin Mehta, *The Score of My Life* (New Delhi: Roli Books, 2008), p. 79.
12. Michaela Williams, 'For Nancy Mehta, Wife of the Conductor, Life Is a Gilded Cage', *The New York Times*, 7 November 1978.
13. Kristin McMurran, 'Don't Argue with This Man on Cricket, Reagan or the Dodgers: Conductor Zubin Mehta Knows the Score', *People*, 12 October 1981.
14. Mehta, *The Score of My Life*, p. 80.
15. Mike Fleeman, 'Swindler's List', *Los Angeles Magazine*, April 1997.

## THE ISRAEL PHILHARMONIC ORCHESTRA

1. Howard Taubman, 'Israel Philharmonic Explores Fiscal Help in the West', *The New York Times*, 25 February 1970.
2. Yaacov Mishori, *Smiles, Pranks and Coughs at the Israel Philharmonic Orchestra* (Tel Aviv: Graphisoft Systems, 2002), pp. 54–55.
3. Ibid., p. 70.
4. C. Robert Jennings, 'Zubin Mehta: Allegro Con Brio', *Los Angeles Times*, 5 April 1970.
5. Ibid., p. 69.
6. Zubin Mehta, *The Score of My Life* (New Delhi: Roli Books, 2008), pp. 117–18.
7. Martin Bernheimer, 'Mehta Conducting in War-Torn Israel', *Los Angeles Times*, 19 October 1973.
8. Greer Fay Cashman, 'Worthy of a Diplomatic Note: Zubin Mehta Recalls the Yom Kippur War', *Jerusalem Post*, 22 July 2011.
9. Mehta, *The Score of My Life*, p. 111.
10. Dorit Gabai, 'The Conductor Dares', *Maariv*, 29 July 2009.
11. *The New York Times,* 'Mehta Gets Life Post in Israel', 2 November 1981.
12. Ibid.
13. Mehta, *The Score of My Life*, p. 112.
14. Zubin Mehta, interviewed by the author.

15. Corinna Da Fonseca-Wollheim, 'The Mystic Maestro', *Jerusalem Post*, 21 November 2003.
16. Ibid.
17. Clyde Haberman, 'Old Agonies Revive: Israel Philharmonic to Perform Wagner', *The New York Times*, 16 December 1981.
18. Daniel Barenboim, *A Life in Music* (New York: Arcade Publishing, 2002), p. 230.
19. Ibid.
20. Zubin Mehta, 'Star Conductor Zubin Mehta Receives Furtwängler Prize', interview by Anastassia Boutsko, 11 September 2011.
21. Amit Slonim, 'Zubin Mehta: Israel Has Lost Europe. Now It Is Losing America', The JC.com, 16 April 2015.
22. Zubin Mehta, interviewed by the author.
23. Peter Marck, email to author.
24. Ibid.

## 'THE MAESTRO OF OUR HEARTS'

1. Nechemia Meyers, 'The Accent Is Russian', *Chicago Jewish Star*, 12 January 2007.
2. Avi Shoshani, email to author.
3. Peter Marck, email to author.
4. Corinna Da Fonseca-Wollheim, 'The Mystic Maestro', *Jerusalem Post*, 21 November 2003.
5. Ibid.
6. Ibid.
7. Ibid.
8. Mark Swed, 'Zubin Mehta: A Celebration', *Los Angeles Times*, 11 March 2000.
9. Israel Philharmonic Orchestra, *The Israel Philharmonic Orchestra: 70th Anniversary*, Tel Aviv, 2006.
10. Linda Gradstein, 'Mahler at Masada; A Concert Spectacle to Honour Israel's 40th', *The Washington Post*, 15 October 1988.
11. Ibid.
12. Ibid.
13. Howard Goller, 'Conductor Zubin Mehta Leads Orchestra on Soviet Dream Tour', *Chicago Sun-Times*, 1 May 1990.

14. Zubin Mehta, interviewed by the author.
15. Zubin Mehta, '*The Score of My Life*' (Roli Books, New Delhi, 2008), p. 113.
16. *The New York Times*, 'Topics for the Times; A Triumph of the Spirit', 25 February 1991.
17. The Delhi Symphony Society was founded in 1965 by Gen. J.N. Chaudhuri who was an excellent violinist, and an American concert artiste Caroline Craig. The founder's association with the ministry of defence led to a tradition of succeeding Chiefs of Army Staff becoming president of the Society. Manekshaw had been president since 1972.
18. *The New York Times,* 'Violins for Finale of Jerusalem 3000', 3 November 1996.
19. Michael Ajzenstadt, 'Meteoric Midori', *Jerusalem Post*, 17 October 1997.
20. Roger Cohen, 'Israelis Join Germans in Concert at Buchenwald', *The New York Times,* 31 August 1999.
21. Ibid.
22. Ibid.
23. Peter Marck, email to author.
24. Ibid.
25. Shesh-Besh is a Turkish game, very similar to Western backgammon.
26. *The New York Times*, 'Political Views Test Harmony', 19 March 2014.
27. Peter Marck, email to author.
28. Greer Fay Cashman, 'Zoom In', *Jerusalem Post*, 14 November 2003.
29. Ben Jacobson, 'The Food Expert—Reena Pushkarna', *Jerusalem Post*, 5 April 2007.
30. Marion Fischel, 'Sophia Loren Here to Celebrate Zubin Mehta's 70th Birthday', *Jerusalem Post*, 11 April 2006.
31. Elana Estrin, 'Israel Philharmonic Marks Zubin Mehta's 40th Year as Music Director', *Jerusalem Post*, 16 July 2009.
32. Greer Fay Cashman, 'Worthy of a Diplomatic Note, Zubin Mehta Recalls the Yom Kippur War', *Jerusalem Post*, 22 July 2011.
33. AP Worldstream, 'Famed Conductor Honoured by Israel's President', 15 October 2012.
34. Peter Marck, email to author.
35. Zubin Mehta, interviewed by the author.
36. Peter Marck, email to author.
37. Henry Chu, 'A Different Valour', *Los Angeles Times*, 7 December 2003.

38. Alex Ross, 'Mehta and Israel in Similar Spirit', *The New York Times*, 15 February 1995.
39. Ibid.
40. Bernard Holland, 'An Opinionated Orchestra, and Indulgent Conductor', *The New York Times*, 3 February 2007.
41. John Rockwell, 'Mehta Conducts Israelis', *The New York Times*, 11 March 1989.
42. Holland, 'An Opinionated Orchestra, and Indulgent Conductor', *The New York Times*.
43. Zubin Mehta, interviewed by the author.
44. Gwen Ackerman, 'Mehta Gala with Perlman Opens $38 Million Concert Hall', www.bloomberg.com, 27 May 2013.
45. Ibid.
46. Zubin Mehta, interviewed by the author.

## A PODIUM ON OFFER

1. An article in *The New York Times* published in October 1970 was headlined 'Mehta's Mystique: Baton in Hand, Foot in Mouth?'.
2. Robert Windeler, 'Mehta Prefers Los Angeles Job to Bernstein's at Philharmonic', *The New York Times*, 12 December 1967.
3. Ibid.
4. Ibid.
5. Ibid.
6. *The New York Times*, 'Mehta Tells Union He Respects the Philharmonic', 10 January 1968.
7. C. Robert Jennings, 'Zubin Mehta: Allegro Con Brio', *Los Angeles Times*, 5 April 1970.
8. Zubin Mehta, 'Mad about Music', interview by Gilbert Kaplan, 4 February 2007.
9. Donal Henahan, 'Union Asks Mehta to Explain His Remarks on Philharmonic', *The New York Times*, 4 January 1968.
10. Ibid.
11. Stephen E. Rubin, 'From Mehta—with Chutzpah and Love', *The New York Times*, 5 September 1976.
12. Henahan, 'Union Asks Mehta to Explain His Remarks on Philharmonic',

*The New York Times*.

13. *The New York Times,* 'Mehta Tells Union He Respects the Philharmonic'.
14. Ibid.
15. Ibid.
16. Ibid.
17. Martin Bernheimer, 'New York Philharmonic Drops Mehta's Name', *Los Angeles Times*, 1 May 1968.
18. Marie Winn, 'Zubin Comes to Town', *The New York Times*, 19 November 1978.
19. Ibid.
20. Martin Bernheimer, 'Mehta Braves the N.Y. Philharmonic', *Los Angeles Times*, 17 May 1974.
21. John Rockwell, 'Mehta Battles Image of Glamour Boy', *The New York Times*, 26 November 1975.
22. Ibid.
23. Winn, 'Zubin Comes to Town', *The New York Times*.
24. Ibid.
25. Ibid.
26. Ibid.
27. Ibid.
28. Martin Bookspan and Ross Yockey, *Zubin: The Zubin Mehta Story* (New York: Harper and Row, 1978), p. 213.
29. Winn, 'Zubin Comes to Town', *The New York Times*.
30. Ibid.
31. Martin Bernheimer, 'Mehta Resigns from LA Philharmonic for NY Post', *Los Angeles Times*, 25 February 1976.
32. *The New York Times*, 'Tells Colleagues on Coast', 26 February 1976.
33. Robert Lindsey, 'Zubin Mehta in a Farewell Concert', *The New York Times*, 6 May 1978.
34. Ibid.
35. Ibid.
36. *Time,* '"Zubi Baby" Switches', 8 March 1976.
37. Martin Bernheimer, 'Solti Paves Way for Mehta', *Los Angeles Times*, 21 May 1976.
38. Martin Bernheimer, 'A Difficult Season Ends for Philharmonic', *Los Angeles Times*, 28 April 1974.

39. Martin Bernheimer, 'Life with Mehta: Some Critical Reflections', *Los Angeles Times*, 7 May 1978.
40. Bernheimer, 'A Difficult Season Ends for Philharmonic', *Los Angeles Times*.
41. Ibid.
42. Ibid.
43. John Rockwell, 'A Perfectionist on the Podium', *The New York Times*, 21 November 1982.
44. (Quoted in) Philip Hart, *Conductors: A New Generation* (London: Robson Books, 1980), p. 145.
45. Bookspan and Yockey, *Zubin*, p. 127.
46. Rubin, 'From Mehta—with Chutzpah and Love', *The New York Times*.
47. Martin Bernheimer, 'The Philharmonic Season in Retrospect', *Los Angeles Times*, 8 May 1966.
48. Bernheimer, 'Life with Mehta: Some Critical Reflections', *Los Angeles Times*.
49. Zubin Mehta, interviewed by the author.
50. Rockwell, 'Mehta Battles Image of Glamour Boy', *The New York Times*.
51. *Time*, '"Zubi Baby" Switches'.
52. *Time*, 'Musical Chairs for the Maestros', 11 September 1978.
53. Rubin, 'From Mehta—with Chutzpah and Love', *The New York Times*.
54. Winn, 'Zubin Comes to Town', *The New York Times*.
55. *Time*, 'Musical Chairs for the Maestros'.
56. Ibid.
57. Conrad Wilson, 'Ernest Fleischmann', *Herald*, 10 July 2010.
58. *Time*, 'Musical Chairs for the Maestros'.
59. Philharmonic-Symphony Society of New York Inc., *The New York Philharmonic: The Mehta Years* (New York, 1990), p. 9.

## THE NEW YORK PHILHARMONIC

1. *New Yorker*, 'Zubin Mehta', 4 September 1978.
2. (Quoted in) Philip Hart, *Conductors: A New Generation* (London: Robson Books, 1980), p. 161.
3. Philharmonic-Symphony Society of New York, Inc., *The New York Philharmonic: The Mehta Years* (New York, 1990), p. 13.

4. Marie Winn, 'Zubin Comes to Town', *The New York Times*, 19 November 1978.
5. (Quoted in) Ibid.
6. (Quoted in) Ibid.
7. Ibid.
8. Kristin McMurran, 'Don't Argue with This Man on Cricket, Reagan or the Dodgers: Conductor Zubin Mehta Knows the Score', *People*, 12 October 1981.
9. Stephen E. Rubin, 'From Mehta—With Chutzpah and Love', *The New York Times*, 5 September 1976.
10. Philharmonic-Symphony Society of New York, Inc., *The New York Philharmonic: The Mehta Years* (New York, 1990), p. 30.
11. Ibid., p. 35.
12. John Rockwell, 'Philharmonic Presents Soloists from the Ranks', *The New York Times,* 25 April 1986.
13. Philharmonic-Symphony Society of New York, Inc., *The New York Philharmonic: The Mehta Years*, p. 94.
14. Ibid., p. 102.
15. Harold C. Schonberg, 'A Leader No Orchestra Can Resist', *The New York Times*, 24 September 1981.
16. Ibid.
17. Donal Henahan, 'Concert: Israelis Join New Yorkers at Benefit', *The New York Times*, 4 June 1982.
18. *Time,* 'Music: Harlem Bash', 5 May 1980.
19. Ibid.
20. Philharmonic-Symphony Society of New York, Inc., *The New York Philharmonic: The Mehta Years*, p. 55.
21. *Time*, 'Music: Harlem Bash'.
22. Philharmonic-Symphony Society of New York, Inc., *The New York Philharmonic: The Mehta Years*, p. 56.
23. John Rockwell, 'Ravi Shankar Brings His Sitar to the Philharmonic', *The New York Times*, 19 April 1981.
24. John Rockwell, 'Philharmonic: Shankar's "Raga Mala"', *The New York Times*, 25 April 1981.
25. Donal Henahan, 'Music: Shankar and the Philharmonic', *The New York Times*, 12 September 1985.

26. Rockwell, 'Ravi Shankar Brings His Sitar to the Philharmonic', *The New York Times*.
27. Donal Henahan, 'Mehta Has a Mandate Now to Change the Philharmonic', *The New York Times*, 13 November 1983.
28. Ibid.
29. John Rockwell, 'Actor Couldn't Make It, "Unemployed" Mehta Did', *The New York Times*, 14 April 1984.
30. John Rockwell, 'Zubin Mehta Will Appear in a Film about Zoroaster', *The New York Times*, 10 April 1983.
31. Cyrus Bharucha, interviewed by the author in Mumbai, 15 March 2015.

## THE NEW YORK PHILHARMONIC ON TOUR

1. Philharmonic-Symphony Society of New York, Inc., *The New York Philharmonic: The Mehta Years* (New York, 1990), p. 70.
2. *The New York Times*, 'Mehta Shifts Position in Performing in India', 15 September 1984.
3. Harold C. Schonberg, 'Zubin Mehta Plans to Go Home Again', *The New York Times*, 12 August 1984.
4. Helena Matheopoulos, *Maestro: Encounters with Conductors of Today* (New York: Harper & Row, 1982), p. 236.
5. William K. Stevens, 'Cheers for Mehta, Bombay's Favorite Son', *The New York Times*, 17 September 1984.
6. Ibid.
7. Ibid.
8. Sanjoy Hazarika, 'Elephants Greet Orchestra in India', *The New York Times*, 12 September 1984.
9. Philharmonic-Symphony Society of New York, Inc., *The New York Philharmonic: The Mehta Years*, p. 70.
10. Stevens, 'Cheers for Mehta, Bombay's Favorite Son', *The New York Times*.
11. Philharmonic-Symphony Society of New York, Inc., *New York Philharmonic: The Mehta Years*, p. 13.
12. John Rockwell, 'Music: For Mehta, the Sabbatical Wasn't All Play', *The New York Times*, 27 December 1987.
13. Ibid.
14. Ibid.

15. Ibid.
16. Ibid.
17. J.Y. Smith, 'J. Du Pre, Famed Cellist, Dies at 42', *The Washington Post*, 21 October 1987.
18. Esther B. Fein, 'An Exultant Zubin Mehta Offers Mahler in Moscow', *The New York Times*, 6 June 1988.
19. Ibid.
20. Ibid.
21. Clyde Haberman, 'Rome Is Big Enough for 3 Tenors', *The New York Times*, 9 July 1990.
22. Zubin Mehta, *The Score of My Life* (New Delhi: Roli Books, 2008), p. 163.
23. Ibid.
24. Barbara Isenberg, 'Escape Artist: Zubin Mehta—Back for a Spell with the L.A. Philharmonic—Acknowledges a Love for the New York Orchestra He Led 13 Years. . . but Not the City', *Los Angeles Times,* 29 December 1991.
25. John Rockwell, 'Music: Mehta to Step Down as Music Director of the Philharmonic After '90-'91 Season', *The New York Times*, 3 November 1988.
26. John Rockwell, 'Mehta Bids Farewell to the Philharmonic', *The New York Times*, 29 May 1991.
27. Ajit Hutheesing, email to author.

## THE BITTERSWEET YEARS IN NEW YORK

1. John Rockwell, 'Music: Mehta to Step Down as Music Director of the Philharmonic After '90-'91 Season', *The New York Times*, 3 November 1988.
2. John Rockwell, 'Why Isn't the Philharmonic Better', *The New York Times,* 19 September 1982.
3. Roger Vaughan, *Herbert von Karajan* (New York: W.W. Norton & Co., 1986), p. 10.
4. James R. Oestreich, 'For Mehta, the Final Melody Is Bittersweet', *The New York Times,* 26 May 1991.
5. Rockwell, 'Why Isn't the Philharmonic Better', *The New York Times*.
6. Ibid.

7. Donal Henahan, 'Music View; Cities Get the Conductors They Deserve', *The New York Times*, 16 September 1990.
8. Harold C. Schonberg, 'Zubin Mehta Plans to Go Home Again', *The New York Times*, 12 August 1984.
9. Ibid.
10. Edward Rothstein, 'Philharmonic Musicians Complain', *The New York Times*, 30 June 1983.
11. John Rockwell, 'New York Philharmonic under Various Batons', *The New York Times,* 18 January 1987.
12. Barbara Isenberg, 'Escape Artist: Zubin Mehta—Back for a Spell with the L.A. Philharmonic—Acknowledges a Love for the New York Orchestra He Led 13 Years . . . but Not the City', *Los Angeles Times*, 29 December 1991.
13. Donal Henahan, 'Acoustical Problems Still Plague the Philharmonic', *The New York Times*, 20 May 1984.
14. Ibid.
15. John Rockwell, 'Music View; Wanted: Leadership for the Philharmonic,' *The New York Times,* 16 September 1984.
16. Schonberg, 'Zubin Mehta Plans to Go Home Again', *The New York Times*.
17. Bernard Holland, 'Critics Notebook: The Many Aspects of Zubin Mehta's Job with Philharmonic', *The New York Times*, 4 August 1983.
18. Donal Henahan, 'Guessing Begins: Who's Next on the Podium', *The New York Times*, 3 November 1988.
19. Ibid.
20. Donal Henahan, 'Music View; Competence Was the Rule at the Philharmonic', *The New York Times*, 19 May 1985.
21. Donal Henahan, 'Music View; Ruffles and Flourishes on an Old Tune', *The New York Times*, 5 April 1981.
22. Ibid.
23. Schonberg, 'Zubin Mehta Plans to Go Home Again', *The New York Times*.
24. Ralph Blumenthal, 'Mehta's Way to Carnegie: Patience, Patience, Patience', *The New York Times*, 21 January 1998.
25. Zubin Mehta, *The Score of My Life* (New Delhi: Roli Books, 2008), p. 144.
26. Isenberg, 'Escape Artist: Zubin Mehta—Back for a Spell with the L.A. Philharmonic', *Los Angeles Times*.
27. Judy Pasternak, 'The Pit and the Podium', *Los Angeles Times*, 28 April 1996.

28. Zubin Mehta, interviewed by the author.
29. Schonberg, 'Zubin Mehta Plans to Go Home Again', *The New York Times*.
30. John Rockwell, 'Mehta: Joy in the Music-Making Now', *The New York Times,* 29 January 1980.
31. Zubin Mehta, interviewed by the author.
32. Isenberg, 'Escape Artist: Zubin Mehta—Back for a Spell with the L.A. Philharmonic', *Los Angeles Times*.
33. Ibid.
34. Blumenthal, 'Mehta's Way to Carnegie', *The New York Times*.
35. Oestreich, 'For Mehta, the Final Melody Is Bittersweet', *The New York Times*.
36. Ibid.
37. Ibid.
38. Ibid.
39. Ibid.
40. *The New York Times*, 'Cities and Orchestras: Thinly Disguised Hostility', 7 October 1990.
41. Sholto Byrnes, 'Zubin Mehta: Lightning Conductor', *The Independent*, 29 November 2005.
42. Oestreich, 'For Mehta, the Final Melody Is Bittersweet', *The New York Times*.
43. Ibid.
44. Ibid.
45. Bernard Holland, 'An Enduring Union of Opposites', *The New York Times*, 27 February 1996.
46. Oestreich, 'For Mehta, the Final Melody Is Bittersweet', *The New York Times*.
47. Ibid.

## FLORENCE

1. Zubin Mehta, interview by Franco Manfriani, *Maggio Musicale Fiorentino: Photographic Display and Chronology* (original in Italian), 2002.
2. Ibid.
3. Ibid.
4. Ibid.
5. Ibid.

6. Zubin Mehta, *The Score of My Life* (New Delhi: Roli Books, 2008), p. 160.
7. Ibid., p. 159.
8. Michael Steen, *A Guide to 25 of the World's Finest Musical Experiences* (London: Icon Books, 2013), p. 417.
9. Ibid., p. 419.
10. James Roberts, 'Turandot to Be Staged in Forbidden City', *The Independent,* 28 August 1998.
11. Ibid.
12. Steven Spielberg, 'Zhang Yimou', *Time*, 17 December 2008.
13. Zubin Mehta, interview by Franco Manfriani, *Maggio Musicale Fiorentino.*
14. Zubin Mehta, interviewed by the author.

## THE PODIUM AND THE PIT

1. Zubin Mehta, *The Score of My Life* (New Delhi: Roli Books, 2008), p. 188.
2. Edward Rothstein, 'The Lyric in Chicago Starts Its "Ring"', *The New York Times*, 9 February 1993.
3. Tim Page, 'Opera of the Big Shoulders; Chicago Lyric's Mighty "Ring" Cycle', *The Washington Post*, 31 March 1996.
4. Judy Pasternak, 'The Pit and the Podium', *Los Angeles Times*, 28 April 1996.
5. Zubin Mehta, interviewed by the author.
6. Mehta, *The Score of My Life,* p. 190.
7. Ibid., pp. 97–98.
8. Chuck Sudetic, 'Sarajevo Journal: In the Very Ashes of War, a Requiem for 10,000', *The New York Times*, 20 June 1994.
9. Michael Ajzenstadt, 'Time to Bring Curtain Down on Three Tenors', *Jerusalem Post*, 2 September 1998.
10. Mira Advani, 'Grandiose Show of Three Tenors with Mehta', *India Abroad*, 22 July 1994.
11. Ajzenstadt, 'Time to Bring Curtain Down on Three Tenors', *Jerusalem Post.*
12. Joseph McLellan, 'Music', *Washington Post*, 18 July 1994.
13. Mehta, *The Score of My Life*, p. 135.
14. Zubin Mehta, interviewed by the author.

15. Stephen Moss, 'I Wanted to Be the One That Got Away', *The Guardian*, 28 July 2006.
16. Mehta, *The Score of My Life*, p. 193.
17. John Allison, 'Three Times Lucky', *Opera*, June 2006.
18. Ibid.
19. Ibid.
20. Mehta, *The Score of My Life*, p. 200.
21. Natalia Ritzkowsky, interviewed by the author.
22. Geoff Pingree, 'Valencia's Big Bet', *Time*, 6 February 2007.
23. Ibid.
24. George Loomis, 'Palau Crowns Valencia's New Riverside', *International Herald Tribune*, 1 November 2006.
25. John Allison, 'Zubin Mehta', *Opera*, June 2009.
26. Roberto Herrscher, 'In Review: Valencia', *Opera News*, 1 August 2007.
27. *The Sunday Times,* 'Spain's First Full All-in-One Ring Cycle', 5 July 2009.
28. Ibid.
29. Zubin Mehta, interview in *GBOpera* magazine, 21 April 2012.
30. Zubin Mehta, interviewed by the author.

## MUSIC IN THE FAMILY

1. Zubin Mehta, *The Score of My Life* (New Delhi: Roli Books, 2008), p. 73.
2. John Hall, 'In Memoriam', UCLA, 2002.
3. Chris Pasles, 'Obituaries; Mehli Mehta, 94; Youth Symphony Conductor', *Los Angeles Times*, 20 October 2002.
4. Hall, 'In Memoriam', UCLA.
5. Harold Schonberg, 'Jascha Heifetz Is Dead at 86; A Virtuoso since Childhood', *The New York Times*, 12 December 1987.
6. Libby Slate, 'Mehli Mehta Marks 80 Musical Years', *Los Angeles Times*, 24 September 1998.
7. Cyrus Bharucha, interviewed by the author in Mumbai, 7 May 2015.
8. Pasles, 'Obituaries; Mehli Mehta, 94; Youth Symphony Conductor', *Los Angeles Times*.
9. Ibid.
10. *The Independent*, 'Obituary: Mehli Mehta, Conductor of Intensity and Passion', 23 October 2002.

11. Ibid.
12. Martin Bernheimer, 'The "Other" Mehta Conquers Montreal', *Los Angeles Times*, 11 April 1968.
13. Edward Rothstein, 'Concert: Mehli Mehta', *The New York Times*, 17 March 1983.
14. Mira Advani, 'Mehta Lauded at Concert', *India Abroad*, 18 March 1994.
15. *India Abroad*, 'Maestro Mehta to Pass on the Baton', 21 March 1997.
16. *The Independent*, 'Obituary: Mehli Mehta, Conductor of Intensity and Passion'.
17. Ibid.
18. Pasles, 'Obituaries; Mehli Mehta, 94; Youth Symphony Conductor', *Los Angeles Times*.
19. Dorit Gabai, 'The Conductor Dares', *Maariv*, 29 July 2009.
20. John Rockwell, 'Mehli Mehta: Zubin's Father—and More', *Los Angeles Times*, 22 March 1972.
21. *Los Angeles Times*, 'Obituaries; Tehmina Mehta; Matriarch of Leading Classical Music Family', 26 April 2005.
22. Ibid.
23. Ibid.
24. Mehroo Jeejeebhoy, interviewed by the author in Mumbai, 25 March 2015.
25. Mehli Mehta Music Foundation, Mumbai (brochure, 2015).
26. Zubin Mehta, interviewed by the author.
27. Khushroo Suntook, interviewed by the author.
28. Ibid.
29. James R. Oestreich, 'The Big Fish That Didn't Get Away', *The New York Times*, 17 September 2000.
30. Andrew Partner, 'Bachanalia at Ravinia', *Chicago Sun-Times*, 9 June 2000.
31. *India Abroad*, 'Zarin Mehta, Brother of Zubin, Is Named Executive Director of New York Philharmonic', 9 June 2000.
32. Oestreich, 'The Big Fish That Didn't Get Away', *The New York Times*.
33. *India Abroad*, 'Zarin Mehta, Brother of Zubin, Is Named Executive Director of New York Philharmonic'.
34. *India Abroad*, 'Zarin Mehta Takes Over as President of New York Philharmonic', 11 June 2004.

## THE MAESTRO ON TOUR

1. Bakhtiar K. Dadabhoy, *Sugar in Milk* (New Delhi: Rupa & Co, 2008), p. 421.
2. Peter Marck blog, https://ipotours.wordpress.com.
3. Ibid.
4. Zubin Mehta, interviewed by the author.
5. Anastassia Boutsko, 'Star Conductor Zubin Mehta Receives Furtwängler Prize', *Deutsche Welle*, 14 September 2011.
6. Ibid.
7. Peter Marck blog.

## 'CONDUCTING IS COMMUNICATION'

1. Roger Vaughan, *Herbert von Karajan* (New York: W.W. Norton & Company, 1986), p. 20.
2. Ibid., p. 188.
3. Zubin Mehta, interviewed by the author.
4. Harold C. Schonberg, *Great Conductors* (New York: Simon & Schuster, 1967), p. 280.
5. Harold C. Schonberg, 'A New Maestro for the Philharmonic', *The New York Times*, 7 March 1976.
6. Martin Kettle, 'Second Coming', *The Guardian*, 26 November 2004.
7. Zubin Mehta, interviewed by the author.
8. Schonberg, *Great Conductors,* pp. 276–77.
9. Zubin Mehta, interviewed by the author.
10. Vaughan, *Herbert von Karajan,* p. 22.
11. Ibid.
12. Schonberg, *Great Conductors,* p. 165.
13. Zubin Mehta, interviewed by the author.
14. C. Robert Jennings, 'Zubin Mehta: Allegro Con Brio', *Los Angeles Times*, 5 April 1970.
15. Harold C. Schonberg, 'Philharmonic Picks Mehta as Conductor', *New York Times*, 26 February 1976.
16. Zubin Mehta, interviewed by the author.
17. Vaughan, *Herbert von Karajan,* p. 121.

18. Zubin Mehta, interviewed by the author.
19. Harold C. Schonberg, 'A Lifetime of Listening', *New York Times*, 8 February 1981.
20. Vaughan, *Herbert von Karajan,* p. 209.
21. Zubin Mehta, interviewed by the author.
22. Bruno Walter, *Of Music and Music-Making* (London: Faber & Faber, 1961), p. 81.
23. Ibid., p. 112.
24. Daniel Barenboim, *A Life in Music* (New York: Arcade Publishing, 2013).
25. Walter, *Of Music and Music-Making,* p. 116.
26. Stephen E. Rubin, 'From Mehta—With Chutzpah and Love', *The New York Times*, 5 September 1976.
27. Jennings, 'Zubin Mehta: Allegro Con Brio', *Los Angeles Times.*
28. Zubin Mehta, interviewed by the author.
29. Albert Goldberg, 'Zubin Mehta's Plans and Dreams for L.A.', *Los Angeles Times*, 15 December 1963.
30. *Time*, 'The Next Toscanini', 14 August 1964.
31. Goldberg, 'Zubin Mehta's Plans and Dreams for L.A.', *Los Angeles Times.*
32. Kristin McMurran, 'Don't Argue with This Man on Cricket, Reagan or the Dodgers: Conductor Zubin Mehta Knows the Score', *People*, 12 October 1981.
33. Vaughan, *Herbert von Karajan,* p. 205.
34. Jennings, 'Zubin Mehta: Allegro Con Brio', *Los Angeles Times.*
35. Zubin Mehta, interviewed by the author.
36. Walter, *Of Music and Music-Making,* p. 146.
37. Zubin Mehta interview, *GBOpera* magazine, 21 April 2012.
38. Ibid.

## EPILOGUE

1. Sheryar Ookerjee, 'Wielding the Magic Wand', Nawaz B. Mody ed., *Enduring Legacy: Parsis of the 20th Century*, vol. II (Mumbai: Published by the author, 2005), p. 708.
2. Martin Bookspan and Ross Yockey, *Zubin: The Zubin Mehta Story* (New York: Harper and Row, 1978), p. 219.
3. Zubin Mehta, interviewed by the author.

# Select Bibliography


Barenboim, Daniel. *A Life in Music.* New York: Arcade Publishing, 2002.

Bookspan, Martin and Ross Yockey. *Zubin: The Zubin Mehta Story*. New York: Harper & Row, 1978.

Boult, Sir Adrian. *Thoughts on Conducting*. London: Phoenix House Ltd, 1963.

Brook, Donald. *International Gallery of Conductors*. London: Rockliff Publishing Corporation Ltd, 1951.

Chatfield-Taylor, Joan. *Backstage at the Opera*. London: Secker and Warburg, 1983.

Dadabhoy, Bakhtiar K. *Sugar in Milk*. New Delhi: Rupa & Co., 2008.

Dastoor, Homi. *Musical Journeys*. Mumbai: 49/50 Books, 2014.

Fernandes, Naresh. *Taj Mahal Foxtrot: The Story of Bombay's Jazz Age*. New Delhi: Roli Books, 2012.

Hart, Philip. *Conductors: A New Generation*. London: Robson Books Ltd, 1980.

Israel Philharmonic Orchestra. *The Israel Philharmonic Orchestra: 70th Anniversary*. Tel Aviv, 2006.

Johnson, Paul. *Mozart: A Life*. New York: Penguin Books, 2014.

Lavezzoli, Peter. *Bhairavi: The Global Impact of Music*. Noida: HarperCollins Publisher, 2009.

Matheopoulos, Helena. *Maestro: Encounters with Conductors of Today*. New York: Harper & Row, 1982.

Mehli Mehta Music Foundation. *Applause: A Tribute to Zubin Mehta*. Mumbai, 2011.

Menuhin, Yehudi. *Unfinished Journey*. London: Macdonald and Jane's Publishers Ltd, 1977.

Mishori, Yaacov. *Smiles, Pranks and Coughs at the Israel Philharmonic Orchestra*. Tel Aviv: Graphisoft Systems, 2002.

Mehta, Zubin. *The Score of My Life*. New Delhi: Roli Books Pvt. Ltd, 2008.

Mody, Nawaz B. (ed.). *Enduring Legacy, Parsis of the 20th Century*, vol. III. Mumbai: published by the author, 2005.

Philharmonic-Symphony Society of New York Inc. *The New York Philharmonic: The Mehta Years*. New York, 1990.

Schonberg, Harold C. *The Great Conductors*. New York: Simon & Schuster, 1967.

Schrade, Leo. *Monteverdi: Creator of Modern Music.* London: Victor Gollancz Ltd, 1972.

Steen, Michael. *A Guide to 25 of the World's Finest Musical Experiences.* London: Icon Books Ltd, 2013.

Thomas, Henry and Dana Lee Thomas. *Living Biographies of Great Composers*. New York: Blue Ribbon Books, 1946.

Vaughan, Roger. *Herbert von Karajan.* New York: W.W. Norton & Co. Inc., 1986.

Walter, Bruno. *Of Music and Music-Making*. London: Faber & Faber, 1961.

**Newspapers and magazines**

*The New York Times*
*Los Angeles Times*
*The Times of India*
*Hindustan Times*
*Chicago Jewish Star*
*Jerusalem Post*
*The Washington Post*
*Chicago Sun-Times*
*The Herald*
*People*
*The New Yorker*
*The Milwaukee Journal Sentinel*
*Little India*
*Daily News*
*The Independent*
*India Abroad*
*The Sunday Times*
*International Herald Tribune*

# List of Sources *for* Photographs

Grateful acknowledgement is made to the following for permission to reprint copyright material:

Mehli Mehta Music Foundation for photographs 1, 2, 3, 4, 6, 7, 42, 43, 44, 45, 46, 47, 48, 49, 50, 53, 56, 57, 60, 61 and 63.

Murray S. Katz Photo Archives of the Israel Philharmonic Orchestra for photographs 8, 9, 12, 16, 17, 18, 19, 21, 23, 24, 25, 28, 29, 30, 37, 51, 52, 59, 66 and 67.

The Mehtas' private archives for photographs 5, 10, 11, 13, 14, 15, 54 and 55.

New York Philharmonic Archive for photographs 20, 26, 27, 31, 32, 39 and 41.

Zionist Archives and Government Press Office for photographs 22, 38 and 58.

Maggio Musicale Fiorentino for photographs 40 and 62.

Cyrus Bharucha for photograph 36.

The author for photograph 33.

# Index

# A Note *on the* Type

Bembo, an elegant and eminently legible old-style serif typeface, is based on a design first cut by Francesco Griffo in 1495 for Venetian printer Aldus Manutius. The typeface owes its name to the poet and cleric Cardinal Bembo, the author of the book in which it was first used. Drawing on pure Roman forms, Griffo's design introduced an italic form based on a cursive handwritten style. Still as popular as it was five centuries ago, the font as we know it today was created by Stanley Morison for Monotype Corporation in 1929. The company produced a faithful digital rendition of the typeface in the 1980s, continuing the legacy of this classic, fresh font.

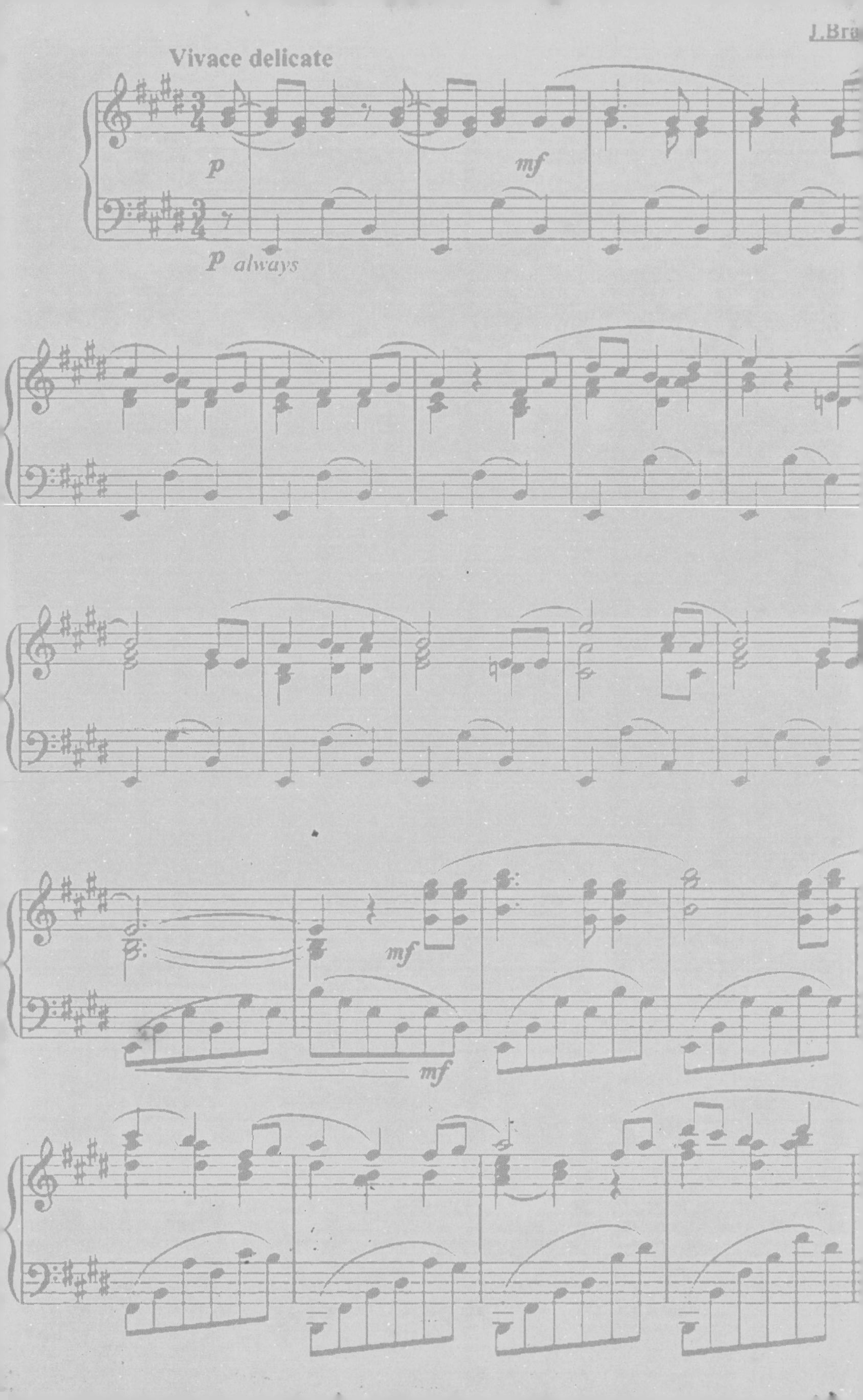
J.Bra
Vivace delicate
p
mf
p always
mf
mf